AF740585

Whither China?

Whither China?

Restarting the Reform Agenda

Wu Jinglian and Ma Guochuan

Translated by
Xiaofeng Hua and Nancy Hearst

OXFORD
UNIVERSITY PRESS

OXFORD
UNIVERSITY PRESS

Oxford University Press is a department of the University of Oxford. It furthers the University's objective of excellence in research, scholarship, and education by publishing worldwide. Oxford is a registered trade mark of Oxford University Press in the UK and certain other countries.

Published in the United States of America by Oxford University Press
198 Madison Avenue, New York, NY 10016, United States of America.

© Wu Jinglian and Ma Guochuan 2016

All rights reserved. No part of this publication may be reproduced, stored in a retrieval system, or transmitted, in any form or by any means, without the prior permission in writing of Oxford University Press, or as expressly permitted by law, by license, or under terms agreed with the appropriate reproduction rights organization. Inquiries concerning reproduction outside the scope of the above should be sent to the Rights Department, Oxford University Press, at the address above.

You must not circulate this work in any other form
and you must impose this same condition on any acquirer.

Cataloging-in-Publication Data is on file with the Library of Congress
ISBN 978–0–19–022315–1

CONTENTS

PREFACE

In the last two decades of the twentieth century China achieved important progress in its market-oriented economic reforms. However, shortly after the turn of this century, an intense debate on "Whither China?" erupted in parallel with the deceleration of the reforms. The intensity and level of participation in this debate exceeded that of any of the previous debates since the late 1970s. At its center were two options: whether China should continue on the path of economic and political reforms or whether it should reinforce the so-called "China model," whereby a powerful government is in command of everything. The latter option may also include a return to practices of the Maoist era. This book reflects the arguments of the authors during the course of this debate.

In the face of many historical crossroads since the beginning of the late nineteenth century, China has had to address the question, whither China? For example, after the initial launch of the reform and opening in 1978, this question (which is similar to one of the questions that the great ancient Chinese poet Qu Yuan directed to Heaven) was raised at many critical turning points. This time, however, the question was being asked just as China was becoming a prosperous, democratic, civilized, and harmonious society. Because of the high stakes and the fact that the question had not been addressed for a long time, it produced much anxiety in society.

As I state in this book's dialogues with Ma Guochuan, by the end of the twentieth century China had established a preliminary framework for a socialist market economy. Under this framework, market exchanges have become the main form of transaction, greatly encouraging the creativity of the private sector and leading to high economic growth. However, in many respects the economic system is still under the influence of the old command economy. Even the functioning of the market remains reined in by the government. Therefore, the current economy is a transitional mix of a semi-command, semi-market economy. There are two possible futures for such an economy. In the first scenario, if the government gradually phases out its interventions in microeconomic activities and strengthens its public-service functions, a rule-governed modern market economy might come into existence. We call this a *market economy based on rule of law*. In the second scenario, if the government continuously enhances its controls and interventions in the market and continues to strengthen the "control capacity" of the state sector, then China's economy might evolve into state capitalism whereby an authoritarian government controls socioeconomic development. Given China's current social and historical conditions, it is possible that this scenario will lead to crony capitalism.

Faced with these two destinies, where should China go from here?

After the onset of the debates, advocates of the second scenario took advantage of the fact that the general public was seriously distressed about the rampant corruption and the sharp divide between the rich and poor, but it did not necessarily understand the deeper roots of the problems. These advocates attempted to employ some demagogic populist and nationalist slogans to lead the public astray. For a while, such attempts, first known as the "Beijing consensus" and then as the so-called "China model," gained momentum. Advocates of this view held that China's remarkable economic performance since the end of the 1970s had been due to its strong government and its powerful control of the state sector. According to such thinking, this model had enabled China to concentrate its resources on doing big things and to enforce the will of the state. They did not accept that the various social ills were due to the "excessive placement, misplacement, or absence of the role of government" (that is, "the government managed many things that it should not manage or that it could not manage well, while it failed to manage many other things that it should manage and that it could manage well"). They claimed that the problems were due to the impacts and obstacles created by the market forces and the limited and ineffective government control over the economy and society. Their conclusion was to further expand government power, enhance control over the economy by state-owned enterprises, and reinforce an authoritarian developmentalism model in which GDP growth is driven by a powerful government, large state-owned enterprises, and massive investments.

In this book, we review the history of the contemporary Chinese economy to provide an objective and in-depth analysis of its evolution—from the establishment by Mao Zedong and his colleagues of a command economy under proletarian dictatorship to the entire process of reform and opening over the last thirty-plus years. We also explore the institutional causes for the social maladies and the correct ways to overcome them. Through such reviews we have come to a conclusion that differs completely from the foregoing argument. The facts show that it has been the Chinese people's creativity and entrepreneurship, unleashed by the market-oriented reform and opening, that have sustained China's strong economic growth for more than three decades. We strongly believe that in the face of the various social ills caused by the delays in reform, the only way out for China is to restart and firmly promote the market-oriented economic reforms and to advance the rule-of-law and democracy-oriented political reforms.

We are pleased to note that the Chinese version of our book immediately became a best-seller, and within two years more than 100,000 copies had been sold. This enthusiastic reception indicates that hundreds of thousands of ordinary readers found strong resonance with these views. After 2011, the realities of the so-called "miracle of high-speed railways" and the "Chongqing miracle," which had been highly praised by advocates of the so-called "China model," were revealed in succession and the negative effects of authoritarian developmentalism gradually surfaced. Debates about China's future direction intensified. More and more people came to realize that if China were to turn back, it would face a dead-end, and the only way to achieve long-term stability and prosperity would be to continue the reform and opening.

Against this backdrop and promoted by the joint efforts of people with keen insight, the November 2012 Eighteenth National Communist Party Congress met the people's expectations by providing a clear answer to the question, whither China? The answer is: "We must, with greater political courage and vision, lose no time in deepening reform in key sectors." With respect to the economic reforms, the Party Congress declared the need to adhere to the reform orientation of the socialist market economy, to "strike a balance between the role of the government and that of the market," and to "leverage to a greater extent and in a wider scope the basic role of the market in allocating resources." With regard to political reforms, the Eighteenth National Communist Party Congress reiterated the statements of the Sixteenth and Seventeenth National Communist Party Congresses to "work harder to enhance socialist democracy" and to "build a socialist country based on the rule of law."

After the conclusion of the Eighteenth National Communist Party Congress, active and heated discussions regarding the design of an overall reform program took place among government officials, the business community, and academics, as well as among many individual citizens. Participants in the debate from academic circles included both those "within-the-system"—that is, those employed in government-affiliated research institutions and nongovernment academic bodies—as well as domestic scholars and overseas experts. This phenomenon of broad participation in the design of the reform has rarely been seen in China's thirty-five-year history of the reform and opening. The participants took an issue-driven approach and scrutinized the main social problems. They identified the institutional causes of the problems and suggested the required reforms. Various lists of proposed institutional reforms were then drawn up.

Wu Jinglian, an active participant in these activities, holds the view that the core task of economic reform is to establish a competitive market system. Specifically, he advocates that the reform should: (a) clarify a property-rights system for the market economy; (b) provide equal protection of property rights and equal access to the factors of production for all economic entities under different ownerships; (c) let the market determine the prices of goods and production factors; (d) improve competitiveness and eliminate local protectionism and administrative monopolies that obstruct the proper functioning of the market; (e) follow the principle of "let the market do what it can and let the society do what it is capable of" to readjust the relationships between the government, the market, and the society, and prohibit governments at various administrative levels from engaging in for-profit activities; (f) establish the rule of law and ensure the powers of the judiciary; and (g) forbid various administrations from intervening in microeconomic activities, and change from prior reviews and licensing of market activities to compliance supervision during or after the activities are completed.

After extensive efforts to collect feedback, the Third Plenary Session of the Eighteenth Communist Party Central Committee, held in November 2013, adopted the "Decision of the Central Committee of the Communist Party of China on Some Major Issues Concerning Comprehensively Deepening the Reform" that spells out the overall design and roadmap for reform from 2014 to 2020.

Most importantly, this decision clarifies the relationship between the government and the market. In elaborating upon the decision of the Communist Party Central Committee's plenary session, General Secretary Xi Jinping pointed out that "the underlying issue is how to strike a balance between the role of the government and that of the market, and let the market play the decisive role in allocating resources and let the government play its functions better."

While highlighting the role of the market in resource allocations, this decision also calls for a better role for the government. Because the visible hand of government has extended too long and into too many areas, the decision defines a "better role" for government to include proper administrative functions to "maintain the stability of the macroeconomy, strengthen and improve public services, safeguard fair competition, strengthen oversight of the market, maintain market order, promote sustainable development and common prosperity, and intervene in situations where market failure occurs." The decision calls for "deepen[ing] the reform of the system concerning matters subject to government examination and licensing" and "cancel[ing] all administrative licensing procedures for economic activities under the effective regulation of the market mechanism." For the first time, an official Communist Party/government document clearly mentions a negative list; that is, "on the basis of making a negative list, all kinds of market players may enter areas that are not on the negative list on an equal basis and according to law."

The decision not only refers to the "decisive role of the market in allocating resources" but also states that "establishing a unified, open, competitive, and orderly market system is the basis for the market to play a decisive role in the allocation of resources." The decision calls for the establishment of such an institutional foundation through comprehensive reforms.

The establishment of a unified, open, competitive, and orderly market system was first called for in the early 1990s and was endorsed in the "Decision of the CCP Central Committee on Issues of Building a Socialist Market Economy" of the 1993 Third

Plenary Session of the Fourteenth Communist Party Central Committee. Twenty years later, the decision of another Third Plenary Session has reiterated this call, which is the correct prescription for curing the chronic diseases in the current system.

This pivotal requirement targets a series of systemic defects that are caused by excessive government interference, which has suppressed the role of the market. The first defect is the "vertical" (sectoral) and "spatial" (geographic) segmentation of the market, under which the market has been cut, sliced, and minced into scattered fragments. The second defect is that market entities are not treated equally and cannot compete fairly under equal market conditions. The third defect is the loss of market competitiveness due to local protectionism, monopolies in certain sectors, and a lack of effective enforcement of the Anti-Monopoly Law. The fourth defect is the lack of order in the market and the absence of the rule of law, leading to failure to ensure rule-based market transactions. Lastly, the uneven development of various markets, in particular the factors market that is critical to modern economic development, has seriously blocked improvements in the efficiency of resource allocations.

The essence of these four defects is a lack of market competition. Free competition is the "soul" of market institutions. This is because only through free competition can price signals that reflect the scarcity of resources be formed and direct resources to the most effective areas of the economy, and only through free competition can a compatible system of incentives be established. In recent years, the government, rather than the market, has become the main force in allocating resources owing to its continuous interventions in microeconomic activities. A market without free competition is a "bogus market," or merely a superficial market. This problem must be resolved in order to establish modern market institutions.

The 2013 decision contains several hundred specific reform steps, most of which center around two overarching principles: "letting the market play the decisive role in resource allocations" and "establishing a unified, open, competitive, and orderly market system."

While celebrating the new breakthrough in reform, people who are concerned about China's future should be aware that although reform has been restored to the top of the government's political agenda, this progress does not necessarily guarantee future smooth sailing. As the saying goes, "easier said than done." Although it is not painless to design a good general program, it is even more challenging to implement such a program. Compared to the previous rounds of reform, this time the reforms will be more broad-ranging and will have higher requirements. It is inevitable that the reforms will encounter many obstacles and their implementation will face many difficulties. Such obstacles and difficulties will come from three main directions.

First, there will be resistance from the traditional ideology. This is due to the introduction of Soviet theories and implementation of the Soviet system during the first three decades of the People's Republic. It can also be attributed to the prolonged influence of despotism in Chinese history. Although many years have passed, people who are still under the influence and shackles of the old ideologies are not cooperative or even hostile with respect to the reforms.

Second, there will be resistance from privileged interests. Systemic reform entails a significant reconfiguration of existing interests. During such readjustments, special groups with privileged interests that abuse power for their own self-interest will try everything they can to obstruct the progress of the reforms. The astonishing cases that have been exposed during the latest round of the anti-corruption drive reveal that these groups have penetrated deep into the Communist Party, government, and military organizations. Without a doubt, they will resort to all possible means to resist or to distort the reforms.

Third, in addition to the obstacles created by the traditional ideology and the privileged interests, a systemic transition will also encounter various practical difficulties. Due to the many years of authoritarian developmentalism and an extensive growth model, China's socioeconomic development is challenged by many deep-rooted contradictions. Even though there were also incompatible contradictions among the different parts of the old system, after years of implementation the various parts of the former system became more or less coordinated. But when some parts of the system are changed and the system can no longer function, many practical problems will arise. For instance, at present the leverage ratio on the national balance sheet is too high because for a long time some local governments survived by mortgaging and selling land. Once interest rates are determined by the market, budget constraints are hardened, and property rights for land are clearly defined, there could be widespread (or limited) problems of insolvency. Given the reduced growth rate, it is crucial that the macroeconomic management authorities avoid systemic risks while deflating the government's balance sheet so that such deflation will not become an obstacle to comprehensive and deepened reforms.

The Chinese version of this book was written several years ago for a Chinese readership to facilitate their understanding of China's realities and to explore the necessary remedies. To date, the main problems covered in the volume have not changed fundamentally; hence the book may help readers in the English-speaking world better understand China. We look forward to receiving comments and feedback from our readers.

Our sincere thanks go to Ms. Hua Xiaofeng and Ms. Nancy Hearst. They have demonstrated great enthusiasm and patience during the process of translating the book and have assisted in the correction of omissions and errors in the Chinese version. Without their efforts, this English version would not have been possible. We would also like to thank Ms. Susan Su and Ms. Liu Lili for their excellent coordination as well as Dr. Fan Shitao, Ms. Wu Suping, Dr. Chen Ruoying, and Dr. Liu Yunpeng for their careful proofreading of both the English and the Chinese versions. Finally, we express our sincere gratitude to the Beijing Cairncross Economic Research Foundation and to the China Europe International Business School (CEIBS) Education Foundation for their generous support..

Wu Jinglian

ACKNOWLEDGMENTS

This book is published in association with the Beijing Cairncross Economic Research Foundation (http://www.cairncrossfund.org/en-index.htm), which was established in 2007 in tribute to the late Sir Alec Cairncross (1911–1998) who provided important advice on Chinese economic policy making, and promoted the training of Chinese economists and the development of contemporary Chinese Studies in the United Kingdom. The mission of the Beijing Cairncross Economic Research Foundation, a nonprofit body registered in China, is to contribute to Chinese economic policy making through international collaborative research and dialogues between Chinese and international experts. The Foundation provided financial and logistical support for the translation and editing of the text, undertaken by Hua Xiaofeng and Nancy Hearst. Acknowledgment is also extended to the China Europe International Business School (CEIBS) Education Foundation for its financial support.

ABOUT THE AUTHORS

For more than thirty years, **Wu Jinglian** has been widely regarded as China's most celebrated and influential economist. In recent years, he has emerged as a prominent public intellectual fighting for market reforms and a democratic society backed by the rule of law. He won an award for making an outstanding contribution to China's economy in 2005 and was named Honorary President of the International Economics Association (IEA) in 2011.

He is currently Senior Research Fellow at the Development Research Center under the State Council of the People's Republic of China, and Bao Steel Chair Professor of Economics at the China Europe International Business School (CEIBS). His main research interests include comparative institutional analysis and theory and policy on the transformation of Chinese society.

Ma Guochuan is Chief Commentator of *Caijing* Business Magazine.

ABOUT THE TRANSLATORS

Xiaofeng Hua is a retiree from the World Bank. She has worked on economic development issues related to China and other Asian and African countries for the last thirty years.

Nancy Hearst is Research Librarian at the Fairbank Center for Chinese Studies in the H.C. Fung Library of Harvard University. She has been visiting China regularly since 1980.

Whither China?

DIALOGUE 1

"WHITHER CHINA?" IN A NEW CONTEXT

Ma Guochuan (Ma): The thirty years of reform and opening have changed China's socioeconomic structure, raised the country's position in the global economy, and deeply influenced the course of world history.

In more recent years, however, it appears that China has reached a new crossroads. On the one hand, the economy has experienced continuous growth due to the dynamism released by the reform and opening. On the other hand, corruption has spread to almost every level of society. The extent of the disparities between the rich and the poor has shocked ordinary people. In recent years, these problems have become increasingly serious.

Such phenomena raise the following important question: Whither China?

Wu Jinglian (Wu): At present, the contrast between light and dark that you just described is indeed striking. On the bright side, the Chinese economy has undergone thirty years of continuous high growth. In 2010, China's GDP surpassed that of Japan to become the world's second-largest economy. China also replaced Germany as the world's largest exporting country. In addition, per capita disposable income has increased by a large margin, and over 100 million people have been lifted out of absolute poverty.

When comparing present conditions with those in the past, people like me who experienced the earlier difficult times see two very different worlds. Within a short span of only thirty years, the economy has registered dramatic changes. Today's youth cannot imagine living on rations. In the 1950s and 1960s, one could not buy grain, cloth, meat, cooking oil, or even female sanitary napkins without the various ration coupons. Dozens of daily necessities were rationed.

However, there is also another side to this situation. There have been high costs due to the rapid economic growth. In recent years, resource shortages and damage to the environment have become ever more serious. Corruption has penetrated the entire society, and the widening gap between the rich and poor presents a threat to social stability.

Ma: The question we should try to answer now is why this contrast between the two extremes is intensifying, for only when we understand the root causes of the problems can we begin to formulate an effective solution.

Wu: In my view, these phenomena can be attributed to the reform process that was initiated in China in the late 1970s. In other words, it is related to the approach that was adopted for the transition from a Soviet-type social system to a modern system. The question whither China? has had different meanings during the various phases of the reform process.

Ma: You have just provided a new analytical approach for answering my question. Perhaps we should begin our dialogue from the situation in the country on the eve of the reforms.

At the end of the 1970s, China faced a serious crisis and the entire nation was in peril. At that time, there was a consensus among most Chinese about what direction the country should take.

Wu: You are right. In 1966, when the great famine caused by the so-called Great Leap Forward of the late 1950s was finally overcome and the economy was gradually recovering, the ultra-leftist leader (that is, Mao Zedong) launched the Great Proletarian Cultural Revolution, which would inflict chaos on the country for the next ten years. If the general public—workers, farmers, and intellectuals—shouldered most of the suffering during the earlier political and economic campaigns, then the Cultural Revolution extended the persecution to those implementing the ultra-leftist policies, including senior officials in the Chinese Communist Party and the government. Even the state president was not spared. Ye Jianying, chairman of the National People's Congress in the late 1970s, pointed out at a Communist Party Politburo meeting that "during the Cultural Revolution those in control of the government usurped power to impose a fascist dictatorship. They made life very difficult for both government officials and ordinary people. Many old revolutionaries lost their positions based on wrongly judged cases or false evidence. A great number of officials and ordinary people were labeled 'capitalist roaders' or 'counterrevolutionary elements,' and thus they were subjected to cruel treatment. If those who suffered because of their ties with the persecuted are also included, then the total number of victims would reach 100 million, or one-ninth of the total population." This is an accurate description of the social and economic situation in our country at the end of 1970s.

After that huge disaster and in the face of such a serious situation, it was relatively easy to reach a consensus, both within and outside the government—the ultra-leftist policies had to be abandoned and the "economic administration system" at that time had to be changed as soon as possible. In a summary of a brainstorming meeting of the State Council in the summer of 1978, Li Xiannian, who was then a vice premier, commented, "It is imperative not only to greatly modify the backward forces of production, but we must also change the production relations and improve the superstructure of society. It is urgent that we change the management mechanism for industrial and agricultural enterprises, the government's mode of administration for industrial and agricultural enterprises, and the behavior and mindset of the people." However, there was no clear or unanimous agreement among the people about the future direction or the desired goals of these changes.

Under these circumstances, the country's leaders adopted a practical approach, which was characterized by "taking one step at a time," "crossing the river by feeling for the stones," and "it doesn't matter whether the cat is black or white, as long as it catches mice, it is a good cat." Any policy or institution could be implemented as long as it was conducive to providing an economic recovery and social stability.

A strategy was introduced to allow some flexibility in the economy so there would be room for entrepreneurial activities by the private sector that until then had been strictly prohibited, while at the same time retaining the dominant role of the command economy and the state-owned economic entities.

These flexible institutional arrangements included the following. First, farming was returned to family-based production by contracting with rural households but land remained under collective ownership. Second, a new fiscal system, called "eating in separate kitchens" (referring to the fiscal autonomy of local governments), was introduced to improve incentives for lower-level governments to promote local economic development, even though public and enterprise finance remained combined. Third, a "dual-track" approach was adopted whereby, in addition to maintaining the command economy under which production materials were allocated and priced administratively, a second "track" of market mechanisms was developed to allow trading through negotiated pricing of production materials. Lastly, even though the overall environment was not conducive to market development, a more pro-market microclimate was created in selected localities to enable them to become integrated with international markets.

The "supporting role" of the private sector facilitated stabilization, recovery, and development of the national economy.

Ma: It appears that theoretical circles were also fumbling around in an attempt to find a way to resolve the problems during this period.

Wu: With respect to coming up with applicable theories, the first "stone" was the "market-socialism reform" that the Soviet Union and the Eastern European

Communist countries had carried out from the 1960s to the 1980s. But the objective of these reforms was not to establish a market economy. Instead, the goal was to introduce some market mechanisms, while at the same time maintaining the dominant position of state ownership and subjecting the national economy to coordination and allocation by the planning authorities. In the late 1970s, a number of Chinese economists were studying the Soviet Union's Liberman proposals and Kosygin reforms, Yugoslavia's "self-managing socialism," Czechoslovakia's Prague Spring, and Hungary's New Economic Mechanisms.

In China, there was a similar reform idea, which was to maintain a planned economy, or, more accurately, a command economy, supplemented by market forces.

Ma: The documents of the 1982 Twelfth National Communist Party Congress defined the reform objective as "maintaining the primary role of the planned economy while giving play to the supplementary role of market forces in economic regulation."

Hence, in the early 1980s a reform strategy was developed in China that was acceptable to the various factions. This strategy, which can be considered an answer to the question, whither China? was quite different from the reform strategies in the Soviet Union and the Eastern European countries. Instead of giving priority to the reform of state-owned enterprises (SOEs), the Chinese strategy focused on facilitating bottom-up development of the private sector. You used to call that a *strategy of incremental reforms*. Can you elaborate on the pros and cons, and the consequences, of this strategy?

Wu: On the one hand, it was a highly successful reform strategy. Because of this strategy, China was able to avoid the "quagmire of state-sector reform" that had bogged down the Soviet Union and the Eastern European countries. The existing size of the state sector was maintained, more or less, but at the same time, the beginning of the development of a private sector was allowed. Rapid economic growth was achieved by relying on the competitiveness of the private sector.

On the other hand, the strategy did not reduce the dominance of the government or the state sector in resource allocations. Furthermore, prolonged application of this strategy led to the coexistence of both a command economy and a market economy, thus creating much room for rent seeking by those in power. Corruption began to spread. Some government officials used their access to resources, allocated by the plan at government-controlled prices, to reap exorbitant profits in the market. By the mid-1980s, *guandao* (that is, profiteering by government officials) had become a frequent topic in daily conversations.

Against this background, a new round of discussions came to the fore regarding whether the reform strategy should be readjusted and the reform objectives clarified.

Ma: The Third Plenary Session of the Twelfth Communist Party Central Committee in 1984 redefined the reform objective to be the establishment of a "socialist planned commodity economy," replacing the previous goal of maintaining the dominance of the planned economy while allowing the market to play a supplementary role. Without a doubt, the new strategy was a major breakthrough in answering the question, whither China? Nevertheless, it still did not completely negate the role of the command economy. But the mode of implementation began to change from incremental reforms to comprehensive reforms.

Wu: Both the selection of a model to define the reform objective and the development of an implementation strategy took quite a while. Only gradually did they become more explicit.

With respect to which model should be followed, by the mid-1980s the reforms in Eastern Europe were no longer popular because those that had been perceived as the most successful—that is, those in Hungary—were facing many difficulties. Even prominent advocates of market socialism, such as Włozimierz Brus, began to reject the earlier proposals. In 1989, Brus and fellow-Polish-exile-in-London Kazimierz Łaski, who was another prominent advocate of market socialism, published the book *From Marx to the Market,* which clearly repudiated market socialism and explored other ways to develop the market.

Under these circumstances, Chinese economists gradually lost interest in market socialism and, instead, turned their attention to the market economies for applicable models. There were two influential market-economy models at the time: the government-driven market economies in East Asia and the free-market economies in the West. In general, Chinese government officials were more inclined toward the East Asian model. Deng Xiaoping highly praised the Four Little Dragons (Hong Kong, Singapore, South Korea, and Taiwan [China]), in particular Singapore, whereas academics armed with modern economics admired the Western model. Although the two models are quite different when it comes to defining the role of government, the differences between the two were not so apparent when the command economy still remained dominant. Because the market was still underdeveloped, even supporters of the development of a free-market economy recognized that the government would have to play a major coordinating role. They tended to agree with Alexander Gerschenkron, who had suggested that a powerful government was needed when a country was attempting to become a developed economy and escape economic backwardness. It was felt that the government would be more effective in bringing out the advantages of the late developers. The supporters of reform, in both academic circles and the government, finally reached a consensus on the preliminary objective of the reform, which was to establish a type of market economy in which the government would play a greater role than that of the governments in the industrialized nations in terms of resource allocations. This is what became known as the "1980s consensus on reform."

Ma: Even after reaching a consensus, it still took a long time, and many ups and downs, to adopt a mode of execution and a strategy to achieve this institutional objective.

Wu: You are right. The core market institution is free prices. To let the "market mechanism play a fundamental role in resource allocations" means that the flow of resources should be determined by prices that are formed through free competition and that reflect the scarcity of supply and demand. Therefore, regardless of what type of market economy is to be established, the key is to build a market institution that enables free competition. But during this process, many technical issues must be addressed. Furthermore, the process will encounter many obstacles and resistance from the privileged groups of rent-seekers.

The overall reform process that sought to establish a competitive market institution underwent many rounds of experimentation and setbacks. In November 1993, the Third Plenary Session of the Fourteenth Communist Party Central Committee adopted the "Decision of the CCP Central Committee on Issues of Building a Socialist Market Economy," which clearly articulated a roadmap for establishing a socialist market economy by combining the overall reform with breakthroughs in priority areas. It was only then that China's economic reform strategy begin to shift from an incremental approach to a more comprehensive approach.

Ma: The reform initiatives launched by Third Plenary Session were quite effective and played a crucial role in sustaining the high economic growth.

Wu: For a number of years thereafter, China's economic reforms made impressive progress based on the overall program and implementation plan of the 1993 Third Plenary Session.

First, the ownership structure of the national economy was improved for the better—from a structure dominated by the state sector to a structure composed of various ownership types. With the exception of several industries still under the state monopoly, the private sector became the main driving force in the economy. By 2006, jobs provided by private businesses accounted for 72 percent of total employment in urban areas. The SOE reforms also made significant progress by reorganizing most nonfinancial SOEs that were not directly held by the central government into state-controlled joint-stock companies. Additionally, the big four state-owned commercial banks were listed on the overseas stock exchanges in the early 2000s. These companies established a basic corporate-governance framework based on diversified ownership.

Second, a preliminary market institution was established. At the end of the twentieth century, a goods market had been established, and in the early 2000s the development of a financial market began to accelerate. The free-price market mechanism made the allocation of scarce resources more efficient, which in turn underpinned the sustained economic growth.

Third, the combination of market-oriented reforms and the opening up to the outside world enabled China to take advantage of the opportunities of globalization and to expand its market to all corners of the globe. By the turn of the century, China had become the world's most powerful base for the processing industries.

Ma: Why was there still vast room for rent seeking by those connected to power, even though a basic market institution had already been established by the end of the twentieth century? And why was it so difficult to rein in the corruption?

Wu: I believe the problem was due to the fact that the reforms remained incomplete. As noted before, the reform objective that was accepted by the majority of people in the mid-1980s was to establish a government-driven market economy, similar to that in Japan and the other East Asian countries. However, under this economic model, for instance, as in Japan, government interventions were executed through the central bank's "window guidance" for the provision of banking credits and through the Ministry of International Trade and Industry's industrial guidance policy for economic development. Unlike in China, however, governments in the other East Asian countries did not directly intervene in business activities. This is because the existing Chinese economy had emerged from Leninist state syndicates (referred to by some Eastern European economists as the "Party-State, Inc."). This mighty state machine still directly managed economic activities, and the powerful state sector still controlled major parts of the national economy. Although the East Asian countries faced many hurdles when attempting to further reform their economies as well as the corresponding "authoritarian development model," the difficulties were nothing when compared to the obstacles and resistance that China has encountered in trying to change its former Soviet-style system into a market-oriented system based on rule of law and democracy.

The new economic system, established by the turn of the twenty-first century, is quite different from those in the other emerging markets of East Asia—China's economy is a semi-command, semi-market economy, in which the government and the state sector still maintain powerful control over the economy and the society. Such an economic model is characterized by the continuing dominance of the state sector, including government agencies and SOEs, in terms of resource allocations. This is specifically reflected in the following. First, although it no longer accounts for a majority share of GNP, the state sector still controls the lifelines of the economy and enjoys a monopoly position in the oil, telecommunications, and railway industries as well as the financial sector. Second, central and local governments continue to hold huge power over the allocation of important economic resources, such as land and financial support. Third, although it is a critical element in a modern market economy, the rule of law has not yet been established. Frequent interventions in the microeconomic activities of enterprises are possible because of the huge discretionary power granted to government officials and because of the procedures for approving investment projects, including issuing market-entry permits and controlling prices.

The semi-command, semi-market economy is transitional. It includes elements of both the new free-market economy and the former command (or controlled) economy. It may develop into a modern market economy by restraining the administrative powers and gradually phasing out government interventions in microeconomic activities, with the government focusing on the provision of public services. Alternatively, if the government's power over resource allocations and its interventions in microeconomic activities are further enhanced, it might develop into state capitalism. Since the beginning of the twenty-first century, the focus of debates in China has been on the future direction of the development of the current economy.

Ma: Perhaps that is why, why in 2003 the Third Plenary Session of the Communist Party's Sixteenth Central Committee passed the "Decision of the CCP Central Committee on a Number of Issues Concerning the Improvement of the Socialist Market Economy."

Wu: Unfortunately, implementation of that decision was unsatisfactory.

The reform went smoothly in terms of changing the ownership structure and increasing the autonomy of small enterprises. By the early 2000s, the ownership reform had been completed for small and medium-sized enterprises and for rural and township collectives affiliated with grassroots governments. Most of these enterprises became proprietary or corporatized firms. However, when the reform moved to the SOEs that held monopolies in the energy, telecommunications, oil, and financial sectors, the pace slowed down significantly. In some places, the SOE reforms were distorted and cases of crony capitalism emerged during the privatization process: "those in charge of cooking took all the food" (that is, asset stripping by management). In recent years, debate has been rekindled about whether the state should make further inroads into the strategic sectors or should retreat from these sectors. Some people have even suggested that the state share in these sectors should be increased. After 2004, there was some backsliding, or what the Chinese media called "re-nationalization" or "new nationalization."

Second, administrative interventions in microeconomic activities in the name of "macroeconomic management" were strengthened. In the fourth quarter of 2003, the economy showed signs of overheating, but the majority view at the time was that the macroeconomic situation was only "partially overheating." The response was to let the line ministries issue joint requirements to restrain investment and production in the iron and steel, electrolytic aluminum, and cement industries. Beginning at that time, various parts of the government intensified control by increasing interventions in microeconomic activities at the enterprise level. The capability and means of the administrative agencies to allocate resources were significantly reinforced, at the expense of a weakening of the fundamental role of the market. As Lord Acton once said, "Power corrupts, and absolute power corrupts absolutely." The expansion of administrative powers led to an expansion of rent-seeking activities in the institutional infrastructure, which, in turn, aggravated corruption.

Third, political reforms lagged. Shortly after the launch of the economic reforms, Deng Xiaoping delivered his well-known "August 18 talk" at a meeting of the Politburo in 1980, signaling the beginning of political reforms. In 1986, he repeatedly pointed out that without political reforms, it would be difficult to implement the economic reforms, so he called for accelerated political reforms. However, neither in 1980 nor in 1986 were political reforms carried out. After Deng Xiaoping's death in 1997, at his memorial service the new leadership reiterated the call for political reforms. The 1997 Fifteenth National Communist Party Congress articulated the need to develop a Communist country ruled by law. The 2002 Sixteenth National Communist Party Congress reasserted this call and drew attention to the need to develop political democracy and to improve the political civilization. However, little progress has been made during the last ten years. For example, it took more than thirteen years to adopt some basic statutes for a market economy, such as the Property Rights Law and the Anti-Monopoly Law. In a modern market economy, where impersonalized transactions prevail, the enforcement of contracts cannot be secure without commonly accepted and equitable laws and a fair and independent judiciary system. In the absence of these conditions, participants in economic activities must "befriend government officials" in order to safeguard their property. This has led to increased momentum in rent-seeking activities and widespread buying and selling of government managerial jobs.

Ma: Since the 1990s, the Chinese economy has been characterized by a high growth rate. Although people's living standards have improved, there is resentment of the status quo. A main reason for the social discontent is the prevalence and spread of corruption, and the source of such corruption is the rent-seeking activities by the administrative powers when they intervene in the market and engage in microeconomic activities.

The expansion of rent seeking has resulted in the worsening corruption. According to Chinese economist Wang Xiaolu, in 2005 the amount of gray income in China totaled RMB 4.8 trillion, but three years later, in 2008, it had reached RMB 5.4 trillion. Total economic rent was estimated at 20 percent to 30 percent of GDP. The huge economic rent and the inability to lower the Gini coefficient are decisive factors in accelerating the polarization between rich and poor.

A serious social consequence of the corruption has been the sharp widening of the gap in household income and wealth. Various studies reveal that the Gini coefficient for family income in China has increased from 0.16 during the pre-reform period to 0.5, indicating that China has joined the group of countries in which there is significant inequality in terms of income distribution. The ongoing widening of the income gap has not only created social contradictions, it has also divided opinion regarding the future direction of the reforms. Furthermore, such differences of opinion appear to be intensifying. This situation has given rise to an unavoidable historical question: Where should China's reforms go from here? People with keen insight have warned of the approaching danger of crony capitalism, or, as referred to by Mao Zedong, of "bureaucratic capitalism" and "comprador, feudal state-monopoly capitalism."

I recall that on the occasion commemorating the twentieth anniversary of the launch of the reforms, you quoted the British writer Charles Dickens to describe the state of the reforms, "It was the best of times, it was the worst of times . . . it was the season of Light, it was the season of Darkness, it was the spring of hope, it was the winter of despair, we had everything before us, we had nothing before us, we were all going direct to heaven, we were all going direct the other way." At the time, you also pointed out that "there are two destinies before us: one is a market economy based on rule of law under a political civilization, and the other is privatization under crony capitalism. The two paths are clashing and the trend of going down the latter path is becoming more aggressive. We have to clearly recognize the threat to the future of our nation. It is imperative that we start from the basics when facing these deep social problems and that we establish the foundation for a society ruled by law." I think that what you meant at the time was that there was a race between these two different trends.

More than a decade has now passed, but it appears that there still is no winner.

Wu: At present, it is particularly important to realize that the ultra-left is a punishment for the ultra-right.[1] The income gap is widening, corruption has become more rampant, and there is an increasingly obvious trend toward crony capitalism. Under these circumstances, some people have tried to hide the truth about the problems and have

[1] "Left and "right" are subtle and polemical concepts in Chinese politics that can only be understood within the specific historical contexts. In general, ultra-leftists seek to strengthen Communist rule by

attempted to mislead the general public. They are advocating a negation of the reforms and a return to statism.

Since the early 2000s there have been two completely different views on the causes of the crony capitalism. For instance, supporters of the reforms have attributed the social inequalities to the unfinished market-oriented reforms and the very slow pace of political reforms, whereas others believe that the market-oriented reforms are the main reason for the spread of corruption and the widening of the income gap. Those who hold the latter opinion are following the traditional political-economy interpretation that claims that a market economy, by default, will widen the gap between the rich and poor and will lower the living standards of the working people.

The existence of these opposite views is a normal phenomenon. However, when the debate reached a stalemate, the supporters of the pre-reform system, who were traditional Communist Party ideologues, resorted to calls for populism and nationalism. They tried to ride the waves of the people's resentment against corruption and shift the target from the privileged groups that were oppressing and exploiting the people to the market-oriented reforms, as if the reforms were the causes of the social and economic problems.

They criticized the reforms for having "betrayed the Leninist theory of permanent revolution under the dictatorship of the proletariat."[2] With respect to economic policies, they complained that, first, "the central leadership has pushed from top down to make great efforts to develop the part of the economy under nonpublic ownership but has said nothing about the efforts needed to develop the public ownership part of the economy" and, second, "the policy to keep large enterprises under public ownership and leave smaller enterprises to other forms of ownership has led to serious adverse consequences." With regard to the political policies, they voiced discontent about the "constant support for liberal policies" and the "abandonment of the Marxist theory of class struggle and the betrayal of the dictatorship of the proletariat." They went on to protest that "during the last two years, the central leadership has put forward some inexplicable propositions that contradict the theories of class struggle and revolution,

resorting to a powerful state to realize absolute egalitarianism. They hope to resume "continuing the revolution under the dictatorship of the proletariat." In contrast, ultra-rightists seek to promote privatization and democratization at any cost and they are undeterred by open and transparent processes and procedural reforms.

[2] This was an attempt by the Chinese Communist Party to legitimize the Cultural Revolution. Claiming that the risk of capitalism restoration always exists in a socialist society, the proletariat should carry out a "cultural revolution" to recapture those powers seized by "capitalist roaders within the Party." The theory was first put forward in November 1967 and was incorporated into the Communist Party Constitution adopted at the Ninth National Communist Party Congress in 1969.

such as 'putting people first,' 'a peaceful rise,' 'a harmonious society,' and 'a moderately prosperous society.' "

With respect to foreign policy, these people alleged that the Communist Party had "continuously implemented policies of surrender and compromise." They argued, "In recent years our Party has stopped advocating Marxist internationalism. There has been no mention of imperialism. The new leadership followed this practice." They complained that "over the years there have been national democratic revolutions and struggles against imperialists. . . . We not only have stopped supporting the revolutions, but also we are following behind the backsides of the imperialists to vilify the revolutionary movements as 'terrorist organizations' and 'destabilizing forces.' " Furthermore, they stated that "reform has privatized, Westernized, corrupted, and divided the country. Efforts are being repeated to institutionalize these changes in the name of reform and opening and a new class of pro-American capitalists is being nurtured." They also pointed their fingers at the market-oriented reforms as the culprit for all the social and economic ills—from the rampant corruption and inequalities in income distribution to the unaffordable medical bills and limited opportunities to attend school, and even the stripping of state assets and the spread of mining accidents.

In essence, what those advocates proposed was a return to the former system dominated by ultra-leftist policies. For instance, they advocated that "in the urban areas all the previously publicly owned assets that were privatized during the period of reform and opening should be confiscated and returned to socialist ownership by the whole people. Rural policy should promote nationalization of land, collectivization of agricultural production, and socialization of the farmers' lifestyles." With regard to the political system, they called for once again raising the banner of "taking class struggle as the key link," "permanent revolution under the dictatorship of the proletariat," and imposing "all-round dictatorship over the bourgeoisie inside and outside the Party."

Ma: Under the influence of these ideological propositions, the pace of the reform of large SOEs has slowed down, and the position of the state sector's administrative monopoly remains untouched. There is a call to "maintain absolute state-sector control over seven industries, including power, oil, petrochemicals, telecommunications, coal, civil aviation, and shipping," and to "maintain strong control" over nine other industries, including equipment and manufacturing, automobiles, information technology, construction, iron and steel, nonferrous metals, chemicals, prospecting and design, and scientific and technological research. In some localities and sectors, there have been signs of "the state advancing and the private sector retreating" and "renewed nationalization."

Wu: In addition to the widely denounced incidents of "the state advancing and the private sector retreating" in the mining industry and the real-estate market, there have been disturbing cases of the private sector being crowded out from land ownership. The relevant law provides that urban land is owned by the state and rural land is collectively owned by the farmers. In the early 1990s, as urbanization began to accelerate, a large amount of rural land was expropriated by the government for urban construction. Since then, more than 80 percent of the land available for urban construction has come from collectively owned land expropriated from the farmers. Transactions between farmers as property owners and the government are not carried out on an equal footing. Rather, the government has used its exclusive powers to simply take over the land. Under this institutional arrangement, compensation for the farmers is not determined by the market value of the land but by the value of its annual produce, and the maximum level of compensation is set at thirty times the produce value. As a matter of fact, in some places the ceiling is no more than ten times. Governments at various levels practice "buying low and selling high," allowing as much as RMB 20 to 30 trillion to be transferred from the farmers to the government. The amount of the de facto free transfer of farmers' property is shocking.

In addition, in 2009 the government adopted an economic stimulus program to ensure that GDP would continue to grow at more than 8 percent. The stimulus program included RMB 4 trillion in funding for planned investments and RMB 10 trillion in loans, mainly provided to large SOEs and government projects. Since money creation is eventually "paid for" by residents who hold currency, the supply of a massive amount of funds for investment projects and loans meant that a huge quantity of wealth was transferred from households to the government.

Hence, a vicious cycle has emerged in recent years: monopolies, administrative allocations of resources, and interventions in microeconomic activities have all enlarged the space for rent seeking, leading to a worsening of corruption. But because of the manipulation of public opinion, the market-oriented reforms are regarded as the culprits, thus providing further "justification" for reinforcing the administrative interventions and state monopolies.

Ma: Amid the resurgence of these practices, calls for a return to the former statist system have become more vociferous since 2004. This trend became more apparent after the global financial crisis erupted in 2008. The government was widely praised for its responses, capabilities, and efficiencies in reacting to the crisis, and the "China miracle" gained currency in certain circles. According to the "miracle advocates," China's success was due to the administrative means of the powerful state. These means were considered to be China's political advantage. Some scholars even elevated state control of the national economy to a so-called "China model," while criticizing the free-market economies and today's mainstream economics. They preached that the excessive administrative interventions in the economy were strengths, not weaknesses, that had allowed for the creation of the "miracles" of the Beijing Olympics and the high-speed railways. According to this argument, the developed market economies should learn from and copy this model. Some people even believe that the world can only be saved by the so-called "China model," characterized by powerful government control of the economy and the entire society.

Wu: After the onset of the global financial crisis, relationships between creditors and debtors were seriously damaged. In some countries, the government supplemented business creditworthiness with its own credibility, or even borrowed on behalf of businesses in order to end the contagion of the systemic risks and to prevent the collapse of the financial system. These were short-term responses, but in China's social environment, some people interpreted them as long-term trends of social development. The "Beijing consensus," coined as an alternative to the "Washington consensus," was said to describe the Chinese economic development model. Advocates predicted that this model, characterized by a powerful government controlling the entire socioeconomic system, was a prime example that the rest of the world should follow. What are the effects of such administrative instruments? Has there been a bias toward excessive use of administrative readjustments in China? Are these instruments in line with the nature of a market economy? Historically, it has been common practice for a government to use its powers to stabilize the economy. In China, the government's discretionary powers are unlimited, and therefore its interventions are all the more powerful. In 2009, the Chinese government raised the GDP growth rate to 9.1 percent through massive investments and lending, something that no other government was able to do. In the short run, the highly intensified government interventions in the economy have achieved many successes, but in the long run, it is not clear whether they will be a blessing or a curse.

It is dangerous to further enhance state control over the economy and the society, to allow administrative powers to intervene in the market at will, and, for the sake of legitimacy, to package all such behavior into some kind of theory. If China is to take this path, the end result will be state capitalism and crony capitalism rather than "socialism with Chinese characteristics."

Ma: In a country like China with a long history of highly centralized power, government agencies and officials are more likely to use their authority to create huge space for rent seeking. The expansion of administrative powers is especially beneficial to corrupt officials. That is why state capitalism will lead to crony capitalism.

Wu: Then the ultra-left path and the ultra-right path will reach the same end.

Ma: The sixty-year history of the People's Republic of China demonstrates that either there will be a bright future for a prosperous, democratic, civilized, and harmonious modern country, to be achieved through market-oriented, rule-of-law, and democracy-based reform, or China will have a bleak fate in which the minority rules and the masses suffer from widespread poverty.

Wu: To summarize our discussion, China has now arrived at a fork in the path of history and once again faces the question, whither China? Whether China can write another brilliant chapter in history will depend on which path it takes. As Francis Bacon once commented, "Histories make men wise." We should learn from our historical experiences to explore where we should go from here: let history shed light on China's future path.

DIALOGUE 2

WHY SHOULD THE SOVIET-TYPE ECONOMIC SYSTEM BE REFORMED?

Ma Guochuan (Ma): The transformation from a traditional socialist economy to a new system in various countries, be it the reforms in the former Soviet Union (USSR), the East European countries, and China or the postsocialist transitions in the aftermath of the dramatic changes in the region, share one common feature, that is, a shift from the USSR's centrally planned-economy model (or, from the perspective of implementation of the state plan, the "command economy") to a market economy. To resolve the current problems facing China, we should start from scratch. How did the command economy come into being, and what were its defects that led to calls for reform within those countries where it had been established?

Wu Jinglian (Wu): Socialism was first proposed as a social ideal. To clearly explain the origins of the Soviet type of socialist system, we need to trace back and review the evolution of socialism step by step, from its birth as an ideal to its transformation into a specific economic institution.

The term *socialism* gained currency in England and France after the 1840s. However, socialist aspirations were raised by philosophical forerunners as early as the beginning of the sixteenth century, when the feudal manorial system in medieval Western Europe began to decline and capitalism was beginning to emerge.

From the late medieval period onward, capitalism, as an economic institution characterized by the employment of labor, grew stronger as it destroyed the feudal manorial system that had prevailed for a millennium. By the seventeenth and eighteenth centuries, capitalism had been established in a number of Western European countries, enabling those countries to make great strides during the following centuries. As Marx and Engels point out in *The Communist Manifesto*, as if by magic, within less than one hundred years, the capitalists awakened the social productivity of labor, which was much greater than the total of all productive forces created in the past.

However, the birth of the new society negatively affected those people living at the bottom of the society. The socialist pioneers, driven by a sense of responsibility and mission, sharply criticized this phenomenon and called for the establishment of a better society.

Ma: An archetypical example demonstrating the transition's adverse impacts on the toiling masses was the enclosure movement in England. At the end of the fifteenth century, as the woolen textile industry was on the rise in England and Italy, the price of wool increased sharply. Driven by a yearning for profits, noblemen and abbots divided and fenced in the common land to graze livestock, as if the enclosed land were their own property. They hired laborers to attend to the herds. Hundreds of thousands of peasants gained personal freedoms, but lost the land on which they had depended for their livelihoods. As penniless vagrants, they migrated to the cities in search of earning a living. But the government greeted them with whippings, cutting off their ears, hangings, and other types of torture. Those who found jobs in workshops or factories labored under miserable working conditions and earned meager pay.

Wu: The capitalist economy as an institution came into being first by dissolving the bondage of the serfs to their feudal lords, so that they were lifted off the land of the feudal lords and entered the labor market. At the time, when there still was no winner between the old and new systems, and when the feudalist order was collapsing but a basic market order had not yet taken root, a small group of wealthy scions and oligarchs preyed upon small producers and gained massive wealth, power, and social status.

A number of early philosophers at the time stood up against the widespread social inequalities and called for the establishment of an ideal society. Their propositions were in response to both the protests by the toiling masses, who were suffering during the dramatic social transition, and to people's desires for a better world. But due to the economic circumstances at that time, they could not design a socialist economic system; instead, they resorted to ancient myths about a better society. In 1516 Sir Thomas More published a fictional work that became known as *Utopia*, with the subtitle *A Truly Golden Little Book, No Less Beneficial Than Entertaining, of the Best State of a Republic*. In this book, through the words of a traveler, Sir Thomas More strongly criticizes unbridled looting by the unscrupulous rich and calls for an end to the coexistence of "hideous poverty" and "wanton luxury." He imagines a perfect fictional state, called "Utopia," to describe his ideals of social equity and common prosperity. In this perfect state, property is jointly owned by all residents who work together and share what they produce.

After Sir Thomas More, several other Western European philosophers proposed their own social ideals. The main appeal of these early socialists was social equity and common prosperity. Their imaginary socioeconomic systems shared one common feature: collective possession of wealth. According to Sir Thomas More, "I am entirely convinced that no just and even distribution of goods can be made, nor any perfect happiness be found . . . until private property is utterly abolished."

Ma: The embryonic form of a socialist system as an institution did not emerge until the first half of the nineteenth century. It was formulated by the "Utopians" in Western Europe.

Wu: As we know, the first Industrial Revolution based on the use of steam engines and fossil fuel, took place in Western Europe in the late 1800s with the use of machines giving birth to a mode of large-scale industrial production. Mankind entered a new era of greatly accelerated economic growth that was accompanied by aspirations for social equity and common prosperity. The new generation, called the Utopians, such as Henri de Saint-Simon, Charles Fourier, and Robert Owen, in succession designed their own blueprints for socialism, and some of them attempted to put them into practice. However, at that time, the mode of large-scale industrial production was just emerging and the socialists could not imagine a production mode different from that of petty industry. When contemplating an ideal future society, their benchmark was self-sustaining small communities under patriarchal control. Because their ideas were replete with idealism, the experiments of the Utopians could not but fail.

Ma: Marx and Engels shared the same values as the Utopians. But they went further in terms of their moral criticism of capitalism and in their aspirations for a legendary utopia. Analyzing the contradictions in capitalist society, they concluded that socialism would eventually replace capitalism. Marx and Engels both believed that their efforts would transform socialism from a utopian ideal to a scientifically proven blueprint for a new society—what they called "scientific socialism."

Wu: Engels, in a well-known 1877 statement in his *Anti-Dühring*, notes, "So now modern industry, in its more complete development, comes into collision with the bounds within which the capitalistic mode of production holds it confined. The new productive forces have already outgrown the capitalistic mode of using them. Modern socialism is nothing but the reflex, in thought, of this conflict in fact; its ideal reflection in the minds, first, of the class directly suffering under it, the working class." The completion of the Industrial Revolution and the further division of labor in the mid-nineteenth century changed production from an individual activity to a series of social activities, and from individual products to social products. Production became more socialized, but the growing capitalist system of private ownership advanced as well. Serious conflicts between the two phenomena emerged. The conflicts were visible everywhere, for example, in the contradiction between the seemingly ever-expanding production and the lack of consumption (the final purchase of goods and services), the periodic economic crises, the poverty endured by the proletariat class, and the sharpening of class antagonisms. Engels thus concluded that highly socialized production requires that the society impose unified management on production. This can only be achieved when the general public possesses the means of production. In his magnum opus, *Das Kapital*, Marx provides further arguments for the inevitable replacement of capitalism by socialism, based on his development of two concepts: "the absolute general law of capitalist accumulation" and "the historical trend of capitalist accumulation."

The absolute general law of capitalist accumulation refers to the inevitable pauperization of the working people and the sharpening of class antagonisms due to the continuous increase in the ratio of capital to labor during the process of capital accumulation (or, in Marx's words, progressive increases in the share of constant capital to total capital, or continuous increases in the "organic composition of capital"); the continuous decline in labor income to national income; and the increased unemployment (Marx called this "the relative surplus of population").

The second concept refers to the development of capitalist expropriations once the capitalist mode of production takes root and production is further socialized. Marx wrote, "What is now to be expropriated is not the self-employed worker, but the capitalist who exploits a large number of workers. This expropriation is accomplished . . . through the centralization of capitals. One capitalist always strikes down many others . . . this expropriation of many capitalists by a few. . . . Along with the constant decrease in the number of capitalist magnates . . . the mass of misery, oppression, slavery, degradation, and exploitation too grows; but with this also grows the revolt of the working class."

Marx predicted that "the centralization of the means of production and the socialization of labor reach a point at which they become incompatible with their capitalist integument. This integument is burst asunder. The knell of capitalist private property sounds. The expropriators are expropriated."

Marx did not believe that socialism as a socioeconomic system would be imposed by external factors. Instead, he believed that the replacement of capitalism by socialism was a "natural historical process," driven by the contradictions inherent in capitalism. This was because capital accumulation entailed a monopoly by a few or even by a single enterprise. As Marx stated, when all capital inputs are consolidated into a single capital in a production unit, concentration will reach its extreme; and when all capital is consolidated under a single capitalist or in a single capitalist enterprise in a society, concentration will reach its extreme. In such a case, the socialist revolution will need to seek "the expropriation of a few usurpers by the mass of the people" and to change the ownership base of a single or a few monopolistic firm(s).

It is said that when the expropriation of the few capitalists was completed, the entire society would become a big factory built on the foundation of common ownership of the means of production. Marx called this the "social factory," or "Robinson Crusoe on a social scale," and he foresaw "a community of free individuals, carrying on their work with the means of production in common, in which the labor-power of all the different individuals is consciously applied as the combined labor-power of the community. All the characteristics of Robinson's labor are here repeated, but with this difference, that they are social instead of individual." Therefore, Marx's socialist economic model may also be called a *social factory model.*

Ma: It is interesting to ask the following question: because the social factory envisaged by Marx would be gigantic, how would it be organized and managed?

Wu: Marx's future society would be quite different from the Communist countries as we know them: there would be no "special oppressive force" of the state. Marx and Engels had serious doubts about the "coercive power" of the state. The state was seen as "at best, an evil inherited by the proletariat after its victorious struggle for class supremacy," and Engels even argued that conditions should be created to "throw the entire lumber of the state on the scrap heap." He thought that the first act in which the state really comes forward as the representative of society as a whole—taking possession of the means of production in the name of society—is at the same time its last independent act as a state and the interference of state power in social relations becomes superfluous in one sphere after another and then becomes dormant.

What would the new society look like without the state's coercive power? Marx's answer was, "In place of the old bourgeois society, with its classes and class antagonisms, we shall have an association in which the free development of each is the condition for the free development of all."

Ma: As you pointed out in *Understanding and Interpreting China's Economic Reform,* the nineteenth-century Marxist forerunners criticized and analyzed the injustices rendered by the "robber barons" and the contradictions in capitalist economies. Today, their analyses still shine as prophetic inspirations. Nevertheless, even though more than one hundred years have passed since the deaths of Marx and Engels, their prediction that socialism would first be established in the developed capitalist countries has not materialized. Communist countries, like the Soviet Union in the twentieth century, were born in backward economies. Instead of discarding all the waste of the state, as Engels had predicted, those countries maximized the coercive power of the state. Why is there such a huge difference between the visions of the pioneers and the practices of those who followed them?

Wu: I believe there are three reasons.

First, Marx's analysis of capitalist society was based on the economic growth model of the Western countries at that time. Under such an investment-driven growth model, the ratio of capital to labor—that is, the "organic composition of capital"— inevitably rose, and there were periodic economic crises. In the political arena, the working class was pauperized and class antagonisms were sharpened. However, the second Industrial Revolution in the latter half of the nineteenth century brought about drastic changes. Under the new economic growth model, which is also called *modern economic growth,* the main driving force was technological progress and rising productivity. Although the investment rate and the unemployment rate did not register obvious increases, the overall income of the working people rose due to the enlarged role of human capital (knowledge and skills) and the increased number of white-collar workers. Because the division of labor in the market was becoming increasingly efficient, the role of economies of scale was becoming less important and Marx's prediction of a social factory did not materialize. During the first Industrial Revolution the archetypical technology was the steam engine, and the top priority was to achieve economies of scale. Before the early twentieth century, increases in the size of enterprises and in large-scale production were considered the driving forces behind industrial development. The subsequent technological revolution, such as the use of electricity, changed the undercurrents to expand the scale of production. The development of the services sector in the mid-twentieth century and the emergence of the high-tech industries at the end of the twentieth century enabled small enterprises in a number of sectors to utilize their advantages: small became beautiful. The socialization of production was driven not solely by increases in the size of enterprises. This is why modern small enterprises still account for the majority of enterprises in the developed countries.

Second, Marx did not foresee that the Western countries would act to oppose monopolies or would adopt progressive social policies. In 1890, seven years after Marx's death, the United States Congress passed the Sherman Antitrust Act. In 1914, the Clayton Antitrust Act was enacted. These acts outlawed monopolistic practices. Against the background of a progressive general public at the turn of the twentieth century, President Theodore Roosevelt strengthened power to enforce the Sherman Act and overruled some attempts by syndicates to establish monopolies through mergers. Under President Franklin D. Roosevelt's New Dea in the 1930s, the J. P. Morgan and Rockefeller empires were broken up. After the Second World War, almost all developed countries strengthened enforcement of anti-monopoly legislation, and monopolies were prohibited by law. Even though, economically, there was a trend in the direction of capital concentration and an increase in the size of enterprises, the society could not be reduced to several or to a single monopolistic factory. In parallel with progress toward democracy and rule of law, governments in the developed countries implemented various social reforms in response to demand. In general, people's living standards and democratic rights improved.

Last, in Marx's socialist society there would be no need for state coercion, as "the free development of each is the condition for the free development of all," and the society would be managed by a community of freely associated individuals. This is an ideal, but it can only be achieved when there are no conflicts of interest among individuals or among individuals and the people as a whole, when wealth pours in without any resource scarcities, and, as Mao Zedong put it, when everyone is "devoted to others without any thought of oneself."

Ma: Apparently these conditions do not exist in real life, and Marx's vision of a free association without state coercion was doomed. The idealized goal might not have blocked the spread of socialism in the nineteenth century when conditions for socialist revolution were not ripe. But the revolutionaries of the twentieth century had to be more practical, as they were tasked with establishing a socialist institution.

Wu: You are right. At the turn of the twentieth century, the leaders of the socialist revolution, when faced with the issue of how to establish a socialist institution, adopted a more practical attitude toward the state. Lenin, the head of the Bolshevik faction in Russia's Social Democratic Labor Party, stood out among the leaders. After the February Revolution in 1917, Lenin returned to Russia and published *The State and Revolution*, which established a theoretical foundation for socialist revolution and construction. In this book, Lenin proposes a social model for a "state syndicate" that is very different from Marx's social factory. In essence, the "state syndicate" would turn the entire society into one big corporation, monopolized and managed by a proletarian dictatorship. Lenin believed that in a socialist society there would be a "conversion of all citizens into workers and of other employees into one huge 'syndicate'—the whole state"—and "the whole of society would become a single office and a single factory with equality of labor and pay." Lenin's proposition removed the idealism from Marx's social model, and, for decades, guided the Soviet Communist Party's efforts to establish a socialist economy. Both the achievements and the problems of the Soviet Union were directly linked to Lenin's model.

Ma: After coming to power, did the Bolsheviks immediately attempt to establish a state-syndicate type of socialist system?

Wu: After the Bolsheviks took power, the "peasant economy" remained dominant in Russia. Could an economic foundation for socialism be immediately established in such a country? There were different answers to this question among the leaders of the Bolshevik Party. Even Lenin wavered for a while. At first, he was thinking of a historical stage, of multiple economic elements, and then the economy would gradually transition to "complete socialism" anchored in state ownership. However, because of foreign intervention and the 1918–20 civil war, the Bolsheviks instead turned to overall nationalization and a command economy. Strict military-type control was imposed on the economy under comprehensive rationing. This is a typical emergency response during periods of war. But in 1919, the so-called war communism was written into the policy platform of the Eighth Congress of the Russian Communist Party (Bolshevik). To elaborate on the Communist Party platform, Nicolai Bukharin and Evgenii Preobrazensky, two of the most famous Communist Party theorists at the time, published a brochure called *The ABC of Communism* in which they describe a socialist economy based on the policies and practices of war communism. Hence, copying the model of war communism, the Soviet government established the world's first centrally planned economy.

Ma: This system was quite different from what Marx had envisaged. In the 1920s, *The ABC of Communism* was translated into Chinese, deeply influencing Chinese Communist Party leaders, such as Mao Zedong and Deng Xiaoping. In 1958, Zhang Chunqiao (a Communist Party functionary based in Shanghai) published "Do Away with the Ideology of Bourgeois Legal Thought," which won praise from Mao Zedong and was reprinted in the *People's Daily*. Zhang's article, which was full of tributes to war communism, had a huge effect in the country, both at that time and during the Cultural Revolution, when it was widely quoted.

Wu: It seems that the Chinese Communists did not know that *The ABC of Communism* had been challenged by the reality shortly after its publication. War communism helped the Bolsheviks win the civil war, but it caused serious economic and social problems. The problems were particularly unbearable for the peasants, resulting in their growing resentment. After the civil war, peasant uprisings broke out in many areas. Given this situation, the Soviet government decided to retreat from its so-called military mobilization and command economy. Instead, it implemented its New Economic Policy and resorted to the exchange of commodities and a market system. Commercial principles and commercial accounting were applied to all industrial and trade enterprises.

However, the New Economic Policy was only an expediency for a grim situation. In the short run, the Soviet leaders did not give up on their plan to establish a state syndicate. As Lenin stated in 1922, when responding to doubts in his Party regarding the threat of the new policy to Russia's socialist future: The state capitalism that we have introduced is a special kind. We hold all the commanding heights. Our proletarian state not only owns the land, but also all vital branches of industry. We are trying to form mixed companies in which part of the capital belongs to private capitalists. We are always in a position to dissolve them if we deem it necessary. By 1924, after four years of the new policy, agricultural and industrial production had largely recovered. But new debates then emerged among the Party leadership regarding whether or not to continue the New Economic Policy.

Ma: During these debates, the leadership of the Soviet Communist Party was divided into three factions: the leftists, led by Trotsky in support of immediate termination of the New Economic Policy; the rightists, led by Bukharin in support of continuing to implement the policy; and the centralists, led by Stalin.

The debates did not take place in a relaxed atmosphere, and they ended in ruthless political infighting. After Lenin's death, leaders of the leftists and the rightists—for instance, Trotsky, Zinoviev, Kamenev, and Bukharin—were either executed during the Great Purge or murdered abroad by Stalin's agents.

Wu: Stalin, who emerged as victor from the internal fighting, turned out to be even further inclined to the left than Trotsky. He called Bukharin and his followers "right opportunists," and he purged them for their "superstition about spontaneous market forces." The New Economic Policy was thus rejected. In 1929 Stalin launched a forced collectivization movement on the basis of his Anti-Rightist Movement and he established a centrally planned economy based on state ownership and so-called collective ownership under total state control.

Stalin never offered any systematic economic theory, but he took full advantage of the coercive power of the dictatorship to promote the collectivization of agriculture and national industrialization. The national economy was both controlled and directed by the state plan. Lenin's state syndicate advanced from a theoretical model to a reality. On the one hand, the Soviet type of socialist economy eliminated the idealistic elements in Marx's social factory and in his "community of freely associated individuals," but, on the other hand, it had a serious negative impact due to its implicit oriental statism.

Some Soviet scholars blamed Stalin's abrasive personality for the resultant system. But such an analysis is too simplistic. There was no fundamental difference between Lenin's state syndicate and Stalin's centrally planned economy.

As a matter of fact, Stalin introduced some flexibility after he established the planned economy. When the USSR's First Five-Year Plan (1928–32) encountered implementation difficulties, Stalin added to the state syndicate an "economic accounting system" to allow the law of value to play an "auxiliary role." After World War II, he further admitted that "so long as the two basic production sectors remain, commodity production and commodity circulation must remain in force as a necessary and very useful element in our national economic system." But these were only partial fixes and did not touch upon the basic framework of the state syndicate.

To sum up, although it was tainted by statism, which had been strongly criticized by Marx and Engels, Lenin and Stalin's socialist economy was taken for granted for a long time in many Communist countries as the "heavenly sanctioned" principle of Marxism. Stalin's formula—"socialist economy = dominant state ownership + command economy"—ruled the Communist world for more than half a century.

Ma: One question that is worth pondering is the following: Should people go as far as the Soviets did and worship statism in order to overcome the idealism of Marx's socialist economy?

Wu: Of course not, and there are prominent examples of this in the history of the socialist movement. For instance, after Engel's death in 1895, Bernstein, the leader of Germany's Social Democratic Party, unearthed Engel's idea on the possibility of taking over state power through parliamentary participation. Bernstein suggested that democracy is both a means and an end. According to his thinking, without democracy, socialism will result in new inequalities and totalitarian rule that constitutes a deprivation of freedom. Totalitarian rule is the greatest threat to humanitarianism and human rights. Thus began the period of democratic socialism during the twentieth century.

Modern democratic socialism advocates social improvements based on the principles of the free development of man, common prosperity, and social equity. In the first half of the last century, the democratic socialist parties, such as the Labour Party in the UK, became ruling parties by winning elections in a number of countries.

At first, these parties believed that nationalization was conducive to achieving social equity and common prosperity. Later realities taught them that nationalization and a command economy based on state ownership not only reduced economic efficiencies but also stymied freedom and equity. One by one, these ruling parties abandoned the goal of nationalization and turned to taxation, welfare, and other social policies to realize their social goals.

Ma: In addition to the ideological differences, what were the economists' views of the centrally planned economy?

Wu: The opinions of mainstream economists evolved in three stages. During the first stage, in the early 1900s, when a centrally planned economy had not yet been established in the Soviet Union, economists discussed the feasibility of a command economy based on public ownership. Interestingly, the proposition that a command economy could be efficient was first proposed not by Marxist economists but by

Vilfredo Pareto, the master of neoclassical economics, and his followers. These economists showed that a command economy, as a different means of allocating resources, could be as efficient as market competition, with the assumption of perfect information and zero transaction costs, and thus the institutional arrangements were irrelevant to efficiency.

During the second stage, from the 1920s to the 1930s, academics in the West became involved in the debates on "socialist calculations," focusing on the following question: Was the centrally planned economy efficient? This debate was kindled by economists Ludwig von Mises and F. A. Hayek of the Austrian School. They found that market prices and competition were crucial to allocating resources. Because there were no market mechanisms in the Soviet Union, it was impossible to have reasonable prices and to produce incentives. A group of Western economists who were considered to be socialist sympathizers responded quickly. Among this group, the model introduced by Polish-American economist Oskar R. Lange was the most influential. It was called the *competitive solution*, which was a simulation of market pricing by planning authorities.

Ma: Lange was born in Poland and received his degree in the United States. At the time of these debates, he was an assistant professor of statistics and economics working at an American university.

Wu: The competitive solution was based on an analysis by Vilfredo Pareto and Enrico Barone. In essence, it allowed the central planning authorities to simulate the market: the planning authorities would adjust prices according to the balance of supply and demand, and, based on the prices that they set or adjusted, the enterprises would decide what and how much to produce, hence resolving the efficiency problem in a command economy. Market socialism[1] was formulated during these debates on the efficiency of a socialist command economy. It suggests that the operational efficiency of a state-owned economy can be improved by planning authorities who simulate market pricing and introduce a certain degree of competition among enterprises. In the 1950s, market socialism strongly influenced the reforms in a number of Communist countries.

Hayek proposed a counter-critique of Lange's model, claiming the model was unfeasible. He pointed out that, because of imperfect information and knowledge and

[1] Market socialism, a reformed version of the Soviet model of socialism, was quite popular in Eastern Europe during the 1960s and 1970s. Advocated by Polish economists Oskar Lange and Włodzimierz Brus, market socialists attempted to introduce into a fully nationalized economy quasi-market mechanisms for price setting and enlarging the autonomy of state-owned enterprises in order to improve the vitality of the socialist economy.

uncertain consumer preferences, it is impossible for the central planning authorities to reasonably set prices, and hence it is impossible to effectively allocate resources. Hayek did not believe that the simulation of competition by the central planning authorities could replace real competition and achieve the same efficiencies.

It appears that there was no winner in these debates for two reasons. Theoretically, neoclassical economics, anchored in the assumption of perfect information, remained part of mainstream thought at the time. Hence, Lange's model, based on neoclassical economics, was widely accepted. Hayek's imperfect information was not fully understood.

Furthermore, the West had become bogged down in the global economic crisis that erupted in 1929, when the dark side of the USSR's economy had not yet been fully revealed.

Ma: During the worldwide Great Depression, the Soviet Union achieved industrialization under Stalin's iron fist at a faster-than-normal pace. Many influential international intellectuals were disappointed, or felt disillusioned, about the traditional liberal economic and political systems. They were curious about, and even felt a certain amount of affection toward, the USSR. They believed that the USSR was blazing a new trail for human progress.

It appears to me that, in an era of dramatic changes, it is not easy to clearly foresee the direction of history or to avoid being swayed by contemporary trends. It takes several generations to recognize the nature of a society. At present, a global financial crisis is sweeping across the main market-economy countries. The past tells us that under such circumstances, it is not easy to grasp the truth, and upholding the truth will require courage.

Wu: By the 1970s and the 1980s, new theoretical breakthroughs had been achieved, and modern economics developed further to include a more thorough analysis of the command economy.

As Joseph Stiglitz states in his *Economics*, because of the evolution of economics since the 1950s, economists have surpassed the neoclassical model in several respects. In particular, progress has been made in terms of a better understanding of the informational constraints and in terms of the immediate application of new knowledge. This has had a powerful impact on the development of economics.

When the neoclassical assumption of perfect information was relaxed, people gained a better understanding about the defects of the command economy.

The implicit premises of an effective command economy are, first, the central planning authorities possess perfect information regarding all economic activities, including the state of material and human resources, technical feasibilities, the composition of demand, and so forth. Second, a command economy is a monosociety, without separate interests and different value judgments, and in such a society all grassroots organizations implement the plan without any reservations. In the absence of these two preconditions, a centrally planned economy cannot function effectively because of the high costs of information and incentives. Because these premises are almost nonexistent in real life, the command economy faces insurmountable problems. In the first place, it is difficult to establish an effective information mechanism in a command economy. Modern production is characterized by rapid technological advances, with numerous options for the product mix, processing routes, and production schemes, as well as complex and rapidly changing consumption structures. Together with the deepening division of labor, links among members of a society and economic units are expanding and becoming more complicated. Under these circumstances, there has been an information "explosion." A command economy relies on the central planning authorities to manage a massive volume of information. There is a lack of horizontal linkages and a lack of effective mechanisms for feedback between the producers and the consumers or among the producers. In the administrative system, economic information is shared vertically through top-down directives and bottom-up reports. The transmission of information is often delayed or blocked due to the long distances and narrow channels. Furthermore, because every level of the administrative system has its own interests, the information they each provide cannot but suffer distortions. All these factors increase the costs of information and lead to "planned" misallocations of resources.

Another main problem in a centrally planned economy is the impossibility of establishing an effective incentive system. When resources are primarily allocated by the plan, decisions are made by the central planning authorities on behalf of the entire society and are implemented by members of the society organized according to hierarchical principles. This requires all members and all organizations to act as Marx's "Robinson Crusoe on a social scale": the arms follow the body and the fingers follow the arms. Organizations and workers implement the plan handed down from the upper levels with absolute loyalty. They should not be concerned with their own interests, nor should they deviate from the reality when providing statistics or progress reports to the planning authorities. In real life, this is impossible to achieve. All economic men, including planning authorities and their departments, have their own interests that are not necessarily in complete alignment with the interests of the whole society. The two groups of interests often contradict one another, leading to conflicts among the various entities. The costs of overcoming such distortions and deviations, which include expenses for planning, for implementing monitoring, and for preventing opportunistic behavior, are very high.

Based on the foregoing analysis, we can conclude that the lack of efficiency in a command economy is a fatal defect because of the way in which resources are allocated.

Ma: Most people recognize the problems of a command economy, but there is also no perfect system in this world. So why do we say that a market economy is better?

Wu: It is in the areas of resource allocations and incentive mechanisms that a market economy is much superior to a planned/command economy. The core of a market economy is pricing by the market. The relative prices of various resources formed through market competition embody information on the scarcity of these resources in comparison to the scarcity of hundreds of thousands of other resources. Individual members of the society can gauge the state of competition based on the relative prices, and, on this basis, they can make decisions regarding resource allocations, hence lowering the information costs for the overall effective allocation of resources. At the same time, every market participant is constrained by competition and property rights, hence significantly lowering the cost of incentives. Because of these advantages, a market economy is efficient in terms of resource allocations and operations. Without a market economy, resources will flow to different places without reliable guidance and will not be effectively allocated, and there will be no incentives to work hard. Without high economic efficiency, the ideals of an equitable society are but a mirage due to the absence of a material basis. In the worst-case scenario, "socialist weeds" are preferable to "capitalist seedlings," resulting in a socialist society of widespread poverty. Hence, the choice is clear between a planned economy and a market economy.

A market economy has its own shortcomings, but compared to a command economy it has huge advantages in these two key areas. At the first and last conference on reform economics, held in Vienna in 1988, an East European economist summarized the discussion on establishing the reform objectives by playing on the words of Churchill's famous 1947 dictum on democracy: "The market is the worst form of an economic system, except for all those other systems that have been tried from time to time."

DIALOGUE 3

THE INITIAL EMERGENCE OF REFORM IN 1956

Ma Guochuan (Ma): In the last dialogue we reviewed the origins of the Soviet-style socialist economic system and the reform history of the former Soviet Union and the Eastern European countries. We noted that the theoretical breakthrough that proved the infeasibility of a command economy was not achieved until the 1970s and the 1980s. Then why did these Communist countries begin, one after another, to reform as early as the 1950s?

Wu Jinglian (Wu): This was because the drawbacks of the command economy were becoming increasingly apparent in practice. Although the system suffered a fatal defect—that is, very high information costs and a lack of proper incentives—under extraordinary situations, it did have short-term advantages. Aided by its ability to utilize the state's coercive power, the command economy was highly capable in terms of mobilizing economic resources to satisfy the needs of the state. During the initial stage of economic development, when resources are not in short supply and there is much room for extensive growth, or when a country is threatened by war or is in a state of emergency, or when there are existing regulations regarding resource allocations intended to bring about an economic recovery, a command economy can better achieve the goals of the state because of its ability to mobilize resources and because it is easier to satisfy the desires for material well-being among the economic participants. However, once circumstances change and the primary goal becomes to improve the efficiency and quality of life, the drawbacks of the system quickly come to the fore.

For instance, before World War II and during the postwar rehabilitation period the Soviet Union managed to achieve an economic growth rate that was much higher than that of the capitalist countries. According to official Soviet statistics, by 1950 annual gross industrial output had increased 10.6 times over that in 1928, which was the first year of the First Five-Year Plan. Heavy industry had grown 19.5 times and light industry 4.1 times. However, in 1953 annual gross agricultural output and the yield of staple grains had still not reached the 1913 levels. After the postwar rehabilitation period, when technological progress and efficiency improvements were the decisive factors for sustained growth, the growth rates in the Soviet Union and the Eastern European countries began to falter. Their technologies and living standards increasingly lagged behind those of the capitalist countries. It was against this background that the need for reform in these countries became apparent.

Ma: An important distinction between China, on the one hand, and the Soviet Union and the Eastern European countries, on the other, is timing. The need for reform in the latter was raised after the command economy had already been in operation for a long period of time and had already demonstrated its low efficiency. In China, the need for reform was raised shortly after the establishment of the People's Republic in response to the overwhelming criticism of the system by Communist Party and government officials. Why did this somewhat special phenomenon occur in China?

Wu: I have also thought about this. It may be related to the different domestic and external environments when the command economy was first put into practice.

Ma: What was China's domestic environment back then?

Wu: I believe the most important factor in China at that time was the lack of preparedness on the part of Communist Party functionaries, including senior officials, to implement a Soviet-style economic system.

The Communist Party platform before 1949 did not call for the immediate establishment of such a system after taking power. Adoption of the system was first phased into the New Democracy period and then into the period of construction.

As early as 1940, in his "On New Democracy," Mao Zedong had suggested that socialism would be established in two steps after the victory of the democratic revolution. The first step was to establish the New Democracy and to carry out a transformation from an agricultural to an industrial society. The transition from the New Democracy to a socialist country would only be realized during the second step. The 1945 Seventh National Communist Party Congress reiterated this two-step strategy. With regard to the political system, Mao proposed that, in essence, the New Democracy would consist of joint dictatorship by the proletariat, the peasantry, the petty bourgeoisie, and the national bourgeoisie, led by the proletariat and based on an alliance of the proletariat and the peasantry. With respect to the economic system, he clearly stated that "there is a need to extensively develop capitalism," because "extensive development of capitalism will have some positive effects and will not have any negative effects."

Based on this, Mao called for "building an independent, free, democratic, united, prosperous, and powerful New China," which was a distinctive representation of his New Democracy. It was this representation that attracted many intellectuals and patriotic youths to join the revolution. The Communist Party Central Committee developed a specific plan for this two-step revolution. At an expanded meeting of the Politburo in September 1948, when nationwide victory was close at hand, Liu Shaoqi (who ranked second to Mao within the Communist Party) announced a plan, on instructions from Mao, for a two-step transition to the New Democracy. This was to include a three-year preparatory period and a ten-year construction period. It was only at the end of these two stages that planning for the transition to socialism would begin. At the Politburo meeting, Liu stated that in order to develop the economy during the New Democracy period, it was possible that the Communist Party would partner for ten to fifteen years with the bourgeoisie. Mao added, "When should an all-out offensive be launched? It may be fifteen years after the victory." All these plans led many Communist Party functionaries, in particular the intellectuals among them, to believe that the New Democracy stage would last for a long while.

Ma: What you have just described is only one aspect of the Communist Party's agenda and policy. Actually, at the meeting you just mentioned, Mao and Liu clearly pointed out that with the victory of the democratic revolution, the main social contradictions would change. Liu said, "Once we take power, the democratic revolution will be over—be concluded. Our contradiction with imperialism and feudalism will no longer exist; then there will only be a contradiction between the proletariat and the bourgeoisie." In his concluding remarks at the meeting, Mao also "revealed" to senior Communist Party officials that "after the completion of our bourgeois democratic revolution, the main contradiction will be between the proletariat and the bourgeoisie." This remark shows that even before the establishment of the People's Republic, Mao had made it crystal clear that the victory of the democratic revolution and the assumption of power by the proletariat would mark the beginning of an all-out offensive against the bourgeoisie and the transition to socialism.

Wu: These are two different issues: the first was the basic policy, and the second was the tactics.

When the regime was not strong enough for battle, maintaining a certain type of alliance with the bourgeoisie was a tactic. But this had nothing to do with the basic policy. In 1955 Mao said, "At the Third Plenary Session in 1950, I spoke against hitting out in all directions. The agrarian reform had not yet been carried out in vast areas of the country, nor had peasants come over entirely to our side. If we had opened fire on the bourgeoisie then, it would have been out of order. After the agrarian reform, when the peasants had entirely come over to our side, it was possible and necessary for us to start the movements against the 'three evils' and the 'five evils.' "[1] Mao also said that agricultural cooperation "will isolate the bourgeoisie once and for all and facilitate the final elimination of capitalism. On this matter we are quite heartless! On this matter Marxism is indeed cruel and has little mercy, for it is determined to exterminate imperialism, feudalism, capitalism, and small production to boot."

Although he was very clear about relegating capitalism to extinction, Mao skillfully used a tactic advocated by Lenin in 1905, in *Two Tactics of Social-Democracy in the Democratic Revolution*, that had been successfully applied during the Russian Revolution. Lenin wrote, "The proletariat must carry to completion the democratic revolution, by allying to itself the mass of the peasantry in order to crush by force the resistance of the autocracy and to paralyze the instability of the bourgeoisie." After the proletariat takes power through democratic revolution, according to Lenin, "from the democratic revolution we should at once . . . begin to pass to the socialist revolution. We stand for uninterrupted revolution. We shall not stop half-way."

The Chinese Communist Party adopted this tactic and before 1952, when land reform had not yet been completed, it emphasized that the newly established People's Republic was a New Democracy (it was only years later that the nature of the "people's democratic dictatorship" was described as a "dictatorship by the proletariat").

At a September 1949 meeting of the Chinese People's Consultative Conference on the draft Common Program, which in essence was the interim constitution, delegates of the democratic parties (eight smaller political parties allied with the Communist Party) suggested that the Common Program should describe the socialist future. But this suggestion was not accepted by the Communist Party leaders.

Ma: It appears that the tactic was hugely successful. Did it have any side effects?

Wu: Yes, indeed. The economic institution established in China in 1949 was not the same as the command economy established in the Soviet Union in the 1930s; rather, it was a market-economy institution similar to that of the New Economic Policy in the Soviet Union in the 1920s. In other words, it was a system with state control of all "commanding heights," or "*jingji mingmai*" (economic lifelines), but accompanied by the coexistence of different ownerships.

[1] Translators' note: The "three evils" refer to corruption, squandering, and bureaucracy among Communist Party and government officials, and the "five evils" refer to bribery, tax fraud, the stripping of state property, producing shoddy products, and the stealing of state economic information by private-sector businesspeople. These movements were political campaigns launched by the Communist Party in 1951 and 1952, respectively.

The smooth operation of the New Democracy economic system helped China quickly heal the wounds of years of war and achieve an economic boom in the first half of the 1950s.

Because of this success, however, a certain number of Communist Party and government officials in charge of economic administration did not proceed to make the transition from the democratic revolution to the socialist revolution that had been called for by Mao. This was particularly true of many officials from intellectual backgrounds. They had joined the revolutionary forces because of the New Democracy platform rather than because of any "Communist consciousness" (Mao later described these officials as "fellow travelers" of the Communist Party, or "democratic revolutionaries"). Because of the initial success of the New Democracy, the establishment of a society featuring the New Democracy became the goal of these officials. This triggered a debate within the Communist Party leadership in the mid-1950s.

Ma: Do you mean the debate as to whether to "strengthen the New Democracy order" and regarding agricultural co-operativization?

Wu: Yes, you are right. By 1952, land reform had been successfully completed, and the parties to the Korean War had begun to negotiate an armistice. Mao believed the time had come to launch an all-out offensive against the bourgeoisie. On June 6, 1952, Mao commented that "the contradiction between the working class and the national bourgeoisie has become the principle contradiction in China." He stressed that "the national bourgeoisie should no longer be defined as an intermediate class." According to Bo Yibo, then vice chairman of the Finance and Economic Committee of the Government Administrative Council (the highest executive body in the early 1950s), on September 24, 1952, Mao proposed that "we should initiate the transition to socialism and by and large complete it within ten to fifteen years rather than wait ten or more years." In Moscow in October 1952, Liu Shaoqi, again on instructions from Mao, reported to Stalin the specific ideas of the Central Committee of the Chinese Communist Party on "how to transition to socialism" and "how to confiscate the factories of the capitalists," to which Stalin offered his consent.

Ma: Mao's ideas obviously sounded very different at that time in comparison to his ideas before the Communists took over the main cities.

Wu: His ideas then were significantly different. He moved up the timing of the transition to the socialist revolution by a large margin. At a June 15, 1953 Politburo meeting, Mao officially put forward the Party's "General Line for the Transition Period." Meanwhile, he criticized Liu Shaoqi for his approach to "firmly establish a new democratic social order," calling such an approach "erroneous views of rightist opportunism which deviate from the General Line." According to Mao, the transition period began when the People's Republic was established, and it would end when the socialist transformation was largely complete. According to his thinking, the General Line and the related tasks were basically to realize a rather long period of industrialization and to complete the transformation of agriculture, the handicraft industries, and capitalist industry and commerce. He considered the General Line to be the beacon of all tasks that the Communist Party had to carry out, and he believed that any departure from this beacon would result in rightist or leftist deviations.

Ma: In August 1953, the General Line was officially adopted as the only path for the Communist Party to follow. In your view, what were the main impacts of this decision?

Wu: The greatest effect was the change in the course of the history of the "socialist transformation" of the private-sector economy.

In a conversation on October 15, 1953, with Chen Boda and Liao Luyan (both of whom were Communist Party theorists), Mao pointed out that the main point of the General Line was "a solution to the problem of ownership"—that is, to turn private ownership into collective and state ownership. "Only thus can the productive forces be expanded and China's industrialization be accomplished." At a later meeting of the Secretariat of the Central Committee, Mao officially proposed that a call be issued to eliminate the bourgeoisie as well as the enterprises owned by capitalists. In his revisions to the "Outline for Study and Promotion of the General Line during the Transition Period," drafted by the Propaganda Department of the Communist Party Central Committee, Mao wrote that the nature of the General Line is to make socialist ownership of production materials the only economic basis of the country and society. What is socialist ownership of production materials? It is collective ownership and state ownership.

Ma: During the development of the General Line, a specific plan was formulated to "address the ownership issue"—that is, the "Three Great Socialist Transformations" of agriculture, the handicraft industries, and capitalist industry and commerce.

Wu: The transformation of household agriculture was to be carried out first. In 1955 Mao launched the so-called socialist upsurge movement in the rural areas. This began with criticism of the "rightist deviation" of Deng Zihui, the director of the Central Rural Work Department. The movement quickly grew into a national campaign to denounce "rightist conservatism." After about a year, household farms were merged into agricultural production cooperatives. Thereafter, the

1958 Great Leap Forward turned the cooperatives into people's communes, which integrated government administrative functions with the cooperatives' role in economic management, and factory production, farming, military training, education, and commerce all became part of one institution. This is how the private ownership of land came to be abolished.

The individual handicraft industry was based on private ownership and individual labor. In 1952, its output accounted for 21 percent of the annual gross industrial output, and a large part of the production materials and means of livelihood in the rural areas came from the handicraft industry. The transformation of this industry began in 1953, in the form of co-operativization. Handicraft production was first organized into "cooperative groups," then into "supply and marketing cooperatives," and, finally, into production cooperatives. By the end of 1956, more than 90 percent of handicraft workers had joined such cooperatives.

The socialist transformation of capitalist industry and commerce was also accelerated. This transformation took place in a two-stage shift to a joint public-private operational structure. Public elements were initially introduced into the ownership and operation of individual enterprises on a case-by-case basis. These enterprises were jointly held by the state and by the private owners at different levels, managed jointly by the two parties and headed by representatives of the state. Later on, whole sectors were converted into this model. Enterprises were subject to state administration, and the previous owners maintained equity only in the form of the distribution of fixed dividends. In October 1955, Mao convened a discussion session with members of the Executive Committee of the All-China Federation of Industry and Commerce and alerted businesspeople to "be prepared to be communized." Since there was no alternative option, in succession businesspeople applied to the government for "socialist transformation" through a sectorwide approach.

Ma: On January 15, 1956, Beijing municipality held a mass meeting in Tiananmen Square. Amid the cheers of some 200,000 people, the chairman of the city's Federation of Industry and Commerce reported to Mao the following good news: Beijing had completed a sectorwide transition to a joint public-private operational structure and had become the first "socialist city" in the country. Thereafter, good news began flowing in from other places as people celebrated the "entry of socialism" with drums and gongs.

Wu: According to statistics, by the end of 1956 the number of households in agricultural production cooperatives had reached 117 million, accounting for 96.3 percent of all households in the rural areas, and the number of households in advanced cooperatives accounted for 87.8 percent. In the industrial sector, state-owned enterprises contributed 67.5 percent of the annual gross industrial output, and joint public-private enterprises contributed 32.5 percent. In comparison, the contribution of private enterprises was very small. State-owned enterprises, supply and marketing cooperatives, and joint public-private enterprises accounted for 99.9 percent of wholesale businesses and 95.8 percent of retail businesses. Privately owned enterprises accounted for only 0.1 percent and 4.2 percent, respectively.

This socialist transformation was achieved in less than three years, even though the 1953 General Line had envisaged completion in fifteen years or more. State ownership and quasi-state collective ownership became the sole foundation of the national economy. A comprehensive Soviet-style command economy was established on top of this foundation.

Ma: The ownership transformation began almost immediately after the success of the democratic revolution and it was completed in merely three years, a clear acceleration from the plan of "three years of preparation and ten years of construction" that had been promoted in the early years of the People's Republic. It was also an acceleration from the 1953 proposal to complete the transformation within ten to fifteen years. Although Mao controlled the momentum, most people, including senior Communist Party leaders, were not prepared for the hastened process. How could this transformation be carried out so smoothly within only a few years?

Wu: I believe there were four reasons. With respect to ideology, both before and after 1949, the Communist Party instilled into the people's minds the idea that the Soviet Union was "our infinitely bright and beautiful ultimate ideal," and that "today's Soviet Union is tomorrow's China." On the economic front, the establishment of a command economy was considered an unalterable principle of socialism.

Second, the Chinese people had suffered a century of humiliation due to colonialism and semi-colonialism. Based on this experience, there was a shared desire among the people to surpass the developed countries of the West. This led the leaders to believe that the people would support the adoption of a command economy modeled after the Soviet system, because such a system could fully mobilize human, material, and financial resources and centralize their utilization in order to realize industrialization within a very short time.

Third, after the beginning of the Korean War, China faced a blockade by the Western countries and, as a result, the strengthening of defense became a top priority on the agenda of the leadership. Chinese leaders opted for a centralized institutional arrangement to mobilize and allocate resources so as to direct the limited resources to the heavy machinery and chemical sectors on which the military industries depended.

Fourth, during much of its history, China had been populated by small landholding peasants and "control of society by administrative power" was an entrenched tradition. After the establishment of New China in 1949, Mao used the high prestige he had earned during the long revolutionary period to establish an omnipotent government under his leadership.

This enabled him to rely on the mighty state power to complete the socialist transformation and to establish a command economy within a short span of just a few years.

Ma: Among the Communist countries established after World War II, China was a latecomer in terms of establishing a command economy. Other Communist countries, in particular those in Eastern Europe, had been established with the support of the Soviet Red Army. Historically, these countries had belonged to Central Europe and their mentality and cultural traditions were European in nature, and communism had a relatively small influence. The political system imported by the Soviet Red Army distorted their previous cultures and institutions.

China was different. Except for your first reason, the other points that you have just mentioned were unique to China. In particular, Eastern Europe did not have the political basis described in your fourth point, and in this regard the Soviet Union and China shared some similarities, as both were populated by small landholding peasants. Therefore, China was more successful in learning from the Soviet Union, and the economic system established in China came to resemble that in the Soviet Union.

You have used the phrase "control of society by administrative power." This warrants special attention in China studies. Could you please further elaborate on the term?

Wu: This idea was first referred to by Marx in 1852 in his *The Eighteenth Brumaire of Louis Bonaparte*: "The political influence of the small-holding peasants, therefore, finds its final expression in the executive power which subordinates society to itself." Marx believed that because the only connection among the small-holding peasantry was regional proximity, and because they had no common relationships, no nationwide networks, and no political organizations due to the lack of unity of their interests, small-holding peasants could not be considered a single class. Marx thought these peasants could not, in their own name, protect their own interests, either through a parliament or through a citizens' general assembly. Since they could not represent themselves, they had to rely on others. At the same time, their representatives had to be their masters, an authority high above with unlimited government power. This power protected the peasants from encroachments by other social classes, bestowed upon them a boon, just like a rain during a period of drought or sunshine in the darkness. Hence, the political influence of the small-holding peasantry led to administrative control of the society.

This is what Deng Xiaoping meant when he later said that the Communist Party and state leadership system in China were influenced by long-term feudal despotism. According to Deng, under this leadership system, all powers tended to be concentrated in Communist Party committees, which, in turn, saw their powers concentrated in a few Communist Party secretaries, "especially the first secretaries . . . whose patriarchal ways place individuals above the organization. . . . Everyone has to be absolutely obedient and even personally attached to them."

Ma: China became a command economy in 1956. Based on the Soviet political economy, this type of economy could definitely be a powerful impetus for economic development. How did this system perform in China?

Wu: During the 1951–55 period, China's economy recorded a rapid recovery and steady growth under the New Democracy, thus winning high praise. However, after the establishment of the centrally planned economy, the national economy was consolidated into "one big enterprise" on a social scale. Independent and autonomous factories that had previously been independent became workshops in this big enterprise. In such an enterprise, the central-planning authorities controlled human, financial, and physical resources and set supply, production, and sales targets, which were then handed down, in the form of administrative economic plans, to various workshops for implementation. This was an extremely intricate top-down system requiring unanimous collective action. The plan was very complex, but it was weak in terms of accuracy and it was rigid in terms of regulation. As a result, the bureaucracy prevailed, the quality of services declined, and the national economy suffered ossification and low efficiency.

Ma: Economist Gao Shangquan once told the following story. After graduation he was assigned to work in the Research Department of the First Ministry of Machine Industry. One day in October 1956, he found that the ministry's guest house had received 1,140 guests from all of its affiliated factories. Their visits to Beijing all shared one common goal: to obtain human, financial, and physical resources from the Center. Gao's investigations discovered that within one year, a single department in the ministry had consumed eight tons of paper merely to produce various types of documents.

Wu: Under the New Democracy, state-owned enterprises (SOEs) were guided by the market and their managers retained some autonomy. After the establishment of the new system, however, enterprises lost their autonomy as they became appendages of the upper-level administrative agencies and their hands were tightly bound; their supplies, production, and sales were all determined by the state plan, and the upper-level agencies always had the last word. People sharply criticized this system. In particular, SOE managers and government officials in charge of economic affairs who were equipped with modern economic knowledge were the most dissatisfied.

Ma: Earlier, you mentioned the international environment when China was establishing a command economy. What were you referring to?

Wu: At that time, China faced a domestic and external environment that was very different from that faced by the Soviet Union in the 1930s. There had been debates in the Soviet Union during the period when the centrally planned economy was first being established. But after Stalin assumed absolute authority through bloody internal and external fighting in the 1920s and the 1930s, no one dared to voice opposing views. The Eastern European countries had no say because their economic systems had been established under the tight control of the Soviet Union. However, when a similar system was established in China in 1956, the Soviet Union had started to denounce and criticize Stalin. The truth about the Soviet economy had already become known, thus destroying any illusions. On top of this, efficiency in the Chinese economy was declining. There were increasing voices of dissatisfaction.

Stalin died in 1953. In 1956 Khrushchev criticized Stalin for his political and economic mistakes. Thus, in China discussions about the shortcomings of the Soviet model were no longer considered a political taboo. In autumn of 1956, Mao initiated a short-lived period of "letting one hundred flowers bloom and one hundred schools of thought contend" (that is, letting people vent their criticisms). The political environment was relatively relaxed, thus encouraging lively discussions. Within economic and academic circles, the main complaints were about the plan's mandatory targets. Many government officials and SOE managers were highly critical of the Soviet system, which was stifled by excessive controls and rigid commands.

Two well-known economists who sharply criticized the command economy were Sun Yefang and Gu Zhun.

Sun Yefang was an old revolutionary who had joined the Communist Party in 1924 when he was sixteen years old. After liberation, he held many important positions, including chief of the industrial division of the Military Control Committee of Shanghai municipality, deputy minister of the Ministry of Industry of the East Region, and deputy director of the State Statistical Bureau. In these positions Sun accumulated firsthand experience about the problems in the economic system. In 1956, as deputy director of the State Statistical Bureau, he began to write essays criticizing the ossified, inefficient economic system, and he began to conceive of his own socialist-economy model. Having received his first education in political economy as a student at Sun Yatsen University in Moscow in 1924, Sun was a firm believer in the Marxist economic model. However, when facing practical problems, Sun was inclined toward letting the "rule of value" play a greater role. This was in part because he had grown up in the market environment of Wuxi, where he had learned about market forces by osmosis. However, Sun's theory suffered from some deep inherent contradictions. On the one hand, he was opposed to the views of the "natural economy" and he came up with some brilliant ideas that were completely different from the doctrines of the Soviet-type central planned economy. On the other hand, he opposed the view of a "commodity economy." He stated that his rule of value was not the same as the rule of the market, but rather it was a rule by which average socially necessary labor determines the value of commodities. In the early 1960s, Sun designed a new economic model that advocated "centralizing the main decisions and decentralizing the small decisions." Simply put, this model gave enterprises more autonomy in day-to-day decision-making regarding simple reproduction (that is, recurrent or cyclical production processes), while maintaining state ownership and plan administration over supplies and sales. Sun's model comes closest to that of market socialism.

Although Sun stressed the importance of the rule of value and profit targets only in terms of accounting and calculations, he was the first economist to be persecuted in the purge against "revisionists" that began in the mid-1960s. Kang Sheng, the Communist Party ideological boss at the time, called Sun "a revisionist who is more Liberman than the Soviet Union's Liberman."

Ma: Compared to Sun Yefang, Gu Zhun suffered many more ups and downs. After the establishment of the People's Republic, Gu was appointed the first director of the Finance Bureau of Shanghai municipality and, at the same time, director in charge of tax administration. Later on, he concurrently held a higher position, as deputy minister of the East Region Ministry of Finance. During the 1951–52 movements against the three evils and the five evils, Gu was accused of "being self-righteous and defying the authority of the Party organization," and thus he was removed from all his Communist Party and other positions. But after 1953, he was appointed director of the Finance Department of the central Ministry of Construction and Engineering and deputy director of the Engineering Department of Luoyang municipality. In 1956, he was transferred to the Institute of Economics in the Department of Philosophy and Social Sciences of the Chinese Academy of Sciences as a research fellow.

Wu: Gu Zhun's analysis of China's economic problems was deeper than Sun's. As early as 1956, Gu had pointed out that the problem of a socialist economy was the elimination of the market. In order to improve efficiency, socialism required an economic system in which enterprises have autonomy to make decisions based on fluctuations in market prices. In other words, he suggested letting market forces play a decisive role in resource allocations. Regrettably, at that time most economists did not pay attention to Gu's proposal, as they still clung to the traditional socialist-economy theory. Shortly thereafter, Gu was labeled a "bourgeois rightist" because he had defended the national interest on an issue related to a Sino-Soviet joint-development project on the Heilongjiang River. His views were judged to be heretical and were condemned to oblivion. Nevertheless, in the development of China's reform theory, Gu Zhun was the first person to advocate market-oriented reforms.

Ma: Apart from the ideas of academics, what were the reactions of the government officials who were in charge of economic work?

Wu: The most important reaction was the economic readjustment program of the "three mainstays and three supplements," put forward by Chen Yun after the previously mentioned Three Great Socialist Transformations (of agriculture, handicraft industries, and capitalist industry and commerce) had resulted in a recession. The program covered three aspects of the economy. First, the state and collective sectors should be the main part of the industrial and commercial sectors, but they should be supplemented by a certain number of individual firms. Second, planned production should be the main part of agricultural and industrial production, but it should be supplemented by autonomous production within the scope of the plan but according to changes in the market. Third, the state sector should be the main part of a unified socialist market, but it should be supplemented by a free market operating within clearly set limits.

Chen's ideas guided the national economic readjustment, which was launched to address the problem of the excessive high-speed growth targets of the Three Great Socialist Transformations. In a later debate on the pros and cons of the Soviet model, these ideas were accepted by many government officials as a substitute for the Soviet model. After 1979, such ideas were summarized as "ensuring the leading role of the planned economy supplemented by market regulation," and they became a key proposition in the debates about the objectives of China's economic reforms.

Ma: Both the academic propositions and the government officials' proposals sought to reform the established economic management system. The final word that set the tone for the reform policy was a speech by Mao, at a Communist Party Politburo meeting in April 1956, which later became known as "On the Ten Major Relationships." Mao's critique of the Soviet model and his views on how to improve the operational mode of the socialist economy were confirmed by the Communist Party's Eighth

National Congress and became the guiding principle for China's reform of the economic administration system.

Wu: Mao's speech should be carefully studied, as it influenced China's economic reform and development for a long period of time.

The following is the background to the speech. After successful completion of the Three Great Socialist Transformations, from the end of 1955 to the beginning of 1956, Mao began to consider how to accelerate China's economic development based on the established socialist-economy system. Meanwhile, the myths about Stalin had already been shattered, and the Soviet Union's status as a model Communist country within the International Communist Movement was weakened. Chinese leaders sought to provide a new and different model for socialist construction. At the beginning of 1956, Mao Zedong and Liu Shaoqi held a number of meetings, at which they received briefings by thirty-four ministries and several provincial governments in preparation for the Eighth National Communist Party Congress, scheduled for August of that year, that was to summarize the experiences of the First Five-Year Plan period.

After the briefings, the Politburo held several rounds of discussions. The Politburo members reaffirmed the basic path of the Soviet Union, but sought improvements so as to accelerate China's industrialization. Liu Shaoqi had earlier pointed out that more attention should be paid to the development of light industry and agriculture, the potential of the coastal industries, incentives for local governments, and the role of technical staff. He had also noted that there were both positive and negative lessons to be drawn from the Soviet Union. These views reappeared in Mao's speech on the handling of the ten major relationships.

In April/May 1956, based on the government agencies' briefings and the Politburo discussions, Mao spoke at an expanded Politburo meeting and again at a meeting of the Supreme State Conference (the highest government coordination body at the time) to elaborate on the ten relationships, including, among others, the relationships "between heavy and light industry," "industry in the coastal regions and industry in the interior," "between economic construction and defense construction," "between the state, the units of production, and the producers," and "between central and local authorities." Mao stated that the main problem of the Soviet-type economy was an "excessive centralization of power." For example, he pointed out that the problem in the relationship between central and local governments was "centralizing everything in the hands of the central authorities and shackling the hands of the local authorities and denying them the right to independent action." On the problem in the relationship between the state, the production entities, and the producers, he stated, "It's not right, I'm afraid, to place everything in the hands of the central or the provincial and municipal authorities without leaving the factories any power of their own, any room for independent action, any benefits." In accordance with his idea that proactive motivation on the part of the people was a fundamental factor behind good economic performance, Mao believed that in order to enhance the people's enthusiasm, the main steps should be the implementation of decentralization to local governments and enterprises, the sharing of profits, and increasing the benefits for individual workers.

Based on Mao's analysis, the First Plenary Session of the Eighth Communist Party Central Committee decided to carry out a "reform of the economic administration system." Mao's comments on how to handle the relationship between the state, the enterprises, and the individual workers, as well as how to handle the relationship between central and local governments, became the guiding principles of this reform. Later on, Mao's thoughts were modified to focus on decentralization and profit-sharing, thus leading to the formulation of an "administrative decentralization" strategy. In 1958, based on this strategy, reform of the economic administration system was launched.

DIALOGUE 4

REFORMS OF THE ECONOMIC ADMINISTRATION SYSTEM DURING THE MAOIST ERA

Ma Guochuan (Ma): In September 1956, the First Plenary Session of the Eighth Communist Party Central Committee summarized the Communist Party's experience in winning the domestic revolutionary war, establishing the People's Republic, and completing the Three Great Socialist Transformations. More importantly, it adopted a blueprint for China's economic development. But, as Mao Zedong stated in March 1958, "This [blueprint] was similar to that of the Soviet Union in principle, but it had our own content." A key detail was the "reform of the economic administration system," based on Mao's April 1956 speech "On the Ten Major Relationships." In 1957, the government developed a reform program that focused on the decentralization of authority to the local governments. The program, which was implemented in 1958, marked the beginning of China's reform of the economic administration system.

Wu Jinglian (Wu): You are right. I call this reform an "administrative decentralization." This type of reform, which began in 1958 (though experiencing a number of stops and starts), lasted almost twenty years until the end of the Cultural Revolution in 1976.

Ma: A careful review will reveal that in his speech "On the Ten Major Relationships," Mao proposed decentralizing and sharing interests with lower-level governments and "production units" (later called "enterprises") and increasing welfare benefits for individual workers, including employees of state-owned enterprises (SOEs) and members of cooperatives. But why were the above proposals about production and individual workers no longer included in the 1958 program that was intended mainly to benefit local governments?

Wu: The main reason was the changed political situation in the country in 1957–58. Because of the changes, it was regarded as politically unacceptable to decentralize and share interests for the benefit of SOEs and workers.

First, with respect to decentralization and interest-sharing, before the Eighth National Communist Party Congress, the Yugoslav experience had been very attractive to Chinese leaders and managers. They hoped that China would learn from the Yugoslav experience in terms of granting more autonomy to enterprises and allowing Workers Councils to elect enterprise managers. At the Eighth National Communist Party Congress "enterprise self-management" was a hot topic. However, with the escalation of Chinese Communist Party's criticism of "socialist self-management," as practiced by the League of Communists of Yugoslavia, the phrase "decentralization and interest-sharing with enterprises" disappeared from the 1957 reform program.

Second, in terms of increases in benefits for individual workers, during the 1956 period of de-Stalinization the USSR and many Eastern European countries had attempted to motivate workers by increasing their welfare benefits. For instance, in sharp criticism of Stalin's economic policies, Khrushchev used the slogan "enhancing material incentives." Similarly, in "On the Ten Major Relationships," Mao proposed granting individual workers more autonomy and benefits. However, Mao was opposed to "material incentives." Instead, he advocated offering nonmaterial incentives to motivate people to work hard. The resolution of the Communist Party's Eighth National Congress in September 1956 points out that "the contradiction between the proletariat and the bourgeoisie has been fundamentally resolved. . . . The major contradiction in our country is between people's demand for the building of an advanced industrial country and the realities of a still backward agricultural country, between the people's needs for rapid economic and cultural development and the inability of our present economy and culture to meet that need." The resolution further notes that "this contradiction in essence is between the advanced socialist system and the backward production forces of society. The chief task now facing the Communist Party and people is to concentrate all efforts on resolving this contradiction and transforming China as quickly as possible from a backward agricultural country into an advanced industrial one." But as soon as the Eighth National Communist Party Congress was adjourned, Mao dispensed with this formal statement on the nature of the main contradiction. After the 1957 Anti-Rightist Movement, he reiterated that the contradiction between the proletariat and the bourgeoisie was the main contradiction, based on which he retained the policy of "taking class struggle as the key link." In 1957, differences between the Communist Party of China and the Communist Party of the Soviet Union in terms of their treatment of Stalinism began to emerge. Meanwhile, during the later phase of the Anti-Rightist Movement individualism was considered to be the source of "anti-Party and anti-socialist rightist thoughts." People were asked to snuff out their longings for fame and material benefits. Motivating individual workers through material incentives clearly contradicted the mainstream ideology at that time.

Ma: The specific political environment dictated the give and take of the reform.

Wu: You are right. When we review the later phases of China's reform, we will continue to see that the specific political environments and the ideological preferences of the times had an influence on the reform steps.

Thus, in the political circumstances of 1957–58, decentralization could only be targeted at local governments, and the 1958 reform mainly consisted of decentralizing power to local governments and expanding their related interests. Thus "institutional reform" at the time referred to an "institutional decentralization."

This approach, to decentralize decision-making power to local governments within the existing administrative framework, had far-reaching effects on China's economic system and economic development in later years.

Ma: What were the main components of the institutional decentralization in 1958?

Wu: There were six main changes. First, planning authority was decentralized. Formulation of the plan had formerly been centralized under the State Planning Commission (SPC), and plan targets were handed top down through the administrative system. After the change, the regions had autonomy to formulate their own plans, which were then later balanced by the SPC. This enabled each local economy to become a "self-contained system."

Second, authority to control enterprises was also decentralized. With the exception of a very few important, special, or experimental enterprises that remained under the central government, the administration of enterprises that had previously been governed by the line ministries was handed over to the local governments.

Third, authority over the allocation of material supplies was decentralized. The quantity and variety of materials allocated centrally by the SPC were reduced, as was the amount of materials managed by the line ministries. Furthermore, the central government no longer directly allocated those supplies still under its control; instead, it only filled in for gaps when the local governments could not balance the supply and demand for materials within their respective jurisdictions. Enterprise supplies were allocated and transferred by the local governments.

Fourth, licensing authority for basic capital projects and control of credit were decentralized. If the size of locally sponsored projects exceeded a certain threshold, the local governments were required to submit a summary proposal to the SPC for licensing. But if the size was below the threshold, decision-making authority rested with the local governments based on a "contract responsibility" system. The previous highly centralized credit-administration system was also abandoned, and decision-making power with respect to loans was decentralized. Local governments could "satisfy the need for loans regardless of the size or the timing."

Fifth, fiscal and taxation authority was decentralized and a "contract responsibility system" for taxation was put in place. In order to increase the fiscal resources of local governments and to expand their fiscal power, 20 percent of the profits of central-government enterprises was shared with the local governments that hosted those enterprises. Local governments were also allowed broad discretion in terms of tax increases, reductions, and exemptions.

Sixth, authority for labor administration was decentralized. Planning for labor had previously been centralized under the SPC, and plan targets were handed down from the top. After this change, local hiring plans could be implemented after confirmation by the provincial governments.

The purpose of increasing the power of local governments to allocate physical and financial resources was to further motivate these administrative bodies.

Ma: Such measures, indeed, increased the power of local governments, especially the power of provincial governments.

Wu: You are right, but these measures also increased the power of enterprises. Although decentralization to enterprises as a main reform measure was removed from the formal program, in practice there were still some changes to that effect. First, the number of mandatory targets handed down by the SPC through the administrative system was reduced from six to four. Second, the previous small "enterprise reward fund" (that is, the factory director's fund), which had been financed by the retention of profits based on industry-specific ratios, was changed to a "whole profit-retention system" based on a per factory ratio. Third, the rights of enterprises to assign human resources were expanded. With the exception of managers and core technical staff, and as long as the total number of employees was not increased, enterprises could manage their workforces on their own, and they had the right to readjust their organizational setup and the placement of their workers. Fourth, enterprises had the right to allocate and reallocate a certain portion of their funding, and to increase, decrease, or scrap their fixed assets.

Ma: After this institutional decentralization, the power of local governments was expanded, and, to a certain extent, the rights of enterprises were increased. But the basic feature of a strict command economy did not change, and resources continued to be allocated by administrative fiat. The only result of these changes was that the highly centrally planned economy became a decentralized and locally based planned economy.

Wu: This is correct if you think that any economy operating according to a government plan is a planned economy. Strictly speaking, however, the decentralized economy after 1958 was not a planned economy. By default, a "planned economy" refers to the allocation of scarce economic resources according to a plan, which is based on thorough mathematical calculations in advance rather than on the basis of prices that are spontaneously formed through market exchanges. However, the calculations must be carried out by a central planning authority that possesses all the information regarding supply and demand in the country. (Italian economist Enrico Barone, who tested the effectiveness of a planned economy, called this central agency the "ministry of production.") In a decentralized situation, the plan is formulated by many local governments (there are more than 2,000 counties in China). Because these local governments do not have information about supply and demand throughout the country, they are unable to carry out nationwide consolidation and balancing. Resource allocations according to a plan formulated by individual local governments thus result in fierce turf wars for limited resources. From the perspective of resource allocations, a planned economy is also called a *command economy*. A decentralized planned economy shares only one feature with a centrally planned economy: they both use administrative commands to allocate resources. Therefore, it may be more accurate to refer to China's economy after 1958 as a *decentralized command economy*.

Another factor contributing to the economic chaos after 1958 was that Mao believed that the SPC was engaging in scholasticism when formulating the plan, because it used Soviet methodology that relied on computing devices to prepare tables to balance the supply and demand of materials. Mao argued that the SPC should only focus on "big things," and, for this purpose, "a staff of 50 people should suffice." In 1965 Mao instructed that a "little planning commission," consisting of about twenty people, be established to substitute for the more than 1,000 staff persons in the SPC. As a result, after the First Five-Year Plan China no longer prepared plans based on careful calculations and balancing, even though the resultant documents were still called five-year plans and annual plans. In any case, after the main authority for preparing the command plans was shifted from the central government to the local governments, the previously centralized command economy became a locally decentralized command economy.

Ma: At the April 1958 Second Plenary Session of the Eighth Communist Party Central Committee, Mao's ideas in the "On the Ten Major Relationships" speech became part of general Communist Party policy. The "General Line of Socialist Construction," which emerged at the Second Plenary Session, sought to "go all out, aim high, and achieve greater, faster, better, and more economical results in socialist construction."

Wu: The "General Line of Socialist Construction" was a more comprehensive representation of Mao's economic thoughts.

As you know, an important characteristic of Mao's philosophy was his stress on the "conscious initiative" of humans, and his belief that "spiritual thoughts can turn into material matters," that is, "the reaction of consciousness to the physical being." In 1949 he announced that "of all the beings in the world, human beings are the most valuable. Under the leadership of the Communist Party, as long as we have people, we can create any miracle." Mao combined these philosophical ideas with policies for properly handling the various contradictions referred to in "On the Ten Major Relationships" as well as with the institutional arrangements to motivate all involved parties, thereby forming the basis for the "General Line of Socialist Construction." Under the guidance of this General Line, the Great Leap Forward movement was launched.

Ma: In addition to the General Line and the Great Leap Forward, in 1958 Mao also took a major step to launch the "people's commune" movement, which consolidated more than 740,000 agricultural production cooperatives into 26,000 people's communes, thus integrating the administrative role of the government and the economic administration role of the cooperatives. One institution was responsible for five functions: factory production, farming, military activities, education, and commerce. Over 99 percent of the farmers became commune members, and all property belonging to the agricultural production cooperatives was taken over by the people's communes. The policy that allowed household plots (small plots of land allocated to households for growing produce to meet their own livelihood needs) was abolished, and the livestock and forests of the members of the cooperatives became commonly owned. This meant that farmers were subject to a tight administrative system and the tentacles of state power reached all the way down to the villages.

Wu: A locally decentralized command economy and a grassroots institution that integrated the functions of administrative and economic management created an economic system that some scholars of comparative economics have called a *mobilization and command-economy system*. This was the institutional foundation for the Great Leap Forward movement that Mao launched in 1958. During this movement, local governments responded to Mao's call to surpass Great Britain and the United States by fully utilizing their newly gained power to mobilize resources. Local governments initiated basic construction projects and hired workers on a massive scale. Farmers' resources were appropriated without remuneration. The purpose was to fulfill the task of "taking steel as the key link, leap forward in all fields," and "take grain production as the key link and ensure all-round development." Short-term successes led Chinese leaders to believe that Mao's "path to industrialization" had made great strides, so they formulated the ambitious goal of catching up with Great Britain and surpassing the United States. Blinded by belief in this goal, their ambitions became inflated and on several occasions the milestones for achieving the goal were shortened—from fifteen years for catching up with Great Britain (in November 1957) to ten years for catching up with Great Britain, and twenty years for catching up with the United States (in April 1958). Then, in June 1958, Mao announced, "It looks as if in three more years we can overtake and surpass Great Britain, and the United States within ten years." In order to achieve such an impossible goal, local governments, line ministries, and various agencies began to compete with one another in terms of fighting for resources and appropriating the property of farmers without providing remuneration. As a result, there was widespread economic chaos.

In 1959–60, fixed investments registered an average annual growth rate of 39.5 percent. During this period, total investments reached RMB 100.74 billion, which was 71 percent more than the total investments during the entire First Five-Year Plan period (RMB 58.85 billion). Because of the decentralization of labor administration, in 1958 the number of SOE employees jumped from 24.51 million to 45.32 million, and by 1960, the number reached 59.69 million, a net increase of 143.5 percent from 1958. This huge consumption of human and physical resources resulted in forged or inflated statistics. We now know that these so-called heroic feats in fulfilling the grain and iron and steel production targets were simply fabricated.

Ma: However, some leaders continued to be deluded by their illusions. During an August 1958 trip to Xushui county, in Hebei province, Mao commented, "What shall we do when we have a grain surplus? Members of the cooperatives can eat more—five meals a day should be fine." Mao also suggested adopting a system for the land to remain fallow and for farmers to work only part time. In accordance with Mao's instructions, one after another the people's communes offered so-called Communist-style distributions, such as free food, free clothing, free medical treatment, free burials, free weddings, free education, free housing, free heating, free haircuts, and free entertainment. A famous slogan at the time was "the people's communes are a golden bridge to paradise."

Wu: This "good fortune" did not last for long. By the end of 1958, the negative results of these practices, which lacked any common sense, began to surface. Production declined, many enterprises suffered losses, daily necessities were in short supply, and the economy encountered great difficulties. Faced with this serious situation, at the end of 1958 and in early 1959 the Central Committee of the Communist Party held a number of meetings calling for a correction to the "leftist deviations."

Ma: In April 1959, the Seventh Plenary Session of the Eighth Communist Party Central Committee (also known as the "Shanghai meeting") proposed that the plan targets be lowered. Mao circulated a "Letter to the Inner Circles of the Party," calling for telling the truth and resisting the trend to falsify the facts. It was decided that a meeting would be held at Lushan (a famous mountain resort in Jiangxi province) to summarize the lessons of the past years. The Lushan meetings (that is, an expanded Politburo meeting and the Eighth Plenary Session of the Eighth Communist Party Central Committee) were held in July/August 1959. Initially, the focus was on correcting the "leftist deviations." At the time, Mao admitted that the Great Leap Forward had suffered from some drawbacks, such as a lack of concern for overall balance in the national economy, thus destroying economic relations. He also admitted that industry and commerce as well as administrative power over human and fiscal resources had suffered from an excess of decentralization to the lower levels.

Wu: Unfortunately, after Politburo member Peng Dehuai wrote a letter to Mao expressing the hope that a serious summary of the lessons of the Great Leap Forward and the people's commune movement be carried out, Mao decided to extend the Lushan meetings, and he proceeded to sharply criticize Peng Dehuai's "right opportunist, anti-Party activities," hence marking the inception of a nationwide campaign against "anti-rightist opportunism." The political atmosphere changed from an anti-leftist deviation to an anti-rightist deviation, and a precious opportunity to correct the earlier mistakes was lost. Furthermore, the campaign led to a second round of communist-style distributions, further exacerbating the socioeconomic situation.

According to official statistics, in 1959 total grain production in the country was 170 billion kilograms, which was lower than the state's planned target and 30 billion kilograms short of production in 1958 (200 billion kilograms). In 1960 grain production declined further, to 143.5 billion kilograms, 0.2 billion kilograms less than that in 1951 (143.7 billion kilograms).

Any news about the sharp drops in grain production was blocked. Because of a lack of adequate remedies, malnutrition and edema broke out in the urban areas. In the rural areas, tens of millions of people died of "abnormal causes." From October 1959 to January 1960, Gu Zhun, who was undergoing *laogai* (that is, reform through labor) in Shangcheng county, of Xinyang prefecture in Henan province, described in his diary the miserable scenes of "land filled with starving people and people eating people."

By early 1960, "death visited villagers one after another, and entire families were wiped out." There were cases in which people killed their relatives in order to feed themselves. At the time, Xinyang prefecture had a population of 8.5 million people. According to official statistics, from the winter of 1959 to the spring of 1960, at least one million people in Xinyang died of hunger, the equivalent of one-eighth of the prefecture's total population. Many villages became a "no-man's land."

Ma: After the locally decentralized command-economy system was established, it demonstrated its prowess during the Great Leap Forward, resulting in an unprecedented "great famine." According to various reports, victims of the famine numbered between 22 million, as estimated by Li Chengrui (former director of the State Statistical Bureau) and 37 million, as estimated by Yang Jisheng (author of *Tombstone: The Great Chinese Famine, 1958–1962*). The sheer size of the number of victims is unparalleled in recorded human history.

Wu: In a comparison of the number of deaths during China's great famine with similar situations in other developing countries, Nobel economics laureate Amartya Sen found that the number of deaths from the famine in China was equal to the sum of all deaths in India during a period of forty years. Sen concludes that the extended duration of the widespread famine was due to institutional and policy-related issues rather than natural disasters. He also points out that without freedom of information, freedom of speech, and popular participation, economic development became a distorted process that did not contribute to sustained improvements in the living standards of the general public or of those living at the bottom rungs of society. To date, these words are still thought-provoking warnings. We should never forget the painful lessons of the past.

In 1962, in order to address the serious economic difficulties caused by the Great Leap Forward and the people's commune movement, President Liu Shaoqi asked Chen Yun, a veteran leader of economic affairs, to pick up the pieces.

Chen's first move after resuming office was to require the establishment of a fiscal and financial system that was "stricter and tighter" than the 1950 system. Based on this requirement, the line ministries re-assumed power over government finance, credit, and enterprises. For instance, the financial sector, government finance, and statistical work were all placed directly under the central government, and enterprises that had been decentralized to local governments were returned to the line ministries. With this highly centralized institutional arrangement, an economic readjustment policy known as the "eight Chinese-word policy," consisting of "readjustment, reform, consolidation, and improvement," was implemented. Specifically, the small smelters using either indigenous or foreign methods that had been established during the massive iron and steel production campaign were closed; about twenty million rural workers who had been hired during the Great Leap Forward were released from their work units and sent back to their villages; and many industrial enterprises in the urban areas were either shut down, suspended, amalgamated, or required to manufacture different products. During this readjustment, which lasted several months, the economy gradually stabilized. But a general economic recovery was not achieved until 1964.

Ma: Obviously, this round of economic recovery can mainly be attributed to the "iron fist" of the highly centralized system. Along with the recovery, China's centrally planned economy that had existed prior to 1958 replaced the locally decentralized planned economy.

Wu: While celebrating the restoration of economic order, people found that all the shortcomings of the centralized command economy were staging a comeback, so another round of reform was considered. Because of the ideology that equated socialism with a command economy and resource allocations by administrative command, market-oriented reforms were politically unacceptable. Once again, the only viable option was a decentralization of planning power to the local governments. Several rounds of reforms, similar to the 1958 institutional decentralization, were attempted during the following years.

For instance, in 1970, under the banner "decentralization is revolution, and the more that is decentralized, the more revolutionary one becomes," there was large-scale decentralization of the economic administration system. In the same year, Mao believed that war was imminent, so the paramount central task was to prepare for a massive foreign invasion. The purpose of the decentralization in 1970 thus had a clear military objective. The entire country was divided into ten "coordination regions," and the provinces in each region were instructed to establish an independent and comprehensive industrial sector so that they would be better prepared to defend themselves.

Ma: What was the result of this second round of large-scale decentralization?

Wu: Very similar to the results of the 1958 institutional decentralization. From the coordination regions to the people's communes, everyone became engaged in developing industries for high-speed growth. Hundreds of thousands of small enterprises were established, but within a matter of only a few years, most of them collapsed. Those that did manage to survive became important forces for the development of the township and village enterprises that emerged after China launched its reform and opening policy in 1978. The national economy became bogged down in chaos because the localities put their own interests first and competed among themselves for resources. But resources were allocated based on "the will of the bosses." The 1984 book *Contemporary China's Economic System Reform*, compiled by several high-ranking officials in charge of economic affairs, highlights the adverse effects caused by this blind decentralization and summarizes the history of the reforms in three areas. First, "enterprises were decentralized without clear guidance, thus exacerbating the chaotic state of production and operations." Second, "the contract responsibility arrangement for fiscal revenues and expenditures, allocations of physical resources, and basic construction did not achieve the anticipated results." Third, "simplification of the taxation, credit, and labor and wage systems weakened their economic leverage."

After the death of Lin Biao (Mao Zedong's designated successor) in a plane crash in 1971, efforts were made to once again centralize the economic administration system— for instance, during the 1971–73 campaign managed by Premier Zhou Enlai to "criticize Lin Biao and rectify incorrect work styles," and during the 1975 "comprehensive consolidation" (to restore order and economic activities in key areas and to readjust the underlying ideological and policy approaches) presided over by Deng Xiaoping.

Ma: In the almost two decades between 1958 and 1976, the main reform measures consisted of an institutional decentralization of the command economy. But the measures resulted in a vicious cycle: once powers were decentralized, chaos ensued, leading to another round of centralization, and as soon as powers were again centralized, the economy lost its vitality.

Wu: As we discussed earlier, a prerequisite for the plan to work is for it to be based on centralized economic calculations and for it to be implemented by a central government that has adequate authority. I once said that the command economy would need a person such as Qin Shi Huang (China's first emperor who unified the country with an iron fist in 221 BC). In a large country like China, this person would have to rely on a strict and comprehensive administrative system to coordinate the economy and to allocate resources. In other words, in order for a command economy to function it needs a decision-making center and a central command, with the lower levels completely obeying the next higher level, and local governments deferring to the central government.

Ma: Why was China's hierarchical system so clear-cut, from the central government to the provincial, municipal, and county governments, and then farther down to the people's communes and the commune brigades? This appears to have been a requirement of the command economy. In turn, the hierarchical administrative system supported and strengthened the command economy.

Wu: The administrative decentralizations of 1958 and 1970 resulted in economic turmoil. What were the origins of the problems? The two rounds of decentralization were carried out within the framework of the command economy. Microdecisions at the enterprise level were made by upper-level line agencies, even though enterprise administration was decentralized. Except for the defense industry and some experimental firms, enterprises remained subject to decisions by lower-level governments. Powers for production planning, fixed-asset investments, material allocations, government financing, tax administration, and even credit were all decentralized from one level to the next. As a result, there were too many "centers." Because local governments did not want to appear to lag behind their counterparts, they began to compete with one another for higher plan targets and each administrative level proceeded to raise its targets. This triggered various so-called output satellites.[1] Predictably, the decentralization resulted in chaos. The only way to address the situation within the command-economy framework was to return to centralization. The subsequent readjustments centralized the economy by issuing regulations that restored the vertical lines of reporting. This was an inevitable result of the administrative decentralization within the command-economy framework.

Ma: After comparing the Chinese and Soviet systems, some foreign scholars have noted that if the Soviet Union is said to have had a Stalinist economic system, then China can be said to have had more than two dozen such systems. What they are referring to is the relatively greater powers that Chinese provincial and lower-level governments enjoyed.

Wu: Compared to the economic system in the Soviet Union, China's traditional system was different in terms of its decentralization of administrative power. However, even though the distribution of administrative power was more rational in China, the traditional system could not solve the problem of inefficient resource allocations. After powers were decentralized to local agencies, the latter were generally reluctant to hand power over to the enterprises. This is similar to what occurred in the *Dream of the Red Chamber*: when Wang Xifeng was out, Jia Tanchun was in.[2] When a command is issued by many local agencies, instead of by one central administration, economic turmoil is likely to occur because the national economy is no longer unified.

Ma: The 1957–76 reform of the economic administration system in China failed, just as the experimental decentralization efforts within the command-economy framework

[1] Translators' note: The term originally referred to the launch of the USSR's first man-made satellite in 1957. During the Great Leap Forward, it was widely used to refer to the fantastic reports of unbelievably high agricultural and industrial output.

[2] Translators' note: Wang and Jia are fictional figures in *Dream of the Red Chamber*, a masterpiece of Chinese literature. In the novel, Wang Xifeng rules a huge aristocratic house with an iron fist. After she becomes ill, Jia Tanchun, who turns out to be even more merciless than Wang in running the household, is asked to take over.

of the other Communist command-economy countries had failed. For instance, in 1957 Khrushchev tried to institute a reform whereby economic administration by the central government and the line ministries would be decentralized to the local administrations. This resulted in colossal changes: twenty-five ministries at the union level and 113 ministries at the republic level were dissolved. Their functions were taken over by 105 commissions in the economic administrative regions. Enterprises previously affiliated with the government of the USSR and its republics were decentralized to lower-level governments. The share of centrally controlled enterprises in the gross industrial output dropped from 45 percent to 6 percent. Supply and demand of materials were supposed to be balanced by local governments, with the central government consolidating what was done at the local levels. What did this reform achieve? The result was economic chaos caused by the enhanced local capture because instead of initiating substantive changes and overcoming the previous shortcomings, the reform threw the entire economic system into turmoil by breaking up the previous relations and distribution patterns. This is why, shortly thereafter, Khrushchev was driven out of office and the Soviet Union returned to centralized administration of the economy.

What we have just talked about are local decentralizations within a command-economy framework. Although such an institutional decentralization was no longer the main thrust of the reform after the Cultural Revolution, from time to time similar measures were adopted. For instance, an institutional arrangement in 1980, called "breaking up the single kitchen for better distribution of food," was widely adopted for the fiscal and tax systems. In the area of macroeconomic management and monetary policy, an arrangement of "two-level macro regulation" by the central and provincial governments remained in effect for a long while. In terms of planning administration, a number of municipalities became stand-alone entities in the plan so as to allow them to have planning authority similar to that of the provincial governments.

These measures had a significant impact on the course of the reform. How did those economists who favored the market-oriented reforms view the local decentralizations?

Wu: In this regard, there were great differences of opinion.

One group found that the institutional decentralization was an important driver behind China's economic development. In particular, the decentralization of fiscal power to local governments led to competition among localities, thus fostering the birth and growth of private businesses. In 1998 Professor Zhang Weiying of Peking University and Professor Li Shuhe of City University of Hong Kong pointed out that when local governments enjoy a certain degree of fiscal independence, local officials, in their pursuit of local interests, provide protection or facilitation to township and village enterprises in terms of funding, production, and sales. This was thus an important factor in the rapid development of China's nonstate economic sector. In a review of the thirty years of market-oriented reforms, Professor Steven N. S. Cheung, a Hong Kong–born American economist, highly praised the "inter-county competition," which he attributed to the decentralization and sharing of interests with local governments. He argued that this institutional arrangement was the secret behind China's economic miracle.

Other researchers have pointed out that competition driven by local-government power, rather than by rule of law, blocks the development of an integrated, competitive market. For instance, Chinese jurist Cai Dingjian has sharply criticized the statement that "intercounty competition is the reason for China's thirty years of economic growth" and he has called for the adoption of constitutionalism. He has noted that for more than twenty years, the means by which many county governments promoted economic development were tainted by illegal operations. County governments plundered land, resources, and tax revenue in violation of the law, such as by giving tax exemptions at will to promote investments, allowing the free use of resources, and not carrying out inspections so that enterprises could continue to unscrupulously pollute the environment. Many incidents in violation of the law in various localities, such as the forced demolition of homes and the free appropriation of land, can be attributed to these actions by county governments. If this type of intercounty competition is credited with creating China's economic miracle, the economy will remain bogged down in chaos and unfair competition.

Professor Xu Chenggang of Hong Kong University has proposed a more balanced view. He calls the system formed through local decentralization a "locally centralized authoritarian system," or a "decentralized authoritarian system." This system, generating a powerful impetus for local governments when market institutions were not well developed, led to thirty years of high economic growth in China. However, the system was also a mighty double-edged sword. On the one hand, it was an effective mechanism for growth, but, on the other hand, it could become a formidable instrument of destruction. When China was no longer mired in poverty and social objectives, rather than GDP targets, became increasingly important, this mechanism that initially had been constructive became destructive. The system could not help resolve the serious structural problems, such as the imbalances between investment and consumption and between exports and imports, as well as the worsening of the economic disparities. Thus, the defects of the decentralized authoritarian system were increasingly exposed. For Professor Xu, the only way out for China is to reform this system—that is, to gradually replace the administrative mechanisms with a governance mechanism that is based on the rule of law; to provide constitutional protections of property rights, including that of land; and to allow the judicial system to be independent of the government.

DIALOGUE 5

THE FAILURE OF STATE-OWNED ENTERPRISE REFORMS UNDER MARKET SOCIALISM

Ma Guochuan (Ma): Almost all of the economic reforms in the Communist countries gravitated toward reform of the state-owned enterprises (SOEs) because they had been the strongholds of the command economy. For example, the thrust of the 1965 reforms launched by Alexei Kosygin, chairman of the Council of Ministers of the USSR, was to grant the SOEs "rights for complete cost accounting." The 1968 New Economic Mechanism in Hungary focused on granting autonomy to the SOEs so that, to a certain extent, they could respond to fluctuations in market prices. In this respect, China was not an exception. The Chinese economic reforms during the post–Cultural Revolution years began from an "experiment in expanding enterprise autonomy" in Sichuan province in 1978. In 1980, the reform was extended to 6,000 large SOEs throughout the country that accounted for a significant share of the national economy. Although such reforms were not successful, it is worthwhile to explore why these countries all began with SOE reforms.

Wu Jinglian (Wu): According to my observations, this type of economic reform became common practice in the Communist countries from the 1960s to the 1980s for the following reasons: first, it resulted from the influence of the prevailing reform theory—that is, *market socialism*, and, second, important line agency leaders and SOE managers were appealing for "relaxed constraints and decentralization" as well as for "expanded enterprise autonomy." Because both these dynamics pointed in the same direction, the state sector was the logical starting point for the economic reforms.

Ma: In Dialogue 2, you mentioned that Oskar Lange proposed a "competitive solution" during the "socialist calculation" debates of the 1920s and the 1930s. Lange had proposed that as long as the planning authorities set prices according to market supply and demand to guide the SOEs in making their own decisions, a planned economy can be as efficient as a market economy. Later on, Lange's proposition evolved into the "market-socialism" reform platform. Today, some people believe that China's efforts after the 1990s to establish a "socialist market economy" are the same as the market-socialism reforms in Poland, Hungary, and the other Eastern European countries. But this requires some clarification.

Wu: You have just raised an issue about which researchers on economic reforms in the Communist countries should be very clear.

Market socialism was quite influential in China in the 1980s. The reform programs influenced by the market socialism in Eastern Europe and the USSR contained certain market-oriented measures, but the "market" referred to in these programs differed sharply from the "market" targeted by China's "socialist market economy." According to Polish economist Włozimierz Brus, under market socialism the means of production are owned by the state or the collective, and command planning for the allocation of resources is replaced by "economic leveraging" based on the "law of the market," such as prices, wages, interest rates, and taxation, as well as additional market regulation. In other words, the "market" in the theory and practice of market socialism is a simulated market developed by the planning authorities, and prices are formed through regulation and control by the planning authorities. In contrast, the market under China's socialist market economy is a real market, whereby prices are formed through free-market competition.

Under market socialism, the central planning authorities had three functions: (a) to determine the prices of the means of production according to supply and demand; (b) to make investment decisions; and (c) to allocate net income (that is, rent and profits) from the use of the means of production. Guided by the authorities' pricing signals, production was expected to follow two principles: first, output should reach a level whereby prices are equal to the marginal costs of the products, and, second, production costs should be the lowest at this level of output. Households and individuals had freedom to decide the volume of their workloads, and they also had discretion to decide how to spend their income.

During the 1960s and the 1970s, Brus had been the research director of the State Planning Commission and the vice chairman of the Economic Council in Poland. He was also one of the most influential reform economists in Eastern Europe. Based on Lange's market-socialism theory and taking into consideration the economic conditions in the Eastern European countries, Brus developed a model for "a planned economy with a built-in market mechanism." For short, this is referred to as a *decentralization model*. In this model, economic decision-making takes place at three levels. At the top is the macro level, where decisions on the pricing of the means of production are made by the central government based on supply and demand. This level also determines allocations of state income obtained from the means of production. The middle level consists of decision-making decentralized to the individual enterprises; the goal of decisions made at this level is to maximize profits, but the decisions are based on the prices set by the state planning authorities. Households, constituting the bottom level, make decisions regarding the selection of jobs and the allocation of individual or household income. Although to a certain extent market-based pricing influences enterprise decision-making in this market-socialism model, the state continues to play a dominant role. Through macroeconomic decision-making—for instance, regarding investment decisions—the state sets the scope of microeconomic activities for households and individuals. The state also regulates microeconomic activities by establishing "economic parameters" with respect to prices, wages, credit, and taxation.

Ma: The reforms in the Soviet Union and Eastern Europe more or less reflected the propositions of market socialism, with the main objective being to enhance SOE market incentives. But these reforms were not successful.

Wu: Kosygin's 1965 complete economic accounting reform in the Soviet Union was the first attempt to be guided by market socialism. The reform was preceded in 1962–63 by discussions on the so-called Liberman proposals. On September 9, 1962, Evsei Liberman, a professor at Kharkov Engineering and Economics Institute, published an article in *Pravda* in which he proposed that economic guidance and planning be reformed. While maintaining the basic framework of the planned economy, the main measures in Liberman's proposals included the expansion of SOE autonomy and the establishment of planned profit targets as a central valuation indicator. Supported by Nikita Khrushchev, first secretary of the Soviet Communist Party, Soviet economists and academics engaged in lively discussions about Liberman's proposals.

In accordance with Khrushchev's instructions, a special committee was established to summarize the discussions and to prepare a reform proposal. Although Khrushchev was ousted by a "palace coup" in October 1964, his successor, General Secretary Leonid Brezhnev, requested that Kosygin, as the chairman of the Council of Ministers, preside over a complete economic accounting reform. There were two main parts to this reform. The first part was to reduce the number of mandatory targets, relax controls under the plan, and grant enterprises autonomy to use a fixed amount of working capital and to apply depreciations for major repairs. The second part sought to enhance material incentives for enterprises and their workforces by expanding the self-managed funds of the enterprises and increasing their profit retention ratios.

Initially, the reform made enterprises more proactive in terms of increasing production and revenue. However, because there were no basic systemic economic and institutional changes, it was difficult to cure the chronic economic problems in the USSR. In addition, as the reform softened the budget constraints, enterprises became adept at avoiding to fulfill the plan, while taking for themselves generous remunerations and bonuses. As a result, economic chaos, dysfunctional planning, and fiscal difficulties ensued. The Kosygin reforms did not materialize not only because of the economic problems, but also because of the power struggle within the Soviet Communist Party. By the end of the 1970s, the administrative means had returned, and the mainstream faction in the Communist Party strongly criticized the Kosygin reforms that had been influenced by market socialism.

Ma: From the 1960s to the 1980s, Poland, Czechoslovakia, and Hungary also carried out market-socialism reforms. In particular, Poland was the initial home of market socialism, as Polish reform theorists like Brus were considered to be protégés of Oskar Lange. However, all of these reforms failed as well, including the Hungarian reforms that lasted until the collapse of the regime in 1989.

Wu: In 1989, Brus coauthored with Kazimierz Laski, another Polish reform economist, an analysis of market socialism, entitled *From Marx to the Market*, in which they retrospectively criticize Brus's own proposition for enhancing the planned economy through market regulation. They explain that this economic model attempted to combine centralized macroeconomic planning and SOE autonomy with market regulation. But the postulated combination was not viable. If a market orientation is the correct direction of change, it should be steadfastly upheld. Brus also examines whether market socialism's concept of completely independent enterprises and entrepreneurship are compatible with the dominant role of state ownership. He maintains that, first, the state and state-owned enterprises cannot be completely separated. State ownership means that the state must retain the power to control the enterprises, and if this power were to be removed, then state ownership would exist in name only. In addition, if the SOEs really became independent and were allowed to compete among themselves, the so-called benefits of state ownership would disappear. Furthermore, if the state played a coordinating role, the market would become distorted and the command-economy institution would continue to exist behind the scenes. Second, even if the two could be completely separated, the SOEs still could not operate as holistic market participants. SOE managers were agents of the state, hence there was no material basis for their shouldering any responsibility for enterprise failures. For this reason, as Friedrich Hayek put it, SOE managers were likely either to act rashly or to use excessive caution. However, if an enterprise were truly autonomous and could select its own managers, this independence would render state ownership meaningless. Therefore, the more a SOE behaved in accordance with the requirements of an effective market mechanism, the more it would deviate from the traditional concept of state ownership. Brus believed that a perfect market mechanism would have to discard any sort of dogma regarding ownership. Thus, the only option for realizing market socialism was to develop a mixed economy based on private ownership. It is obvious that Brus's redefinition of market socialism was a departure from his previous theory.

Ma: In fact, no economic school in China advocated market socialism and the term remained unknown for a long time to those outside the profession. However, similar views did exist at the time. The outstanding economist Sun Yefang may be considered the most prominent representative of market socialism. Sun is known for his persistence, despite the repressive circumstances, in advocating reform of the command-economy system and the expansion of SOE autonomy.

Wu: Sun Yefang strongly supported the role of the rule of value as a mechanism to provide incentives to enterprises, and he regarded the rule of value as the key link to improve the socialist economy. This is why he once said that "whether there are hundreds of rules or thousands of rules, the rule of value is first and foremost." However, it should be noted that Sun's rule of value is not the commonly understood rule under which market supply and demand determine the price. Sun believed that a "socialist economy is different from not only a natural economy but also from a commodity economy" and he maintained that economics should "destroy the theory of a natural economy and the theory of a commodity economy." He called for researchers to study the socialist political economy based on the definition of value provided by the classical Marxist authors. Therefore, Sun's rule of value is not the rule of the market (Sun called this the "number-one rule") but, rather, the rule, as elaborated upon by Marx in the first volume of his *Das Kapital*, and described as "the value . . . determined by its socially necessary labour time." (Sun called this the "number-two rule.") This rule is realized by the planning authorities by establishing prices based on the "value."

Consistent with these arguments, as early as 1956 Sun Yefang proposed to "base the plan on the rule of value" and to "advance the role of profit-targeting in the management of the planned economy." Equipped with this core proposal, Sun designed his socialist-economy model. According to Sun, the main feature of his model was to "centralize the major powers and decentralize the minor powers," using the amount of available funding as a yardstick. "Major powers" referred to "decision-making powers to expand economic reproduction based on available funding," such as decisions on investments, supplies for new projects, and sales of products. The so-called minor powers referred to "decision-making powers for simple economic reproduction based on the original funding," such as enterprise authority to readjust the product mix. The major-power decisions should be made by the government and the minor-power decisions should be made by the enterprises based on the "rule of value."

Sun Yefang was critical of administrative decentralization. In 1961 he wrote directly to a senior national economic leader to point out that the core issue in the economic administration system was not the relationship between the central government and the local governments. Thus, it was not the division of power among the administrative authorities at different levels. Rather, the core issue was "the autonomy and responsibility of enterprises as independent accounting units as well as their relationship with the state, or, in other words, the enterprises' power to operate and manage independently." Sun believed that only if enterprises have autonomy "can the state arouse [enterprise] enthusiasm to shoulder the responsibility given to them by the state," and only when enterprises obtain operational independence can the assignment of responsibilities for enterprises be clarified between the central authorities and the local governments, or, in other words, only then can the issue of "vertical vs. horizontal relationships" be resolved.

Although Sun used language different from that of Brus to describe his model, a thorough comparison will reveal that the two models are actually quite similar. In 1980, during his first visit to China, Brus visited Sun Yefang, who was hospitalized at the time. Even though it was their first meeting, they immediately developed a fond kinship and remained close friends thereafter.

Ma: Obviously, Sun's proposal regarding market socialism was intolerable to the Chinese political leadership at the time. Beginning in 1964, Sun was criticized and persecuted as "China's primary revisionist." He was imprisoned in 1968 during the Cultural Revolution on charges of being a "counterrevolutionary revisionist" who was anti-Party, anti-socialism, and anti–Mao Zedong Thought.

Did the situation change after the Cultural Revolution?

Wu: Yes, indeed, and significant changes took place. After the end of the Cultural Revolution, many economists and most officials in charge of economic work expressed agreement with Sun Yefang's ideas about economic administration. They agreed that the reform should focus on expanding operational autonomy so as to increase enterprise vitality.

In this atmosphere, authorities involved in economic decision-making responded positively. At a September 1978 brainstorming session called by the State Council, Vice Premier Li Xiannian pointed out that "a major flaw in the economic system reform of the past twenty years was to put too much emphasis on the division and transfer of administrative powers, leading to a cycle of 'decentralization-recentralization-decentralization.' It is necessary that independence be granted to all enterprises in any future reforms, allowing them to actively instead of passively carry out economic accounting so as to increase overall economic efficiency."

Ma: Based on the available records, it appears that some academics also appealed for decentralization and interest-sharing with the SOEs. In a 1979 paper, Professor Dong Fureng, deputy director of the Institute of Economics of the Chinese Academy of Social Sciences (CASS), proposed changing "the mode of state ownership under the system of ownership by the whole people." He advocated that economic units under ownership of the whole people should "possess, under unified guidance, a sense of independence and autonomy. They themselves must carry out comprehensive, independent, and strict economic accounting of their own. . . . The workers in an economic organization should have the right, on the premise of defending and promoting the common interests of the working people as a whole and under the guidance of unified planning to integrate the interests of the unit with their own personal interests, to directly take part in management." In September 1979, Professor Ma Hong, director of the Institute of Industrial Economics of CASS, commented that "the entry point for the reform of the economic administration system should be an expansion of enterprise autonomy. Enterprises should be given more decision-making power with respect to human and physical resources, finance, and planning." In early 1980, Jiang Yiwei, deputy director of the Institute of Industrial Economics, published an article calling for replacing the previous "state-centered thinking" and "local-government–centered thinking" in the state sector with "enterprise-centered thinking." Jiang suggested that "an enterprise is an association of all workers . . . it should be controlled by all its employees . . . under the unified leadership and supervision of the Communist Party organization," and enterprises should operate independently, implement independent economic accounting, and enjoy their rights as well as fulfill their duties to the state.

These proposals, reflecting the ongoing trends at the time, were warmly welcomed by enterprise managers, who cherished a strong desire for a loosening of constraints and decentralization.

Wu: It was against this background that an SOE reform was initiated after the end of the Cultural Revolution. At the time, it was referred to as an "experiment to expand enterprise autonomy."

As early as October 1978, Sichuan province experimented with this reform in six enterprises, including Chongqing Iron and Steel Works. Sichuan's experiment was very similar to the 1965 complete economic accounting in the USSR. The Sichuan reform consisted of two parts. First, planned targets were streamlined and control by the plan was relaxed. For instance, as long as the targets of the state plan were achieved, enterprises were allowed to increase their output according to market demand, to engage in processing trade, and to sell supplies and products outside of the plan. Second, the size of the enterprise bonus fund was enlarged and enterprises could retain a certain portion of their profits. Enterprises had authority to select and appoint mid-level managers, thus enhancing incentives for both the enterprises and their workers. During the first several months of the experiment, the reform recorded remarkable results as the workers' enthusiasm to increase production and revenue grew considerably.

Ma: It appears that the reform was initially quite effective.

Wu: You are right. Because the experiment was obviously successful in increasing production and revenue within a short period of time, Sichuan province extended the experiment to one hundred enterprises. In 1979, the Sichuan experiment won the support of the central government and it was quickly introduced in state-owned enterprises throughout the country. In July 1979, based on a Sichuan provincial government regulation, the State Council issued a regulation regarding expansion of the autonomy of industrial enterprises, requiring local governments and line agencies to select enterprises for similar experiments. By the end of 1979, the number of pilots had reached 4,200, and in 1980, this number was increased to 6,600. The pilots accounted for 60 percent of total industrial output of "on-budget" enterprises and 70 percent of total profits of industrial enterprises nationwide.

Ma: However, several months into the nationwide extension of the experiment, problems began to emerge. These were similar to the problems the USSR had encountered during the "Kosygin reforms." Because the enterprises were still affiliated with the administrative authorities, they lacked operational autonomy. At the same time, the enterprises could be "reinvigorated," because they were granted more benefits and were accountable only for profits and not for losses. But such measures distorted enterprise behavior. Enterprises under the new system were constrained neither by property rights nor by market competition. In addition, they were not guided by price signals. The increased enthusiasm did not lead to improved efficiency in terms of resource allocations, nor did it increase overall income in the society. As a result, aggregate demand grew out of control and fiscal deficits increased, resulting in turbulence in the economy. Within two years (1979–80), fiscal deficits exceeded the critical threshold of 3 percent of GDP, and by 1980, the retail price index had increased by 6 percent. After a comprehensive review of the economic situation, the December 1980 Central Work Conference announced that "readjustment" should be the priority of the new "eight Chinese-word policy" that had been adopted in 1979—that is, "readjustment, reform, consolidation, and improvement." The work conference decided that beginning from 1981 efforts would focus on "further readjusting the national economy." Under this situation, the reform to expand enterprise autonomy was halted and enhancement of an SOE "responsibility system" became the new driving force to ensure fulfilment of plan targets.

Wu: A more serious consequence was the resurgence of some former ideas as the opposition was emboldened by growing doubts about the market-oriented reforms. Some Communist Party and government leaders, together with several economists, believed that the economic difficulties were caused by an excessive preference for the role of the market and enterprise autonomy. They advocated replacing the market orientation with a "plan orientation," that is, improving the plan and tightening its disciplinary controls. Some people strongly criticized the proposed "enterprise-centered thinking," claiming that the pursuit of independence would separate enterprises from the state plan.

Ma: People who firmly believed in the plan and who were opposed to the market had always regarded the reform as a source of macroeconomic instability. According to their logic, the plan itself was good; it had merely not been implemented correctly due to imperfections and poor discipline. So it would suffice simply to correct these shortcomings. Some people today still hold such a belief.

Wu: Reform advocates were against the "plan-oriented" views you just mentioned. They believed that the difficulties were not caused by the market orientation but, rather, by the narrow focus on enterprise independence and autonomy. As early as 1980, Xue Muqiao, adviser to the System Reform Office of the State Council, highlighted the limitations of an approach that centered on decentralization and interest-sharing with enterprises. Xue believed that most important was to reform the "circulation sector" (that is, services for the supply and distribution of goods). He proposed to gradually remove administratively fixed prices and to establish a goods market and a financial market. In essence, Xue upheld the correct reform direction, which was to establish an economic system based on a competitive market institution. In the fall of 1980, guided by these ideas and on behalf of the System Reform Office, Xue took the lead in drafting a document entitled "Preliminary Opinions on Economic System Reform," which advocated the development of a commodity economy and different types of economic ownership. The proposal was submitted to a meeting of provincial Communist Party secretaries in September 1980 and won the approval of some of the participants as well as of Communist Party General Secretary Hu Yaobang.

However, against the backdrop of the political and economic situation in 1980–82, those officials and academics in favor of the plan-oriented approach gained the upper hand. The idea that a "socialist economy is a commodity economy" was rejected for political reasons. The official document of the 1982

Twelfth National Communist Party Congress confirmed the principle that "the state ensures proportionate and coordinated growth of the national economy by means of comprehensive balance of the planned economy and the supplementary role of market regulation." The idea of economic reform was dropped, and the need for true enterprise independence and a commodity economy was almost abandoned.

Ma: Although the market-socialism reforms to expand enterprise autonomy with market regulation were not successful in the late 1970s, they were later attempted on several occasions during China's reform process. For instance, in May 1984 the State Council issued the "Interim Provisions on the Further Expansion of the Autonomy of State-Owned Industrial Enterprises" (also known as the "Ten Articles on the Expansion of Autonomy"). In July 1992, the State Council issued the "Ordinance on the Transformation of the Operational Mechanism for State-Owned Industrial Enterprises," reassigning autonomy to SOEs in fourteen areas, including operations, sales, pricing, procurement, imports and exports, and even investments and asset management.

Wu: Another form of expansion of enterprise autonomy involved adoption of the "enterprise contract responsibility system," which was based on profits and revenue-sharing, for example, "a fixed base amount, a guaranteed turnover, retention of the surplus, and self-compensation for shortfalls." This represented the maximum mode of expansion of enterprise autonomy under state ownership.

In May 1979 the State Economic Commission, together with five other ministries, selected eight enterprises, including Capital Iron and Steel Works, as pilots for the contract responsibility system. In these pilots a certain portion of the profits was retained, and the enterprises had a certain amount of authority to make decisions regarding production, sales, funding, employee assignments, and distribution of bonuses. Workers' representative conferences were established to allow workers to participate in the "democratic management" of the enterprises.

Ma: In early 1983, with catchy slogans such as "It also works in the urban areas as soon as you try it" and "Contract responsibility for each and every level," some members of the Secretariat of the Communist Party's Central Committee called for all urban enterprises to comprehensively implement a contract responsibility system. Within two to three months, SOEs throughout the country had adopted such a system. Management of enterprises was handed over by the relevant agencies to contractors based on agreements regarding the amount of revenue and profits to be turned over to the owner (the state). Surplus income would be either left to the discretion of the contractors or would be allocated between the two parties based on a given ratio. However, before long, this experiment was halted amid economic disorder and rising prices.

Wu: Another reason for ending the experiment before it was extended nationwide was the existence of differing views among the central leaders regarding whether a contract responsibility system was appropriate for SOEs. Thus, the enterprise contract responsibility experiment was short-lived.

In December 1986 the State Council called for "implementation of various forms of an operational contract system to grant adequate autonomy to managers." These various forms included: (a) the handover of a fixed amount of profits; (b) profit-sharing based on a given ratio; (c) guaranteed tax payments, profit handovers, and priority for technological upgrading; and (d) total wages linked to realized taxes and profits. During the next year, these forms of a contract responsibility system were quickly adopted by all SOEs, and the newspapers were full of praise of this practice. Some people believed that, given the existing conditions in China, this was the only option for advancing the reform. They felt that the contract responsibility system could be regarded as a "second milestone" in China's reform. Some suggested that if the preliminary phase of socialism were to last for one hundred years, it should rely on the enterprise contract system throughout this period.

In 1988, the National People's Congress promulgated the "Law of the People's Republic of China on State-Owned Industrial Enterprises," which was modeled after the institutional arrangements of the SOE reform. The law recognizes the following principles: state-owned assets shall be owned by the state, that is, owned by the whole people; based on the principle of the separation of government bodies and enterprises, the state shall grant enterprises the rights of operation and management; and enterprises shall enjoy the rights to possess, use, profit from, and dispose of their properties according to the law. Later on, concepts such as "state ownership should be separated from legal person [enterprise] property rights" and "enterprise directors represent the legal persons" became the prevailing beliefs.

Ma: For some officials, the reform did not achieve the expected results, mainly because the SOEs had not been granted adequate operational autonomy. This is why they proposed entering into a contractual relationship with the managers of the state-owned industrial and commercial enterprises modeled after the successful "household contract responsibility system" that had been adopted as part of the rural reforms in the early 1980s.

Wu: However, the SOE contract responsibility system experiment was fundamentally different from the system implemented in the rural areas (the latter was also called "all-round contracting"). The system in the rural areas restored the institution of household farming, whereas the SOE reform did not alter the existing institution. The enterprise contract responsibility system was limited to delegating power to managers, thus leading to many problems.

Contrary to the high expectations of the political leaders, implementation of the enterprise contract responsibility system did not result in higher SOE efficiency or improvements in the economic situation. After a brief period of increases in output and revenue, short-term behavior and lax financial management became prevalent. At the time, "the ten classes of people," a jingle about the number of undesirable social phenomena, was widely circulated, which contained a verse to the effect that "the third class of people are assigned contract responsibilities and are reimbursed for meals, drinks, prostitution, and gambling." This so-called third class referred to those SOE directors who took advantage of the shortcomings in the contract responsibility system for their own benefit at the expense of the public interest.

Ma: To address these drawbacks in the enterprise contract responsibility system, the authorities proposed a number of solutions, such as "scientific setting of contract terms and conditions," "adding control indicators," "collateralized contracts," and "guaranteed contracts." However, because of the fundamental defects in the system, the problems only became worse over time.

Wu: This system had the following characteristics with respect to the institutional arrangements. During the term of the contract, the contractee (the owner) granted to the contractor (the operator) residual control rights, including part of the rights to retain the residual income. SOE managers were allowed extensive autonomy. However, because of a lack of ownership constraints, the granting of all the control rights to the enterprise managers (the contractors) led to "insider control." The system did not turn enterprises into independent entities responsible for their own profits and losses, nor did it realize the separation of government from enterprises or equal competition among enterprises. The system blurred the boundaries of enterprise property rights, exacerbating the conflicts of interest between the contractees and the contractors and making it easier for the contractors to expand their own interests at the expense of those of the contractees.

In addition, because the contractors sought to maximize current-period profits during the term of the contract, they were reluctant to make long-term investments, resulting in a lack of momentum for continual enterprise growth. In some cases, the contractors even used the owner's original capital to increase their own profit retentions. At the end of the 1980s and in the early 1990s, as the situation worsened with increasing revelations of managerial misconduct (for example, that of the head of the

Capital Iron and Steel Works, which was a "contract-based" company), almost no one in the enterprise sector or in academic circles still considered the system to be a feasible approach for the reform of the SOEs.

Ma: There was another reason that people abandoned that system. Decentralization and interest-sharing did not lead to an effective enterprise institution, and SOE operations went from bad to worse. By the end of the 1980s, 20 percent of SOEs were suffering losses. In the early 1990s, one-third of SOEs reported losses; another one-third reported profits, but, in actuality, they were really suffering losses; and only the remaining one-third was truly profitable. By the mid-1990s, the entire state sector was recording net losses. The market-socialism reforms focusing on decentralization and interest-sharing with the SOEs had reached a dead end.

Wu: A comparison of the various economic sectors in the 1980s reveals two opposing scenarios. In the SOE sector, there remained lingering "decentralization and interest-sharing" reforms, with unsatisfactory results. An appropriate path had yet to be discovered. But in the private sector, various private (nonstate) firms were emerging and demonstrating great vitality. By the beginning of the 1990s, more and more people began to realize that the market-socialism reforms could not solve the problems of the state sector. Against this backdrop, the 1993 Third Plenary Session of the Fourteenth Communist Party Central Committee adopted a new guiding principle to revitalize small and medium-sized SOEs and to carry out institutional innovations in the large SOEs, with a view to establishing a modern enterprise (that is, corporate) institution. The 1997 Fifteenth Party Congress introduced a strategic readjustment of the state sector by allowing the state to retreat from some sectors while assuming more market shares in others.

Ma: As we discussed earlier, decentralization, interest-sharing, and the revitalization of the SOEs were all reflections of the market-socialism reforms. Perhaps we should make an overall assessment of this type of reforms.

Wu: Market socialism was an important trend that for decades after World War II dominated the economic reforms in many Communist countries. Even today, although most of those countries have abandoned these types of reforms, they still have a significant influence in China.

For me, the most comprehensive and deep assessment of market socialism in academic circles has been the criticism by Hungarian economist János Kornai. Kornai is a well-trained economist and humanitarian. In his early years, he actively supported and had firsthand experience with the market-socialism reforms in Hungary and elsewhere in Eastern Europe. In his well-known 1992 book, *The Socialist System: The Political Economy of Communism*, Kornai devotes an entire chapter to systematically reviewing the market-socialism reforms in Yugoslavia, Hungary, China, Poland, Vietnam, and the USSR. Based on his review, he assesses the theory and practice of this school of economic thinking.

Kornai points out that these reforms achieved some good results, such as weakening administrative control and expanding enterprise autonomy. Product quality improved and SOEs paid more attention to the needs of customers. Many shortages in the economy were alleviated. More importantly, the reforms helped to eliminate the blind faith in centralization and the all-embracing plan; reduced the bias against private ownership and the market; and established an ideological foundation for a deeper and more thorough social movement.

While recognizing the progress made by the market-socialism reforms, Kornai also identifies their limitations. The basic framework of a planned economy and dominance of state ownership were maintained, although there were partial relaxations of control. Because government controlled the market and the national economy through indirect instruments, such as interest rates, tax rates, and prices, SOEs had a "dual dependence," that is, administrative coordination and market regulation. But administrative coordination had the upper hand. Under such circumstances, the SOEs could not eliminate the legacy of the traditional Communist system.

Kornai notes that under market socialism, the horizontal dependence on the market was enhanced, but it was only secondary. The vertical dependence—that is, dependence on the government—was altered because direct administrative controls were replaced by indirect controls. Nevertheless, vertical dependence remained dominant. "The destiny of SOE managers of socialist firms is tied, as has been seen, to those above them in the hierarchy. Although they have one eye on the market and the other on their superiors, the important thing, in fact, is for the eye cast upward to see clearly: their present bonus or penalty and their future promotion depend on their superiors." Although they were more concerned about profits, the reality revealed that "it is not in production or on the market that a firm's profits are decided, but in the offices of the bureaucracy."

Ma: Kornai was right on target with such a keen analysis.

Wu: Kornai also comments that until the budget constraints on enterprises are hardened, there can be no sustained breakthroughs in quality improvements and technological upgrading. In addition, the market-socialism reforms created new stresses and imbalances. For instance, "under the semi-deregulated market-socialist system the flow of informal communications presents an amorphous picture. The relation between firms and superior agencies is full of vague, accidentally or intentionally ambiguous rules, improvisation, exceptional cases, and personal connections that evade the official 'route.'" Because of these problems, "a spirit of cheap commercialism . . . permeates the whole society: personal connections with officials in the bureaucracy are used by state-owned firms and private entrepreneurs in matters of production and by individuals in their own affairs, and bribery is often attempted."

Kornai demonstrates that those phenomena "appear conspicuously in the Chinese economy, where the dual system based on plan instructions and freedom of firms to decide almost entices manipulation. . . . Nominally, a firm of this kind is publicly owned, but, in fact, it becomes more or less the private property of its manager, who puts much of the profit in his or her own pocket. It is the start of interpenetration by the bureaucracy and the private sector, not just in the form of legal joint ventures but through personal contacts. Private enterprises are set up by the dependents of high-ranking Communist Party and state officials or managers of firms, taking advantage of their familiarity with the 'back door.'" Kornai highlights the serious socioeconomic consequences caused by such government-business collusion, "All this ties in with the appearance of high incomes. Some derive from real market success, but others draw on shadier sources: bribery, defrauding the state, or cheating customers. . . . A surge of hatred for 'speculators' and 'corruption' breaks out. . . . Stuck halfway, the reform process digs the ground from under its own feet, alienating a sizable section of the general public."

Ma: How precise and sharp Kornai's criticism is, especially when one considers the earlier general dissatisfaction with "profiteering government officials" that triggered the political turbulence at the end of the 1980s and the anger expressed today against "the rich and the powerful"! The future is full of forks in the road. Are we doing OK? Does the risk of tripping over one's own feet still exist? These are questions that should be taken seriously during China's reforms.

DIALOGUE 6

RURAL HOUSEHOLD CONTRACTING LEADS TO THE INCREMENTAL REFORM STRATEGY

Ma Guochun (Ma): At the end of the 1970s, the market-socialism reforms to expand enterprise autonomy began to falter in China. As a result of a development strategy aimed at high targets and high speed, control over aggregate demand was lost, fiscal deficits rocketed, and the economy was in chaos. In March 1979, with adoption by the State Council of the "eight Chinese-word policy" to "readjust, reform, consolidate, and improve," the Chinese economy entered a period of contraction. At the December 1980 Central Work Conference, Chen Yun quoted from a letter by four young people that proposed a "twenty-four-Chinese-word" principle, which proposed to "suppress demand, stabilize prices, sacrifice opportunities for development, seek stability, slow down reform, give priority to readjustment, and centralize major decisions while decentralizing minor decisions." This marked the beginning of a period of slower reform and further readjustments to the national economy. As a witness during that period, would you please talk about the reform situation at the time?

Wu Jinglian (Wu): After the Communist Party Central Committee confirmed the principle of "slowing down reform and placing priority on readjustment," some so-called theorists and politicians launched criticism of the doctrine of a "commodity economy." In April 1981, the Research Office of the Secretariat of the Central Committee circulated an internal document that divided the main policy researchers and economists into four groups (to receive different political treatment) based on their attitudes toward the plan and the market. Advocates of the market-oriented reforms, including Xue Muqiao, Liao Jili, and Lin Zili, were "classified" in the "fourth group" (that is, those with the most "incorrect" political attitudes).

Shortly after circulation of this document, Communist Party theorist Hu Qiaomu, who was in charge of document preparation for the Twelfth National Communist Party Congress, reported that a letter sent by several members of the drafting team had criticized the views of these economists (members of the fourth group), views such as the role of the rule of value, enterprises as independent economic entities, market regulation of enterprise economic activities, and the establishment of a commodity economy as the essence of the reforms. According to Hu, the response of the drafting team members was that "our economy should never be generalized as a commodity economy. If such a generalization is used, socialist relations of common possession and joint labor will become relations of commodity exchanges of equal value. The main driving force of our economic activities will become the rule of value rather than the basic socialist economic laws and the rule of planned economic development. This will blur the borders between the socialist economy of planned development and the anarchic capitalist economy and will obscure the fundamental differences between the socialist and capitalist economies."

This maneuver succeeded, and the 1982 Twelfth National Communist Party Congress reiterated that China should adhere to the principle of maintaining the dominance of the planned economy and an enabling supportive market. The reforms in the urban areas had lost direction.

However, as the Chinese saying goes, "when the sun sets in the east, it rises in the west." In the fall of 1980, based on appeals by farmers and with the support of some central leaders, the Communist Party Central Committee issued a document allowing farmers to select their own modes of production. This triggered a wave of adopting a rural household contract responsibility system, thus turning a corner in China's reforms and rural economic development. It is safe to say that this rural reform was the first major breakthrough in China's economic transformation.

Ma: On September 20, 1954, the First Session of the First National People's Congress unanimously passed the Constitution of the People's Republic of China, which solemnly announced that "the state protects according to law the right of peasants to own land and other means of production." However, less than one year later the "socialist upsurge" turned the farmers' land and other means of production into quasi-state cooperatives. The provisions of the Constitution had become mere scraps of paper.

Wu: After taking power, the Communist Party did not attach importance to law; instead, it often replaced laws with regulatory policies. We should learn some lessons from this painful experience.

Ma: After the onset of the rural reforms, agricultural production experienced a period of unusually high growth. During a consecutive number of years, there were huge harvests. In 1984 the total output of grain reached a record high of 407.31 million tons, representing an increase of 33.6 percent from 1978. During the same period, the average annual growth rate of grain was 4.95 percent and the average annual growth rate of crops exceeded 10 percent. According to economist Justin Lin, the most important step for significant rural reform is a shift from an institution of production–team–based farming to household contracting. This systemic reform contributed 46.89 percent to the growth in output. Why did the household contracting system achieve these great results within such a short period?

Wu: I believe there are two main reasons. First, farmers had suffered greatly under the collective economy of large-scale production under greater public ownership. They had a strong desire to eliminate this institution as quickly as possible.

The collective economy that had dominated China's rural areas after 1956 was not indigenous. Rather, it had been imported from the Soviet Union. In fact, in his early years Lenin had advocated modernization of agriculture according to "the American way." But once in power, the Soviet Communist Party set out to achieve the "primitive accumulation of socialism" by expropriating the farmers' land. The key instrument for doing this was agricultural collectivization. China embarked on a similar path. Between 1948 and 1952, land reform was rolled out from north to south to realize the promise of returning the "land to the tiller." However, shortly after completion of land reform Mao Zedong initiated the "socialist transformation of agriculture."

Ma: In the summer of 1955, Mao criticized the "rightist deviation" of Deng Zihui, director of the Central Rural Work Department, and initiated a so-called "upsurge of socialism" in the countryside.

Wu: Why did this start from Deng Zihui? It was because after land reform Chinese agriculture faced two alternatives: either to develop individual farming or to realize agricultural collectivization. Deng Zihui and his colleagues believed that socialism could only be realized when the forces of production were highly socialized. This was consistent with the policy platform of the Seventh National Communist Party Congress, which advocated achieving socialism in two steps. Deng Zihui and his colleagues advocated granting farmers the freedom to sell and rent land as well as to hire and borrow so as to develop capitalist farming. They referred to the proposition of immediately shaking up, weakening, or even abandoning private ownership for the sake of agricultural collectivization as "an erroneous, dangerous idea of Utopian socialism in the rural areas." They enjoyed the support of Liu Shaoqi (number two in the leadership at the time), but Mao took the opposite view. He believed that the successful completion of land reform marked the end of the democratic revolution and the next step should be to put socialist construction on the agenda by vigorously carrying out a mutual-aid cooperative movement to achieve the "socialist transformation of agriculture."

The debate ended with Mao's criticism of Deng Zihui. Thereafter, "collectivization" was achieved by administrative directives and social pressures through "mass criticisms."

Ma: According to historical records, in response to the tremendous pressure from the "anti-right-deviationist line" campaign, household farming was abolished within a single year and agriculture was collectivized. By the end of 1955, there were only 500 higher-level agricultural production cooperatives (which did not pay land dividends), and the number of cooperative members accounted for only 3.45 percent of the total number of rural households. But five months after the launch of the cooperative movement, the number of higher-level cooperatives reached 540,000 and 88 percent of rural households had become members.

By winter of 1956, when the government announced completion of the movement, about 120 million farming households had been organized into 750,000 higher-level cooperatives. But the leaders considered these cooperatives still to be too small and too dispersed, making it difficult for the grassroots administrative units to control them. On March 30, 1958, in order to facilitate "leadership" over the cooperatives, the Communist Party Central Committee issued a directive requiring that the cooperatives be merged into larger organizations. In June of the same year, Mao launched the "people's commune movement" to consolidate the higher-level agricultural production cooperatives into people's communes that were characterized by so-called "large-scale production under greater public ownership," a combination of government and cooperative functions and integration of five economic and public-sector activities into one institution. The property of the higher-level cooperatives was taken over by the communes, and the members of the cooperatives handed over the lots of land that they had retained for their self-use as well as their privately owned homestead lots, livestock, and forests.

By the end of October 1958, the movement had consolidated 750,000 higher-level cooperatives into 26,000 people's communes. On average, this was 28.5 cooperatives per one people's commune of 4,500 households. Under the people's communes, production brigades were responsible for production management and economic accounting, but profits and losses were handled by the commune. A fixed work-point system was adopted to measure each member's labor input for the purpose of determining year-end distributions. A free supply system provided grain to households based on a per-head quota. Farmers thus became members of a military-style organization under strict discipline: they were not allowed to cook at home; instead, they had to take all three meals of the day in communal canteens.

Wu: At the time, the people's communes were praised as "the best organizational form for socialist construction and for the gradual transition to communism." Slogans such as "communism is paradise and the people's communes are the bridge to communism" and "the realization of a Communist society in China is not far away" became widespread.

In essence, the cooperatives were quasi–state–owned economic organizations. In the higher-level agricultural production cooperatives, the property of individual farmers was merged into one inseparable collective property and the farmers could not voluntarily leave the cooperatives. Production was managed by cooperative officials who were also in charge of distribution of the produce. The cooperative was no different from a state-owned enterprise, except in terms of wages and welfare benefits. As grain and other products were controlled by officials, there was no longer any concern that farmers would refuse to hand over or to sell their produce to the state.

Ma: Economist Du Runsheng once said that, as a country full of farmers, it was understandable that from time to time China had entertained utopian ideas. However, once such utopian thinking was put into practice in a country of several hundred million people, the costs were very high. This is reminiscent of the Western proverb "the road to hell is paved with good intentions."

How true that is! The promised paradise did not materialize; on the contrary, disastrous results soon surfaced. After a decline of 15 percent in 1959, the output of cereals went down another 10 percent in 1960. Additionally, average national per capita grain consumption dropped from 203 kilograms in 1957 to 163.5 kilograms in 1960, a reduction of 19.5 percent. The drop was even sharper in the rural areas: a 23.4 percent decline in average per capita grain consumption. In the urban areas there was widespread edema. In the rural areas hundreds of thousands of people died of hunger. Agriculture became the biggest victim of the command economy.

Wu: Because the people's communes and the Great Leap Forward movement caused serious economic and social problems, the government had to readjust the organizational structure of the people's communes. The main thrust was to maintain the general institutional framework, reduce the size of the people's communes, and gradually move the basic accounting unit downward to below the commune level. Beginning in 1962, the production teams became the basic accounting unit under a system of "ownership by three levels [the commune, the production brigade, and the production team], with the production team as the basis." This system remained in place until the end of the Cultural Revolution in 1976. But such readjustments failed to achieve fundamental changes in the rural areas. The "Decision on Several Issues of Agricultural Development," adopted by the Fourth Plenary Session of the Eleventh Communist Party Central Committee in 1979, made the following calculations regarding the situation in the rural areas, agriculture, and the farmers' livelihood: "Per capita grain output in 1978 was only equivalent to that in 1957. The average per capita annual income for the agricultural population was only a little over 70 yuan, and that of a commune member in nearly one-quarter of the production teams was less than 50 yuan. On average, the collective fund accumulation (the physical and financial surpluses) of each production brigade was less than 10,000 yuan, and some production brigades could not even sustain simple reproduction."

Ma: Here is another thought-provoking statistic: by 1978, the share of the urban population in the national total had only increased 17.9 percent; whereas, at the same time, the average level of urbanization in the developing countries had increased 27.3 percent. It makes no sense to blame urbanization for the slow growth of per capita grain possession. The root cause was the low economic efficiency of the backward system.

Linguist Zhou Youguang once recalled that, during the 1976 Tangshan earthquake, he returned to Suzhou from Beijing on sick leave and visited an old woman who had been classified as a member of the "poor peasant" class.[1] She lived in a large room that had been allocated to her during land reform. Except for a large bed, there was no other furniture, and she even had to borrow a bench for her visitor. They had a nice chat, and before leaving, Zhou Youguang asked her, "Which is better, your life before liberation in 1949 or at present?" Her answer was "of course, life before liberation." Although this is just one incident, it is an undeniable fact that after thirty years of economic development, the rural areas were still devastated and agriculture remained depressed.

Wu: Indeed, the rural areas were destitute. Farmers worked throughout the year but earned very little. Even during those years when there were no major disasters, farmers could hardly feed and clothe themselves, to say nothing of amassing any savings. In 1978, there were 250 million farmers who were living in absolute poverty, accounting for 30.7 percent of the total number of rural residents.

Ma: How did this miserable situation come about?

Wu: From the perspective of microeconomics, the most important policy is to get the incentives right. However, in China's collective economy there was no incentive mechanism linking remunerations with results. The higher-level cooperatives implemented a system of "variable work-points based on evaluated labor input," but during the people's commune period, most places implemented a fixed system. Production teams set benchmarks for work-points based on age and gender, and work-points were recorded according to the number of workdays. There was no difference between

[1] Translators' note: During land reform, rural residents were grouped into the exploiting classes, i.e., landlords and rich peasants; the exploited classes, i.e., poor peasants and hired laborers; and those neither exploiting nor being exploited, i.e., middle peasants.

more or less labor input or good or bad results. The system seriously damaged the farmers' work ethics. It was common practice for farmers to go to the fields to be present for the attendance records, but not to do any work.

In addition, the people's commune system led to a dual social structure that divided the urban and rural societies. Under the institutional arrangement of combined government and collective functions, there was a household registration system, a food ration system, and a grain quota system, in addition to controls over people's political and ideological beliefs. Farmers were deprived of the right to manage their own assets, their labor input, or their produce. Even their personal freedoms were restricted. It was up to the commune officials to decide what to grow, how much to grow, and where to get the inputs. The officials also determined how much grain one could consume per month and the monthly mix of the quota for coarse and finely-ground grain. Farmers could not move freely about the country, and sometimes they were required to receive permission from the village head even to go to town to shop or to visit friends. Production targets were handed down from one administrative level to the next. Officials from the administrative agencies exerted pressure to sow and reap, but then they took away part of the funds and the grain. Although they were the main source for agricultural production, all the farmers could do was passively accept these administrative directives. The state commerce departments and the quasi-state supply and distribution cooperatives monopolized the procurement and selling of the main agricultural products, such as grain, cotton, and rapeseed, at prices set by the government. Farmers were prohibited from engaging in long-distance shipping or sales of goods.

Ma: Under the feudal manorial system of medieval Europe, serfs were personally attached to their feudal lords and they could not leave the farms without permission from their lords. No wonder in 1979 economist Dong Fureng told a foreign scholar that "in an economic sense, the institution of the people's communes is a contemporary system of serfdom."

Due to the price scissors between the industrial and agricultural sectors, the dual-track system that divided the urban and rural societies extorted funding from agriculture in order to finance the growth of infant industries. According to estimates by some economists, between 1953 and 1981 the price scissors allowed the government to take about RMB 700 billion from farmers through unequal exchanges, amounting to about one-half of the country's total accumulation (RMB 1.5 trillion) during that period. Farmers were the main victims of the institution of "large-scale production under greater public ownership." Thus it is fully understandable why they seized the opportunity in 1978 to eliminate this institution.

In addition to the motivation of the farmers, what was the second reason for the success of the household contracting system?

Wu: Farmers were familiar with this institutional arrangement, so it was easy for them to accept it. It was also the most nimble option: land remained under collective ownership but was contracted (leased) out to farmers for household farming.

China has a long history of combining small-scale household farming with ownership of relatively large lots of land. The Qin and Han dynasties (221 BC–AD 221) implemented an institution of "farmland assignments": land was owned by the state (that is, the imperial court), but it was assigned to farmers for agricultural production. In return, the state collected taxes and levies from the farmers. For a long time, ownership was separate from users' rights. By the Tang dynasty (AD 618–907), a tenancy system had developed. Under this system, regardless of its ownership, land was rented out to farmers, who in turn were obligated to hand over to the government and the landlords a fixed amount of the produce or monetary payments. Starting from the Ming dynasty (AD 1368–1644), the land system matured with the institution of tenancy in perpetuity. This was an institution of "three masters for one *mu* [0.165 acres] of land." The landlords, the big tenants, and the peasants were the three "masters." Landlords owned the land and held the sub-surface rights. Big tenants held tenancy in perpetuity and enjoyed surface rights. They made capital investments, for example, construction of irrigation facilities, land consolidations, and soil fertility improvements, to increase the productivity of the land. Sometimes big tenants subcontracted the land under their tenancy to farmers who engaged in household farming.

After the rural collectivization movement, the farmers became members of higher-level agricultural cooperatives, and their private property was turned over to the collectives, but they still longed for household farming on leased land. Whenever an opportunity occurred, they would ask for a return to household-based contracting. However, during the Mao era their requests were repeatedly rejected, and on each occasion, the farmers were suppressed with a heavy hand. In all, there were three rounds of ups and downs in the treatment of such demands by farmers prior to 1976.

Ma: The first surge in household contracting took place in the fall of 1956, less than one year after the nationwide extension of the higher-level agricultural cooperatives. The practice first emerged in Wenzhou, Zhejiang province; Wuhu, Anhui province; and Chengdu, Sichuan province, where remuneration for farmers was calculated based on their output. The *Zhejiang Daily* carried an article by Li Yunhe, deputy county Communist Party secretary of Wenzhou prefecture, entitled "Individual Responsibility and Household Contracting Are Good Ways to Address

Intra-Cooperative Contradictions." At that time, 15 percent of the farmers in Wenzhou were engaging in a household-contracting type of farming.

After the beginning of the Anti-Rightist Movement in the summer of 1957, the Communist Party Central Committee launched a "big debate on the socialist path versus the capitalist path" in the rural areas. During the debate, household contracting was considered part of the capitalist path. One after another, the *People's Daily* and the newspapers of the provincial Communist Party committees carried sharp criticisms of household contracting. Many local officials were criticized and punished. Li Yunhe was labeled a rightist and sent to "reform through labor." In Wenzhou, more than twenty people were arrested and sentenced for engaging in household contracting, thus suppressing the first surge in household contracting.

Wu: The second surge took place in 1959. During the people's commune movement of 1958, the prevailing trends were "Communist-style living," "exaggerated reporting," "commandism," "the issuance of arbitrary orders," and "pursuit of privileges by officials." Farmers suffered greatly. Facing the devastation of agricultural production and the drastic declines in the farmers' basic livelihood, some localities adopted household contracting to remedy the situation. Shortly thereafter, at the Lushan meetings in July/August 1959, an "anti-rightist deviation" movement was launched. During the movement, the practice of household contracting was criticized as a major example of "right-deviationist opportunism." A commentary in the *People's Daily* called household contracting "a typical proposition and activity of right-deviationist departmentalism, . . . extremely backward, back-peddling, and counterrevolutionary." The article referred to the practice as a "poisonous weed" and called for its "uprooting, burning down, and complete eradication." Thereafter, the criticism escalated and the practice was accused of being part of a plot "to restore capitalism." Many officials who supported the practice were labeled "right-deviationist opportunists." Thus, the second surge in household contracting was also crushed.

The results of the ultra-leftism soon resurfaced, particularly in the rural areas where widespread famine wreaked havoc. The third round of efforts to implement household contracting took place in the early 1960s.

Ma: At that time, farmers in many places could not feed or clothe themselves and mass incidents with abnormal deaths occurred. The collective economy was no longer able to maintain basic living conditions for commune members.

Wu: Under these circumstances, Anhui province adopted an approach of "fixing required output by farmland lot and assigning responsibility per household" in the hopes of restoring agricultural production and providing a basic livelihood for the farmers. By March 1961, 39.3 percent of the production teams in Anhui had implemented this approach. Other provinces followed suit with similar practices.

However, Mao found the approach absolutely unacceptable. He felt that, in order to mobilize farmers to increase production, the basic accounting unit should be set at the production-team level. Household contracting was not to be implemented because of its features of private ownership. For Mao, the bottom line was no private ownership.

Ma: In November 1961, the Communist Party Central Committee issued a directive stating that "household contracting and other disguised practices of dividing the land for individual farming do not comply with the principle of the socialist collective economy and thus are incorrect." The Central Committee mandated that provinces "gradually direct farmers away from these practices." During the January 1962 Central Work Conference (that is, the 7,000 cadres conference), Mao criticized Anhui province for supporting the farmers' household contracting efforts, and Anhui province was forced to issue a "Decision on Correcting Household Contracting."

Wu: But there were diverse views among the top leaders. Some leaders felt that household contracting was a viable option for the situation in the early 1960s. For instance, in the second half of June 1962, at a briefing meeting on the situation in the East China Region for the Secretariat of the Central Committee, one-half of the participants were in favor of implementing household contracting. At the meeting, Deng Xiaoping, in his thick Sichuan dialect, stated that "it doesn't matter whether the cat is black or white; it is a good cat as long as it catches mice." After the meeting, Chen Yun and Deng Zihui proposed to Mao that in some places household contracting could be used to mobilize the farmers in order to rapidly restore the level of agricultural output.

Mao was infuriated that so many Communist Party leaders had agreed to adopt household contracting. In several 1962 speeches, he reiterated the existence of class struggle, and he sharply criticized the so-called trends in "dividing land for individual farming," "reopening concluded cases," and "returning to the dark era." He also declared that the issue of class struggle should be referred to "annually and monthly." In May 1963 the Central Committee decided to launch a large-scale "socialist education movement" in the rural areas. The movement's draft decision stated: "Never forget class struggle; never forget the dictatorship of the proletariat," and "once the theory of class struggle is grasped, all problems can be readily solved." The socialist education movement was a prelude to the Cultural Revolution. During the latter, household contracting was considered a serious criminal offense, similar to the sword of Damocles hanging over the heads of the farmers and rural officials.

Ma: In the more than twenty years from the completion of collectivization in 1955 to the end of the Cultural Revolution in 1976, farmers tried to implement household contracting on a number of occasions, but they were never able to eliminate the people's communes.

What great sufferings Chinese farmers endured during the period of forced industrialization under the people's communes! Rural development was lopsided, agriculture as a source of urban industrial accumulation contracted, and infant industries that were shrouded in the administrative system could not achieve healthy growth, to say nothing of providing a supplement to agriculture. There was an urgent call for change, in particular in the rural areas.

In November 1978, eighteen farmers in Xiaogang village of Fengyang county in Anhui province secretly signed a "death pact," agreeing to launch a household-based farming institution called "all-round contracting."

Wu: Faced with destitution in the rural economy, many local officials were frantically seeking a solution. Wan Li, Communist Party secretary in Anhui province from 1977 to 1979, has recalled how tough life was for farmers in Anhui at the time. "They did not have enough to eat or to keep themselves warm. Their dwellings did not even look like houses: the doorframes and window sills were made of mud bricks, as were the tables and chairs. In their houses, there was no wooden furniture at all. There was nothing but bare walls. I could not imagine that the rural areas were in such an impoverished state even several decades after liberation! I could not help but asking myself: *Why, and was this socialism?*" The farmers' initiatives to implement change gave officials with similar mindsets new hope.

The spontaneous reform of household contracting took three forms: contracting specific tasks to each production group, contracting output quotas to each household, and contracting responsibility to each household, that is, after handing over a sufficient amount to the state and contributing a sufficient amount to the collective, each household kept the remainder of the harvest (also called all-round contracting). The first two forms were ways to organize labor input and to distribute remuneration within the collective, although the contractor under the second form was the individual household rather than the production group. The third form represented a fundamental change. Under this form, the collective, as the owner of the land, contracted out the farmland to households based on the size of the family and/or the number of working-age family members. Under such contracts, farmers were committed to paying taxes, fulfilling the procurement targets of the state or the contract, and handing over a certain amount of the output as a contribution to the collective fund for public accumulation and the fund for public benefits. The remaining produce belonged to the farmers, and they could use it at their own discretion. The all-round contracting eliminated management and distribution at the production-team level. According to the farmers, as long as the state targets were fulfilled and contributions to the collective were made, what was left was one's own. Because of this feature, all-round contracting was also called "dividing the land for individual farming."

All of these practices resulted in significantly higher output, thus resolving the food shortages. As facts speak louder than words, the practice gained the support of open-minded local officials. By 1979, the approach had spread, on a considerably large scale, to Sichuan, Gansu, Inner Mongolia, and Henan provinces, in addition to Anhui.

Ma: Open-minded local officials enjoyed heartfelt support from the farmers. A widely circulated jingle vividly captures popular sentiment at the time. It goes like this: "Go to Wan Li [Anhui Communist Party secretary] for rice and to Ziyang [Zhao Ziyang, Sichuan Communist Party secretary] for grain."

Wu: However, the local experiments encountered significant resistance from the more conservative local officials and from higher-level political officials. At the time, the "two whatevers doctrine"[2] was dominant. Because Mao had rejected the experiments, all-round contracting was deemed unacceptable. A draft decision entitled "Questions Concerning the Acceleration of Agricultural Development," reviewed at the December 1978 Third Plenary Session of the Eleventh Communist Party Central Committee, clearly stipulated that "dividing land for individual farming and contracting output with households were prohibited."

In September 1979, the Fourth Plenary Session of the Eleventh Communist Party Central Committee approved this draft decision, but the phrase "contracting output with households is prohibited" was modified to "do not contract output with households." The tone was somewhat softened, yet all-round contracting was still prohibited.

The following factors probably triggered the above modification. The transformation from the people's communes to the household contracting system had brought about not only substantial gains to farmers but also benefits for other social groups, without harming their interests. Because the people's communes had reached a dead end and the Cultural Revolution had brought the entire society to the brink of collapse, pragmatic Communist Party and government officials felt it was necessary to support the farmers' institutional innovations in order to ameliorate the situation in the rural areas. For rural officials, the contracting system did not reduce much of their power and interests; on the contrary, it increased the benefits for themselves and for

2 Translators' note: The "two whatevers" doctrine maintains: "We should resolutely safeguard whatever decisions Chairman Mao made, and unswervingly abide by whatever instructions Chairman Mao gave."

their families. Therefore, many Communist Party and government officials played an enabling role in the acceptance and implementation of the system.

Ma: In economics, a *Pareto improvement* is any action in which at least one person benefits, while the interests of the others are not harmed. China's rural reform is a typical example of a Pareto improvement.

Wu: Although the social conditions were ripe, nationwide adoption of the household contracting system depended on the decision of the top leadership because of the differing views within the Communist Party. In February 1980, Hu Yaobang (a supporter of Deng Xiaoping) replaced Hua Guofeng as general secretary of the Communist Party and began to preside over the work of the Central Committee. This meant that Deng Xiaoping had gained an upper hand in control of the top leadership. In May 1980 Deng affirmed the local experiments with household contracting and all-round contracting. In September of the same year, a Central Committee document pointed out that in remote and impoverished areas "where the masses have lost faith in the collective," household contracting "is permitted and is nothing to be afraid of." This included contracting output or production with households. The document opened the door for a nationwide rollout of the system.

Thereafter, the farmers' enthusiasm for household contracting burst forth, and various forms of the system soon came into being.

In January 1982, the Communist Party Central Committee and the State Council issued the first of a series of annual "No. 1 documents" on economic policy in the rural areas. The 1982 document officially affirmed the household contracting system for farmland, thus putting an end to the related debates that had gone on for some twenty years. Shortly thereafter, household contracting was extended throughout the country. By the end of 1982, the number of production teams that had implemented output and production contracting reached 93 percent of the national total. Chinese agriculture had thus completed the transition from the collective economy of the people's communes to household farming on contracted land.

With the nationwide adoption of the household contracting system, the foundation of the people's communes was shaken. In December 1982, the revised Constitution changed the basic political institutions in the rural areas from people's communes to township governments, signaling the official end of the people's commune movement that had dominated China's rural areas for more than twenty years.

Ma: The adoption of the household contracting system greatly facilitated agricultural development, and the income of farmers registered significant increases. Per capita annual income of rural residents grew from RMB 133.6 in 1978 to RMB 397.6 in 1985.

The rapid increase in income led to a sharp drop in poverty. According to the State Statistical Bureau, there were 120 million people living in poverty in 1978 and the incidence of poverty accounted for 30.8 percent of the total rural population; by 2007, the population living in poverty had dropped to 14.79 million, accounting for only 1.6 percent of the total rural population. In general, farmers had access to adequate daily necessities.

The American economist Theodore Schultz once said, "Successful reform that puts land in the hands of owners . . . has again and again in country after country almost literally 'turned sand into gold.'" What a beautiful remark!

Wu: Another major change was the emergence of farmers' property rights. Before the rural reforms, farmers did not own much property except for their homes (excluding the homestead lots), and most of their homes were sparsely furnished. An investigation by the Research Office of the State Council found that the average property per rural household was valued at about RMB 500, and the average property held by the collective was similarly pathetic. Total fixed assets in the rural collective economy amounted to RMB 72 billion, or less than RMB 240 per work-age farmer. After the reforms, farmers received property rights in three forms. First, farmers gained land-use rights (surface rights), unprecedentedly entitling them to keep the proceeds from the land. Second, in addition to other private property, such as bank deposits and private residences, farmers gained ownership of the means of production for self-use. By 2006, their situation changed from having nothing to gradually accumulating property. Third, farmers had discretion in terms of the use of their own human capital. Through migration and the discretion to select their own employment, the mindsets and attitudes of farmers changed dramatically, and the quality of human capital registered remarkable improvements.

There was also a more far-reaching result: with improvements in rural labor productivity and partial rights to migrate, the surplus labor in the rural areas began to move to urban jobs in the non-agricultural sectors. China's rural areas thus became integrated with the ongoing trends of industrialization and the modernization of agriculture.

Ma: After nationwide adoption of the household contracting system, agricultural output increased for a number of consecutive years. However, in the second half of the 1980s, agricultural growth began to stagnate. Between 1978 and 1989, the income gap between urban and rural residents narrowed. But in the 1990s, the urban economy was on a fast track, whereas the standard of living for the rural population was growing much more slowly. By the early 2000s, the so-called problem of the "three rural issues" (related to the development of agriculture, rural areas, and farmers) had resulted in an increase in the incidence of poverty among farmers, agricultural stagnation, and widespread flight from the rural areas. Why did these phenomena occur?

Wu: The varying responses to these issues can be grouped into two points of view. One group, believing that the potential of household contracting was already nearing its end, called for a re-collectivization of agriculture. The other group, believing that the problems were caused by the incomplete reforms, appealed for further rural reforms and urbanization.

Ma: We all remember the first point of view. After the 1989 political turbulence, some people attempted to abolish the rural reforms and to launch a new "socialist education movement" in the rural areas. They wanted farmers to reject the household contracting system and to return to the people's communes—that is, to large-scale production under greater public ownership.

Wu: Obviously, there was no chance to turn back the wheels of history. Such suggestions were unacceptable to the farmers who had gained partial property rights and production autonomy. Thus these ideas were not implemented.

Ma: I am afraid, however, there was some theoretical support for the first point of view. A widespread doctrine in socialist countries maintained that collectivization is an inevitable product of mechanization. Even the more open-minded Communist Party leaders felt that collective agriculture has advantages over individual agriculture. They believed that production relations are determined by the status of the forces of production, thus they were opposed to hurriedly implementing collectivization before the realization of mechanization. These leaders objected to the development of collective farms beyond the existing level of the forces of production. Based on this doctrine, some people were in favor of a re-collectivization after agricultural productivity and mechanization improved. What do you think about this?

Wu: These views were based on a Marxist idea of the 1800s. Based on conditions in England at the time, Marx concluded that, similar to what had occurred in industry, large-scale production in agriculture was more advantageous than petty production, and, eventually, large-scale production would squeeze out petty production. Therefore, many socialists believed that family-based farming was backward and it would eventually be replaced by either large-scale farms owned by capitalists, who hire laborers to work the fields, or by state-owned (or quasi-state) large farms.

At the end of the 1800s and in the early 1900s, the international socialist movement engaged in debates on the advantages of large-scale versus petty agricultural production. Leaders such as Edward David and Eduard Bernstein, supporters of democratic socialism, questioned Marx's conclusion, as they believed in the development potential of the family-based peasant economy. In contrast, Karl Kautsky defended Marx's view, claiming that developed capitalist large-scale agriculture would increasingly replace petty agriculture, and the direction of social development would be the same in agriculture as it was in industry. Because Lenin supported Kautsky, agricultural collectivization was implemented in the Soviet Union. Other socialist countries followed suit in establishing quasi-state collective farms, agricultural cooperatives, or people's communes. Of course, agriculture in these countries did not fare well, and in some cases the agricultural situation even deteriorated.

Ma: The institution of large capitalist farms had once been popular in some countries, for instance, the United Kingdom. But agricultural development in the developed countries during the twentieth century has revealed that, even with agricultural mechanization and a high degree of socialization, household farming has its own advantages and vitality. Today in the UK, where large farms used to be dominant, family farms still account for 52 percent of all farms and large farms only account for 23 percent. Some scholars have pointed out that private farms at present form the basic farming unit in most market-economy countries. These farms may be large capitalist farms, with employed labor, or family farms, where family members are the main labor force.

Wu: Why did the agricultural production cooperatives fail to improve productivity? Du Runsheng, who had been in charge of rural work for a long time and who made great contributions to the rural reforms in China, was the first to point out that cooperatives under centralized farming are inconsistent with the nature of agricultural production. Agricultural production processes are closely linked to the life cycles of plants and animals. Agriculture has the following characteristics: First, it is constrained by factors that are due to natural changes and it requires intensive care by highly conscientious people who adopt flexible approaches to the changing circumstances. Second, agricultural returns are concentrated in the end products, requiring that the producers' benefits be linked with the final output. Third, land, the main means of production, requires constant nurturing in order to achieve improved production. Thus, the producer must establish a stable and vital relationship with the land so that he is able to nourish the land for his long-term interests. It is because of these characteristics that household farming has great vitality.

Ma: If all that is required is to be in line with these characteristics, it should be feasible and efficient to have the owner manage the farm and to have the hired laborers work in the fields.

Wu: The challenges in providing incentives to hired laborers involved in agricultural production are the following: unlike in the case of industry, agricultural workers cannot measure the quantity and quality of their effective labor input during each step of the production process. It is impossible to measure input if it is not linked with final output. Many types of agricultural work are dispersed and seasonal, which increases the complexity of measuring labor input. It is much easier to allow the family to handle this issue. Since family members are closely linked economically, they share similar objectives and interests. They seldom argue over each member's inputs or income within the family, significantly reducing the costs of decision-making. Furthermore, there are almost no transaction costs for the measurement and supervision of labor input. Hence, household farming has unparalleled advantages over other modes of farming and it is most suitable for agricultural production.

As a result of the previously mentioned debate in the 1990s, the government revised the doctrine that favored large-scale agricultural production. In 1998, the Third Plenary Session of the Fifteenth Communist Party Central Committee pointed out that household farming is suitable not only for traditional manual agriculture but also for modern agriculture equipped with science and technology and advanced production tools. It has high adaptability and strong vitality and should be maintained for a long time.

Ma: Obviously, it is wrong to blame the private ownership, that is, the family farms, for the problems of the three rural issues. But what are the reasons for these problems?

Wu: I agree with some scholars that the root causes are the lack of further rural reforms and the deficiencies in urbanization.

First, the rural reforms are incomplete. The household contracting system is a makeshift system, under which the collective ownership of land continues to exist. Under this system, farmers only have users' rights to the land, in accordance with the terms of the contract, rather than rights in perpetuity with discretion (that is, land surface rights that are the most important aspects of land ownership). Extension of the contract terms is not equal to returning "land to the tiller." Because farmers do not have permanent users' rights, they lack enthusiasm to protect and invest in the farmland. Laws and policies prohibit the use of contracting rights and homestead lots as collateral for loans, nor do they allow cross-village real-estate transactions. The limited users' rights cannot be turned into liquid capital, restricting the ability of farmers to obtain funding for start-up businesses.

Second, urbanization has suffered many setbacks under the current land ownership system, thus reducing opportunities for farmers to share in the returns of industrialization and urbanization. The problems have delayed rural modernization and the transformation of rural residents into urban residents. Furthermore, although land is owned by the collective, it is actually controlled by the localities. This has led to substantial official abuses. Some local governments have developed so-called image projects that consume large investments funded by "land financing" (that is, relying on revenue from the selling of land-use rights to finance their expenditures). Some corrupt officials and businessmen have benefited from the huge differentials between the prices of buying and selling land, and their behavior has greatly damaged state-society relations.

In the forthcoming dialogues, we will further discuss the rural reforms and urbanization.

DIALOGUE 7

THE SUDDEN RISE OF THE PRIVATE SECTOR

Ma Guochuan (Ma): In the last dialogue, on rural reforms, you mentioned that the rural household contract responsibility system ushered in a new reform strategy for China. Why do you take this view?

Wu Jinglian (Wu): This was because the reforms in the Soviet Union and the Eastern European Communist countries all began from the reforms of the state-owned enterprises (SOEs). At the end of the 1970s, China followed suit and launched its own SOE reforms. But the reforms in the Soviet Union and the Eastern European countries met with insurmountable obstacles and eventually became bogged down. China was an exception in this respect because of the adoption of the rural household contracting system in the countryside that enabled the country to overcome some of these obstacles. Although the road of reform and development in China remained bumpy, the reforms continued. This was achieved despite the fact that there was some opposition to the market orientation, rule of law, and democratization. The opposition's suggested solution to the three rural issues (related to the development of agriculture, rural areas, and farmers) was a return to collectivization, and they advocated a policy of state ownership of land, collectivization of labor, and the "socialization" of farmers' lifestyles. Nevertheless, it is appropriate to say that China's successful reform path was triggered by the rural household contracting system.

Ma: But why did the Communist countries select the SOEs as the first step for the reforms?

Wu: On the surface, the reason is straightforward: the objective in these countries was to reform the command economy, and the SOEs were the economic foundation of that system. From this perspective, the SOE reform strategy was entirely appropriate.

But there is a deeper economic reason. Be it explicit or implicit, the objective of the reform in the Communist countries was oriented toward the market: to allow a competitive market to play a role in the allocation of resources. How does a market mechanism effectively allocate resources? It is through a price equilibrium formed from free-market competition. Market prices are important for two reasons. First, they reflect the scarcity of resources. Exchanges based on market prices can direct resources to where they will be most effective. Second, market prices provide the proper incentives. Like Adam Smith's "invisible hand" of the market, market prices direct people's self-interest to provide social benefits. However, market exchanges are transactions between various owners. If the entire society has only one owner—that is, the state (or the government), as in the Leninist-Stalinist models—there will be no real market exchanges and there will be no way to form prices that reflect the relative scarcities of resources. Therefore, sooner or later any market-oriented reforms will be directed to the SOEs to break the monopoly of state ownership.

Ma: Because reform of the SOEs is a prerequisite to reforming the command economy, why did such a reform encounter such insurmountable obstacles?

Wu: In the political sense, the Soviet-style economic system was a state syndicate, or a Party-state corporation. The state sector was the lifeline of the system. The 1954 *Textbook on Political Economy*, a publication compiled by the Institute of Economics of the USSR Academy of Sciences under direct guidance by Stalin, taught that between the two systems of public ownership (that is, the state property system and the cooperative collective farm system) "state property is the . . . most developed form of socialist property. The leading and determining role in the entire national economy belongs to it." Collective ownership is a makeshift system for the period when the forces of agricultural production are still at a low level. After the forces of agricultural production are improved to a certain extent, collective ownership should gradually be transformed into comprehensive, whole-people (state) ownership. The 1996 "Ten-Thousand-Chinese-Word Manifesto" (one of several lengthy tracts that sharply criticized the reform and opening), which opposed state-sector readjustments, stated, "The state economy is the highest form of public ownership, a most sought-after objective of socialism." Under these circumstances if, from their first thrust, the reforms are directed to the state sector, the reforms will inevitably face political problems.

Even if the political difficulties can be overcome under certain conditions, the practical economic problems will not be completely resolved. Because the state sector underpinned the Soviet-style socialist economy, when the benefits produced by the state sector declined during the first phase of the reform, the reform lost support from the society because of the worsening economic conditions. As an example, in 1984 the state sector in the Soviet Union accounted for 95.5 percent of total industrial output and the cooperative sector accounted for only 2.5 percent.

Of the total commercial agricultural output, the share of the SOEs was 48 percent, the share of the cooperatives was 41 percent, and the share of individual sideline production was 11 percent. Among total retail sales, the share of the state sector was 70 percent, the share of the cooperative sector was 27.4 percent, and that of collective farms was 2.6 percent. Such ownership shares were also reflected in the Eastern European countries. Given the economic structure, it proved difficult to reform the SOEs because they were the socioeconomic foundation of the economic system.

This situation was the source of the dilemma for the reforms in the socialist countries. Unless the state-ownership system was fundamentally changed, national economic operations would not be improved. But to make such changes, high political and economic risks were involved. Simply put, this was the most serious problem that these countries failed to resolve: on the one hand, the traditional socialist economic system had to be reformed, but, on the other hand, the system still had to continue operations during the reform process. In other words, although the state sector, as the foundation of the system, had to be reformed, its existence was necessary to sustain the national economy. Because the SOE reforms did not achieve any positive results, the economies in these countries became increasingly overstretched. The countries that did not carry out these reforms as well as those that halted these reforms both faced insurmountable economic declines. Furthermore, even the countries that had undergone ten to twenty years of reforms encountered serious economic problems.

Ota Šik, a Czech economist who had been a Czech deputy prime minister and had presided over the reforms during the 1968 Prague Spring, once used the following analogy to describe this reform dilemma. He pointed out that economic reform is a leap forward from an old to a new system. In order to avoid conflicts among various parts of the system, to succeed one must take a decisive vault in one stride, rather than merely moving step by step. This can be compared to the changing of the traffic rules. After World War II, some countries adopted the US rule and changed from driving on the left side of the road to driving on the right side. The rule was changed at midnight and the change took effect nationwide all at once. If the change had been considered too much of a shock and if the traffic rule had been changed only for important vehicles, for instance ambulances, one can only imagine the results. Similarly, as a huge and complex system involving a maze of relationships, the economic institutions could not be changed overnight. This is why there were so many conflicts and so many pitfalls during the reform process. Šik admitted that the reform economists in Eastern Europe had been unable to come up with a solution to the problem.

Ma: It appears that the success of China's rural reforms provided a feasible option for resolving the problem.

Wu: Yes, indeed. The biggest inspiration was that, rather than launch major reforms in the state sector, it was feasible to make small changes and to focus reform and development on the nonstate economic sector, or what we Chinese call the "privately operated economy." The SOE reforms were to be revisited once the private sector matured and was able to provide stable economic development.

This strategy of incremental reform and of a dual-track transition is very different from what took place in the Soviet Union and the Eastern European countries. It is a reform strategy that places priority on reforms outside of the established system.

More specifically, the strategy was deployed in three areas. First, prohibitions on private enterprises were gradually relaxed to facilitate their growth. Second, a "microclimate" of special economic zones in some areas was created to allow certain localities to gradually expand the scope of market activities by becoming more integrated with international markets. Third, experimental zones to test comprehensive reforms were established so as to promote regional reforms and opening in various regions.

Ma: Obviously, reform in the first area was the core basis of the strategy.

Wu: You are right. This change started shortly after the end of the Cultural Revolution. Because these reforms touched upon the essence of the traditional Communist ideology, initially only baby steps could be taken.

During the socialist transformation movement, the number of individual businesses was reduced to a minimum, and most individual businesses became public-private jointly operated entities. The number of individual businesses in the urban areas dropped from 838,000 in 1953 to 106,000 at the end of 1956, and by 1957, a unitary economic structure had been established. Industrial enterprises were all public-private joint operations. Private enterprises accounted for only 0.1 percent and 2.7 percent, respectively, of the wholesale and retail sectors. During the Cultural Revolution, individual and private industry and commerce almost completely disappeared. By 1978, enterprises under whole-people ownership accounted for 77.6 percent of total industrial output, and collectively owned firms accounted for 22.4 percent. The dominance of state ownership and implementation of a national plan are the most important economic characteristics of communism. Even the collective economy is said to have elements of socialism under the "glow" of state ownership. Other types of ownership were eliminated as elements incompatible with state ownership.

Ma: In terms of ideology, because the private sector was regarded as "sprouts of capitalism," it was hence prohibited. The mainstream ideology preferred "socialist weeds" over "capitalist seedlings." For example, whenever there were attempts to reopen county fairs, to retain land lots for self-use, to reinstitute remuneration systems based on individual responsibility for profits and losses, or to adopt rural household contracting practices, they were labeled "new trends in class struggle" and "movements by dark forces." Ordinary people who peddled some daily necessities to make ends meet were regarded as criminals for "engaging in profiteering." Thus, due to these harsh circumstances, by 1978 there were no privately owned enterprises and only 140,000 individual businessmen.

At the time, many people, both within and outside the government, realized that there was no hope of curing the ailing economy unless private economic activities were restored. However, because of the rigid ideology it proved virtually impossible for the authorities to openly legalize a private economy.

Wu: Unexpectedly, one phenomenon provided a rare historical opportunity to break the dominance of state ownership: the return to the cities of large numbers of sent-down youth after the Cultural Revolution.

In 1968 Mao Zedong had called for young people to go to the countryside "to be re-educated by poor and lower-middle-class peasants." More than sixteen million college and middle-school students and other young people, or one-tenth of the total urban population, were sent to the countryside. After the end of the Cultural Revolution, these people sought to return to the cities, and eventually over 90 percent of them were successful. As a result, the cities were teeming with young people waiting for job assignments. Countless numbers tried to secure jobs in the SOEs. But the system was unable to accommodate so many job seekers. In particular, those who were considered to have come from "bad backgrounds"[1] were unable to find jobs in the formal state sector. The high rate of urban unemployment became a serious problem for the government.

Under these circumstances, economist Xue Muqiao proposed that the job seekers be allowed to set up cooperatives that would be responsible for their own profits and losses or to engage in individual businesses. Although the superior position of state ownership would be maintained, other types of ownership would be allowed to exist. Xue suggested that there be diversified channels for employment—that is, SOEs, collective enterprises, and individual businesses. In 1979, the State Council accepted Xue's proposal and instructed that the administrative bureaus of industry and commerce "approve applications from idle people who hold formal *hukou* registrations (household member residents) to be self-employed in repair businesses, services, and the handicraft industries." However, the relevant State Council document also clearly stated that the "hiring of workers is strictly prohibited."

[1] Translators' note: After 1949, families were assigned class statuses that branded them for generations. Typically, those with bad class backgrounds were members of the exploiting classes.

Ma: This State Council document was the first regulation after the 1978 Third Plenary Session of the Eleventh Communist Party Central Committee to allow for the development of self-employment. People began to work as barbers, cobblers, whetters, umbrella or furniture repairmen, and snack peddlers. Thus, the first group of "self-employed people" was born on the city streets.

By the end of 1979, the total number of self-employed workers had reached 300,000, an increase of more than 100 percent from 1978. In 1980, a national work conference on labor and employment issued a "three-channel" principle supporting a combination of job assignments by labor bureaus, by voluntary organizations, and by self-employment. Thereafter, the individual business sector registered rapid growth. At the end of 1980, the total number of people engaged in individual businesses reached 806,000, more than double the number in the previous year.

The following is an interesting anecdote. One morning Xue Muqiao went to Tiananmen Square to take a walk and he asked a self-employed photographer on the square to take his picture. When the photographer realized who his customer was, he became very excited and took many pictures of Xue for free. Then he gratefully said to Xue, "Thank you for proposing that we can seek jobs on our own. Because of your proposal, I now have this job."

This is a vivid example of a reform that came about as the result of a crisis. If there had been no pressure from the sent-down youth who had returned to the cities, the policy that strictly prohibited individual businesses probably would not have been relaxed so rapidly.

Wu: In June 1981, the Sixth Plenary Session of the Eleventh Communist Party Central Committee adopted the Resolution on Certain Questions in the History of Our Party since the Founding of the People's Republic of China, which confirmed that "the state economy and the collective economy are the basic forms of the Chinese economy. The working people's individual economy within certain prescribed limits is a necessary complement to the public economy." This statement represented official recognition of the legality of individual businesses. By the end of 1981, the total number of self-employed workers had reached 2.27 million, again double the number in the previous year.

Ma: It is this social stratum that contributed to the rebirth of the private sector in the cities, transformed the economy, and fostered the first group of entrepreneurs during the period of reform and opening. However, the Criminal Law, which went into effect on July 1, 1979, stated that the crime of "speculation and profiteering," which was only vaguely defined, applied to all those who were self-employed. An Office for Controlling Speculation and Profiteering, established in local governments, often sent staff persons to either apprehend, extort money from, or confiscate the goods of the street peddlers. Meanwhile, as the general public was still constrained by the traditional ideology and growth of the individual economy was still tightly restricted, "self-employment" remained a derogatory term that was unacceptable to the mainstream, and those who were self-employed were the most denigrated segment of society. At the time, being rich did not give people entrée into the mainstream or lead to acceptance by the general public. Private workers often felt inferior, and some would only appear in public in disguise for fear of being recognized by former classmates and friends.

Wu: Amid these political constraints, the biggest challenge to the development of individual businesses was the prohibition on hiring workers. But many private businessmen were unable to take advantage of further market opportunities unless they were able to hire more regular workers to expand their businesses. Due to the boom in the commercial sector, many households specializing in certain trades, stalls, small workshops, and household factories began to hire helpers and apprentices. As the debate on the rural household contract responsibility system was winding down, a new and more heated debate, regarding whether private businesses should be allowed to hire employees, erupted. Because of the prevailing socialist psychology in New China, this debate came to a full boil.

Ma: It was against this background that the "hiring incident involving Chen Zhixiong" took place. In 1979, Chen, a farmer in Gaoyao county of Guangdong province, received 8 *mu* (1.3 acres) of fish-farming ponds under a household responsibility contract. The ponds provided him with high returns. In the following year, Chen began to expand his business by receiving 14 *mu* of fish-farming ponds from two production brigades, so he hired a regular worker. By 1981, the size of Chen's fish farm had already reached 497 *mu*. He had hired five regular workers as well as employing 1,000 workdays of temporary farm hands. Chen's actions greatly exacerbated the already existing sensitivities: should hiring, which was regarded as a form of exploitation, be allowed to exist in a socialist country?

On May 29, 1981, the *People's Daily* carried an article introducing Chen Zhixiong's fish ponds and describing "the debate on contracted fish farms." The newspaper invited readers to provide their opinions. The main issues were "is hiring equal to exploitation?" and "can one enter into a contract across production brigades?" The debate in the *People's Daily*, consisting of a total of twenty-one articles, lasted for three months. Some writers warmly supported Chen's actions. Others were fiercely critical. Hu Qiaomu, a member of the Secretariat of the Central Committee, wrote to the Communist Party Committee of Guangdong province, "Attached is a report, although I am not sure how true the story is. If it is true, what is the opinion of the provincial committee? In my personal view, if what is reported is true, it is a deviation from the Communist system. The provincial committee should issue a directive to halt and correct this practice and make the directive known throughout the province. As the matter is related to the overall situation in our socialist system, I would like to request that the provincial committee review it." In contrast, Wan Li, vice premier of the State Council, instructed, "Please look into this story. The enthusiasm of farmers to develop a commercial economy should be protected. Caution is in order when using the old framework to make judgments about this practice." Eventually, the Guangdong Provincial Communist Party Committee came out in support of Chen Zhixiong.

Wu: Around the same time, economist Lin Zili in the Research Office of the Secretariat of the Central Committee realized that without a breakthrough on the hiring taboo, there would be no room for private-sector development. The challenge was to receive clearance from the long-time head of Communist Party ideology in the Research Office, so that the issue could be submitted to the senior leadership. As an expert on *Das Kapital*, Lin, using Marx's calculation when elaborating on the notion of "surplus value," suggested that "engaging no more than eight people is hiring helpers. Engaging more than eight people is hiring regular workers. Hiring less than eight people should not be considered exploitative."

This was the demarcation line Marx had used to distinguish "petty property owners" from "capitalists" in chapter 9 ("The Rate of Surplus Value"), book 3, of volume I of *Das Kapital*. According to Marx's estimate, if a person at the time (the mid-1800s) hired fewer than eight people and directly participated in the production process together with the workers, he was considered a transitional figure between a capitalist and a laborer, and he was a petty property owner; but if he hired more than eight people, he then possessed the workers' surplus value and was a capitalist.

The document drafted by Lin Zili was accepted politically and was submitted to the Communist Party Central Committee. Issued on July 7, 1981, "Some Policy Stipulations of the State Council on the Urban Non-Agricultural Individual Economy" pointed out that the individual sector was a necessary supplement to the state and collective sectors, and it permitted individual businessmen to hire one or two helpers. If their businesses were more technical or required special expertise, they could employ two to three apprentices, or a maximum of five. But the document specified that households engaging in special trades and individual businessmen were not allowed to hire more than eight workers. In particular, the general restriction against employing more than eight people applied to Communist Party members.

Ma: Individually owned enterprises were thus "upgraded" from the "other register" to a "supplement" to the "regular register."[2] The wisdom of working around a political obstacle is a typical "Chinese characteristic." This is also indicative of the rigidity of the prevailing ideology at the time.

Wu: Shortly after the gates for hiring workers were opened, individual businessmen began to hire more than eight people. With an increase in the number of such cases, a new round of debates ensued. People who had supported the former policy line derided the emergence of capitalism and called for a "prohibition and a correction." According to their logic, the hiring of more than eight workers constituted a form of capitalism that should be prohibited. In June 1982, the central government issued an urgent notice on "cracking down on serious economic crimes." As a result, a number of people who were "riding the waves" of the market economy were imprisoned. In Wenzhou, the birthplace of the individual-business sector, eight business leaders, including "hardware king" Hu Jinglin, "mine-lamp king" Cheng Buqing, and "screw king" Liu Dayuan, were the main targets of the crackdown. Their suppression was called the incident of the "eight kings." Their purge, the first cold front experienced by the private sector during the new era, seriously slowed the pace of economic development. The impact of this crackdown was most obvious in southern Zhejiang province and in the Zhujiang delta region of Guangdong province, where the private sector had first emerged.

Nevertheless, some local officials resisted the leftist views and approaches. In a direct response to the criticisms, Ren Zhongyi, Communist Party secretary of Guangdong province, announced that there should be a "rectification of names" (that is, calling things by their proper names) for private businesses that hired workers so as to "allow the private sector to develop and become stronger."

Ma: Deng Xiaoping used another tactic. At the October 1984 plenary session of the Central Advisory Commission, Deng stated, "The emergence of privately hired labor was quite shocking a while back. Everybody was very worried about it. In my opinion, that problem can be set aside for a couple of years. Will that affect the overall situation?" In April 1987 when meeting members of the drafting committee for the Basic Law of the Hong Kong Special Administrative Region, Deng again pointed out: "At first I said we could wait two years; now two years have passed, and I'd say we should still wait."

[2] Translators' note: During the Qing dynasty (1644–1911), law-abiding people were registered in a "regular register," and bandits, thieves, and others were registered in the "other register." In the contemporary context, these are metaphors referring to the unfair treatment of certain people or entities.

Wu: Deng adopted his "no debate" tactic to let the passage of time work out the problems. The January 1984 "No. 1" document—that is, the "Notice of the Party Central Committee on Rural Work in 1984"—allowed farmers to establish and invest in enterprises. Wenzhou took advantage of this opportunity to rehabilitate its "business kings" who had been imprisoned.

The October 1987 Thirteenth National Communist Party Congress gave a formal green light to the development of the private sector. Thereafter, an amendment to the Constitution of the People's Republic of China, adopted by the First Session of the Seventh National People's Congress in 1988, added the following provision: "The State permits the private sector of the economy to exist and develop within the limits prescribed by law. The private sector of the economy is a complement to the socialist public economy. The State protects the lawful rights and interests of the private sector of the economy, and exercises guidance, supervision, and control over the private sector of the economy." This amendment signaled recognition of the legality of the private sector in China's socialist ownership structure (although the private sector was still defined as a "supplement to public ownership").

Ma: By 1988, the number of privately owned enterprises had reached 90,000 and they employed a workforce of 1.64 million. The development of individual businesses, and the private sector more generally, affected the dominance of the state sector.

Wu: The rural reforms were the main driver behind this change. As mentioned in the previous dialogue, from 1980 to the end of 1982 household contracting of production was widely adopted, thus ending the institution of people's communes. Although government documents called the new institution of household contracting a "cooperative sector under collective ownership," in reality it was a proprietary economy based on the contracting of land from the collective sector (called *individual proprietary enterprises* according to Chinese law). Between 1981 and 1985, five consecutive "No. 1" documents issued by the Communist Party allowed for an enhancement of the household contracting system. In 1991 and 1993, two decisions by plenary sessions of the Communist Party Central Committee clearly stated that this system would remain in place for a long period of time. This further established the institution of household farming.

After the rural reforms, formerly impoverished farmers who were assigned property rights saw their assets increase enormously. By 2006, the total value of fixed assets of rural households reached RMB 1,928.8 billion, or RMB 7,647.10 per rural household. Among the total rural fixed assets, 50.7 percent was in agriculture, 18.7 percent was in animal husbandry, 12.1 percent in transportation and warehousing, and 7.2 percent in manufacturing.

The biggest and most unexpected effect of the rural reforms was the "sudden rise" (in Deng Xiaoping's own words) of township and village enterprises (TVEs). Before the Cultural Revolution, the government had strictly implemented the *hukou* system that separated the rural areas from the urban areas. Industrialization was achieved through a policy of forced accumulation. There were strict restrictions against individuals changing from an agricultural *hukou* to a non-agricultural urban *hukou*. Even commune and brigade enterprises were required to comply with a "localization" principle (that is, using local resources, processing local resources, and selling local products locally). In other words, industry and commerce could not be developed to target the broader market. Enterprises had to limit production and sales of products to small village communities. The goal of the principle was to prevent the growth of the "spontaneous forces of capitalism among petty producers."

Ma: The theoretical basis for preventing "the spontaneous forces of capitalism" in the rural areas was a remark by Lenin that was highly regarded by Mao: "Small production *engenders* capitalism and the bourgeoisie continuously, daily, hourly, spontaneously, and on a mass scale." These irrefutable words provided the theoretical basis for the several rounds of "socialist education movements" to remove the "reactionary" elements from the Chinese Communist Party bureaucracy and for the political campaigns to "cut off the tail of capitalism."

Worldwide experience in industrialization and analyses by development economists reveal that a shift of surplus labor from rural areas to industry and commerce in urban areas is a building block for industrialization and modernization. It is also an effective path to improving rural living standards. To a large extent, the speed with which this shift is achieved is a determinant of the level of industrialization. The arbitrary limitations on commune and brigade enterprises within the village communities contradicted the general trends of history.

Wu: Compared with the industrial countries, China has a much larger population base and many more farmers. Lacking sufficient arable land, per capita resources for farmers are therefore seriously limited. As a result, there has been an obvious trend toward diminishing returns from the land. Hence, regardless of any government measures to raise the prices of agricultural products, in order to increase production, raise the income level of farmers, and improve their livelihoods, it was imperative that the rural surplus labor be allowed to transfer to the non-agricultural sectors. Prior to the rural reforms, the problems of the three rural issues (stagnant agriculture, destitute rural areas, and a high incidence of poverty among farmers) had been very serious, due in part to the strict restrictions on the business scope of commune and brigade enterprises that resulted in a huge amount of rural surplus labor and disguised unemployment.

The rural household contract responsibility system unexpectedly triggered a boom in the rise TVEs. The TVEs varied considerably in terms of their characteristics and ownership structures depending on where they were located. In general, there were three TVE models. One was the Southern Jiangsu Model, which can be traced back to the commune and brigade enterprises that emerged during the Cultural Revolution. After the onset of the reform and opening, these enterprises were owned by the village or township governments. Because of their proximity to Shanghai, they enjoyed access to technology and marketing networks, and hence they grew rapidly. In the 1980s and 1990s, these TVEs, established and owned by grassroots governments on behalf of local communities, were the most popular in the country. The second group was based on the Zhujiang Delta Model, consisting mainly of TVEs owned by investors from Hong Kong, Macau, and Taiwan (China) (including the so-called bogus foreign devils, that is, mainland-owned businesses based in Hong Kong and Macau) that primarily targeted international markets. The third group was the Wenzhou and Taizhou Model. Located in these two localities of Zhejiang province, these well-developed TVEs mainly grew out of individual businesses that had been created by farmers and handicraftsmen. Although they were often affiliated with state or collectively owned enterprises in order to receive political protection (commonly known as "red-hat companies"), these firms were actually privately owned businesses.

Ma: Although the TVEs based on the Southern Jiangsu Model evolved from commune and brigade enterprises, they were fundamentally different from their quasi-state predecessors. Whereas the commune and brigade enterprises were restricted by a combination of government and enterprise functions and belonged to the government, the Southern Jiangsu Model TVEs, enjoying more independence and autonomy, demonstrated strong market competitiveness.

Wu: The main problem with the commune and brigade enterprises was that they were units with combined functions, thus they were not true enterprises. Because their development was suppressed, their market growth was limited. Nevertheless, they were better than nothing. The rural household contract responsibility system provided a strong impetus for the rapid development of the TVEs. This can be seen in three respects. First, the system revealed the existence of surplus labor that had been hidden within the people's communes. As farmers gained freedom to migrate to non-agricultural sectors, the TVEs were provided with an adequate supply of labor and various self-starters from the villages demonstrated amazing creativity and entrepreneurship. Second, the household contract responsibility system liberated rural productivity that had long been suppressed under the people's communes. The accumulation of agricultural surpluses allowed for the development of rural industries.

Last, with their rising living standards the consumption demands of farmers increased, and with the removal of the institution that separated the rural areas from the urban areas, rural-urban exchanges were facilitated. All of these phenomena provided a market for TVE products.

Ma: According to statistics, the value added by commune and brigade enterprises in 1978 accounted for only 5.7 percent of GDP, but by 1990, this figure had increased to 13.4 percent. By the mid-1990s, after many years of continuous development, the TVEs, accounting for one-third of total industrial production, could no longer be ignored.

As a result, the many surplus rural laborers transferred to jobs in the non-agricultural sectors. Between 1980 and 1990, the number of workers in rural non-agricultural sectors grew from 30.57 million to 86.73 million, an increase of 1.84 times. According to the State Council Development Research Center, in 1983 there were about 2 million migrant workers from various villages and towns; by 1989 this number had exploded to some 30 million. Over one hundred million farmers were working in the non-agricultural sector.

Wu: The Sino-foreign joint ventures and foreign proprietary enterprises were another important driver behind China's economic development. After the onset of the reform and opening, China established special economic zones and open coastal cities, encouraging and promoting foreign direct investments. Foreign enterprises brought in capital and advanced technology and management, and they also introduced marketing channels to global markets. By contributing to the formation of a competitive domestic market, they were an important source for China's further economic development.

Ma: The reforms we have discussed thus far, be they implementation of the rural household contract responsibility system, the rise of the TVEs, the relaxation of the restrictions on individual businesses, the granting of permission to hire workers for the growth of private enterprises, or the opening to foreign investment, all led to gradual increases in new nonstate elements in the national economy. These incremental economic changes are the main reasons for China's sustained high growth rate in the 1980s. Between 1979 and 1990, China's GDP grew by 181.7 percent, or the equivalent of 9 percent per annum.

DIALOGUE 8

OPENING TO THE WORLD: A DRIVER OF DOMESTIC REFORM

Ma Guochuan (Ma): In the last dialogue, you mentioned that the special economic zones (SEZs) and the pilot cities for comprehensive reform of the economic system played important roles in the implementation of the incremental reform strategy. These were critical measures in China's opening to the outside world. As is well known, China's reforms did not take place in a completely closed state. A policy of opening the economy to the outside world was adopted in parallel with the reforms of the domestic economy. The domestic reforms and the opening to the outside world are generally referred to together as the "reform and opening." In this dialogue, I would like to ask you to comment on the relationship between these two policies from a historical perspective.

Wu Jinglian (Wu): In order to elaborate clearly, let us first clarify the external economic relationships of the developing countries based on development economics.

State of the Opening of the Economy	*Inward-Looking Economy*	*Outward-Looking Economy*
Lower level	Closed	Export-oriented (relative opening)
Higher level	Import substitution	Complete opening

From the perspective of external relations, the economic policies in the developing countries can be classified as either *inward-looking* or *outward-looking*. The former can be further divided into a lower-level, closed economy with a higher level of import substitution, whereas the latter can be described as export-oriented or completely open economies.

After World War II, most of the developing countries abandoned the practice of closed economies because it was necessary that they purchase from the developed countries those goods that they could not produce domestically. At the time, external economic relations constituted an important element in the economic development strategies of the newly independent countries. However, many of these countries, although no longer closed, still looked inward and implemented an import-substitution policy. Instead of integrating economically with the outside world, they replaced imports of end products with imports of technologies, equipment, and critical parts, thus substituting producing products on their own for importing them. In other words, their external economic relations were at a higher level than those of the inward-looking economies. In comparison, during the more than twenty years since the establishment of the People's Republic, China was a lower-level, closed economy.

Ma: Historically, China had had extensive economic and cultural exchanges with many countries. The history of the "silk road" is indicative of China's long-time opening to the outside world. However, shortly after Zhu Yuanzhang became the first emperor of the Ming dynasty (1368–1644), the imperial government strictly prohibited coastal residents from "crossing the seas to trade on their own with foreign countries." The *haijin* policy that banned private maritime activities lasted for more than two hundred years. In contrast, the sixteenth century marked the dawn of maritime activities by the Western European countries. After the mid-1600s, the Qing dynasty (1644–1911) continued its strict closed-door policy, under which the flow of ships, personnel, and goods in and out of China was rigorously restricted. As a result, China remained isolated from the rest of the world. In 1793, a British mission, led by Lord Macartney, visited the court of Emperor Qianlong (1711–99) to seek the establishment of trade relations. The Emperor's response was, "Our Celestial Empire possesses all things in prolific abundance and lacks no products within its borders. There is no need therefore to import the manufactures of outside barbarians in exchange for our own produce." At that time, the Western European countries were riding the high tide of the Industrial Revolution, but the Qing dynasty was still mired in the illusion of the "celestial empire." During the several hundred years of the Ming and the Qing dynasties, China became increasingly isolated and backward. At the same time, however, the feudal system collapsed in Western Europe. The capitalist countries developed their own domestic markets, which also led to the formation of international markets. These changes culminated in the Industrial Revolution in the West that began in the late 1700s and greatly facilitated improvements in productivity. What a sharp contrast!

History shows that opening to the outside world contributes to economic development, whereas closed borders result in stagnation. After World War II, many newly independent countries engaged in external economic relations in order to achieve their development goals. Why did China remain closed for such a long time after the Communist Party came to power?

Wu: This is a complex historical issue. To be fair, around the time of the establishment of the People's Republic, Chinese leaders did not intend to adopt a completely closed economic system. They hoped to maintain economic relations with both the Communist camp and the capitalist camp. At the Second Plenary Session of the Seventh Communist Party Central Committee in March 1949, Mao Zedong clearly stated, "As for doing business with foreigners, there is no question; wherever there is business to do, we shall do it and we have already started; the businessmen of several capitalist countries are competing for such business. So far as possible, we must first of all trade with the socialist and people's democratic countries; at the same time, we will also trade with the capitalist countries." However, due to the country's political alliances and international strategy, and given the commitment of the Soviet Union to provide aid, New China adopted a policy of "leaning to one side" and gradually came to depend on the USSR and the other Communist countries for foreign trade. In June 1950, the Korean War broke out, and in October, the Chinese People's Volunteer Army entered the war. In December of the same year, the US Department of Commerce imposed an embargo on China, and on May 18, 1951, the United Nations passed a resolution imposing a comprehensive embargo on China, further isolating China from the West. Therefore, the USSR and the other Communist countries became China's main trade partners. By 1952, trade with these countries had reached 81.26 percent of mainland China's total imports and exports. In terms of basic industrial investments, during the First Five-Year Plan period (1953–57) aid from the USSR supported 153 key projects in the metallurgy, automobile, and weaponry industries.

Under these circumstances, during the Three Great Socialist Transformations (1953–57) of agriculture, the handicraft industries, and capitalist industry and commerce, the government established a highly monopolistic foreign trade system in accordance with the Leninist principle of nationalization. Under this system, state-owned general import and export corporations were established in each industry to "unify" international trade. The State Planning Commission issued mandatory trade targets. Goods to be exported and goods to be imported were procured by the state trade corporations according to these plan targets. The state budget was responsible for all profits and losses.

Ma: Despite its trade relations with the Soviet Union and the other Communist countries, China maintained a certain degree of autonomy and independence. In 1949, the Communist countries established the Council of Mutual Economic Assistance (Comecon), under the Soviet Union, to coordinate the international division of labor, to arrange for specialization and collaboration, and to develop economic cooperation. China was invited to join the organization, but it only attended its meetings as an observer.

Wu: In 1952, in *Economic Problems of Socialism in the USSR*, Stalin asserted that socialism and capitalism represent two parallel but opposing world markets. Comecon supported a closed economic system, as opposed to an open system, and only fostered close trade relations among its members. After the 1958 Great Leap Forward movement and, in particular, as a result of the deterioration in relations with the USSR in the early 1960s, China ended its observer status in Comecon activities. Chinese leaders instead stressed "self-reliance," encouraging the various regions to develop their own independent economic systems but further promoting a closed-door policy in external relations. Economic exchanges with other countries were limited, with the exception of a few selected countries, such as Albania. Among those countries with which China maintained economic relations, China mainly served as a provider of foreign aid and there were very few two-way transactions. As a result, China was basically cut off from the outside world.

Under the closed system, the purpose of foreign trade was to exchange needed goods and to balance between surpluses and deficits. Primary agricultural and mining products were exported in exchange for sorely needed manufactured goods. Nevertheless, the scale of these transactions remained relatively small.

Ma: After the beginning of the Cultural Revolution, the dominant ultra-leftist policy greatly influenced China's position in international affairs. Under slogans like "combating peaceful evolution," "combating and preventing revisionism," and "maintaining self-reliance," a strong anti-foreign bias took hold. Utilization of external capital was attacked as "inviting the wolf into one's house." The country refused to participate in the international division of labor, and Chinese economics textbooks referred to the international division of labor as a division "between hegemonic states and vassal states" and as an "instrument of the imperialists' aggression and expansionism."

In 1972 the State Council approved the import of a color television assembly line. A government delegation went to the United States to visit Corning, Inc., which was considered a global leader in the production of glass and ceramic materials. Before the delegation was to return to China, the company gave each member of the group a Christmas gift that was highly valued by the Americans: a glass snail paperweight. However, the gift was regarded as an insult by the Chinese because it indicated that China was moving at a snail's pace. The relevant Chinese government agencies held a "mass meeting" to denounce the American "attempt" to humiliate the Chinese people and called for an end to the import of color television tubes from the United States. Official statements declared, "We shall never yield to pressure from the imperialists." There were also calls to lodge an official protest with the US Liaison Office in Beijing. This furor over the "Corning snail incident" reflected the twisted mentality of a closed country.

Wu: In an era of increasingly closed economic relations, if a country focuses only on maintaining self-sufficiency, the development of its economy will be retarded. At the end of the 1960s and in the early 1970s, the world economic system underwent several major structural adjustments. The economies of the Four Little Dragons (Hong Kong, Singapore, South Korea, and Taiwan [China]) took off, whereas China, gradually withdrawing behind its closed doors, lost a rare historical opportunity to develop further.

During the late stages of the Cultural Revolution, after tensions with the United States were reduced and diplomatic relations with Japan normalized, China tilted toward developing economic and trade relations with the Western countries. For example, during the 1977–78 "outward leap forward" (120 large projects to introduce foreign technologies) China imported some large industrial and mining equipment, and in 1978 twenty-two contracts, valued at USD 7.8 billion, were signed to import large fertilizer and metal facilities. Imports and exports grew rapidly, and the total volume of trade increased from USD 6.3 billion in 1972 to USD 20.64 billion in 1978. However, the goal was not to develop an open economy to achieve prosperity based on China's comparative advantages in international trade. Instead, the goal was to establish an "independent and self-reliant" economic system through the import of technologies and, eventually, to substitute the imports with China's own products.

This marked the beginning of a shift from a closed-door policy to an import-substitution policy. Nevertheless, in 1978 the volume of Chinese trade ranked twenty-seventh in the world, accounting for only 0.8 percent of global trade. Its trade deficit totaled USD 1.1 billion and its foreign reserves amounted to only USD 1.7 billion.

Ma: After World War II, many newly independent countries sought to catch up with the advanced economies through industrialization and modernization. They relied on import substitution as their main strategy. How did this strategy work?

Wu: Specifically, the following is how import-substitution functions. The size of the domestic market for imports is determined by the accumulated volume of imports over the years. Local producers are encouraged to introduce foreign technologies so as to be able to eventually produce on their own. Import substitution is facilitated by tariff and nontariff barriers and an overvalued local currency that helps to reduce domestic costs.

Globally, the Latin American countries were the first countries to implement this strategy. During World War II, with the emergence of infant industries that were able to substitute for imports, the governments of Argentina, Brazil, Colombia, and Mexico systematically established high tariff and nontariff barriers to restrict or to ban competition from imports. After the war, most of the newly independent countries adopted a similar strategy. However, this industrialization strategy did not meet its initial expectations. Take, as an example, India, which strictly implemented an import-substitution policy. Per capita GDP increased by only a few percentage points, even after four ambitious five-year plans between the 1950s and the 1970s.

Ma: Why did the strategy fail?

Wu: According to economists, the following is the most important reason. In the developing countries, the low level of manufacturing is usually caused by shortages of skilled labor, entrepreneurs, and managerial talent, as well as organizational defects. Instead of improving competitiveness and creativity, trade-protection policies, due to the excessive protectionism, weaken the efficiency of the manufacturing industries. Furthermore, because import substitution enables a minority of elite enterprises to reap monopolistic profits, the policy exacerbates dual-economy problems, widening income disparities and increasing unemployment in the traditional sectors. After the import-substitution strategy was widely criticized for creating these problems, the developing countries in succession turned to the export-oriented strategy that the East Asian economies had adopted.

Ma: What are the differences between the two strategies?

Wu: The export-oriented strategy, also called *neo-mercantilism*, is characterized by a partially open system, a certain degree of government support, and the export of goods with comparative advantages in the international market. Japan was the first country to successfully adopt this policy regime. The strategy consists of two parts: some degree of tariff protections and import limitations, and an undervalued currency to suppress imports and to promote exports. The strategy was an important factor in the high growth rate of the "Japanese economic miracle." In the 1960s, Taiwan (China), South Korea, and Singapore also adopted this policy regime and experienced high economic growth rates.

Ma: After the end of the Cultural Revolution, many government officials visited foreign countries to study strategies that would be helpful to revitalize the Chinese economy. In October 1978, Deng Xiaoping visited Japan, and in November 1978 he visited Thailand, Malaysia, and Singapore. The inspirational success stories in these countries enhanced Deng's determination to adopt a similar export-oriented strategy. He pointed out that after the Industrial Revolution in the West, China had lagged behind the West because it had become self-complacent and had closed its doors to the outside world. The first thirty years of the People's Republic had revealed that closed doors do not work, especially as the outside world is becoming increasingly open. According to Deng, without an opening to the outside, even within fifty years China would not be able to catch up with the economically developed countries.

Wu: Obviously, given the vast size of the country, the longstanding command economy, and the fact that the command economy remained dominant at the beginning of the reform and opening period, it was extremely difficult to adopt an outward-looking policy regime and immediately integrate the country into the global economy. The response of the government was a dual-track approach and a step-by-step transition. On the one hand, the focus of the reform was to improve the business environment in most areas to allow for import substitution. On the other hand, based on international experience in establishing free ports and special economic zones, several regional localities meeting certain conditions were selected as SEZs to implement an export-oriented strategy.

Ma: Both steps required a dismantling of the trade monopoly.

Wu: Beginning in 1978, China gradually implemented changes to its trade monopoly regime. The following were the main steps: (a) Decentralization of the foreign trade licensing authority. The central government gradually expanded the authority of local governments and the line ministries to grant foreign trade rights to exporters and to export producers. These agencies were also authorized to approve the establishment of "enterprises with three types of foreign investment" (equity joint ventures, contractual/cooperative joint ventures, and solely foreign-owned firms). Power to approve "three types of processing trade" (processing of materials, production based on supplied designs, and the assembly of supplied parts) and compensation trade (that is, product buybacks with advance payments) was also decentralized. In succession, provincial governments opened up their coastal areas and granted these localities direct foreign trade rights; (b) The establishment of general trade companies belonging to the line ministries and the granting of foreign trade rights to a number of qualified large and medium-sized enterprises. The foreign trade corporations under the Ministry of Foreign Trade continued to manage the export of bulk commodities, goods that were strategically important to the national economy and the people's livelihood, and products that were highly desirable in the international market or were manufactured according to special requirements. All other exports were managed by local sub-companies of the foreign trade corporations or by line-ministry enterprises that had foreign trade rights; (c) Rights to import raw materials and parts to produce finished products for export were granted to solely foreign-owned firms; and (d) Similar import and export rights were also granted to some private enterprises and research institutes.

Ma: Another important component of China's import-substitution strategy was the establishment of a set of tariff and nontariff barriers to protect the domestic market.

Tariffs had existed prior to 1978, but they played a very limited role because foreign trade was still subject to the state plan, which was implemented by the monopoly of the state trade corporations. Thus there was no need for tariff controls. In the early 1980s, however, after foreign trade was gradually liberalized, the government established a high tariff system, with an average rate as high as 56 percent. Other instruments that were widely used to limit imports included the issuance of quotas and permits. By the end of the 1980s, fifty-three types of imports and exports required permits, accounting for 46 percent of total trade.

Wu: Reform of the foreign trade system was accompanied by reform of the foreign-exchange system.

Under the monopoly of the foreign trade system, imports and exports were regulated by the plan, and the required foreign currencies were allocated directly by the administrative authorities. In general, in order to reduce domestic costs, the foreign-exchange regimes in the Communist countries highly overvalued their domestic currencies. But this was a weak instrument for controlling imports and exports. Such regimes were inconsistent with the development of an export-oriented strategy. After 1979, the government implemented several rounds of foreign-exchange reforms. First, a foreign-exchange retention system was introduced in 1979, allowing enterprises to retain a certain portion of their foreign-exchange earnings at various ratios set by the authorities. Enterprises with surplus foreign exchange were allowed to sell it. Second, a foreign-exchange swap market was introduced, and the market was allowed to expand. Initially, the settlement rates in this market were a markup from the official foreign-exchange rate. After March 1988, however, the pricing regime was liberalized and the settlement rates were determined by the parties to the swap. Third, between 1983 and 1993, the official foreign-exchange rates were adjusted to devalue the RMB.

Ma: In the 1980s, China's manufacturing industries were weak and the educational backgrounds and skills of manufacturing workers were relatively low. In order to expand from the export of primary goods and to provide more jobs for its abundant labor resources, the government adopted a strategy to extensively promote the processing trades. As early as the end of the 1970s, the coastal areas were encouraged to engage in the above-mentioned three types of processing trade plus compensation trade. In 1978 Guangdong province signed China's first-ever agreement to process supplied materials, signaling the beginning of China's processing-trade industry.

Wu: Thereafter, the government adopted a series of policies to promote the processing trade. For instance, in parallel with the expansion of the foreign-exchange swap market and the devaluation of the RMB, bonded warehouses were established. With the exception of a few sensitive goods, imports and exports under processing-trade contracts no longer required permits and were no longer subject to quotas. These measures contributed to the further development of foreign trade, allowing export trade to reach a new level.

In 1981, processing trade totaled USD 2.64 billion, accounting for 6 percent of total imports and exports. By the end of the 1980s, these numbers had increased by about 30 percent. At the same time, exports of manufactured goods as a percentage of the total volume of traded goods increased from 50 percent to 70 percent. In 1978, total imports and exports amounted to USD 20.64 billion. By 1988, total imports and exports exceeded USD 100 billion, the equivalent of an average annual growth rate of 23.7 percent. Exports were increasing by 23.6 percent per annum. Although the volume of total trade was still low, China had become the fifteenth highest-ranked economy in terms world trade, compared to its ranking of twenty-ninth in 1978.

Ma: The most important measure in China's export-oriented strategy was the gradual expansion of areas open to the outside world, starting with the establishment of several SEZs.

Wu: In May 1980 the government decided to apply special policies and flexible measures in Guangdong and Fujian provinces. The provincial governments were the main body for implementing the new economic development plan. The provincial fiscal system adopted a contracting approach and more flexible practices were allowed. Furthermore, enterprises with foreign investment were granted greater autonomy. Market mechanisms were applicable for materials supplies and commerce. One especially significant measure allowed the two provinces to set up special export zones, in which overseas Chinese and businessmen from Hong Kong, Macau, and foreign countries could invest in factories and enjoy preferential tax treatments. Shortly thereafter, the export zones were renamed "special economic zones." In August of the same year, the Standing Committee of the National People's Congress formally approved the first four SEZ pilots, in Shenzhen, Zhuhai, and Shantou, all in Guangdong province, and in Xiamen, in Fujian province, to develop a regional outward-looking economy. The central government allowed the SEZs to implement special economic policies and management systems. In particular, their ownership structure could be diversified; although the public sector remained dominant, market regulation could also play a role. Capital construction was mainly to be financed by foreign and overseas Chinese investors. Preferential treatments were granted to attract investments.

The special economic zones enjoyed more economic administration rights and flexible mechanisms. Goods for self-use were exempt from import duties and from the unified industrial and commercial tax (a turnover tax). The tax rate on imported goods for commercial purposes was cut by one-half, as was the rate on the turnover tax for goods produced and sold within the SEZs.

Ma: Shenzhen, Zhuhai, and the southern coastal cities are all within geographic proximity to Hong Kong, Macau, and Taiwan (China) and they have large populations of overseas Chinese. China took advantage of this situation to create a "microclimate" for international integration. These areas thus became beachheads for China's opening to the outside world. The strategy for opening the economy was similar to the incremental reform strategy. Whereas the "base camp" was maintained, a "forward base" for an opening to the outside world was established in remote areas (where "the mountains are high and the emperor is far away"—that is, where central-government control was weak). This strategy reduced shocks and government intervention.

The economies in the SEZs grew rapidly and within a very short time recorded outstanding achievements. Nevertheless, from their very beginning there had been extensive discussions as to whether the SEZs represented a form of capitalism. They were accused of being "concessions" with capitalistic characteristics. In 1982, the Research Office of the Secretariat of the Communist Party Central Committee prepared an article entitled "The Origins of the Concessions in Old China." Published in an influential newspaper, the article used the past to disparage the present, although it did not explicitly target the present. This debate lasted several years. Regardless, Deng Xiaoping was a strong supporter of the SEZs, and he hoped that the zones could "create a way out" for the obstacles facing China's economic development. In 1984, Deng composed the following inscription for the Shenzhen SEZ: "The development and experiences of Shenzhen have proved the correctness of our policy on the establishment of special economic zones." As a result, the debates gradually subsided.

Wu: After the success of the SEZs, the entire coastal region became a bridgehead for phasing in a multilevel opening to the outside world. In May 1984, the government decided to open fourteen coastal cities, including Dalian, Qinhuangdao, Tianjin, Yantai, Qingdao, Lianyungang, Nantong, Shanghai, Ningbo, Wenzhou, Fuzhou, Guangzhou, Zhanjiang, and Beihai. These cities enjoyed some preferential treatments that were similar to those granted to enterprises with foreign investment in the SEZs. In the next year, the following localities became "open-economy areas": the Changjiang (Yangzi) delta area, the Zhujiang delta area, the southern Fujian delta area, Jiaodong peninsula in Shandong province, and Liaodong peninsula in Liaoning province. In April 1988, Hainan Island became a special economic zone and was granted greater autonomy to adopt more open and flexible policies. By then, all of China's coastal areas had become bases for the opening to the outside world.

Ma: In addition to this development and the reform of the foreign trade system, external capital was introduced and utilized on a massive scale. At the beginning of the reform and opening period, China faced a serious capital deficit for economic construction. In 1978, foreign reserves amounted to only USD 167 million and by 1980 the reading was a negative USD 1,296 million. The limited foreign-exchange reserves could not support the import of equipment, technologies, and products, presenting a serious obstacle to further economic development. Therefore, the core task for the opening to the outside world was to introduce external capital.

Wu: In addition to external capital, China also needed to introduce technologies as well as the operational and managerial experience and marketing channels that foreign enterprises had developed over a long period of time. These objectives could be realized through foreign direct investment (FDI). From the outset, attracting FDI was an important part of the opening strategy. Government leaders often contacted Western businessmen and encouraged them to invest in China. On January 17, 1979, Deng Xiaoping hosted a banquet in the Great Hall of People and invited opinions and comments about the promotion of FDI from his guests, who had been prominent business leaders before 1949, including Hu Juewen, Hu Zi'ang, Rong Yiren, Gu Gengyu, Zhou Shutao, and others. Deng hoped that these businessmen would take the initiative and start businesses in China. Deng also voiced support for using external capital and for allowing overseas Chinese to open factories in China. Shortly after the January 1979 meeting, Rong Yiren set up the China International Trust and Investment Corporation (CITIC). One of the main tasks of CITIC was to attract, guide, and utilize capital from foreign countries.

Ma: At the time, foreign investors remained cautious about investing in China because it still lacked a proper legal framework. Who would want to invest a large amount of money in a place where there were no legal protections?

In July 1979, the Standing Committee of the National People's Congress adopted the Law of the People's Republic of China on Chinese-Foreign Equity Joint Ventures. At a time when such joint ventures still did not exist in China, the law indeed could be considered very forward-looking. Vice Premier Gu Mu, who was in charge of foreign trade, recalls in his memoirs that "from July [1979] to the end of the year, six joint-venture projects were approved, including two restaurants, one pig farm, one plastic packaging manufacturer, one radio assembly factory, and one photo studio. Four of these were in Shenzhen [Guangdong province] and two were in Fuzhou [Fujian province], with a total negotiated foreign investment of USD 8.1 million. This amount can be considered almost pitiful if we compare it to the hundreds of thousands of projects that are being approved nowadays. However, this was the first-ever step for future development. Without this first small step there never could have been the later big steps."

Wu: Based on the experience of the SEZs and the open coastal areas, the government promulgated a number of laws, such as the Income Tax Law for Chinese-Foreign Equity Joint Ventures, the Individual Income Tax Law, the Income Tax Law for Enterprises with Foreign Investment and Foreign Enterprises, and the Regulations on the Special Economic Zones in Guangdong, which formed the legal basis for external borrowing and FDI. In addition, negotiations to secure the protection of investments were conducted with West Germany, Japan, Sweden, Canada, and Switzerland, and several agreements were eventually signed. A favorable environment was thus created for opening to the world and to economic development.

By the end of the 1980s, the FDI promotion strategy had achieved notable results. The coastal areas in particular had attracted a huge amount of foreign investment owing to their enabling environment, low labor costs, vast domestic market, and government policies granting preferential treatment. Equipped with modern technologies, the competitiveness of enterprises with foreign investment improved significantly, eventually leading to the development of modern industries. In 1985, the total industrial output of the four SEZs was only RMB 5.5 billion, but by 1990, it had reached RMB 49.5 billion, a more than eightfold increase. Average annual growth was as high as 50 percent. During the Seventh Five-Year Plan period (1986–90), FDI by more than 2,000 foreign-investment enterprises in the fourteen open coastal cities exceeded USD 10 billion, resulting in dynamic growth of the external-oriented economy. In 1990, exports from the twelve coastal provinces amounted to USD 40 billion, accounting for two-thirds of the national total.

Ma: These great results during the initial phase of the reform and opening can be attributed to two main factors: the partial opening of the domestic market to foreign businessmen and the use of preferential treatments to attract FDI. Statistics reveal that from 1979 to 1991, FDI reached USD 25.06 billion. Some people have referred to this pro-growth practice as a "market for technology." But others have blamed the policy for having negative effects on China's interests and for introducing market losses without producing technological gains. What do you think?

Wu: I do not agree with those who simply reject the policy. China began the period of reform and opening after its doors had been closed to the outside world for a long time and, as a result, it lagged behind the West in terms production technologies and management know-how. The market opening and the promotion of FDI created favorable conditions for attracting modern technologies from abroad. The policy was thus conducive to furthering economic development. But the policy on its own could not narrow the gap with the advanced countries. Eventually, it was up to local enterprises in an enabling business environment to become world-class companies. As a matter of fact, several important industries, such as electronics, communications, and equipment manufacturing, reached world-class levels through the effective utilization of foreign technology and home-grown innovation. Some Chinese companies, such as Huawei Technologies and ZTC Corporation, are today globally competitive firms. But if these privileged enterprises only reap gains from the introduction of foreign investments and foreign technologies and do not make further progress, their technologies likely will not develop further, and eventually, they will lose their market competitiveness. Such disturbing cases are not uncommon.

Enterprises with foreign investment are a new economic phenomenon. They have quickly improved the defects in the market structure, increased market competition, and caused shocks to the former system. They have helped to improve the fragmented domestic market and to accelerate the transition from administrative to market allocations of resources. FDI has not only brought in capital, technology, and know-how, but it has also enhanced market competition, therefore contributing to the market-oriented economic reforms.

Ma: Foreign investment first entered the Chinese market from the coastal areas and it changed the market structure in these areas. It then moved to the inland areas in waves. The SEZs and the coastal areas were pilots for establishing a modern market economy. They absorbed the experiences of the advanced economies and took bold steps to experiment with new economic administration institutions, providing important lessons for a nationwide reform of the economic system.

The global market represents an extension and an integration of national markets. It is a general rule of economic development that a global market starts from the development of domestic markets. However, under the particular circumstances in China, the government implemented a strategy to gradually expand the market opening and step-by-step improve the business environment. Can this be regarded as a good example of using an opening to the outside world to promote the reform of the domestic economy?

Wu: Yes, it can. In terms of sequences, the objective of reforms is to transform the command economy or the natural economy in order to develop a market-economy system. Once a market is formed, the opening will integrate the domestic market with the international market such that the national economy will become an organic part of the global economy. China's "reverse approach" utilized the opening to promote domestic reform. The SEZs are a typical example. Their exceptionally high growth greatly increased the demand for labor. However, when market regulation of labor supply and demand played only a supplemental role, the SEZ authorities could not meet the demand through administrative labor and job-placement allocations. This triggered reforms in the personnel management system, the system of residence registration, and the job-assignment system, with a view to attracting a wide range of talent. These changes gradually eroded the traditional job-placement system and placed pressures on the administrative agencies to implement reform.

An opening to the outside world can also correct distortions in price parameters. One such distortion occurs when prices for raw materials and upstream products are lower than normal prices and when prices for downstream products and consumer goods are higher than normal prices. When foreign trade is well developed, competition from the procurement of primary goods and the sale of imported consumer products can help correct such distortions in the price parameters.

In addition, the SEZs were also pioneers in implementing reforms in plan management, price formation, fiscal policy, taxation and revenue distribution, and investment and finance. The zones established China's first real-estate market, a market for contracting construction projects, a labor market, and a capital market. These groundbreaking initiatives were copied nationwide and effectively facilitated reform of the entire economic system.

China's 2001 accession to the World Trade Organization (WTO) represented a major step in the country's external economic relations. It injected new energy into the drive to normalize the domestic market and to improve rule of law.

Ma: Based on your description, the significance of the opening to the outside world for China's reform cannot be understated. The reform and the opening were mutually complementary. The reverse approach, using the opening to the outside world to create momentum for domestic progress, can be regarded as a "boost" for the reform.

Wu: Yes, indeed, but the role of the reverse approach should also not be exaggerated. Although the opening to the outside world provided an impetus and brought pressures for reform, the progress of the reform also depended on the determination and capability of the authorities to overcome the obstacles to establishing new institutions. Without such political will, a mature market-economy institution will be eroded or diluted by the explicit and implicit rules of the former system. According to a Chinese saying, when an orange tree is replanted in the north, it can only yield bitter fruit for Chinese medicine. Thus the correct way to avoid backpedaling is to uphold the reform and opening and to maintain a virtuous cycle between both opening to the outside world and domestic reform.

DIALOGUE 9

THE ROLE OF THE "DUAL-TRACK" SYSTEM AND ITS CONSEQUENCES

Ma Guochuan (Ma): The incremental reform strategy played an important role in China's reform of the economic system. As you mentioned before, the gist of the strategy was to allow development of the private sector and to introduce partial market mechanisms, while more or less maintaining the command economy. This resulted in a dual-track situation whereby the command economy and the market economy coexisted; the transition was to be achieved through a gradual strengthening of the market and a step-by-step weakening of the plan. However, whenever there is an advantage, there is also a disadvantage. Was this also the case with the incremental reform strategy?

Wu Jinglian (Wu): That is a good question that merits further attention.

The incremental reform strategy characterized by a dual-track and gradual transition had the following advantages: (a) The tactic "quick wins first and uphill battles later" enabled the economically viable enterprises and localities to develop more rapidly. The general public and government officials directly benefited from the changes brought about by this strategy, and they both realized that the only way to reinvigorate the country was to reform; (b) The increasingly active nonstate sector was pivotal in mitigating the inevitable economic shocks from the reforms and in maintaining economic prosperity and political stability; and (c) The demonstration effects and competitive pressures helped promote the reform of the state sector. The dynamic growth of the nonstate sector and the development of the state sector were mutually complementary and generated momentum for the market-oriented reforms. The dual-track system reduced resistance to, and strengthened support for, this reform. As the force of the market gradually expanded in an environment of steady economic growth, a smooth transition from plan to market would eventually be achieved.

However, this is just one side of the coin. On the other side, the dual-track system allowed people, in particular those in power, to reap personal gains. It nurtured a social force that favored maintaining the command system, and even expanding the role of the plan (the command economy), thus blocking the development of further reforms.

Ma: In his *Notes on the One-Hundred-Year History of the Chinese Economy: Chinese Economic Reform (1978–2002)*, economist Yang Xiaokai points out that China's reforms were characterized by making progress along both tracks. Yang lists various phenomena under the dual-track system. In the rural areas, public ownership of land and contracted users' rights for farmers coexisted. The village and township enterprises (TVEs) embodied public ownership and government control as well as private ownership, so they were sometimes referred to as informal joint ventures between the government and the private sector. During the reform process, state-owned enterprises continued to rely on government power and low-priced supplies to reap excess profits.

Professor Yang concludes that these dual-track practices led to large-scale corruption, although it is also possible that the practices helped generate more supporters for the reforms because privileged interests were allowed to benefit from the changes. He states that "perhaps the negative effects of the dual-track system exceeded the positive effects"; in addition, "the system resulted in a highly inequitable distribution of income combined with inefficiencies."

Wu: For me, the various positive and negative effects were based on the stage of the social transformation. When the reform was first introduced, China had just emerged from several decades of struggle to "exterminate capitalism and petty production," and it was facing a vast vacuum. Without the various institutional arrangements under the dual-track system, market relationships could never have been established. Although the system initially suffered from unfair competition and other shortcomings, it opened up opportunities for the development of the private sector. The policy change with respect to the private sector led to bursts of previously suppressed creativity and entrepreneurship, resulting in the high economic growth rates of the 1980s. Compared with the state sector, the private sector could adapt more easily to the market and was more competitive. By the mid-1980s, this sector was playing a crucial role in the national economy. The entire agricultural sector was populated by household farms. Thirty-five percent of industrial output came from the private sector, accounting for more than one-half of the total retail volume. However, because of the lack of institutional changes in the state sector, at about this same time the shortcomings of the dual-track system began to appear.

First, because of the lack of an environment for fair competition, room for the growth of the nascent private sector was limited and private businesses were overshadowed by the powerful state sector. Scarce economic resources could not flow freely through the market to the more efficient enterprises. Because the state sector possessed the main resources, national economic efficiency was low.

Second, the system created an environment for using the power of the public sector to command personal gains. Corruption began to spread in Communist Party organs and government agencies. Some private-sector businessmen gained access to public-sector power by cozying up to government officials or by engaging in bribery.

Ma: At the time, there was a saying that "those in power should read *Zeng Guofan*, and those in business should read *Hu Xueyan*." The first novel depicts the life and death of a well-known senior politician in the Qing government who was very adept in politics. He is regarded as a good example of one who achieved fast-track promotions and secured highly valued jobs. The second novel is a saga about the famous Qing businessman Hu Xueyan. By befriending senior officials and dignitaries, within a little more than ten years Hu rapidly expands his business and transforms himself from a counter-jumper in a money shop to a famous wealthy man. His fortune, no less than that of nobility, was said to be equal to one-half of the total national wealth. The Qing emperor grants Hu special permission to wear the clothing of a level-two government official, and he becomes a "red-hat" businessman, that is, one with close government connections. However, after his supporter in the government is defeated during a political conflict Hu suffers overwhelming losses and, ultimately, he dies in disgrace.

Wu: Many contemporary businessmen only saw the bright part of the Hu Xueyan saga and attempted to collude with the government in order to cut a slice of the huge resources held in the name of the state. This opened up ample room for under-the-table deals by government officials and encouraged bribery by corrupt merchants, enabling them to reap windfall profits.

Ma: These characteristics were symptomatic of the dual-track pricing system and resulted from the simultaneous different pricing mechanisms for the same product. In the late 1980s, the problems associated with the windfalls from the profiteering of the means of production triggered widespread debates about the "profiteering officials."

Wu: It should be noted that the dual-track pricing system not only applied to the means of production. Under the incremental reform strategy, the private sector and the state sector existed in parallel, resulting in dual-track pricing for many of their products and services. For instance, there was a dual track for the cost of funds because of the differences between the lending rates of state-owned banks and the market rates. Foreign exchange also operated under a dual-track regime, with official rates that were different from the rates on the swap market.

Ma: How did this pricing system come about?

Wu: During the period of the command economy, economic activities in industry and commerce were monopolized by the state, and administrative directives reined in resource allocations. Money was a shadow behind the physical allocations and prices were a tool for enterprise accounting. The prices of the main means of production and the prices of consumer goods were both fixed by the administrative authorities, thus prices did not play a role in resource allocations. Under this system, private businesses could not survive because they did not have access to the plan quotas for the supply of raw materials and for working capital, nor did they have access to market channels.

During the initial phase of the new era, the government allowed administrative agencies and affiliated institutions to establish some enterprises whose production would not be subject to the plan. These enterprises could set the prices for their own products and services in accordance with market supply and demand. At the same time, the embryonic private businesses had to buy raw materials and other means of production. In the late 1970s, the state-owned industrial enterprises that at that time had gained a certain degree of exemption from the enterprise reform began to sell products in excess of the plan targets at negotiated prices. The July 1979 State Council Regulations on the Expansion of Operational Management Autonomy for State-Owned Industrial Enterprises allowed the selling of "excess" products, giving birth to the second track (that is, the market) for the circulation and pricing of enterprise output.

At first, the market for goods that were subject to negotiated pricing was small and it did not have much influence. Things started to change, however, as private businesses grew and the autonomy of state-owned enterprises (SOEs) expanded. In 1981, to alleviate shortages in the supply of crude oil, the State Council authorized the Ministry of Petroleum to implement a contracting program with a floor of 100 million tons of crude oil. Output in excess of the floor could be sold at market prices in both the domestic and international markets. In 1983, the State Council adopted a policy that allowed domestic crude-oil producers to retain a portion of their output that was originally slated for export and to refine the oil domestically. The refined oil products could then be sold at international prices in the domestic market. In the same year, the policy "higher prices for better quality" was adopted, allowing up to a 20 percent price hike for fine-quality ferrous and nonferrous metal, chemical, and machinery products. However, the price levels for the planned allocations of key industrial products were fixed too low, and these products were in short supply. In order to address this problem, in May 1984 the State Council issued the "Interim Provisions on the Further Expansion of the Autonomy of State-Owned Industrial Enterprises," allowing SOEs to sell on their own any products in excess of the planned target, at a price no higher than 20 percent of the planned allocation price. Given the short supply of these goods, purchasers often paid much more than the ceiling price and middlemen pocketed the margins. To stop the middlemen from profiteering, the State Council authorized the Price Bureau and the Materials Bureau to remove the 20 percent ceiling, beginning in January 1, 1985. This was soon extended to all means of production and the dual-track pricing system became an official institution, under which each product had two prices, one for the portion of the output allocated by the plan and the other for the remainder of the output that could be sold by the enterprises on their own.

Similar practices had appeared during the mass steel-making movement of the Great Leap Forward in 1958–59 and during the three years of economic difficulties in 1959–61. At the time, economist Sun Yefang pointed out that if the two tracks remained parallel roads that never crossed, there would be no problem of arbitrage resulting from their differences. However, if the market grew in size and the two tracks were not insulated from one another, it would be impossible to prevent the output that was subject to the planned allocations from being sold in the market at higher prices. This is exactly what occurred in the 1980s. Furthermore, starting in January 1985 the dual-track system was applied to the physical inputs of the SOEs. Although the relevant regulation required that the plan for input allocations be kept at the 1983 levels, people always found ways to increase the authorities' plan targets or quotas, and the SOEs found ways to sell in the market supplies they had received under the plan, thus allowing them to make quick fortunes.

Ma: The price differences created huge opportunities for arbitrage by abusing the power to allocate the means of production. Because the price differences were huge, colossal windfall profits could be made by selling in the free market goods that had been obtained at low prices. By the second half of the 1980s, many such "profiteers" were actively engaging in deals between the plan and the market. Some of them rapidly became millionaires. They did not trade products (buying low from the plan allocations and selling high in the market); rather, they bought and sold official authorizations to obtain low-priced resources, including licenses for material allocations, import quotas at the official exchange rates, and lending quotas with the low interest rates of the state-owned banks. Because the secret behind their fortunes was their connection to the government, they were generally called "profiteers."

Although at the time an average annual salary was only between RMB 1,000 and RMB 2,000, the nouveaux riches were able to amass huge wealth, effortlessly and within a short period of time. Naturally this phenomenon triggered widespread debate about the profiteers and corruption, attracting a great amount of attention from the society.

Wu: At first, there were two different views about this phenomenon. One view held that the corruption was a product of the pre-1949 society. The market-oriented reforms had generated greed and had led to a resurgence of corruption. People holding this view advocated a "correction" by shifting back from the market orientation to the plan orientation.

Ma: At that time, *Red Flag*, the official journal of the Communist Party Central Committee, carried several articles in support of this argument. Quoting both Shakespeare and Marx, these articles asserted that money and greed drove people to commit crimes.

Wu: Those holding the second view agreed that the enlarged role of the market might lead to greater greed and more corruption. But they stressed that without the market, China would never become prosperous. The resurgence of corruption was simply an inevitable byproduct of the market reforms. They argued that moral purity should not be pursued at the expense of the fundamental national interest, which was economic development.

Ma: Some economists attempted to theoretically demonstrate the "positive role" of the dual-track system. Their reasoning was the following: although the SOEs continued to enjoy the benefits of low prices, increases or decreases in their products and in their inputs were functions of the market prices. This meant that the market prices were already playing a decisive role in the marginal productivity of enterprise inputs. The marginal changes provided price signals for short-term adjustments in supply and demand that were conducive to stabilizing SOE production and realizing a Pareto improvement.

Wu: Although these were opposite views, by linking corruption with the market economy both regarded the market economy as the source of the corruption. However, history provides no evidence for this judgment. Historians had long ago concluded that corruption had been rampant in Western Europe in the nineteenth century before a market economy was established, a result of the mercantilism by which the state controlled the economy in order to accumulate national wealth. The excessive intervention by the state created favorable conditions for the abuse of power. Unfair competition was also widespread in the underdeveloped markets.

In contrast, after World War II the process of market development in some of the developing countries did not result in serious corruption. As the process accelerated and became more favorable, the spread of corruption was contained.

Ma: Both inside and outside China, there were economists who disagreed with the view that corruption would reduce transaction costs and facilitate the formation of the market. In their view, if prices were not liberalized all at once, there would be distortions in the allocation of resources. Inequalities would occur between the SOEs, which were implicitly subsidized, and private businesses, which could only obtain raw materials, equipment, and financing at market prices. The longer price liberalization was delayed, the more the development of the private sector would suffer.

It appears that with the growth of the market, the expansion of the monetization of the economy, and the broadening of the boundaries of wealth beyond physical possessions, the desire to become rich was enhanced. However, the problem was not the extent of the greed but, rather, whether there were institutional conditions in place that enabled the realization of the greed.

Wu: That's right. Some foreign economists developed a rent-seeking theory that can be considered the theoretical basis for analyzing the profiteering phenomenon. When reviewing the corruption in both the developed and the developing countries in the mid-1970s, those economists who studied political economy or international economics (development economics) found that the root causes of the corruption were government intervention and control of microeconomic activities by enterprises or individuals. The "visible foot" had stepped on the "invisible hand," frustrating the formation of equilibrium prices through market competition. Since access to the market was limited, excess revenue was generated through connections to political power or through bribery. In economics, the excess income is called *rent*, or *nonproductive profits*. Obtaining such profits through political power is called *rent seeking*.

Ma: The introduction of the rent-seeking theory gave Chinese economists a scientific tool to analyze the phenomenon of corruption during the reform era. In 1988, *Comparative Economic and Social Systems*, a journal published by the Central Compilation and Translation Bureau, carried several articles that applied this theory to an analysis of the corruption that was prevalent in China. At a follow-up seminar, economists discussed the nature of the profiteering and other corrupt behavior. The 1989 book *Corruption: The Exchange of Power and Money*, a collection of the papers presented at the seminar, reveals that most of the participating economists, as well as some scholars in the humanities, were using this theory to provide a convincing answer to the question of why corruption had occurred during the reform process. This had been a puzzling question for quite a while.

For instance, in one article, the well-known humanities scholar Wang Yuanhua notes that "during discussions in recent years on the market economy, a number of influential scholars in the mainland (most of whom I know well) offered assumptions without offering any substantiation for them. For instance, they assumed that the market economy will inevitably cause corruption. . . . I took exception to that view and offered my own opinion. However, my analysis was limited to the imperfections in our market-economy system, the shortcomings of our economic laws and regulations, and the phenomenon of collusion between money and power, e.g., providing informal licensing that allows those who hold the slip of paper to grant licenses to get what they want and to sell plan quotas. After reading *Corruption: The Exchange of Power and Money*, I realized that these economists had provided a convincing explanation for many of those issues that had been difficult to explain."

Wu: I still have vivid memories of the discussions at the time. By resorting to rent-seeking theory, the economists provided a scientific analysis of the phenomenon of corruption and also came up with a solution to the problem.

Obviously, the government-dominated dual-track system was the institutional foundation for government intervention in business and for rent seeking. Under this system, both command-economy rules and market-economy rules were in effect. There were two sets of pricing mechanisms for the same product: prices set administratively and prices set by market competition. Under these circumstances, those backed by influential officials could obtain licenses (the embodiment of government power) for supplies of plan-allocated materials and then could gain from arbitrage on the price differentials (rent).

In other words, as long as such an institutional foundation existed, corruptive rent-seeking activities were inevitable. Communist Party and government leaders realized the threat that this situation posed to the survival of the Communist Party and they tried to contain the corruption by tough discipline and strict national laws. However, the measures were not very effective because the institutional foundation that allowed for the corruption was simply too large and "the law cannot be enforced when everyone is an offender."

Furthermore, because of the high returns, the rent seeking was self-reinforcing. As the rent seeking was enabled by certain conditions, people used their administrative powers to create more of those conditions, such as setting up more dual-track arrangements and increasing the layers for obtaining administrative licenses. Hence, a vicious cycle was created: from limited rent seeking to more room for rent seeking and then to even greater space for rent seeking. Corruption through rent seeking spread rapidly; even government positions were being sold at listed prices.

Ma: In 1974, the American economist Anne Krueger, in a paper entitled "The Political Economy of the Rent-Seeking Society," calculated the value of rent to GDP in India and Turkey. Thereafter, this statistic became a widely accepted indicator to measure the level of corruption in a country.

Wu: In 1989, economist Hu Heli revealed in an influential research report that in 1988, the price differentials for goods in China amounted to more than RMB 150 billion; the price differentials for bank lending amounted to over RMB 113.88 billion; and those for foreign-exchange rates used for imports amounted to more than RMB 93.04 billion. These three readings revealed a value of rents exceeding RMB 350 billion, accounting for 30 percent of the national income in that year. The gravity of the corruption was simply horrifying! This huge figure indicated how rampant the corruption had become and that it obviously was playing a decisive role in the widening gap between the rich and the poor and the rapidly rising Gini coefficient.

We should note the remarks by Nobel economics laureate Milton Friedman at a September 1988 meeting with senior Chinese leaders (published in *Reform*, no. 6, 1988). Friedman said that the dual-track pricing system for many products was an open invitation for corruption and waste. He stressed that it was insufficient only to utilize the market and implement privatization; it was even more important to ensure open and free competition, which would prevent corruption and the polarization of wealth.

Ma: To sum up, at the time there were three very different views regarding the emergence of corruption during the reforms: (a) Corruption is a product of the market economy and the pursuit of wealth. The reform and opening were the culprits. Thus, the only way to end the corruption was to restore the dominant position of the plan. Administrative controls had to be strengthened in order to return to the command economy; (b) Corruption is a common phenomenon in a market economy. Since the decision had been made to embark on market-oriented reforms, corruption should be tolerated and it was not to be considered a matter of major concern; and (c) Based on rent-seeking theory and comparative studies, corruption is not an inevitable outcome of a market economy. The corruption in China originated from the administrative controls and government intervention in market activities (that is, the so-called mixing of power and business). It was caused by the wavering efforts and incomplete measures and not by the market-oriented reforms per se. Comprehensive market-oriented reforms that sought to quickly establish a new market order for fair competition were the only way to tackle the root causes of the corruption.

Wu: Initially, the first view attracted little support, since memories of the suffering under the command economy and the "all-round proletarian dictatorship" were still fresh. However, with the worsening of the corruption and the changing political situation, support for this view resurfaced from time to time. Some people even believed that it was not outdated to uphold the principle of "maintaining the dominance of the planned economy and enabling a supportive market."

The second view enjoyed much more support. In addition to confirming the positive effects on the economy, a report by the System Reform Institute of the National Commission for Restructuring the Economic System had found that the political role of the dual-track system was also positive. The report argued that such a system provided an administrative mechanism for resource allocations. According to this view, the monetization of vouchers could shift to the monetization of power. Power could become a currency or could be "capitalized," which was an economically reasonable phenomenon. This view was based on a different guiding principle.

The third view opposed extending support for the dual-track system. Supporters of this view believed that monetization or capitalization of power would entrench institutional rent-seeking arrangements by those holding power. Supporters thus advocated a new overall reform design, with a phased-in plan for implementation in order to eliminate the institutional foundation for corruption.

The debate on the dual-track system and corruption was more than simply part of an academic debate because it was related to the big question: Whither China?

Ma: At the time, what were the attitudes of the leaders? Did they adopt any countermeasures?

Wu: It is not clear whether the leaders reached any consensus on this issue. With the support of Deng Xiaoping and some other leaders, the 1984 Third Plenary Session of the Twelfth Communist Party Central Committee adopted the objective of establishing a socialist planned commodity economy. But there were varying interpretations of what was implied by this objective.

From Deng Xiaoping's explanation, the goal established in the plenary session decision was quite clear.

The main topic of the plenary session was the need to shift the focus of reform from the rural areas to the urban areas—that is, to accelerate the pace of overall reform of the system by giving priority to reforms in the urban areas and developing a socialist commodity economy. In Deng's words (in June 1984), after the success in the rural areas, "we decided to shift the focus of reform from the countryside to the cities"; "the urban reform will include not only industry and commerce but science and technology, education and all other fields of endeavor as well"; and "this should be a comprehensive reform." Obviously, the focal point of the comprehensive reform was the state-owned industrial, commercial, and financial sectors. Deng said it was like "touching the backside of a tiger"—that is, confronting someone in his/her own territory.

In order to establish a market economy, the Decision of the Third Plenary Session of the Twelfth Communist Party Central Committee (October 20, 1984) attached great importance to price-system reforms, stating that reforms of the price system were the key to the success of the overall reforms. The following were listed as the top priorities of these reforms: a gradual reduction in the scope of uniform prices set by the state and an appropriate extension in the scope of floating prices and free prices, within certain limits, to allow prices to respond quickly to changes in labor productivity and to changes in the relations between market supply and demand. The goal of the decision was clearly to have the market determine prices.

The CCP National Congress held in September 1985 further stated that three complementary reforms should be carried out simultaneously: turning enterprises into autonomous commercial producers that would be responsible for their own profits and losses; developing and improving the market system; and establishing an indirect macroeconomic management system. The congress also called for the establishment of an institutional foundation for the new systems within a period of five or more years.

Ma: In March 1986, Premier Zhao Ziyang, who was also head of the Communist Party Central Committee leading group for financial and economic affairs, pointed out at a meeting of the group that many of the problems had originated from the "confrontations, frictions, and conflicts" between the old and new systems, and that this situation should not be allowed to continue for a long time. There was a need to take major steps in 1987 and 1988 to improve the market system and to adopt indirect macroeconomic management methods, so as to create externalities and to enable enterprises to become truly responsible for their profits and losses and to compete with one another under basically equal conditions. The goal was to allow the new economic system to become dominant. To establish a market for fair competition, Zhao suggested "designing and exploring the reform . . . in the following three interrelated areas: prices, taxation, and public finance. . . . The key is the reform of the price system and other reforms should be undertaken around this reform."

Wu: In April 1986, in accordance with Zhao's ideas for developing an overall reform program and plans for its implementation, the State Council established a leading group, headed by Vice Premier Tian Jiyun, for developing a reform program. The leading group, consisting of thirty staff persons, was responsible for designing a program of complementary reforms during the first part of the Seventh Five-Year Plan period.

Ma: You were the deputy director of this office.

Wu: After several rounds of consultations with the relevant agencies, the leading group came up with the following comprehensive reform program: priority would be placed on reforms of the price system, taxation, public finance, the financial sector, and the trade regime. In August, the program was approved by the State Council and by the leading group for financial and economic affairs, and it was to be implemented beginning in early 1987.

Ma: There had been many proposals about to how to carry out the transition from the dual-track pricing system to a single market-pricing system. For instance, at the 1984 Moganshan Seminar of young economists, held at a mountain resort, the participating economists suggested various approaches to reforming the price system. One group was in favor of liberalization, but another group supported a combination of regulation and liberalization. What approach was ultimately adopted for the 1986 program?

Wu: The 1986 program adopted a sequence of "regulation first and liberalization later," which was similar to the approach of the 1967–68 reforms in Czechoslovakia. The plan aimed first to make comprehensive price adjustments based on economic calculations, and later, within one or two years, to liberalize the price system.

When teaching in Beijing in 1981, Ota Šik, who had been deputy prime minister during the Czechoslovak reforms, proposed that China introduce the comprehensive 1967 price adjustments of his country as well as the successful once-and-for-all liberalization of the 1968 Prague Spring. After Zhao Ziyang was briefed on the Czechoslovak experience, he asked that the Czech expert who had been in charge of calculating the price adjustments be invited to give some lectures in China. According to Zhao's instructions, the Price Research Center of the State Council was established to train staff, collect information, and develop calculation models, all in preparation for the reform of the price system.

The 1986 plan to reform the prices of the means of production was thus more or less copied from the Czech experience—that is, first regulation and then liberalization.

Ma: Since the objective of the price reforms was to free up prices, why was a two-step approach adopted? Why were prices not liberalized in one fell swoop?

Wu: This issue was discussed among foreign economists. Because of shortages in the socialist economy, there were huge differences between planned and market prices. If prices were to be liberalized all at once, it would be difficult to avoid sharp economic shocks, as explained by the cobweb theory of economics. The serious consequences of the "shock therapy" in the Soviet Union had proved the correctness of this approach. But if prices were to be liberalized through adjustments as they came closer to equilibrium, then such shocks could be avoided.

Ma: At a September 13, 1986, briefing meeting, Deng Xiaoping highly praised the reform program and gave the State Council a green light to begin implementation. Around the same time, on several occasions Deng also stressed the importance of political reforms. He called for the separation of Communist Party and government functions so that the political system could be adapted to meet the needs of the economic reforms.

Wu: Unfortunately, neither of these reforms was carried out.

With respect to the economic reforms, in October 1986 government priority changed from establishing a market system through mutually complementary reforms to reforming the state-owned enterprises. In 1987 and 1988, several contracting systems were adopted, including the contracting of enterprises, the contracting of the line ministries, the contracting of foreign-exchange earnings, and the contracting of credit. The market-oriented reforms were halted and the economic development model reverted back to the high GDP growth model driven by large-scale fixed investments and excess money supply. At a November 1988 reform seminar held in Fengtai District of Beijing, the participants began to question whether China's reforms were creating stagnation, similar to that which occurred during the Brezhnev era in the Soviet Union.

Ma: Were there any efforts to address the problems associated with the price reforms at the end of the 1980s?

Wu: Yes, there were. Deng Xiaoping had always believed that price reforms were necessary for the development of a market economy. In 1985, he said that the obstacles to the price reforms had to be surmounted. In May 1988, he reiterated that the price reforms were well worth the risk and they had to be carried out. Consequently, in May 1988 the Standing Committee of the Politburo and in June 1988 the entire Politburo decided to "storm the barriers to price reform." The State Planning Commission was tasked with coming up with a plan to liberalize the prices of steel and other means of production within three to five years, or a bit longer. However, as soon as the Politburo's decision was made public in August, bank runs and panic buying of daily necessities spread throughout the country. The Communist Party Central Committee had to halt the plan to "storm the barriers" and subsequently announced that for the time being there would be no price reforms.

Ma: Why did the 1988 price reforms fail?

Wu: There are various explanations.

One view holds that the price reforms were not necessary and in fact would have been impossible to achieve prior to any results from the SOE reforms. When two very different levels of prices coexisted, liberalization within a short period of time would inevitably lead to price hikes. The second view holds that inflation (sustained increases in general price levels) is a monetary phenomenon. The serious inflation in 1988 was not caused by the price reforms but, rather, by mistakes in the timing of the reforms and the specific implementation arrangements. In a summary of the 1948 price reforms in the Federal Republic of Germany that had led to sustained prosperity, Milton Friedman had pointed out that the secret to the German success was the tightening of the money supply and the liberalization of prices. In early 1988, China was already suffering from inflation expectations, but it was still increasing the supply of money. Under these circumstances, announcement of the plan to "storm the barriers to price reform" had quickly resulted in inflation and all-out panic buying had become unavoidable.

I am in agreement with the second opinion.

Ma: It appears that there were heated debates regarding what type of macroeconomic policy should be adopted during the transition period.

Wu: Beginning in the second half of 1987, there were numerous debates focusing on whether inflation was beneficial or detrimental. Mainstream opinion held that inflation was beneficial. But those holding the opposite view remained steadfast in their opinion. One incident highlights the efforts by the latter group. In April 1988, Qian Jiaju, an eighty-year-old economist and a "democratic personage,"[1] delivered a speech at a plenary session of the Chinese People's Political Consultative Conference, in which he sharply criticized the administrative price controls and the dual-track pricing system for the means of production that had led to the rampant corruption. Qian proposed that the exceptionally high level of fixed investments should be drastically reduced; thereafter, price reforms should be launched as soon as possible. His thirty-minute speech was so much on target that it received thirty-one rounds of warm applause from the audience.

On May 25 and 27, 1988, at a senior briefing meeting on the Politburo price reform decision, several economists strongly opposed an immediate launch of the reforms due to the excess money supply and the sporadic cases of panic buying. They warned Communist Party and government leaders that without a tightening of monetary policy and improvements in macroeconomic conditions, the rush to reform prices would increase inflation expectations and ultimately result in serious inflation.

[1] Translators' note: "Democratic personages" refers to those people who did not join a political party but allied with the Chinese Communist Party during the people's democratic movement prior to 1949.

Unfortunately, the leaders were influenced by the argument that inflation was not harmful and thus they did not accept the recommendation that the first step should be to put the macroeconomic environment in order.

What happened subsequently is evidence of the poor timing. During the following three years, from early 1989 to early 1992, the central government did not issue or implement any "storming the barriers" plans. However, in early 1989 the money supply was tightened and in this macroeconomic environment some local governments, in collaboration with some central-government agencies, quietly began to reform the price system. Toward the end of this period, with the exception of petroleum products, the prices of all commercially traded goods were liberalized (but in 1994, grain procurements reverted back to the fixed-target regime and the dual-track pricing system).

Ma: Did these initiatives solve the problems caused by the dual-track system?

Wu: It was not quite so simple. For instance, with respect to foreign-exchange rates and the price of land, because the administrative controls were maintained, the dual-track system continued to exist, either explicitly or implicitly. The dual-track exchange-rate system was not eliminated until 1994, when the overall exchange control regime was reformed and interest-rate liberalization was put on the official reform agenda. As for the pricing of land, because farmers only had users' rights during the terms of their contracts, when rural land owned by the collectives was converted for urban purposes, local governments, as the purchasers, unilaterally set the purchasing prices at very low levels. As China's urbanization began to accelerate in the early 1990s, land transactions became a breeding ground for rent seeking.

Furthermore, as noted earlier, as long as opportunities exist, there will be abuses of power and distortions of the reforms as part of the attempts to establish an institutional foundation for rent seeking. When the old dual-track systems were removed, new dual-track regimes were created and the corruption became even worse.

Ma: In the late 1980s, because of the loss of the opportunity to broaden the reforms and the worsening of rent-seeking activities, corruption and inflation resulted in the economic turbulence of 1988 and the political turbulence of 1989. Thereafter, the political trends were reversed. Between 1986 and 1988, discussions among researchers about the reforms had focused on the appropriateness of the reform path. However, between 1989 and 1992, the bottom line was lowered significantly and the debates about the reforms concentrated on whether to adopt a plan orientation or a market orientation.

DIALOGUE 10

OVERALL PROMOTION OF REFORM: A NEW PHASE

Ma Guochuan (Ma): During the two to three years after the 1989 political turbulence, the prevailing political trends were reversed. Discussions as to whether to accept the plan or to accept a market orientation were elevated to a political struggle between two Party lines, and the market-oriented reforms were criticized. At the end of 1990, the *People's Daily* and the journal *Seeking Truth*, a bimonthly under the Communist Party Central Committee, carried a series of influential articles by pundits who blamed the reforms for the 1988 economic turbulence and the 1989 political turbulence. They claimed that in the final analysis, the reforms "sought to eliminate public ownership as the dominant force and realize privatization, and to replace the planned economy with a market economy." According to the articles, the reforms "attempted to negate the leadership of the Communist Party and socialism and to establish capitalism." After some ten years of arduous efforts to determine the correct path, once again the Chinese reforms had come to a standstill.

Wu Jinglian (Wu): My memories are still very fresh about the situation at that time. In November 1989, the Development Research Center (DRC) under the State Council was informed that Deng Liqun, a Communist Party theorist who had been in charge ideological work for a long time, had been entrusted by the Communist Party Central Committee to summarize the lessons from the seventy days before and after the 1989 political turbulence. As an assistant to Sun Shangqing who represented the DRC, I participated in some of the meetings held to discuss the lessons. The first meeting of the economic work group was held in Zhongnanhai, the seat of the Communist Party Central Committee and the State Council, on the morning of November 7, 1989. At that meeting I had a disagreement with Xu Yi, a former director of the Research Institute of Fiscal Science under the Ministry of Finance.

Director Xu and I had been acquainted since the 1950s. He was my senior and was knowledgeable about how the Chinese economy operated. Our criticisms were similar with regard to the negative phenomena, such as the inflation, embezzlement, corruption, and the regional "feudal economy" practices. We differed, however, about their causes. At the November 7 meeting, Xu spoke first. After listing the negative phenomena and the inequalities in distribution, he attributed these problems to the direction of the reforms. According to his thinking, the reforms should have been oriented toward the plan (that is, strengthening and improving the state plan), but instead they had resulted in a market orientation that had given rise to all of those problems.

I spoke next and expressed my complete disagreement about placing the blame on the market-oriented reforms. I pointed out that instead the problems were due to a certain wavering in terms of the carrying out of the reforms. The high-growth strategy had not been sustained by market-oriented reforms. Instead of expanding the role of the market, the reforms had relied on decentralization, interest-sharing, and contracting to mobilize enthusiasm for increased production and returns. Such measures had been attempted during the Great Leap Forward period of 1958–60, and had they continued they would have resulted in disastrous consequences. First, administrative decentralization led to market fragmentation and a feudal economy. Second, the widespread phenomenon of government intervention in business became a breeding ground for corruption through rent seeking. Third, the soft-budget constraints were the sources of the fiscal deficits, the oversupply of money, and the inflation.

Ma: At the time, the outside world was also undergoing many unexpected changes. Communist parties, which for years had ruled Poland, Hungary, Czechoslovakia, Bulgaria, and Yugoslavia, all fell from power. The future of the USSR was also in jeopardy.

Wu: Between March and June 1990, I was a visiting scholar at St. Antony's College at the University of Oxford. On my return trip to China, I stopped in West Germany, East Germany, Czechoslovakia, and the USSR. When I visited Berlin, the Berlin Wall had already been torn down and currency in the two Germanys had been unified. Traveling on the subway between East and West Berlin, I witnessed the huge differences in the two parts of the city that were due to their being divided for more than twenty years and having existed under two different systems (a planned economy and a market economy). What I saw in Moscow was even worse than what I witnessed in East Berlin and Prague. The menus offered to foreign visitors at luxury hotels and restaurants were pitiful. The magnificent gate of the Lenin State Library of the USSR was attached by a strong spring to lessen the jolt when it was opened, and the library looked like an impoverished household. At the time, I was also not very optimistic about my own country. Since some people were manipulating the political and economic situations in attempts to backpedal into the past, I was unsure about China's future. Meanwhile, I became ever more determined to defend the market-oriented reforms.

Shortly after I returned to Beijing, the two opposing groups confronted one another at a July 5, 1990 seminar on economic issues that had been called by the Communist Party Central Committee.

Ma: Based on available information, the meeting, held in Zhongnanhai, was led by Communist Party General Secretary Jiang Zemin. Premier Li Peng was also present. In addition to you, more than one dozen economists participated in the meeting, including Xue Muqiao, Liu Guoguang, Su Xing, Gui Shiyong, Wu Shuqing, You Lin, Yuan Mu, and Xu Yi.

Wu: Again, Xu Yi spoke first. He insisted that there had been mistakes in terms of the direction of the reform. The reform should have been oriented toward the plan, but because it had been directed toward the market, many problems were created. I spoke next, arguing that although the negative phenomena mentioned by Xu did in fact exist, they were not due to the so-called mistakes in the direction of the reform. Instead, the problems were attributable to the lack of a firm resolve to undertake market-oriented reforms and due to the half-baked reform measures. The proposition of "combining the planned economy with market regulation" was inappropriate. I called for upholding the reform objective as stated in the decision of the Third Plenary Session of the Twelfth Communist Party Central Committee—that is, to establish a "planned commodity economy"—and I pointed out that, in essence, a commodity economy is a market economy.

Heated arguments and counterarguments ensued. Several economists in favor of the plan orientation stressed that socialist countries must implement command economies based on public ownership. Market regulation could only play a supplemental role within the scope provided by the state plan and should not act "as a presumptuous guest who usurps the role of the host." These economists blamed the 1988 inflation and the 1989 political turbulence on an inversion in the relationship between a planned economy and market regulation and the mistaken political line of orienting the reforms toward the market. They insisted that the proposition of combining the planned economy with market regulation must be upheld. On the opposing side, Xue Muqiao, Liu Guoguang, and I proposed that a "socialist commodity economy," or a "socialist planned commodity economy," should be upheld in order to move ahead with the market-oriented reforms.

Although we were in a minority, we fought hard. At the time, Xue Muqiao was already eighty-six years old. He became so excited that he could hardly speak clearly. After the meeting, he felt that he had not adequately expressed his views, so he wrote a long letter to the Politburo (the letter was later published under the title "A Letter to the Politburo of the Communist Party Central Committee"). In his letter, Xue wrote that the main reason for the drastic changes in Eastern Europe had been a lack of thoroughgoing reforms and an inability to break the vicious cycle of chaotic pricing, soft fiscal constraints, and a loose credit policy. Xue advocated that a clear understanding of the situation was necessary so as to promptly implement comprehensive reforms with the aim of establishing a commodity economic system. Only by doing this would China overcome its difficulties and become prosperous.

Ma: The nature of the debates on the reform orientation focused on whether or not China should embark on further reforms. Should a new, market-economy system be established, or should the country return to the former system that was characterized by poverty? This was not merely a theoretical issue. It was a major practical question related to the question, whither China? It would be difficult to avoid ideological confrontations if this question were not addressed.

Wu: The Huangfu Ping Incident in the spring of 1991 represented the climax to these debates.

On December 24, 1990, on the eve of the Seventh Plenary Session of the Thirteenth Communist Party Central Committee, Deng Xiaoping told senior Communist Party leaders not to be afraid of taking some risks to promote the reform and opening. According to Deng, the more the reform and opening progressed, the stronger the economy's capacity would grow to sustain and resist the impacts of any risks. Deng pointed out that socialism also included a market economy. Without a market, one would not be aware of what was occurring in the rest of the world; this would be no different from intentionally falling behind. During the Spring Festival of 1991, Deng Xiaoping, who, at the time, was in Shanghai, reiterated his views to Shanghai Mayor Zhu Rongji and other municipal leaders. Based on Deng's remarks, Zhou Ruijin and researchers in Shanghai wrote a series of four articles that was published in *Liberation Daily*, the official newspaper of the Shanghai Municipal Communist Party Committee, under the pseudonym Huangfu Ping. Shortly thereafter, *Contemporary Trends*, a journal published under the aegis of the Chinese Academy of Social Sciences (CASS), singled out a sentence in one of the articles that read "China will lose a good opportunity if it becomes bogged down on worrying about whether something is capitalist or socialist," and then the journal launched into a criticism of the Huangfu Ping articles. The articles proceeded to come under siege as almost all the mainstream media joined in the criticism. This is what came to be known as the famous Huangfu Ping Incident.

The debate about the Huangfu Ping articles was once again about whether or not a market orientation was correct. The supporters of the reform fought hard to uphold the direction of a market economy. Reform-minded political leaders also spoke out and rejected the backpedaling views of the opposition. From October to December 1991, Communist Party General Secretary Jiang Zemin called eleven meetings with researchers from various central government agencies to discuss the following three issues: first, how the capitalist economic development after World War II should be assessed from a Marxist perspective; second, what are the basic lessons to be learned from the drastic changes in the Soviet Union and Eastern Europe; and third, how should socialism with Chinese characteristics be developed. During discussions on the latter issue, the economists who spoke up at the meetings unanimously supported the market-oriented reforms.

Ma: At the time, in addition to launching theoretical attacks, people in favor of the plan orientation also undertook several concrete economic measures. First, beginning in the fourth quarter of 1989 large loans from state-owned banks were used to "jump-start" the state-owned enterprises (SOEs). Meanwhile, decentralized enterprises in some "priority backbone industries" were recentralized and organized into large national industrial corporations. Second, banks were no longer allowed to provide lending to township and village enterprises, which, in fact, until that time had been surviving on bank loans. Third, private businesses were subject to strict scrutiny for tax evasion and faced stiff penalties for any violations. Fourth, a "socialist education movement" was launched in the rural areas. Remote areas in Beijing municipality became a pilot area for a "second round of cooperativization."

Wu: But these measures did not yield the expected results. This is similar to what is described by a Chinese idiom: when soldiers are first called to battle by the beating of drums, morale is high; but if they do not win or if they have to be called to battle a second time, their morale will decline; by the third time, there will no longer be any morale at all. On the one hand, the SOEs were "jumped," but they could not "start," and they continued to lack any momentum for growth. On the other hand, although many businesses were closed down through consolidation and restructuring, the private sector soon regained its footing. Starting from 1991, the economy began to recover, driven mainly by the private sector.

This was on the eve of Deng Xiaoping's trip to Southern China (in January–February 1992) that launched a new high tide of reform and opening.

Ma: Deng's early 1992 speeches "set the tone with one beat of a gong." He pointed out that "the reason some people hesitate to carry out the reform and opening policy and dare not break new ground is, in essence, they are afraid it will mean introducing too many elements of capitalism and, indeed, taking the capitalist road. The crux of the matter is whether the road is capitalist or socialist. The chief criterion for making such a judgment should be whether it promotes the growth of the productive forces in a socialist society, increases the overall strength of the socialist state, and raises living standards." Deng also said that "a planned economy is not equivalent to socialism, because there is planning under capitalism too; a market economy is not capitalism, because there are markets under socialism too. Planning and market forces are both means for controlling economic activities. The essence of socialism is liberation and development of the productive forces, elimination of exploitation and polarization, and the ultimate achievement of prosperity for all."

Wu: Deng's talks removed the ideological constraints to seek clarity regarding whether a market economy was socialist or capitalist and paved the way for accelerating the market-oriented reforms. On June 9, 1992, at the Central Party School of the Central Committee, Communist Party General Secretary Jiang Zemin made an important speech on the key issues to be discussed at the forthcoming Fourteenth National Communist Party Congress. After comparing the various reform objectives, he stated that he was inclined to use the term *socialist market economy* as the reform objective. He said that some people "rarely considered the positive role of the market in encouraging competition among enterprises and promoting economic development" and that "markets are an effective way to allocate resources and provide incentives. They use competition and price levers to allocate scarce resources to wherever they will have the greatest benefit, and they not only put pressure on but also stimulate the enterprises." Jiang's speech was warmly received and no one voiced any disagreement. The Fourteenth National Communist Party Congress, held during the following October, announced that the objective of China's reform of the economic system was to establish a socialist market economy.

In November 1993, the Third Plenary Session of the Fourteenth Communist Party Central Committee adopted the "Decision of the CCP Central Committee on Issues of Building a Socialist Market Economy," which spelled out the overall plan and developed several key aspects of the program to establish a socialist market economy. This means that, after more than a decade of experimentation, China's reform had finally entered a new stage in which a market-economy institution would be established through a combination of overall reforms and major breakthroughs.

Ma: The decision on "overall reforms" represented a major strategic adjustment from the strategy of "feeling for the stones when crossing the river" that was implemented during the initial stage of the reform and opening. It also marked a huge step forward in the reform process. How did this finally come about?

Wu: This huge stride involved a long and tortuous road.

At the end of the 1970s when the Cultural Revolution had just ended and the great turbulence and disaster were still fresh in people's memories, there was widespread consensus that reform was the only way to save the country and to restore the national economy and basic social order. But people were clueless about where they should turn. The old generation of national leaders, for instance, Deng Xiaoping and Chen Yun, proposed "feeling for the stones" and "looking before taking the next step."

These slogans were reasonable. After the establishment of the People's Republic in 1949, the country underwent a number of rounds of political movements. In particular, after the Anti-Rightist Movement in 1957, many social sciences, including economics, were labeled "bourgeois, counterrevolutionary academic disciplines" and were buried at the "eighteenth level of hell" (the bottom level of hell in Buddhism). Due to the closed-door policy and the tight ideological controls, people knew almost nothing about the outside world. They had only been informed that a socialist planned economy had enabled the Soviet Union to become a powerful industrial nation in its transition to communism. "Today's USSR will be tomorrow's China." But this myth was soon shattered and all the former taboos became acceptable. Although there was a strong desire to take action, people were not sure where to turn or what should be reformed, so they resorted to experimentation and exploration based on the developmental experiences of other countries.

Ma: In order to learn from foreign countries, the government sent many delegations to Europe, the Americas, and East Asia. These trips opened the eyes and minds of the participants. Statistics reveal that in 1978 alone, twelve senior national leaders, including vice chairmen of the National People's Congress and vice premiers of the State Council, made twenty trips to more than fifty countries. During the second half of the 1970s, Deng Xiaoping's four trips to eight foreign countries left a very deep impression on him. According to Deng, after these visits his comrades strongly felt that China had been left behind, and they realized that international modernization in the 1970s was different from that in the 1960s, which, in turn, was not the same as that in the 1950s.

Wu: At the time, everyone was willing and eager to learn and explore. Take the economists as an example. Chinese economists first studied the experiences in the Eastern European countries where the reforms had been introduced earlier. Reform-oriented economists, such as Sun Yefang and Yu Guangyuan, frequently visited Yugoslavia and elsewhere. At the end of 1980 and in early 1981 the Chinese Academy of Social Sciences invited Polish economist Włodzimierz Brus and Czech economist Ota Šik (both were living in exile at the time) to present a series of lectures in China. The lectures attracted many academics and government officials. Their introductions to the reforms in Poland, Czechoslovakia, and Hungary were eye-openers for the Chinese. In particular, Brus's market-socialism theory—that is, introducing some market elements in enterprise decision-making under state ownership and a planned economy—was highly appreciated by those eager for reform. However, the popularity of market socialism did not last for long. On the one hand, after coming in touch with the West, many believers began to question the reforms. On the other hand, at the same time the market-socialism reforms in Eastern Europe were reaching a low ebb. Market socialism thus lost much of its appeal among Chinese economists during the latter part of the 1980s.

However, this led to an unexpected side effect. The tools of modern economics that Brus and Šik had used in their analyses were brand new to economists in China. Many were eager to engage in systematic studies of modern economics.

In the early 1980s, there was a burst of enthusiasm in China to study Western economics (that is, modern economics). Between mid-1980 and the following summer, the Institute of Economics of CASS organized three large training workshops, on econometrics, foreign economics, and development economics, respectively. Well-known domestic and foreign experts were invited to present lectures at the workshops, providing a good opportunity for middle-aged Chinese economists at universities and research institutions to systematically study the latest findings in modern economics and to enable them to observe the Chinese economy from new perspectives.

Ma: In addition to attending these "makeup classes," many people decided to study abroad. The government sent hundreds of thousands of outstanding college graduates abroad to study in postgraduate programs in the UK, the United States, Europe, and Japan. Many of those who were among the initial group to obtain doctoral degrees from world-famous universities are leading economists in China today.

Some middle-aged economists decided to begin from scratch their study of economics. You and your colleague, Professor Zhao Renwei, both already in your fifties, went to Yale and Oxford, respectively.

Wu: Practical needs were another undercurrent driving these explorations. To be fair, although the "feeling for the stones" strategy made progress in weakening the planned economy and expanding private business activities, it did not establish clear institutional targets. There was no comprehensive planning for an overall reform of the system, nor was there a design for complementary measures. No new steps were taken without first carefully looking around. As there were differences in people's understandings and preferences, naturally there was hesitation and backpedaling. In order to promote reform and development, it was necessary to first establish a clear objective based on Chinese realities.

Driven by the theoretical explorations and practical needs, national leaders reached a consensus on the reform objective at the October 1984 Third Plenary Session of the Twelfth Communist Party Central Committee. The goal was to establish a "socialist planned commodity economy."

Ma: How was this objective formed, and what were the differences of opinion before its adoption?

Wu: There were mainly two opposing views in the early 1980s.

The first view held that the reform should be aimed at "maintaining the dominance of the planned economy and enabling a supportive market." In 1979, Chen Yun proposed that throughout the socialist stage of building communism, market regulation was secondary and subordinate but also was necessary, with planning remaining as the main part of the economy.

The other view maintained that the command economy should be transformed into a commodity economy. According to traditional socialist theory, socialist countries should retain command economies because market economies are a legacy of capitalism. In the early days of China's reform, advocates of the market played it safe politically and used the Russian term *commodity economy* to refer to a market economy. An even safer term was a *socialist planned commodity economy*. Deng Xiaoping, the "chief architect of China's reform," was an advocate of this view.

Ma: Although both groups from time to time used the phrase "combining the planned economy and the market economy," they were at opposite poles regarding the basic attributes of the reform objectives: the first group upheld the notion of a command economy, whereas the latter group advocated a market economy.

Wu: In 1980, the "Preliminary Proposal for the Reform of the Economic System," a document drafted by the System Reform Office of the State Council and prepared by senior researcher Xue Muqiao, recommended that the reform objective should be the "establishment of a commodity economy." Supported by Communist Party General Secretary Hu Yaobang, Premier Zhao Ziyang, and other senior leaders, the proposal was considered a breakthrough.

Even though this was a breakthrough, the reform suffered setbacks in 1981, when the Communist Party Central Committee adopted the Resolution on Certain Questions in the History of Our Party since the Founding of the People's Republic of China, and in 1982, when the Twelfth National Communist Party Congress affirmed that China must implement a planned economy based on public ownership, even though market regulation would be allowed to play a supplemental role.

However, this trend was halted in 1984 when the Third Plenary Session of the Twelfth Communist Party Central Committee adopted the "Decision on Reform of the Economic Structure."

The most important conclusion of this decision was the need "to discard the traditional idea of pitting the planned economy against the commodity economy. We should clearly understand that the socialist planned economy is a planned commodity economy based on public ownership, in which the law of value must be consciously followed and applied." The decision established two reform priorities: (1) "invigorating enterprises is the key to restructuring the national economy," and the key link in restructuring the economic system is to increase the dynamism of enterprises through an appropriate separation of ownership and management; and (2) "reform of the price system is the key to the reform of the entire economic structure." This involved reforming the overly centralized system of price controls, gradually reducing the scope of uniform prices set by the state, and appropriately enlarging the scope of free prices and floating prices, within certain limits. Thus, prices would respond rather rapidly to changes in labor productivity and changes in relations between market supply and demand. These conclusions established a commodity market economy as the reform objective in the official language of Communist Party and government documents.

Ma: Because this decision exceeded the limit of "maintaining the dominance of the planned economy and enabling a supportive market" and established a "socialist planned commodity economy" as the reform objective, it won high praise from Deng Xiaoping and other reform-oriented national leaders. However, in all fairness, the objective still suffered from ambiguities, which allowed for varying explanations. The specific framework for the new system required further exploration in order to devise implementation measures.

Wu: Four events took place in 1985 with respect to clarifying the basic path and objective of the reform.

The first event was publication of a comprehensive review of the Chinese economy, prepared jointly by domestic and foreign experts. In 1984, based on a request from Deng Xiaoping, the World Bank assembled a large team of international experts to collaborate with a Chinese working group to carry out a comprehensive review of the Chinese economy. The final report, issued in 1985 under the title *China: Long-Term Development Issues and Options*, consisted of one main volume and six annexes. The national leaders attached great importance to the report because it thoroughly reviewed the problems facing the Chinese economy and recommended options for addressing these problems based on comparisons with international experiences. The senior leaders themselves not only carefully read the report, but also required that officials in the economic administration departments study it as well. The report was an eye-opener for government officials, and it helped improve the decision-making capacity of the various economic departments.

The second event was preparation of the first-ever overall plan for reform of the economic system. In May 1985, Guo Shuqing and two other graduate students who were receiving training in economics at the Chinese Academy of Social Sciences wrote to the State Council calling for an overall plan for comprehensive reforms. Supported by Premier Zhao Ziyang, the State Commission for the Restructuring of the Economic System established a research group composed of nine young economists, including Lou Jiwei and Guo Shuqing, to prepare such an overall plan. An initial draft of "A Conceptual Framework for an Overall Economic Restructuring" was soon produced. Using economics language, the draft report provided a clear description of a commodity economy. It pointed out that in a commodity economy, the market system is the foundation of all economic mechanisms; enterprises have autonomy to decide upon their own activities based on their relationship with the market; workers can freely choose their own jobs; and direct control of economic administration by the government is transformed into indirect control.

The draft also proposed a two-phase sequence for the reform. The first phase would focus on price reforms to be carried out in parallel with enterprise reforms, fiscal and tax reforms, financial reforms, and the establishment of a central bank. During the second phase, an integrated factors market would be formed and the mandatory plan would be eliminated, thereby achieving the transition from a planned economy to a commodity economy.

Ma: The report was far-reaching, as it further defined the objective and basic path of the reforms since their initiation more than ten years earlier.

Wu: The third event was the September 1985 International Symposium on Macroeconomic Management (also known as the "Bashanlun conference," after the name of the cruise ship on which the symposium took place), jointly sponsored by the State Commission for the Restructuring of the Economic System, the Chinese Academy of Social Sciences, and the World Bank. Two main reform issues were discussed at the symposium.

The first issue, which resulted in heated discussions, was the selection of a targeted system. At the conference, Hungarian economist János Kornai pointed out that economic reforms in a Communist country could target either indirect administrative coordination of the economy or market coordination under macroeconomic controls. The Chinese participants who had been trained in modern economics supported Kornai's position, advocating the development of market coordination under macroeconomic management as the preferred reform objective. The second main topic focused on the macroeconomic policies to be adopted during the transitional period. The discussions at the conference ultimately played an important role in the adoption of later policies. Earlier discussions in China had been dominated by the view of Western economics that held that inflation was beneficial. At the Bashanlun conference, however, the Chinese economists, together with Nobel economics laureate James Tobin (of the United States), Sir Alexander Cairncross (who was a government economic adviser and master at St. Peter's College at the University of Oxford), and former Deutsche Bundesbank president Otmar Emminger of West Germany, unanimously agreed that China should adopt policies of fiscal austerity, monetary tightening, and income contraction to combat the economic overheating and inflation.

Ma: In September 1988, Professor Milton Friedman visited China and provided similar advice to China's national leaders. Actually, Friedman and Tobin were the heads of two opposing schools of economic thought: the former was a leading member of the Chicago School, and the latter was a leading member of the Keynesian School.

Wu: During Friedman's visit, I asked him why he agreed with Tobin regarding which policies the Chinese should adopt. He explained that debates among economists were often about secondary issues. In actuality, he and Tobin really did not have fundamental differences regarding the basic issues.

The fourth event was the official adoption of the researchers' findings in the "Recommendations of the Party Central Committee on the Seventh Five-Year Plan (1986–90)," issued at the end of September 1985. This Communist Party document proposed carrying out reforms in three areas. First, the SOEs should be transformed into autonomous commodity producers and should be responsible for their own profits and losses. Second, a market system, composed of goods, capital, and labor markets, should be developed. Third, economic administration by the state should be gradually shifted from direct to indirect control. Focusing on these three areas, price, fiscal, financial, and wage reforms were recommended. The document also suggested that the objective of the Seventh Five-Year Plan should be to establish a basic foundation for a new socialist commodity economy within about five years or a little more.

Ma: It is fair to say that the reforms proposed in this five-year plan were quite complete and, compared to the previous piecemeal approaches, they appeared to be part of a much more comprehensive program.

Wu: In April 1986, in accordance with the five-year plan, the State Council established a research group, headed by Vice Premier Tian Jiyun, to study the reform of the economic system. Within the group, there was an office responsible for designing the reform program. Guided by Premier Zhao Ziyang, the office produced the Economic System Reform Implementation Plan for 1987, which proposed complementary steps. The proposal was approved by the State Council and the leading group for financial and economic affairs under the Communist Party Central Committee. Deng Xiaoping also expressed support for the program. Although the proposed reforms were not implemented because of the economic and political turbulence that occurred in the late 1980s, the process was a good exercise to design comprehensive reforms and an important preparatory step for the later "overall design and phased-in implementation."

From 1987 to 1988, the State Council sponsored research in preparation for the "1988–95 Medium-Term Reform Program." Liu Guoguang, Li Yining, and I, together with five other economists, were invited to set up various research teams to design the program based on our own understanding of which reforms were needed. Dr. Zhou Xiaochuan and I led a core team composed of more than one dozen researchers, with academic backgrounds in economic theory, systems engineering, comparative systems analysis, fiscal and financial sciences, and so forth. Equipped with our respective specializations, the team came up with an overall reform program entailing a huge systemic re-engineering that focused on the establishment of competitive market institutions that would be implemented in phases. In June 1988, a seminar was held to review our eight reform proposals. However, because of the subsequent serious economic fluctuations and the political turbulence, these proposals were never consolidated or implemented.

Ma: As noted in Dialogue 8, in early 1988 when the economists were working on the Medium-Term Reform Program, the Communist Party Central Committee had decided to "storm the barriers to reform the prices of the means of production." The reform sought to completely liberalize prices within three to five years. Shortly after this decision was announced, serious inflation and panic buying broke out, and the decision was tabled. In the aftermath, there were no other major reform activities.

Wu: In the late 1980s there were two main social contradictions in China. First, the state sector remained dominant and controlled most of the economic resources. This economic system was naturally inclined toward large-scale investments for high growth and SOE profitability, which inevitably led to an excess money supply and inflation. During the ten years from 1979 to 1988, China had experienced three rounds of serious inflation. In particular, the last round, in mid-1988, seriously damaged the reputation of the reform. Second, the powerful command economy and the subordinate market economy existed along parallel tracks, which formed an institutional foundation for rent seeking. Abuses of the administrative powers that controlled resources became rampant. The resultant inflation and corruption enraged the general public and led to the political turbulence of 1989.

Ma: After the political and economic turbulence, between 1989 and 1991 debates about a planned economy and a market economy began to re-emerge. As noted at the beginning of this dialogue, at this time reform and development were both stagnating. It was not until 1992, when Deng Xiaoping gave his famous talks in Southern China, that the country returned to the path of market-oriented reforms and the economy began to grow again.

Wu: The serious economic and political consequences of the stalled reforms taught an important lesson. After the winter of 1991, the government began to organize comprehensive studies on the economic reforms; these were warmly received by economists who held varying perspectives.

For example, consider the research I led together with Dr. Zhou Xiaochuan. Even though the market-oriented reforms were halted after 1988, we did not stop our research. Between 1989 and 1992, we completed a number of reports, such as "The System of SOE Asset Management and the Corporatization of Enterprises," "The Restructuring of the SOE Ownership Structure," "Reform of the Fiscal System," "Reform of the Financial System," "The Transition to RMB Convertibility," "The Development of a Social-Security System," and "The Positioning of the Role of Government and the Path for Transformation." We then consolidated our findings into a comprehensive plan for further reforms called "An Overall Plan for Restructuring the Economic System in the Near to Medium Term." These reports were sent as reference to government agencies in charge of reform planning and were later published.

As noted earlier, the decision of the November 1993 Third Plenary Session of the Fourteenth Communist Party Central Committee (the "50-article decision") represented some important progress. First, a new strategy of "overall promotion of reform with key breakthroughs" was adopted. In other words, the reform would address not only the marginal difficulties, but it would also tackle the major problems of the state sector. Second, objectives were established and plans were formulated for reforms in priority areas, including the fiscal and tax systems, the financial sector, the foreign-exchange regime, the enterprise sector, and the social-security system.

Ma: The decision included an overall program for market-oriented reforms and a conceptual design for priority actions. It provided details on the basic content, sequencing, and relationships of enterprise reform, the development of market institutions, and improvements in macroeconomic management by the government. Judged even from today's perspective, it was a good reform program.

Wu: This reform program was based on the basic principles of modern economics and on a good understanding of Chinese realities. Beginning in 1994, China undertook various reforms in accordance with this blueprint. The main reforms included: (a) establishment of a market system for goods, labor, financial products, and services; (b) managed convertibility of the RMB under the current account; (c) the transformation of one million small enterprises from state and township ownership to private ownership; (d) adoption of a macroeconomic management system using indirect instruments; (e) development of a social-security system; and (f) transformation of government functions and the strengthening of the legal system.

China had thus entered a new phase in its comprehensive reforms.

DIALOGUE 11

REDEFINING PROPERTY RIGHTS

Ma Guochuan (Ma): Beginning in 1994, China implemented a new reform strategy to advance the development of the market economy. Clearly assigned property ownership and well-defined property rights and responsibilities as well as other institutional arrangements are part of the foundation of a market economy. In 1959, economist Ronald Coase pointed out that well-defined property rights are a crucial prerequisite for market transactions. This is obvious and simple to understand: so-called market transactions are nothing more than exchanges of property rights. If property rights are not well defined, then there are no true market transactions. However, under the command economy and "ownership by the whole people," which had been described in China as the "universal shining light" and the "highest form of public ownership," property belong to an abstract body—the "people"—instead of being assigned to specific persons. In an economy with ownership by the whole people (that is, state ownership) market transactions among property owners do not exist.

Wu Jinglian (Wu): Therefore, an important task in the transition from a planned economy to a market economy was to thoroughly transform the ownership structure.

However, unlike in the Soviet Union and the Eastern European countries, where mass privatization quickly transformed the ownership of former state-owned enterprises (SOEs) and collective farms, the transformation in China underwent a long and gradual process.

The incremental reform strategy to which we have referred was applied during the initial phase of this process. There was no fundamental transformation of the national economy, that is, the state sector; rather, conditions were created for the private sector (that is, the nonstate sector, or the incremental part of the national economy) to grow from bottom up. Even the collective sector that had adopted a "family contract" approach retained the collective ownership of land. This approach enabled farmers to establish family farms through household contracting. It was not until the private sector was capable of supporting the economy to a certain extent that transformation of the state sector was initiated.

Ma: When did this occur?

Wu: In the mid-1980s the private sector accounted for about one-third of China's GDP and a market economy was operating in certain areas. Many people at the time believed that reform of the state sector should be included on the government's political agenda. The "Decision on Reform of the Economic Structure," adopted at the Third Plenary Session of the Twelfth Communist Party Central Committee in 1984, was a milestone in shifting the priority from the rural reforms to the urban reforms and to making more systemic changes. One important task was to "slap the tiger's ass"—that is, the state sector—and to transform the SOEs.

There were two main forms of SOE reform in the 1980s: an expansion of enterprise autonomy and an enterprise contracting system that also granted the SOEs more autonomy. However, as we discussed in Dialogue 5, neither step was successful. They both failed to improve SOE efficiency, and they softened the budget constraints. The financial status of the state sector went from bad to worse. Before 1988, loss-making SOEs accounted for less than 20 percent of the state sector, but by the early 1990s, they accounted for one-third. Another one-third of the SOEs reported profits but were actually incurring losses. Only the remaining one-third of the SOEs were profitable. In the first quarter of 1996, the state sector suffered its first net losses since 1949, with some entire industries operating at a loss.

The lack of a breakthrough in the reform of the state sector resulted in a failure to improve the SOEs. Under these circumstances, even national leaders were beginning to question whether state ownership was a higher form of public ownership and whether it was a goal to be pursued by socialism.

Ma: It appears that because of this change in attitude, the Third Plenary Session of the Fourteenth Communist Party Central Committee (in November 1993) adopted a new interpretation of the objective of maintaining the dominance of public ownership. The decision of the plenary session, "On Some Issues of Building a Socialist Market Economy," pointed out that "nationwide public ownership should be the mainstay in the national economy but it may vary in different places and trades."

Wu: Most importantly, for the first time, a Central Committee document adopted a decision to change the ownership structure of small enterprises ("letting go of the small"). The decision states that "as for the small state-owned enterprises, the management of some can be contracted out or leased; others can be shifted to the partnership system in the form of stock sharing, or sold to collectives or individuals."

Why was it necessary to let go of the small enterprises? They constituted the absolute majority of the SOEs. In 1995, the number of state-owned industrial enterprises that were independent accounting units totaled 87,900. According to the criteria of the State Statistical Bureau, among these, large and medium-sized SOEs totaled about 17,500 and the remainder (72,200) were all small enterprises. There were also more than a half million township and village enterprises (TVEs) owned by local governments. Thus, in total, there were 600,000 small and medium-sized enterprises. It was therefore impossible for the government to effectively manage all these SOEs.

In light of this, national economic leaders decided to replace the earlier principle of "managing the SOEs well" with a new principle—to "reinvigorate the entire state sector." The approach toward SOEs was changed to a "differentiated provision of guidance" and "keeping the large enterprises and letting go of the small enterprises." In his speech at the Fifth Plenary Session of the Fourteenth Communist Party Central Committee (September 1995), General Secretary Jiang Zemin pointed out, "We need to formulate strategies and plans for developing the state sector, vigorously carry out SOE reform based on the objective of creating a modern corporate structure, and concentrate our efforts on invigorating large SOEs while deregulating and invigorating small ones." Among these proposed reforms for the large and small SOEs, many economists and local-government officials placed an emphasis on letting go of and reinvigorating the small firms.

Ma: After this Central Committee decision, some local leaders who were more sensitive to the new trends responded quickly, but overall implementation of the decision did not proceed smoothly.

In 1993, Zhucheng municipality, in Shandong province, decided to promote a "joint-stock responsibility system" (later called a "joint-stock cooperative system"), whereby shares of small SOEs were sold to their employees and then the firms were restructured. In the same year, Shunde municipality, in Guangdong province, initiated a reform that focused on transformation of the "main ownership structure." Under this reform, the local-government-owned SOEs and the township-government-owned collectives were restructured into joint-stock cooperatives, Sino-foreign joint ventures, or corporations. But these initiatives were met with both suspicion and criticism. Some people who had resisted departing from the traditional ideology criticized the reforms for being politically incorrect. Political pressures blocked wider implementation of the transformation of the small SOEs.

In particular, growth of the private sector during the reform and opening period created great uneasiness among some politicians and theorists. Between 1995 and 1997, these people wrote four long articles (commonly known as the

"Ten-Thousand-Chinese-Word Manifestos"). Although each of these so-called manifestos had a different target, they shared the same political inclinations and were sharply critical of the reform and opening policies.

Wu: The first two manifestos were circulated as typescripts instead of being published in the mass media. The first, entitled "Several Factors Affecting Our National Security," appeared in the spring of 1995. It warned that "once the share of the private sector in the national economy exceeds a certain level, it will have a serious impact on our economic foundation . . . and will negatively affect national security." The second, appearing the following autumn and entitled "A Preliminary Exploration of the Shape of Our Domestic and Foreign National Security in the Next Ten or Twenty Years and the Primary Threats It Faces," discussed the drastic changes in the former Soviet Union and Eastern Europe and predicted that a similar "peaceful evolution" would take place in China. It called for "focusing all efforts to oppose peaceful evolution." The latter two manifestos appeared in 1996, with the final one highlighting protection of state ownership and criticism of the SOE reforms.

The third and the most highly pointed manifesto, entitled "Several Theoretical and Policy Issues for Upholding the Dominant Role of Public Ownership," was circulated toward the end of 1996, on the eve of the Fifteenth National Communist Party Congress. It was an extension of an article that had been published in 1996 in the fourth issue of *Contemporary Trends*, a journal published under the aegis of the Chinese Academy of Social Sciences. A typescript of this manifesto was widely circulated. It noted that it was very unfortunate that the new interpretation of the dominance of public ownership provided by the Third Plenary Session of the Fourteenth Communist Party Central Committee had been accepted. The document, providing a comprehensive description of its authors' views on socialism, maintained that "socialist public ownership (that is, state ownership), as an advanced form of public ownership, is the foremost goal to be pursued."

The authors claimed that upholding socialism required adherence to the following principles. First, the state sector—that is, the several hundred thousand large, medium, and small industrial enterprises (at the level of independent accounting units) and a number of industries that represented the lifelines of the economy—should be maintained as one unified and complete system. Second, the state sector should remain dominant over the collective sector. Third, nonpublic entities should play only a supplemental role to the public sector. The document sharply criticized the government for letting nonstate industry grow faster than state industry and for the dramatic decline in the share of the state sector in the national economy. Finally, the document insisted that a socialist country that possessed political power and held ownership but could not use its power to defend the state-owned enterprises was no different from a socialist country implementing "Gorbachev's erroneous line."

Ma: Amid the surging leftist waves, Communist Party and government officials in favor of the market-oriented reforms fought back.

In autumn of 1996, Li Youwei, Communist Party secretary of Shenzhen municipality in Guangdong province, completed his graduation paper at the Central Party School. Entitled "Thoughts on Several Issues Concerning Ownership," the paper called for breakthroughs in dealing with the ownership issue. Li proposed that in addition to public and private ownership, there should also be "social ownership" under which the majority of workers would possess most of the means of production. He pointed out that the private sector was an organic part of the foundation of a socialist economy. The paper was sharply criticized and referred to as "a timely negative example." Critics even called the paper "a carefully prepared and well-timed political manifesto and economic program to completely change the direction of our socialist reforms."

Wu: The research team on the strategic restructuring of the state sector at the Development Research Center (DRC) under the State Council provided an alternative view.

Shortly after the Central Committee's announcement that the Fifteenth Natitonal Communist Party Congress would be held in the fourth quarter of the year, a team was established by the DRC to study the "strategic restructuring of the state sector." I was asked to lead this team of ten members, who included Zhang Junkuo and Liu Shijin. Taking into consideration the situation at the time, I selected two research goals. The first was to achieve common development of diverse forms of ownership by dismantling the ideological doctrine, copied from the Soviet Union, that maintained that "socialist public ownership" (that is, state ownership), an advanced form of public ownership, was the foremost goal to be pursued." The second goal was to take bold actions in order to restructure the state sector at a strategic level by utilizing different operational modes and organizational set-ups as long as they reflected the scale of socialized production. Our team prepared two reports. One, a policy paper entitled "The Strategic Restructuring of the State Sector" was submitted to the Document Drafting Group for the Fifteenth National Communist Party Congress. The second, "On a Redefinition of Socialism," was more academic. Because it was more sensitive politically, it was sent, under my name, to General Secretary Jiang Zemin and Premier Zhu Rongji.

Ma: What was the main content of the first report?

Wu: Anchored in Chinese reality, the first report confirmed that the limited state financial resources could not afford to support the huge state sector, and thus the SOEs should retreat from the competitive industries. It reported that, according to the State Assets Management Bureau, by the end of 1995 the assets of profit-making state-owned entities totaled RMB 4.5 trillion. If the assets of the military, posts and telecommunications, and railways were excluded, the total was only RMB 3.16 trillion. Further, if the 20 percent of nonproductive assets of industrial and commercial entities (that is, employee dwellings, schools, and hospitals) were also excluded, productive state assets totaled less than RMB 3 trillion. These assets were stretched thin in almost all sectors, from retail to the long-distance missile industry. Among the 290,000 industrial and commercial enterprises, each SOE held only about RMB 10 million in productive assets.

These statistics revealed two serious problems in terms of the scale and structure of the state sector. First, although the state sector was omnipresent, it was clear that some industries were unsuitable to be run by the state. They suffered from low efficiency, poor services, and even widespread losses. Second, the state sector was dispersed too widely, and the funding available for each enterprise was inadequate. Because of this problem, it was difficult to realize economies of scale or to make technological innovations even in areas that were suitable for SOE operations. Furthermore, because the profit-making entities used so much of the state's financial resources, the government was unable to ensure the provision of basic public services. For instance, although the Law on Compulsory Education of the People's Republic of China clearly states that the state will implement a system of nine years of compulsory education, because of budget constraints many localities demanded that the parents pay the tuition before their children would be admitted to school.

Ma: A popular slogan at the time was "the people's education should be run by the people." This meant that when the state could not provide budgetary support, ordinary people would have to pay for their children's education out of their own pockets. Such a situation contradicted the nature of compulsory education, which should be provided free by the state. In some areas, because schools collected all kinds of arbitrary fees, the number of student dropouts increased dramatically. Even worse, victims of crimes were charged fees for legal recourse because of the insufficient budget for the judiciary. This obviously resulted in judicial corruption.

Wu: The most effective way to resolve these problems was to proactively allow the state sector to withdraw—that is, to retreat—from the general competitive industries in order to focus on the strategic sectors where state control was necessary.

Our second report was a direct theoretical response to the third Ten-Thousand-Chinese-Word Manifesto. The following were our main arguments: (a) The claims that state ownership is a more advanced form of public ownership and is the foremost goal of socialism were nothing but a repetition of the basic economic characteristics of socialism, as provided for in the Soviet Union's *Textbook on Political Economy*. This doctrine was the main obstacle to further reform and opening. Thus, a clearer definition of socialism was required to break the shackles of the Soviet model; (b) Public ownership can have multiple forms. Experiments with these forms of ownership (for example, ownership by foundations, cooperatives, or communities) should be encouraged. Public ownership should not be confined to state ownership or to Soviet-style collective ownership, nor should state ownership be considered a higher form of ownership or the foremost goal of socialism; and (c) The nature of socialism was to pursue social equity and common prosperity. The shares of different ownerships in a national economy were not yardsticks by which to judge whether a country was socialist. As long as the Chinese Communist Party adopted the correct policies to effectively prevent a polarization of wealth, China would remain a socialist country.

Ma: It appears the focus of the debate was on the relationship between state ownership and socialism.

Wu: You are right. The authors of the third Ten-Thousand-Chinese-Word Manifesto, based on their definition of state ownership, had suggested that the decline in the contribution of state ownership to the economy had weakened the socialist nature of the nation and this was a sign of peaceful evolution from socialism to capitalism. Accordingly, the authors were opposed to state-sector reforms and to providing equal opportunities for other economic elements to compete with the state sector. They called for increasing the shares of the state sector and strengthening control over the national economy.

Ma: What was the result of the debate?

Wu: The Fifteenth National Communist Party Congress, held in September 1997, provided an important conclusion. The National Communist Party Congress declared that public ownership was dominant in China's basic economic system, but other forms of ownership could also coexist. The congress recognized the private sector as an important part of a socialist market economy. A criterion of "three benefits" for judging the merits of the different forms of ownership was adopted. These benefits included whether an ownership form is conducive to development of the productive forces in a socialist society, to an increase in the overall strength of a socialist country, and to improvements in the people's living standards. The congress decided that the ownership structure of the national economy should be readjusted based on these principles. The specific steps to be taken were as follows: (a) To adopt a policy of "some retreats and some advances" to restructure the national economy. The state only had to control the lifeline industries and the key economic sectors. The reduced shares of the state sector would not necessarily affect the socialist nature of the country; and (b) To seek a mixture of public ownership forms that would maximize development of the productive forces. Bold efforts were to be taken to utilize all operational modes and organizational setups that reflected the rules of social production.

This decision differed from the traditional understanding of socialism and blazed the way to change the ownership structure and to enhance the property-rights regime of the socialist market economy.

Ma: This was achieved through the retreat of the state sector from the nonstrategic sectors and the development of the private sector. Did it imply a dismantling of all SOEs?

Wu: Of course not. In today's world, there is no country that does not have SOEs. However, in most countries the reason for the existence of SOEs is that they can provide those goods that private firms are unable or unwilling to provide. These are the noncompetitive or non-excludable public goods. In terms of general competitive sectors, however, SOEs do not have the flexibility and competitiveness of private enterprises and cannot provide good-quality products and services at reasonable prices.

As was pointed out at the 1997 Fifteenth National Communist Party Congress, the state sector should only remain dominant in important industries and key economic areas. The remainder of the industries should be subject to asset restructuring in order to focus on improving the overall quality of the national economy.

The "Decision on Several Major Issues Concerning the Reform and Development of State-Owned Enterprises," adopted at the Fourth Plenary Session of the Fifteenth Communist Party Central Committee in September 1999, further defined the strategic industries that are the lifelines of the economy. They include industries related to national security and natural monopolies, industries that provide important public goods and services, and important backbone enterprises in pillar and high-tech industries.

Ma: We mentioned earlier that implementation of the 1993 decision of the Third Plenary Session of the Fourteenth Communist Party Central Committee to let go of the small enterprises did not proceed smoothly. Did the situation change after the Fifteenth National Communist Party Congress?

Wu: The most important effect of the decision of the Fifteenth National Communist Party Congress was that it enabled widespread restructuring of the small SOEs. In general, these were the small formal SOEs owned by local governments and the TVEs owned by local grassroots governments (that is, collectives based on the Southern Jiangsu Model). This restructuring was quickly implemented after the Fifteenth National Communist Party Congress.

Ma: The TVEs were directly under local governments, and most were 100 percent owned by these governments. At the beginning of the reform and opening, such firms were quite dynamic due to government protection and favorable financing conditions. During the 1990s, why was there a precipitous drop in their growth rate and why did an increasing number of these firms begin to face difficulties?

Wu: In my view, the Southern Jiangsu Model was no longer advantageous because when the TVEs matured, they exhibited weaknesses that were similar to those of the SOEs. In general, when small SOEs, including TVEs, grew, they were contracted to their managers. This was conducive to mobilizing enterprise directors to increase production and revenue, but it also led to insider control and short-term behavior by management. In Shunde municipality of Guangdong province, for example, it was common practice among local TVEs to distribute all the earnings, to rely on bank loans for production, and to leave all the debts to the future managers. Considering the adverse effects of these practices, the local government decided to accelerate the reform of letting go of the small enterprises. In some areas, TVE directors misappropriated enterprise funding for high-risk investments in the stock market, the futures market, or the real-estate market. Some kept secret accounts, reported forged profits, made under-the-table deals, and embezzled public property. The contract responsibility system became a "factory director ownership system" and a system of "ownership through nepotism."

Owing to the reduced ideological pressures after the Fifteenth National Communist Party Congress, reform of the state sector was implemented throughout the country. This involved five main approaches: (a) Part or all of the property rights of enterprises were transferred to the employees to turn the small and medium enterprises (SMEs) into joint-stock cooperatives; (b) Whole firms were sold to nonpublic legal persons or individuals and became independent (or affiliated) private businesses, joint ventures, or foreign-owned enterprises; (c) In accordance with The Company Law, small enterprises were reorganized into limited liability companies or joint-stock companies. Some of these companies retained state shares, in others shares were held by the employees, and still others became Sino-foreign joint ventures; (d) The SMEs were merged, consolidated, or became subsidiaries of other enterprises; and (e) Part or all of the assets of these firms were leased out to their managers, employees, or other enterprises. The first approach was a transitional arrangement, and most of the joint-stock cooperatives became corporatized within two years after the employee shares were transferred. By the early 2000s, the ownership structure of the entire small and medium SOE sector had been transformed into proprietary or corporatized enterprises.

Ma: This was a major economic change. Because of the lack of a capital market and control by managers over asset pricing, some enterprises were sold at such low prices that it was equivalent to giving away the enterprises for free. In addition, some managers acted as both buyer and seller, or pretended to pay for the enterprises but actually received them for free without providing any compensation to the laid-off employees. All these practices damaged the interests of the employees and other related parties.

Wu: You are right. As soon as the reform was initiated, two major problems emerged: first, those in control gave away the enterprises to their own people at very low prices; second, unless they bought shares of the restructured enterprises, the employees or members of the cooperatives were laid off without receiving compensation for their accumulated pensions and health insurance. These problems produced strong reactions among the employees. At the time, I wrote several articles calling for government action to prevent the spread of these abominable practices.

Nevertheless, reform of the small enterprises in the early 2000s was in general a significant impetus for China's economic development. Within a short span of only several years after the reform, a plethora of viable enterprises emerged. These private firms generated new jobs and helped to reduce the jobless rate in China during the 1997 Asian financial crisis.

Ma: In the mid-1990s, China's SOEs were stuck in a dead-end alley, with about half of them operating in the red. Some industries operated at a loss for months on end. In July 1997, the Asian financial crisis broke out, further exacerbating the situation. Against this backdrop, the government implemented a three-year (1998–2000) program to increase SOE efficiency by trimming employment (through layoffs or downsizing). Between 1998 and 2001, the state sector laid off 25.5 million employees, equivalent to three-fourths of its work force.

The rapidly growing SMEs absorbed many of the laid-off workers. According to the DRC and the China Enterprise Survey, at the end of 2001 China reported a total of 29.3 million SMEs, employing 173 million workers. This sector created more than 75 percent of the new jobs and accounted for 43.2 percent of the total tax revenue.

Wu: The reform of small enterprises greatly improved the economic ownership structure and reinforced the microeconomic foundation for the market economy. In particular, after the establishment of this multi-ownership system, the coastal areas in southeast China registered high economic growth.

Zhejiang province was a pioneer in this respect. Before the reform and opening, the province was in the middle-level group of provinces in terms of economic development. In 1980 Zhejiang's total industrial output was RMB 21 billion, of which only 0.035 percent (RMB 7 million) was contributed by private SMEs. But the province's SMEs took off between 1981 and 1985. Usually beginning as household-based workshops or curbside shops with backyard factories, they gradually grew into industrial clusters offering specialty products for both domestic and international markets. By 1985, there were 264,000 small enterprises either individually or jointly owned by farmers. During the same period, the average annual net income of rural residents increased by 20.14 percent. By 1986, the per capita income of rural residents in Zhejiang was the highest among all provinces, except for Beijing, Shanghai, and Tianjin. In 2000, urban and rural private businesses contributed 49 percent of Zhejiang's total industrial output. During these twenty years, the amount of rural surplus labor declined from 67.7 percent in 1980 to 37.2 percent in 2000, a drop of 30.5 percent. During the same period, the urbanization rate went up from 14.9 percent to 48.7 percent, an increase of 33.8 percent and 12.5 percent higher than the national average. The province also ranked first among all provinces, except for Beijing, Shanghai, and the other mega-municipalities in terms of annual per capita GDP and income. By the turn of the century, the state of the economy in Zhejiang province was quite gratifying: multiple ownership forms coexisted and urban and rural areas were growing side by side.

Ma: Compared to Zhejiang, development of the private sector in Jiangsu province experienced more twists and turns. In the 1980s, the TVEs based on the Southern Jiangsu Model had demonstrated a competitive advantage compared to the dominant SOEs. The model was considered a good example for emulation in the rest of the country. However, by the mid-1990s, although they had grown larger, these "quasi-state" TVE enterprises encountered problems that were similar to those encountered by firms in the state sector: declining efficiency and weak momentum for growth.

In the past, Jiangsu had always been the first to recover from economic recessions, and its growth rate had always ranked much higher than that of the other provinces. However, in 2000, when the Chinese economy was improving, performance in Jiangsu lagged behind the national average and was surpassed by that in Zhejiang.

Wu: In the late 1990s, there was a consensus that the TVEs following the Southern Jiangsu Model should be reformed and replaced by a new institutional arrangement. However, initially the provincial government was hesitant about the reform of letting go of the small enterprises, given their "past glorious history" and the earlier mistakes made during the reform that had resulted in national leaders calling for an end to the "unhealthy trend" of asset stripping by enterprise managers. However, suspension of the small-enterprise reform did not improve local economic conditions. When they could not make ends meet, some local governments in Jiangsu turned to Wenzhou and Taizhou in Zhejiang province and copied their enterprise institutional arrangements. In the early 2000s, these localities carried out an ownership restructuring, and most of their TVEs were transformed into proprietary or corporatized companies. After adoption of the new institutional arrangements, the economy of southern Jiangsu underwent dramatic changes and demonstrated rising dynamism: GDP grew, industrial production increased, and all sorts of investments began to flow into the region. The regional external sector recorded even better results.

Another good example is Guangdong province. Characterized by its export-oriented TVEs, Guangdong had been a seasoned pilot for the reforms. For a period, multiple systems of ownership had coexisted in the province. However, toward the end of the 1990s, the province's external and internal sectors began to lag behind those in the Yangzi delta region, owing to delays both in reforming the state sector and in improving the legal framework. In more recent years, some localities in the province have started to catch up in terms of the investment climate and state-sector reform. The province will have a very promising future if it learns from the experience of the adjacent Hong Kong Special Administrative Region in terms of how to maintain an enabling environment for market competition and if it can complement Hong Kong through economic integration.

To sum up, by the turn of the century the private sector in the southeastern coastal regions, after enlarging in scale and improving in quality, had become an important driver of economic growth. Empirical studies reveal that the higher the share of the private sector, the faster GDP will grow. At present, the private sector accounts for the largest share of the national economy and is the main pillar of China's economic development. The sector is also the foundation of the market economy and the most dynamic player driving the deepening of the new economic system. More importantly, this sector is fostering a large middle class, which is a basic force for social stability. The private sector is also a main source of technological innovation.

Ma: In the early 2000s, when the SMEs were transformed into proprietary or corporatized companies, did the reform of the large SOEs make any progress?

Wu: That reform also made significant progress. The decisions of the 1997 Fifteenth National Communist Party Congress and of its 1999 Fourth Plenary Session called for a transformation of most of the large SOEs, with the exception of a few corporations that were to remain under the state monopoly, into multiparty owned, limited liability companies. By the early 2000s, the majority of nonfinancial SOEs that were members of enterprise groups had become joint-stock, limited-liability companies under the relative or absolute control of the state. Among the financial SOEs, the big four state-owned banks were listed publicly overseas, providing a microlevel basis for China's financial market.

However, there still remain numerous important tasks for the state-sector reform. The restructuring of the sector has not yet been completed and many competitive industries are still controlled by the large SOEs. Most of the primary SOEs (that is, industrial and commercial groups) continue to be solely state owned. It is not clear how the State Assets Supervision and Administration Commission will exercise owners' rights over these SOEs.

In short, the state-sector reform still has a long way to go.

Ma: Starting in early 1994, the government implemented a series of important reforms, readjusted the structure of the state sector, and took state capital out of the competitive industries. By the turn of the century, a multi-ownership institution had already been established in the coastal areas of southeast China and was being extended to the central and western regions. This institutional arrangement is now the most important driver behind China's economic growth.

DIALOGUE 12

FINANCIAL INSTITUTIONS

Ma Guochuan (Ma): Financial institutions are an important part of a modern economy, but the traditional theory of socialism does not recognize the existence of commercial or monetary relations under public ownership. There was no financial sector in the command economy. Hence, a key task in the transition from a planned to a market economy was to re-establish financial institutions in accordance with the tenets of a market economy.

Wu Jinglian (Wu): Although terms like "money" and "banks" were used under the command economy, these were bogus terms because they meant something completely different from what they mean in the market economies. Under the command economy, there were no financial assets other than money, which was only an inactive measurement unit for accounting purposes and hence a mere shadow of the real economy. Except for opening savings accounts at banks, residents were not allowed to engage in any financial activities. The government exercised cash restrictions and controls to prevent "spontaneous" allocations of resources by monetary exchanges. Only commercial and industrial enterprises could establish borrowing relationships with the state banks (that is, banking credit). Credit offered by enterprises among themselves (that is, trade credit) was strictly forbidden. Banks were but the cashiers of the government, playing a negligible role in providing funding at various times. Bank lending to enterprises was limited to the provision of "nonregular" working capital (that is, nonperennial working capital). This was because the Leninist state syndicate did not distinguish the macroeconomy from the microeconomy. There was a monobanking system under which the People's Bank of China (PBoC) was responsible for the issuance of currency and the implementation of monetary policy as well as for the maintenance of household deposits and the extension of commercial loans.

With the completion of the 1956 Three Great Socialist Transformations, private financial institutions were merged into the PBoC, which concurrently regulated the banks, issued currency, and provided all commercial banking business. The PBoC established a vertical organizational structure throughout the country and regulated money supply through the issuance of currency and a credit plan.

Ma: After the Great Leap Forward and the people's commune movements in 1958, economic life was further dematerialized. Money became a coupon to obtain from the government a certain portion of the products of the society. Similar to the widely used coupons for grain, clothing, and meat, money could not be circulated freely in the market. Using money for commercial buying and selling was considered a criminal act of profiteering. During the Cultural Revolution, the PBoC was merged into the Ministry of Finance.

Wu: The government began to re-establish the banking system as soon as the Cultural Revolution ended in 1976. In January 1978, the PBoC was separated from the Ministry of Finance, and thereafter the Bank of China and the Agricultural Bank of China were reopened. The People's Construction Bank of China, specializing in fixed-assets lending, was also separated from the Ministry of Finance. In September 1983, the State Council issued the "Decision Concerning the People's Bank of China Exclusively Performing Central Bank Functions." In early 1984, the Industrial and Commercial Bank of China was established to lend to industrial and commercial enterprises and to take deposits in the urban areas. Thus, the banking system consisted of the central bank, four specialized banks, and other banks and nonbank financial institutions. In the 1980s, insurance companies were restored and several overseas insurance companies were also opened. In 1987, two joint-stock commercial banks at the national level, the Bank of Communications and CITIC Industrial Bank, were opened for business. These financial institutions, existing between the two economic systems, attempted to operate in accordance with the rules of a market economy.

Ma: After these reforms, the rudimentary financial system was more similar to the financial systems in the market economies.

Wu: But these were only superficial similarities. In essence, China's financial system was quite different.

In a mature market economy, the central bank enjoys independence to maintain monetary stability. Other banks are profit-making institutions and they maintain an arm's-length relationship with the central bank. In China, however, the specialized banks lacked independence because they were managed as lower-level units of the PBoC and they were subject to intervention by local governments. The PBoC too was not independent; it was directly under the State Council and had to follow government instructions in terms of formulating and implementing credit policy.

For the following reasons, the PBoC, as a central bank, was unable to effectively exercise its basic function of maintaining monetary stability. First, the functions of the central bank were not well defined. The 1986 "Provisional Regulations of the People's Republic of China on the Control of Banks" states that the following are the goals of the PBoC, the specialized banks, and other financial institutions: economic development, monetary stability, and improvements in socioeconomic efficiency. In practice, however, according to the government requirements, the banks implemented an expansionary monetary policy to achieve their mandate of attaching top priority to "economic development." Therefore, the central bank could not effectively maintain monetary stability.

Second, the internal structure of the PBoC matched that of the government, with a branch at each administrative level throughout the country. Macroeconomic management was conducted at two levels—the central and provincial governments. Monetary policy and control over aggregate money supply were affected by local government influence over the PBoC branches.

Third, the main PBoC monetary policy instrument consisted of credit quotas. But there were many loopholes in their implementation. The instrument was ineffective because of the various externalities and privileged interests in the banking system.

Fourth, the profit-retention system of the PBoC branches contributed to an excess supply of money. Both the head office and the branches owned profit-making enterprises—a practice inconsistent with the role of a central bank. These were the endogenous factors contributing to the monetary expansion.

Ma: Although there was progress and the financial market was becoming increasingly diversified, bank credit remained the primary financing channel, a legacy of the command economy. The specialized banks only served the state-owned enterprises (SOEs). They performed a commercial role, but at the same time, they had to extend policy loans, thus confounding their institutional objectives and obscuring their functions. Policy lending was not backed by adequate funding, and banks used the policy lending to hide their commercial risks and losses. Credit expansions were in the interest of those banks that were not subject to risk-control mechanisms. On the one hand, the planned targets for lending suffered shortages of funding, and, on the other hand, loans were increased through interbank transactions. These shortages were caused by the low official rates (prices) for funding. For a number of years during the 1985–94 period, real interest rates were negative. But rates in the gray and black markets were exceptionally high. This huge interest-rate differential enabled widespread rent-seeking activities. Massive quantities of funding were leaked to the gray and black markets.

Wu: The 1980s witnessed abnormalities and disorder in the development of the financial sector as a result of these serious problems. In general, capital was still allocated by administrative decisions rather than by the financial market. It was thus difficult to ensure effective economic growth and macroeconomic stability. Drastic ups and downs in the economy were commonplace.

During the ten years from the early 1980s to the early 1990s, there were several large economic fluctuations characterized by overheating and inflation that can be attributed to the immaturity of the financial system. Although it was responsible for regulating the financial sector, the central bank did not have the independence or the expertise to supervise financial institutions. It was thus unable to prevent regulatory institutional violations and unethical conduct by the staff. The abnormal development of some nonbank financial institutions, such as local-government-owned trust and investment corporations and credit cooperatives, adversely affected the standardization of the financial system and resulted in serious consequences for social stability.

Ma: Another round of economic overheating and high inflation during the 1992–94 period further exposed these problems and forced the government to deepen the financial-sector reforms.

Wu: China began to implement an overall reform of the financial system in 1994 in accordance with the "Decision on Issues of Building a Socialist Market Economy" that was adopted by the 1993 Third Plenary Session of the Fourteenth Communist Party Central Committee. An important step in this reform was to establish a central bank institution.

The main function of the PBoC (that is, the central bank) was to independently implement monetary policy under the leadership of the State Council. In 1997, in order to strengthen the PBoC's role in the formulation of monetary policy, the Monetary Policy Committee of the PBoC was established as an advisory body for policy decision-making. In 1998, with a view to further eliminating the possibility of local government intervention in monetary-policy decisions and financial regulation and supervision, the thirty-one provincial PBoC branches were merged into nine regional branches, located in key cities. Meanwhile, the intermediate targets of monetary policy began to shift from the size of credit expansions to the level of money supply. From 1994 to 1996, the PBoC adopted money-supply indicators, as commonly used by other central banks, engaged in open market operations, and established a unified national interbank credit market. In 1998, the restrictions on the size of lending by state-owned commercial banks were replaced by indirect controls based on asset-liability management and risk management.

Ma: Another important measure in the financial-sector reform was to promote the commercialization of the specialized banks (the Bank of China, the Agricultural Bank of China, the Industrial and Commercial Bank of China, and the People's Construction

Bank of China). Several joint-stock commercial banks (not owned solely by the state) were also established. In May 1995, the National People's Congress adopted the Law of the People's Republic of China on Commercial Banks. The law specifies the requirements for the establishment, separation, and consolidation of commercial banks and their branches and clearly spells out the principles for the protection of the rights of commercial banks to independently conduct their business, thus providing legal safeguards for the further reform of commercial banks.

Wu: The objective of this round of commercial-bank reform was to transform them into real banks guided by the price of funding (deposit and lending rates) and operating entirely in accordance with commercial principles. However, this made it difficult for projects with beneficial externalities, for example, infrastructure projects necessary for developing countries, to obtain loans at market rates. This problem was addressed during the financial-sector reform that was initiated in 1994. Three policy banks were established: the China Development Bank, the Export-Import Bank of China, and the Agricultural Development Bank of China. The policy banks extended loans to certain projects at low or subsidized interest rates in accordance with the relevant regulations.

The third step was to establish several joint-stock commercial banks, such as the China Minsheng Bank and the Hainan Development Bank. The state was merely one of the owners of these banks. There were also initiatives to consolidate the urban credit cooperatives into city commercial banks.

Implementation of the first and third reforms proceeded smoothly. The second reform, however, did not yield obvious results and had a negative effect on the two other reforms.

Ma: This lack of progress also affected the financial system in the 1990s. As lending grew, new problems emerged. Bad debts and nonperforming loans (NPLs) accumulated due to inappropriate government interventions, poor management, and weak internal controls.

In 1998, in order to reduce the NPLs and to improve the capital adequacy ratio of the state-owned commercial banks, the government issued special bonds in the amount of RMB 270 billion to increase the capital of the state-owned commercial banks. In 1999, four asset management companies (Cinda, Huarong, China Orient, and China Great Wall) were established to handle the RMB 1,400 billion in NPLs that had been transferred from the big four state-owned commercial banks.

Wu: Although on more than one occasion the state provided additional capital, these banks continued to suffer from financial difficulties. According to statistics at the end of 2002, the state-owned commercial banks, with the exception of the Bank of China, did not meet the requirements of the Basel Accords regarding their capital adequacy ratios. The NPLs of the big four amounted to RMB 2,077 billion, accounting for 26.12 percent of their total loans. By the turn of the century, China's financial industry was operating in de facto default.

Because the banks' basic institutional arrangements had not been transformed, efforts to improve the state-owned commercial banks could not ameliorate their asset situation. Although a systemic payment crisis was avoided due the backing of the state, sporadic incidents involving small and medium banks took place here and there, seriously threatening the safety of the entire financial system.

In 1998 and 1999, two large state-owned nonbank financial institutions (Guangdong International Trust and Investment Corporation and Yuehai Business Group) declared bankruptcy, with each company's debt exceeding RMB 10 billion. This was a clear warning about the state of the financial system.

In the early 1990s, the government had planned to complete the banking-system reform in three steps. These steps included: first, to commercialize the specialized banks and to improve their operations; second, to restructure these banks into solely state-owned companies; and third, to list the joint-stock banks to further diversify their ownership structures. However, because the basic institutional arrangements had not been changed, it was impossible to turn the banks into commercial entities.

Ma: According to a 2003 PBoC study, out of the total NPLs of the state-owned commercial banks, about 30 percent involved lending to SOEs due to government policy and another 30 percent was due to the requirements of the plan and administrative interventions. Of the remainder, 10 percent was attributable to state-sponsored restructurings, under which the borrowers were shut down, suspended, merged, or ordered to change their business lines, and another 10 percent was due to local government interventions or to a lack of judicial enforcement and protection of the creditors. Only the remaining 20 percent of the NPLs was due to the various internal weaknesses of the state-owned commercial banks. These statistics revealed that unless the intrinsic mechanism for generating bad loans were to be eliminated, it would be difficult to mitigate the risks in the banking system simply by transferring or writing off part of the bad loans.

Another factor intensified the need to reform the banking sector. In January 2002 China became a member of the World Trade Organization and thus was committed to further opening up its financial market. It was imperative that the risks be reduced and the competitiveness of the financial enterprises be strengthened.

Wu: Against this backdrop, the government initiated a new round of banking reforms in 2003. The key was to transform the state-owned commercial banks by introducing ownership reforms, corporatization, and the establishment of effective corporate governance in order to transform these institutions into modern commercial banks.

Most noteworthy was the abandonment of the approach widely used for the transformation of industrial and commercial enterprises, that is, separating the bad assets from the good assets and then listing the latter on the stock market. Instead, the banks first addressed the NPL problems and then listed on the stock market as a whole. More specifically, the following steps were taken: (a) In order to resolve the historical problems, financial restructuring, including the provision of additional capital by the state and the separation of nonperforming assets, was carried out. Central Huijing Investment Ltd., a state-owned investment company established for the purpose of transforming the state-owned commercial banks, invested USD 79 billion in the big four banks that were funded by China's foreign-exchange reserves. A total of RMB 1,900 billion in NPLs was transferred from these banks; and (b) With a view to hardening the property-rights constraints, enhancing corporate governance, and improving operations, the banks were partially sold off to several overseas strategic investors and went public through initial public offerings (IPOs). These measures strengthened the ownership structure of the state-owned commercial banks and raised their equity levels.

Ma: After these reforms, the big four state-owned commercial banks were listed on the Hong Kong Stock Exchange and the Shanghai Stock Exchange. Their ownership structures were diversified, and a mechanism of checks and balances between owners and management was put in place. The banks also signed strategic cooperation agreements with their overseas investors.

Wu: Based on the diversified ownership structure, a relatively standard corporate-governance system was put in place in the main commercial banks. Rules and procedures for decision-making were clarified, operations were gradually standardized, and internal controls were strengthened. Meanwhile, disclosure by the banks was institutionalized to improve their transparency.

Ma: In addition to the transformation of the four state-owned commercial banks, reforms of the joint-stock banks, city commercial banks, policy banks, postal savings institutions, and the rural credit cooperatives were all accelerated. Their competitiveness was improved by separating the bad assets from the good assets, increasing their capital (funded by strategic investors or by public listings), and restructuring their management systems, thereby reducing the risks in the financial system.

Wu: The reforms obviously improved the financials in the banking system, largely mitigated the accumulated risks, and significantly strengthened the banks' resilience. The enhanced corporate governance and the improved environment for better creditworthiness contributed to the banks' improved capacity to manage risks and to provide better services.

However, problems that had accumulated over the years required a further deepening of the financial-sector reforms. The commercial banks' corporate-governance structures that were established after their public listings are more similar to international practices in form than in practice. For instance, state-held stakes are too high and the traditional administrative appointments of senior bank managers have been retained, contrary to the rules in a market economy. During the latest wave of credit expansions that began at the end of 2008, banks, propelled by the various levels of government, provided a huge amount of loans to the funding platforms of local governments or to infrastructure projects. The most serious problem is the bureaucratic culture within the financial institutions that has weakened their identification with the role of service provider and has affected their capability for innovation.

Ma: The financial-sector reforms were an attempt to change the financial institutions and to develop a financing market. Although the market became increasingly diversified, bank loans remained the main financing channel in the economy. Until the early 2000s bank loans accounted for over 90 percent of total financing. A major drawback of China's financial market was the very low share of direct financing (for example, equity investments and bond issuances) due to the underdevelopment of the capital market.

Wu: Before the just-mentioned reforms, fixed-investment funds and the regular working capital of the SOEs were provided by the state free of charge. Firms thus did not have to worry about funding. But in the 1980s, the system of free appropriations was gradually transformed. Beginning in June 1983, shortfalls in the SOEs' regular working capital were financed by the banks, and beginning in 1985, the funding sources of basic construction investments were changed from government appropriations to bank loans (the so-called "loans for appropriations"). The People's Construction Bank was entrusted with extending loans in accordance with the state plan for basic construction. Borrowers had to pay the interest on time and to repay the principal in annual installments. The amount of investments in enterprises financed by the budget gradually decreased and the amount of investments funded by bank loans increased.

Ma: Statistics reveal that before 1979, close to two-thirds of SOE fixed investments were financed through budget appropriations, but by the mid-1980s, this share had declined to one-fourth.

Wu: At that time, the objectives and functions of the specialized banks were not clarified and their management systems remained underdeveloped. A huge amount of funding for loans was leaked to the gray and black markets. On the one hand, bad loans and nonperforming bank assets were increasing, revealing the accumulation of problems in the financial system. On the other, as mentioned in the last dialogue, by the early 1990s, because of the lack of progress in the SOE reforms, one-third of all SOEs were incurring losses, another one-third were reporting paper profits, and only the remainder were truly profitable. Funding was the tightest for the SOEs.

It was under these circumstances that the stock markets first emerged. The Shanghai Stock Exchange was officially opened on December 19, 1990, followed by the Shenzhen Stock Exchange on July 3, 1991. At the end of November 2000, a total of 1,063 enterprises were listed on the two exchanges, raising a total of RMB 480 billion. Enterprises also raised more than USD 60 billion from international markets by listing H-shares (of mainland-incorporated companies) and red-chip stocks (of mainland companies incorporated outside of China) on the Hong Kong Stock Exchange.

Ma: In modern economics the basic role of the stock market is to optimize the allocation of capital through transactions and price changes on the stock exchanges that will direct capital to where efficiency is higher. Another fundamental role of the stock market is to evaluate company performance through changes in stock prices and to monitor company management. However, the mandate of the Chinese stock market was quite different. For a long time after the market was established, its guiding principle was "the securities market should serve the SOEs." The basic function of the market was to mobilize funding for enterprises, primarily for the SOEs.

Wu: This unique role created a special stock market with Chinese characteristics. First, the licensing procedures for issuances and listings favored the SOEs in order to help them overcome their financial difficulties. In mature market economies, companies are established and public placements are conducted through registration with the authorities. But for a long time, IPOs and listings in China first had to be approved by the provincial governments. Based on the approvals, the China Securities Regulatory Commission (CSRC) would assign listing quotas and determine the number of shares to be listed and their listing prices. In most cases, only the SOEs could survive these multiple layers of reviews and approvals. Private businesses did not have much of a chance. A large number of private-sector firms went public by "purchasing the shell of a listed company," that is, through back-door listings.

Second, stock prices were artificially raised on both the supply and demand sides, so that the companies that survived the approval process could raise more funds through share premiums. On the supply side, both the pace of the issuance of new shares and the number of shares to be listed were controlled. A public company's shares were divided into transferable and nontransferable shares, but only about one-third belonged to the former category. These restrictions significantly reduced the supply of new shares. On the demand side, various sources of funding were encouraged or required to finance the purchase of securities on the market; hence, when a large SOE issued new shares, the amount of subscriptions often reached trillions of yuan. These practices resulted in great price differentials between the primary market (the issuance market for new shares) and the secondary market (the trading market for listed shares). Those who were authorized to issue new shares and those who obtained rights to subscribe to new shares reaped enormous nonproductive profits. Small investors also rushed in despite the risk of bubbles.

Ma: To a large extent, the stock market abandoned its basic function, which is to provide opportunities for investors, in particular small investors, and to efficiently allocate capital through investment decisions by market participants.

Wu: Aside from the misplaced role of the market, these problems can also be directly attributed to deviations from a standard regulatory philosophy.

The securities market is characterized by high informational asymmetries. For instance, the knowledge among small investors about a public company is vastly different from the knowledge among insiders. Without strict regulations and supervision, the interests of the less-informed parties are negatively affected. Such information asymmetries will lead to market failures.

Ma: The informational asymmetries require that the stock market be regulated. The question is what should be regulated and how.

Wu: Under a market economy, regulation mainly refers to compliance-based supervision to address the asymmetry problems through mandatory disclosure requirements, so that informed investment decisions can be made. However, for a while the philosophy in China was to use administrative clearances as the main regulatory instrument. In May 1993, the State Council issued the Provisional Regulations on the Administration of Share Issues and Trading, which established approval processes, including rules for the acquisition of listed companies.

The biggest problem of this regulatory regime was the creation of vast room for rent seeking. It was a policy-based market in which entries and stock prices depended on the regulatory authorities. Because the approval powers could determine profits and losses, corruption became rampant. As Peking University's Professor Zhang Weiying once put it, China's stock market was a "rent-seeking game."

Ma: Compliance supervision is quite effective in the developed countries. Why did China adopt a problematic administrative approval regime? This is difficult to understand.

Wu: In addition to the differences in the regulatory philosophy, perhaps the most important factor was the various privileged interests. Professor Gao Xiqing, a former senior CSRC executive, pointed out in a 1996 paper that "the substantive approval power remains a 'sharp sword' held by the regulatory authorities of China's stock market. In the four years after the China Securities Regulatory Commission was established, 360 companies have received approval and are publicly listed. Month after month and year after year, local government officials from the thirty-one provinces (including the municipalities directly under the central government and the autonomous regions), the fourteen municipalities separately listed in the state plan, and the various government agencies, as well as enterprise directors, stream in and out of the China Securities Regulatory Commission and the other regulatory agencies trying to obtain listing rights for their enterprises. It might take 'a revolution deep in the soul' for an organ born out of the traditional centrally planned economy to cede such broad and far-reaching powers."

The misplaced role of the stock market and the deviations in the regulatory philosophy resulted in persistently high price levels on the secondary market and unbridled violations of the laws and regulations. In the United States, the average price-earnings ratio (P/E) is 14 times. From the 1990s to the early 2000s, the average P/E ratio of transferable shares on China's stock market reached an absurdly high level of close to 100 times. Most of the shares lost their value as investment opportunities. In the developed countries, cash dividend payouts from listed companies are about one-third of their profits, but in China there were almost no distributions of cash dividends. Under these circumstances, as they could not receive steady income from their investments, investors turned to speculation and short-term trading to gain from the price differentials. It seemed that everyone in China was becoming a short-term investor and the stock market was filled with a speculative atmosphere. At the time, there was a popular jingle about "the eight silliest people in the capital," one of the eight consisting of short-term traders who accidentally became longer-term shareholders.

Ma: Given the nature of the capital market, it was difficult to avoid speculation.

Wu: You are right. Speculation is indispensable for an effective market. If there are only long-term investors, the market will lose liquidity and the market clearing prices cannot be discovered in a timely manner. Speculators seek better returns at higher risks, thus enabling continuous trading. However, speculators can only play a positive role when there are other investment activities in the market. If such conditions are in place, the securities market can optimize the allocation of capital, increase investment returns, and contribute to the development of enterprises and economic growth. But speculation alone cannot improve efficiency or increase wealth. Without other investment activities, speculation will be a zero-sum game to move monies from one person's pockets to another's. This is why the following rings true: "You are sure to lose if you long remain in stock speculation."

Excessive speculation also results in soaring prices that are detached from the basic value of a stock, that is, the future profitability of the issuer. These circumstances will lead to the growth of bubbles. But bubbles cannot inflate forever, and once a peak is reached, prices will drop. A decline in prices may result in positive fluctuations, that is, market corrections, or a crash in the market. In the latter case, wealth in the amount of hundreds of millions of yuan or any other currency obtained from speculation in a bull market that is accumulated on paper will immediately become worthless. This so-called wealth effect will actually have an "adverse effect on wealth." Some deep-pocketed speculators, acting as "bookmakers" at the expense of small investors, reaped staggering fortunes by taking advantage of this special characteristic in Chinese financial markets.

Ma: From the Dutch Tulipomania of the 1600s, the British South Seas Bubble, and the French Mississippi Bubble of the 1700s, the "greatest bull market" and the subsequent Wall Street crash in the United States in the 1920s, and the bubble economy of Japan and Taiwan (China) in the 1980s–90s to the Internet bubble in the United States in the early 2000s, dramas and tragedies of "speculation frenzy, panic selling, and market crashes" have been played out in succession in the financial sector. China's securities market in the 1990s shared some similarities with the market economies during their early days. Privileged investors were able to escape from punishment for compliance violations and they feverishly engaged in speculation, "making wind and waves," that is, fomenting trouble, in the stock market, the futures market, and the real-estate market. Their activities accelerated the formation of market bubbles and when those bubbles burst, the monies of the small investors went down the drain.

At that time, China's stock market was characterized by its small size, many administrative interventions, widespread speculation, and dramatic ups and downs. The SSE Composite Index (of all stocks traded on the Shanghai Stock Exchange) was very volatile. At its height, the index was over 1,500 points, and at its low, it registered under 350 points. Compliance violations were rampant, such as the "Qiongminyuan case," the "Zhongke Chuangye market manipulation case," and the "Yinguangxia case."[1] People brazenly violated the law and blatantly engaged in false filings, insider deals, and market manipulations. The stock market became what you once called a "casino without rules." Criminals, easily amassing huge amounts of wealth, were able to escape legal punishment. The interests of investors were not effectively protected and the market did not play its role of better allocating funding.

Wu: There were different views and attitudes toward these phenomena. Some people believed that the market bubbles and compliance violations were detrimental to growth and social stability because the country was at a preliminary stage of economic development that required thrift and hard work. In particular, small investors were drawn into a bull market with expectations of high returns. When the bubbles burst, they risked becoming penniless, and there was a danger of serious social consequences. Another group of people found that the capital market lacked speculation. They were against strict regulation and supervision as well as actions to suppress excessive speculation. Whenever the prices of assets, such as the prices of securities or real estate, declined, these people would issue calls for government bailouts. They turned away when the bubbles were clearly visible, claiming that any comment on the bubble economy "was not only talk by alarmists but also instances of calling something white that is black."

Although the market bubbles did not last for long, in the short run all market participants reaped returns. High stock prices were hailed by both the rent-seekers and the small investors. Given these factors, it is particularly regrettable that people who called for government support to maintain the high market prices enjoyed the "support of the masses."

Ma: During the evolution of China's stock market, the government stepped in on several occasions. On May 19, 1999, the regulatory authorities staged a "blowout" on the Shanghai and Shenzhen stock exchanges. Over the next twenty days, the SSE Composite Index increased from 1,059 points to 1,427 points. On June 15, the *People's Daily* carried a commentary stating that the increases were in line with the inherent

[1] Translators' note: These companies were listed on the Shenzhen Stock Exchange but were later de-listed and subject to criminal investigations for fraud, forgery, and market manipulation.

requirements of the macroeconomic trends and the market, and thus were restorative. Accordingly, "At present, China's macroeconomy remains healthy and the securities market enjoys a good basis for long-term and stable development. . . . Let us be unified in our views, reinforce our confidence, and make joint efforts in order to bring a standardized and vigorous securities market into the twenty-first century." This government statement clearly lowered the investors' guard, resulting in many more investors entering the market. Stock prices climbed from high to higher. On June 29, 1999, the SSE Composite Index reached a high of 1,739.2 points. On June 14, 2001, the index reached yet another record high of 2,245.44 points. But thereafter, the index dropped sharply and the market entered a four-year adjustment period. Stock prices declined sharply and many investors suffered heavy losses.

Wu: Similar dramas and tragedies were played and replayed many times on the stock market. The solution to the root of these problems was the establishment of a healthy market based on rule of law. To achieve this, however, the role of the market and the regulatory philosophy had to be redefined.

In the face of the stock market chaos in the early 2000s, the authorities adopted and implemented a series of rules and regulations to strengthen the regulatory and supervisory framework. The most meaningful reform was the shift from quota-based approvals for issuances to qualifications-based approvals. The new regime also made improvements in the following four areas: (a) removal of quota controls on paper; (b) abolition of required recommendations for listings by local governments or line agencies; (c) establishment of issue prices at least nominally based on the issuers' and their underwriters' understandings of the market and the price quotes from the institutional investors; and (d) the highlighting of disclosure requirements.

Ma: In March 2003, the Securities Crimes Investigation Bureau of the Ministry of Public Security was established to collaborate with the CSRC. The latter also adopted a number of regulations to enhance the corporate governance of listed companies, such as requiring inclusion of independent member(s) on the boards of directors and specification of the internal-control responsibilities of the boards of directors. In addition, new requirements regarding information disclosures were promulgated.

Wu: However, these reforms are inadequate to prevent the expansion of rent-seeking activities. They too are affected by privileged interests. Take as an example the reform of the licensing regime. At present, under the current qualification-based licensing system, the regulatory authorities retain many administrative controls. Misappropriations and rent seeking still occur on the Shanghai and Shenzhen stock exchanges. The growth of the enterprise market (the second board), which was opened in October

2009, also suffers from many abnormalities. Its issue price, P/E, and issuance volume are all very high. Some people become owners at the last minute, just before the companies go public. The performance of some companies turns sour shortly after the listings and their shares are traded at below IPO prices. The issuers then cash in and flee. These practices have robbed the poor to feed the rich and have generated strong discontent among the general public.

In general, a modern financial system is a large and sophisticated institution. China has a long way to go before it can establish a financial system that is compatible with a developed market economy. Such reforms have still not been completed.

DIALOGUE 13

RETURNING TO PUBLIC FINANCE

Ma Guochuan (Ma): In addition to establishing a competitive market system, the reform also entails major changes to the fiscal system and to the institutional arrangements for the central bank. What were the main reform measures for the fiscal system in the 1990s?

Wu Jinglian (Wu): The key step was to replace the previous fiscal contracting system of the 1980s with a system that divided taxation responsibilities and benefits between the central government and local governments (that is, a tax-sharing system). After this reform, China's fiscal and taxation system was compatible with institutions in the market economies.

Ma: What was fiscal contracting, and why was it necessary that it be replaced by a tax-sharing system?

Wu: Well, that's a long story. The previous system was the result of the reform of the fiscal system in the command economy. In order to clearly understand the problems of fiscal contracting, we should first review the original system.

In the command economy, the entire country consisted of one large corporation. The fiscal system was mainly characterized by a high level of centralization, the inseparability of public finance and enterprise finance, and entangled government and enterprise budgets. Government finance was responsible for distribution both within and outside the production sector. This unified state fiscal system integrated the state budget, the banking credit plan, and enterprise finance.

Ma: As soon as the People's Republic of China was established, efforts were made to develop a fiscal system similar to what you have just described. The February 1950 national finance conference proposed the unification of "national economic and fiscal work." Hence, a strict unified taxation and spending system was implemented. With the exception of a 5 to 15 percent surtax on "grain due to the state" (the agricultural tax paid in grain) and several other small taxes, all grain due to the state and all tax revenue were allocated by the central government. Government spending had to comply with staffing quotas and the standard supply criteria set by the central government.

Wu: After the beginning of the First Five-Year Plan period in 1953, a less-centralized three-level (central, provincial, and county) fiscal system was put in place. In 1954, a sharing arrangement, based on revenue classifications, including fixed income, income to be shared per fixed ratios, and income to be adjusted between the various levels, was implemented. Expenditures were also classified based on their administrative affiliations. Expenditures by state-owned enterprises (SOEs), public-sector institutions (nonprofit government affiliates), and administrative agencies under the central government were included in the central-government budget, and expenditures by local governments were covered by the local-government budgets. Of total government expenditures during the period of the First Five-Year Plan, central-government expenditures accounted for 74.1 percent and local-government expenditures accounted for only 25.9 percent. Key construction projects and the main state expenditures were financed from the central-government budget. Essentially, the three-level system remained centralized.

After completion of the Three Great Socialist Transformations in 1956, the entire society became a large corporation managed by the government (a state syndicate). As the head office of this corporation, the central government was responsible for the supply of both public and private goods. But in 1958 various administrative decentralization approaches were adopted. Revenue was shared between the central and local governments based on certain ratios that were fixed for three years, and investment projects were open for all-round contracting, with enterprises allowed to retain all the profits. However, this period represented but a brief hiatus and, in general, the fiscal system remained highly centralized until the end of 1978.

Ma: How was this huge fiscal system funded?

Wu: Unlike in the market economies, in China most government revenue did not come from tax proceeds. Instead, government revenue mainly came from the industrial sector. Between 1955 and 1980, profit handovers and taxation on the industrial sector accounted for 50 to 60 percent of total government revenue.

How could the industrial sector be the main funding source? Under the command economy, the government used its power to set the prices of primary goods (for example, agricultural raw materials and grain) at very low levels. Using the price scissors between industrial and agricultural products, the government transferred the surplus from the nonstate sector, mainly the rural collective sector, to the industrial and commercial SOEs. Then, based on the profit handovers and the taxation on these enterprises, the government appropriated almost the entire economic surplus for its own budget. Compared to other countries undergoing industrialization, after 1956, when the command-economy system was in place, China's industrial sector maintained higher profitability and provided a sizable source of funding for government finance.

Ma: Since the entire country was a large corporation, those economic units called "enterprises" were simply workshops or working groups of the state syndicate. From the very beginning, their tax payments and profits belonged to the state. Then why was there a distinction between profits and taxes?

Wu: That was to facilitate enterprise "economic accounting" so that taxes would apply pressure for profit-making, and profits would induce cost savings. The design of the tax rates incorporated the principle of "reasonable profit retentions." By leveraging the tax rates, enterprises were allowed to retain some of their profits, equal to their assumed average social profitability. In addition, the government used the tax policy to realize its industrial-development goals. Tax rates varied greatly depending on the industry and the product.

Ma: The developed economies apply a principle of "tax equality." In contrast, in China there were huge differences in the various complex tax-rate schedules. For instance, in 1980 the average rate of the industrial and commercial tax applied to light industries was 18.9 percent (it was as much as 31.7 percent for the cigarette industry). The average rate of the same tax levied on heavy industries was 4.6 percent. Thus the tax burdens were not fairly distributed among sectors and enterprises. This was the main reason for the underdevelopment of China's long-neglected light-industry sector. As a result, people faced livelihood shortages and the sustainable development of the heavy industries was adversely affected.

Wu: The highly centralized fiscal system had a negative effect in motivating local governments and enterprises to increase revenue and to reduce costs. As soon as it was adopted, the system met with criticism and calls for reform. Mao Zedong's 1956 speech, "On the Ten Major Relationships," reveals his criticism of the excessive centralization of power. Thus, the 1958 administrative decentralization adopted local-government contracting of profits and taxes as a major measure to address this problem.

After the end of the Cultural Revolution, various factors led to an increase in spending and a decline in revenue. The economy was essentially in shatters. A number of steps had to be taken to compensate for the weak growth in production and to make improvements in living standards. During the "outward leap forward" at the end of the 1970s, the government continuously injected new funding into basic construction projects. At the same time, the expansion of SOE autonomy increased enterprise financing power. However, this also resulted in lower profitability because payments of wages and bonuses were higher than what had been stipulated in the plan. In 1979, the government budget registered huge deficits, exceeding the widely accepted threshold of 3 percent of GDP. All these deficits were in the central-government budget, adding burdens at the central level. In order to mobilize local governments to increase their revenue and to reduce spending, as well as to rein in the decline in their own revenue, beginning in 1980s the central government decided to decentralize fiscal power. A new system, called "eating from separate kitchens," was implemented. This fiscal contracting system remained in place for the next thirteen years.

Ma: It appears that the 1980 fiscal reform was a practical response to the existing difficulties. What were the components of the fiscal contracting and the "eating from separate kitchens" reforms?

Wu: The latter can be summarized as dividing revenue and expenditures among the various levels of government, with each level responsible for its own revenue and expenditures. On the revenue side, revenue from central-government enterprises and customs went to the central budget as regular income. Revenue contributed by local-government enterprises, the salt tax, the agricultural and animal husbandry tax, the income tax on industrial and commercial enterprises, the taxes levied by local governments, and other sources of revenue from local governments were designated as the regular income of local governments. The industrial and commercial tax, the most important turnover tax, was categorized as "adjustment revenue." On the expenditure side, defense spending, investments in basic construction projects, and financing for the incremental working capital of enterprises under the central government were part of the central-level budget. Funding for investment in basic construction mobilized by local governments and financing of the incremental working capital of local enterprises were part of local-government expenditures. Special expenditures, such as disaster relief and support for underdeveloped regions, were funded by the special-purpose funds of the central government.

This split clearly separated the revenue and expenditures of the central government from the income and spending of the local governments. The figures for 1979 constituted the baseline for the contracting. If the revenue of a local government exceeded its expenditures in the baseline year, the ratio of handovers to the central government would be fixed based on that surplus as a percentage of the locality's total expenditures. If the expenditures of a local government exceeded its revenue, the central government would compensate for the shortfall based on a certain ratio of the industrial and commercial tax. If, after all the receipts of the industrial and commercial taxes from a locality were given to the local government, the revenue was still less than expenditures, the central government would provide a fixed-amount subsidy. Once these ratios and amounts were set, they would be retained for five years. During this period, local governments were expected to balance their budgets on their own; if they collected more revenue, then they could spend more, and vice versa.

Ma: The system was characterized by income distributions between the central and local budgets based on fixed ratios and amounts. It represented an adjustment of the previous fiscal system in line with the reform philosophy under the command economy, that is, decentralization and interest-sharing. Certain decision-making powers were decentralized to local governments. Because these governments became entities with independent economic interests, they were more enthusiastic about developing their local economies.

Wu: In Dialogue 4 we referred to the results of the administrative decentralization. The economy was changed from a mono (U-shaped) entity to multiple and relatively independent departments (M-shaped), or a head office–subsidiary structure (H-shaped). Under the new structure, local governments, as independent economic entities, were motivated to protect and support local businesses. When local gross output increased, the revenue of the local government and the personal income of local officials increased as well. However, the new fiscal system was negatively affected because of an increase in the burdens of the central government and the growing local protectionism. In 1984, the Third Plenary Session of the Twelfth Communist Party Central Committee established a market orientation as the basic reform objective. In 1986, a comprehensive program for coordinated reforms of prices, taxation, and the fiscal system was prepared, with a view to replacing the fiscal contracting system with a tax-sharing system. However, the plans for the comprehensive reform program were aborted and the "eating from separate kitchens" arrangements continued. In 1988 they were formalized as "all-round fiscal contracting."

Ma: What were the main differences between these two arrangements?

Wu: For me, there were no fundamental differences. The all-round fiscal contracting was a continuation and further development of the 1980 arrangement. It covered all thirty-seven provinces (including the municipalities directly under the central government, autonomous regions, and quasi-provincial-level cities specifically designated in the state plan). The types of contracting were increased from four to six. They included progressive rates for revenue contracting, the inclusion of incremental income in revenue sharing, incremental increases in handovers, fixed-amount handovers, and fixed-amount subsidies. With the implementation of fiscal contracting, the relationship between the government and the SOEs was readjusted. In the past, the SOEs had to hand over all of their profits and to pay all taxes due in return for the financing of their investments by the Ministry of Finance. Under the contracting system, the enterprises could retain a certain portion of their profits or utilize any income that exceeded the contract targets.

In 1987 profit contracting was widely adopted in the state sector. Thereafter, the central government repeatedly prohibited the contracting of tax proceeds. However, in addition to enterprise profits, local governments continued to include in the contracting all of the tax payables, including the turnover taxes and the corporate income tax. When the SOEs incurred losses, state taxation would be squeezed. In such a situation, a policy of "when there were excess profits, there was greater retention" was implemented without any problems, but the requirement that one would have to make up for one's own shortfalls was ignored. It was general practice to assume responsibility for profits but not for losses. According to statistics, between 1987 and 1991 enterprises under the contracting system incurred total losses of RMB 5.1 billion, of which 37 percent (RMB 1.9 billion) was funded by the enterprises themselves, and the remainder (RMB 3.2 billion) was regarded as fiscal deficits and recorded as inactive bank loans.

Ma: At the end of the 1980s, the practice of contracting reached a peak, as fiscal contracting and enterprise contracting were both implemented. The result was a complex fiscal system: the sharing arrangements and ratios varied by locality because they were set by one-on-one negotiations with the central government based on their various historical baselines. It was thus difficult to make the system both fair and reasonable.

Some localities had low historical baselines because formerly they had been underdeveloped, but they had achieved higher growth and a more rapid increase in revenue after becoming pilots for the reform and opening. They therefore benefited immensely from the fiscal contracting system. In contrast, some old industrial bases had high baselines. Although the pace of their economic development was slow, these places had higher handover targets and thus suffered financing difficulties. The unfair sharing ratios led to unequal treatment among the regions, as described by the Chinese saying, "the faster ox was whipped harder." Hence, rich governments became richer and poor governments became poorer. This was obviously inconsistent with the fiscal principle of equalizing regional public services.

Wu: As the American economist Nicholas Lardy once put it, because the sharing ratios were determined arbitrarily, fiscal contracting resulted in a rent-seeking system that encouraged the amassing of benefits from the differentiated contracting terms rather than from spending cuts or public-service reforms.

In the short run, the administrative decentralization produced positive results. However, from the longer-term perspective, one cannot ignore the "path dependency" of the institutional transformation. Efforts were needed to prevent the reform from creating obstacles for the next steps. Because it benefited local officials, the fiscal contracting system reduced local resistance to the reform and increased the momentum for reform; however, it also fostered local protectionism and market fragmentation. The arrangement of "eating from separate kitchens" and the "all-round fiscal contracting system" divided SOE profits and income taxes based on administrative affiliations. To increase their revenue, local governments did everything possible to expand investments, including setting up new enterprises. Meanwhile, they engaged in widespread local protectionism, featuring market blockades, tax discrimination, and disguised subsidies to protect "their" enterprises from competition by outsiders. These practices led to the creation of a "feudal economy" that fragmented the market and polarized the regions in terms of their possession of wealth. Pressure groups, which were formed around the various privileged interests, attempted to block progress toward a more standardized fiscal system based on equalized public services.

Furthermore, the fiscal decentralization arrangements and the all-round fiscal contracting shared the same objectives, that is, to clarify the rights and responsibilities of the government at different levels while maintaining the stability of the central budget in order to mobilize both the central and local governments. However, these measures failed to stabilize central-government revenue. As soon as they were granted significant fiscal powers, local governments sought to hand over less revenue while applying *ultra vires* tax reductions and exemptions. Their tax administration was also slack. Initially, central-government revenue was stabilized, but starting in 1986, it began to decline.

Ma: According to a Chinese proverb, a ship rises with the tide, but central-government revenue did not rise with the economic development. Because of the inflation, revenue declined in real terms. For instance, in 1988 the amount of revenue handed over from the regions in which all-round fiscal contracting was being implemented increased by 6.5 percent. However, general price levels in that year increased by 18.5 percent. Thus, in real terms local handovers decreased. In the 1980s and the 1990s, government revenue as a share of the national economy suffered sustained declines. In 1979, government revenue to GDP was 28.4 percent and in 1980, it was 25.7 percent. But by 1993, this figure had dropped to 12.6 percent, a total decrease of 15.8 percent, or an average annual reduction of more than 1 percent over the course of fourteen years.

Wu: The problem was more obvious in the sharing of the incremental revenue. The central-government share of the total increase in revenue routinely declined. In 1988 and 1989, less than 5 percent of the annual increase in revenue collected by local agencies went to the central government, and more than 90 percent of the increase was kept by the local governments. As a result, the central-government share of total government revenue dropped from 41.5 percent in 1984 to 22 percent in 1993.

Although its revenue was declining, the responsibility of the central government for expenditures remained largely unchanged. With its budget overstretched, the central government was oftentimes unable to provide basic public services. It coped with such difficulties in the following ways: (a) requesting that rich local governments make contributions in excess of the amounts of the fixed ratios; (b) creating new levies, such as the "energy and transportation fund" in the mid-1980s and the "budgetary adjustment fund" in 1989, resulting in an ever-expanding scale of extrabudgetary revenue and spending; (c) decentralizing certain responsibilities for expenditures (what is called in Chinese "powers for carrying out certain tasks"); and (d) requiring that certain expenditure responsibilities, such as expenses for some administrative entities and spending for basic education be taken over by public-service institutions and SOEs, which then had to mobilize funding or generate income on their own in order to finance these expenditures. Many government agencies and state-owned entities established their own coffers. Despite growing resentment by the general public, educational and public-health institutions began to charge arbitrary fees,

Ma: Because of these serious shortfalls, on two occasions, once at the end of the 1980s and once in the early 1990s, the central government was forced to borrow from local governments. But it did not repay them. Shortages were everywhere: funds were unavailable to subsidize grain procurements or to invest in key basic construction projects in the railway, port, and civil aviation sectors. Some central-government agencies had to borrow monies to pay salaries. Finance Minister Liu Zhongli once joked that even his shirt was about to be stripped off his back.

At the July 1993 national work conference on government finance and tax administration, Vice Premier Zhu Rongji reported to the participants that the central government was facing serious financing difficulties, and if no reforms were undertaken, the government would not be able to make ends meet. He stated that if this situation were allowed to continue, the central-government budget would collapse before the year 2000!

Wu: The central government realized the seriousness of the threat to systemic stability and thus was eager to implement a reform of the fiscal system.

During the 1992–93 period, there was a new round of economic overheating. It was generally agreed that the economic fluctuations were the result of both the chaos in the financial sector and the defects in the fiscal system. Reform of the fiscal system was thus placed on the government agenda. In November 1993, the Decision of the Third Plenary Session of the Fourteenth Communist Party Central Committee specified the key tasks for government finance: first, all-round fiscal contracting would be replaced by a tax-sharing system based on a reasonable division of revenue and expenditures between the central and local governments; second, the reform would follow the principles of unified tax laws, fair taxation, a simplified tax system, and reasonable decentralization.

Tax sharing sought to divide responsibilities for tax administration and tax revenue between the central and local governments based on a reasonable division of expenditure responsibilities and taking into account the characteristics of the various taxes. The system was to be supplemented by a fiscal transfer system. The model for the decentralization of the budget system was the fiscal federalism that is found in the large market economies. A main feature of fiscal federalism is that it seeks to determine jurisdictions for revenue and responsibilities for expenditures based on the different types of revenue and expenditures.

A basic design for the new system, proposed in 1986 during preparations for a comprehensive reform of the price, taxation, and government finance systems, was implemented during the 1994 reform. Those taxes that were relevant to national sovereignty (for example, customs duties) would become exclusive taxes of the central government; those taxes relevant to national economic development (for example, value-added taxes) would be shared by the central and local governments; and those taxes relevant to local economic development or more suitable for collection by local administrations were categorized as local taxes.

Ma: However, China is a large country with great regional disparities in terms of the level of economic development and government revenue. Under these circumstances, would the division of revenue per types of taxes result in huge gaps in local finance and polarization in the level of public-sector services among localities?

Wu: To overcome these problems, the design of the new system included an institutional arrangement that allowed for numerous intra-government transfers to facilitate the equitable provision of public services. Under the new structure, 60 percent of revenue and 40 percent of expenditures were under the jurisdiction of the central government, and the remainder was under the jurisdiction of the local governments. In other words, among the total government revenue, the central government would collect a higher proportion from the rich regions (20 percent) and would make transfer payments to the underdeveloped regions. In practice, there were actually more transfer payments than what was stipulated in the design of the system.

Ma: Obviously, the rich regions with privileged interests under the fiscal contracting system resisted the reform. Taking this factor into consideration, Vice Premier Zhu Rongji, who at the time was in charge of the fiscal reform, and his team visited thirteen provinces to review the figures with the provincial officials. These face-to-face visits continued for more than two months. The team's patience and attention to detail eventually won the support of the provincial governments.

Wu: To reduce the resistance, the 1994 reform adopted the 1986 reform proposal that was similar to tax rebates so as to protect the existing interests of the rich regions. The baseline for calculating the rebates was the level of revenue in these regions in 1993. Any amount handed over to the central government that exceeded the baseline would be refunded to the local governments. When revenue from the value-added tax and the consumption tax increased by 1 percent, the central government would add 0.3 percent to the rebate. This 1993 baseline was welcomed by the provinces and reduced their resistance to the reform. However, because some local governments artificially raised the baseline in the fourth quarter of 1993, during the first several years after implementation of the new system most of the revenue from the two taxes that was sent to the central government was refunded to the provincial governments, leaving the central government with insufficient funding to make the transfer payments to the poorer provinces. This problem was not completely resolved until the end of the 1990s.

Ma: The tax-sharing reform was the most far-reaching institutional change after the establishment of the People's Republic because it adjusted the distribution of existing interests. Based on this reform, a basic fiscal framework suitable for a market economy was established. This was of major significance.

Wu: You are right.

First, the new system eliminated the coexistence of the different arrangements under the old system. Intragovernmental income-distribution relations were standardized. The system included a restraining mechanism by which each level of government was responsible for its functions in return for its related interests. Expenditures were shared and benefits were clearly designated. The rights and responsibilities among the levels of government were clarified.

Second, the scale of central-government transfer payments was significantly increased. Horizontal equalization among regions became more standardized and vertical income distribution between the central government and local governments became more reasonable. These changes were conducive to narrowing the gaps in government services.

Third, the new system effectively facilitated industrial structural changes and improvements in the allocation of resources. The budget constraints on local governments were hardened, contributing to improvements in the rationalization of their economic behavior. Most of the revenue from the value-added tax on industrial products and the consumption tax went to the central government, thus greatly reducing local protectionism and market blockades. Taxes on services and special agricultural products became local levies, which increased the enthusiasm of local governments to develop the services sector and specialty agriculture. Government revenue as a share of GDP declined in 1995 because of inertia, but it began to increase in 1996. The ratio of the annual budget deficits to GDP was gradually reduced.

Ma: Statistics on government revenue reveal a completely different state of government finance in 2010 as compared to that in 1994, when the reform of the fiscal system was first introduced. During the course of these sixteen years, government revenue increased by RMB 7,873.1 billion, from RMB 434.9 billion in 1993 to RMB 8,308 billion in 2010. This is a remarkable achievement.

Wu: However, we should not evaluate the fiscal reforms too highly. The 1994 reforms established a basic fiscal framework. But there are still many problems left over from history, and further improvements are required. It will take some time to complete the development of a federal fiscal system.

The most urgent problem to be addressed after the success of the tax-sharing reform was the lack of standardization in the various extrabudgetary incomes that had existed since the early years of the People's Republic when the centralized fiscal system was in place. However, during that period the amount of extrabudgetary revenue was small because it was limited to the agricultural surtax and the income from production activities by administrative agencies. In 1957, such income accounted for only 8.5 percent of total budgetary revenue. During the Great Leap Forward in 1958, the scale of the extrabudgetary levies was expanded as a result of the fiscal-power and economic-system decentralizations. But after 1978, as budgetary revenue was shrinking, different levels of government collected more extrabudgetary funds to finance expenditures that had not been reduced. By the early 1990s, it was a commonplace for both the central government and local governments to seek extrabudgetary resources. The expansion of extrabudgetary collections gave rise to corruption, resulted in additional burdens on both enterprises and residents due to the increased levies, and produced a strong reaction from the society.

Ma: In 1998 Premier Zhu Rongji announced the decision to streamline and consolidate the extrabudgetary revenue, and by the early 2000s obvious results had been achieved. The ratio of extrabudgetary funds to budgetary revenue dropped from a peak of 1:1 in 1992 to 0.28:1 in 2000. In 2001, the Ministry of Finance began to reform the administration of extrabudgetary funding. Budget units were required to de-link extrabudgetary revenue from expenditures and to separate collections from payments, with a view to phasing out this type of funding and eventually putting these funds on the budget. In 2002, the Ministry of Finance issued a regulation requiring that agencies manage all extrabudgetary revenue under the budget or under a special account for government finance. Beginning in 2003, all administrative fees and penalty payments collected by government agencies had to be handed over to the special government account.

Wu: Although significant progress was made by the central government in streamlining the extrabudgetary revenue, after the consolidation new collections emerged. As old items were eliminated, new levies were introduced. Many local governments relied on revenue from the selling of rural land that had been acquired at low prices. Others borrowed from their local financing platforms, such as the city construction investment corporations, to make up for the budget shortfalls.

Ma: To prevent a repetition of such practices, it is necessary to determine the causes. The prescription must be based on an accurate diagnosis to cure the disease. There is a popular view that the reason for the fiscal deficits of the local governments is a lack of revenue. Of the total government revenue, the central government takes the lion's share (about 60 percent), leaving the local governments with far too little to finance their expenditures. Based on this view, a thorough solution, entailing "taking away the firewood from under the cauldron," would be to give the local governments more revenue.

Wu: But this view only focuses on government-revenue statistics. It overlooks the transfer payments, financed by the revenue from the richer regions, that the central government makes to the underdeveloped regions. In recent years, expenditures have consumed only about 20 percent of the revenue of the central government, and the remainder had consisted of transfer payments to various local governments. If this factor is taken into account, the ratio between central and local revenues would be 20:80.

Compared with other large countries, China's central-government expenditures as a share of total government expenditures are among the lowest. Thus it will be very difficult to further reduce the share of central-government expenditures. When studying the mismatch between local revenue and local expenditures, one should also look at the expenditure side. An unfinished task of the 1994 tax-sharing reform is to improve the expenditure structure.

Based on available findings, there are two major problems in the structure of government expenditures. First, much of the spending is not the responsibility of public finance, such as investments in competitive industries. The other problem is the excessive decentralization for the provision of public goods, such as social security and compulsory education.

Ma: Although local-government finance is not as overstretched as it was at the beginning of the reform era, many local governments are still engaging in "construction finance" rather than "public finance." The current fiscal system has retained one important characteristic of the command economy—that is, the mixing of public finance and enterprise finance. Large amounts of fiscal resources are spent on the competitive industries. This produces many adverse results. One is a shortage of funding for various local governments.

Wu: You are right. In 2002 Vice Premier Li Lanqing, who at the time was in charge of government finance, reported that he had found numerous cases of violations of public-finance principles. He pointed out that "in the name of satisfying public needs, some local governments are busy spending on 'image projects' and 'projects to showcase their political achievements,' which are out of touch with reality. Meanwhile, they are not satisfying public needs, such as salary payments to government officials and school teachers. They are still under the influence of the command economy and prefer to take care of everything on their own. Too many government resources are being invested in the productive and profit-making sectors, and many investment-promotion initiatives and commercial-purpose enterprises are owned by the local governments. The shortfall has had to be compensated for by arbitrary fundraising, and the result has been that local governments have assumed heavy debts."

Corresponding to these problems was a lack of resources to provide services for public security, compulsory education, and public health. For instance, until the early 2000s the legally required nine-year compulsory education program had not been realized in most of the rural areas because of funding shortages. The outbreak of SARS (severe acute respiratory syndrome) revealed the serious defects in the funding of the public-health system. But among the competitive industries, even though some large state-owned enterprises did not have the same adaptability and competitiveness as the nonstate sector, they reaped huge profits through government policy biases, explicit or implicit subsidies, and administrative monopolies. Obviously, such allocations of government funding were a waste of social resources.

Ma: Under these circumstances, there have been appeals to return to public finance. In a market economy, the function of the state is to provide public goods that are funded by public finance. In this sense, a complete market economy will not be established until public finance is implemented.

Wu: To establish a public-financing system means to adjust and optimize the structure of government expenditures, standardize their scope, and gradually withdraw from the general competitive industries. It also means to significantly reduce the expenses of government administrative affiliates and to encourage profit-making affiliates to move to the market. Fiscal resources should be mainly used to enhance basic education, scientific research, public health, social security, infrastructural development, and other public needs.

In the Fifteenth Five-Year Plan (2001–5) the government clearly focused on the establishment of a public-financing system. Starting in 2001, a number of fiscal-system reforms were introduced. The most important step was the adoption of the treasury single account (TSA). Prior to this reform, the government's cash resources were scattered in various bank accounts that were held by different agencies and the state treasury had no control over them. Because these funds circulated outside the fiscal system, the central government faced resource allocation problems. After the reform, all receipts and payments were centralized in the TSA. The cash balance of the government increased dramatically, enabling payments at any time. Furthermore, payments were made directly to the service providers and the goods suppliers. The removal of the intermediate layers in the payment process solved the problems of skimping and arbitrary appropriations by various government agencies.

Another important reform was the establishment of a transfer-payments system. Public finance cannot completely solve the problem of unequal economic development, but basic expenditures should be relatively equal. Transfer payments are an important instrument for adjusting for regional differences. In 1994 transfer payments (called "special appropriations") made by the central government only amounted to RMB 40–50 billion. But by 2011, they had reached almost RMB 4 trillion. At present, per capita government expenditures in the western provinces, which formerly faced many government payment difficulties, are approaching the level of the developed regions. The most notorious problem, wage arrears owed to primary and middle-school teachers, has been resolved.

Ma: Although huge transfer payments have been made, many come with pre-set purposes, or, as referred to in Chinese, they "come with distinctive hats." Local governments, in particularly those at the county levels, still have many grievances. It has been said that "while the central finance authorities are jubilant, the provincial authorities live from hand to mouth, the municipal authorities have to demolish the east wall to repair the west wall, and the county authorities are crying out from hunger and pain." Although this is somewhat exaggerated, government finance at the county and township levels has indeed encountered many difficulties. Local governments, in particular the two lowest levels of local governments, must provide many national-level public services, including financing the nine-year compulsory education and public health. The expenditures are not matched by corresponding sources of revenue and the transfer payments are usually insufficient to fill the gaps.

Wu: The 1994 reform did not make any changes to the division of responsibilities for expenditures. Small adjustments were made thereafter, but mainly in terms of responsibility-sharing between the central and local governments. The latter are still burdened with many national-level expenditures. The combination of heavy expenditure responsibilities and insufficient sources of revenue has resulted in vast regional differences in the provision of public services. The mismatch at the local levels has also reduced administrative efficiencies. These problems should be addressed as soon as possible.

Some Ministry of Finance officials and fiscal economists have proposed that the central government should be responsible for expenditures on national-level public services. After the mismatch between the sources of revenue and the responsibility for expenditures is eliminated, the remaining shortages of some local governments should be made up for by central transfer payments. Current transfers should be standardized. If transfer payments are made arbitrarily, irregularities and corruption will be encouraged, such as "running between ministries to allow monies to flow in" (that is, obtaining central-government appropriations by paying frequent visits to the agencies in charge). When redefining the expenditure responsibilities between the central government and the local governments based on the nature of the various public goods, efforts should be made to establish a standard transfer system to bring about an equalization of public services.

Ma: In addition, the budgetary system of the sectoral agencies and the government procurement system also need to be improved.

Wu: The reform of public finance has not been smooth sailing. First, some Communist Party and government officials have not recognized the importance of public finance. Second, some officials are still keen to spend on wasteful projects to showcase their political achievements. They are resistant to the reform because it amounts to their forgoing certain powers to allocate resources and relinquishing economic control. These factors have slowed down this reform even though it was initiated more than ten years ago. In recent years, the practice of taking care of everything has been revived. Massive public-sector resources are increasingly spent on various investment projects. There is still a long way to go for China's fiscal system to return to public finance.

DIALOGUE 14

THE LONG AND BUMPY ROAD TO A SOCIAL-SECURITY SYSTEM

Ma Guochuan (Ma): Among the comprehensive reforms since 1994 regarding the fiscal system, the financial sector, the foreign-exchange management regime, state-owned enterprises (SOEs), and the establishment of a social-security system, which was the most successful and which was the least successful?

Wu Jinglian (Wu): The most successful and smooth was the reform of the foreign-exchange management regime, which we will discuss in the next dialogue.

The least successful was the reform of the social-security system. The 1993 Third Plenary Session of the Fourteenth Communist Party Central Committee called for the establishment of a universal and multitiered social-security system to safeguard the people's basic livelihood. Because the reform would also bring changes to administrative powers and interests, it took a long time before the new system could be established.

Ma: The market-oriented reforms have been represented by a process of broad interest readjustments and major reorganizations of the social structure. It was thus imperative that a social-security system be established as soon as possible in order to provide a social safety net. In particular, during a transition period a society will undergo dramatic changes and will need an institutional arrangement that can safeguard the citizens' livelihoods and mitigate the related risks. If there is no such institutional arrangement, the reforms may destabilize the society and create resistance to change, especially among those who stand to lose their privileged interests. However, the development of a new social-security system was delayed in China for a long time and this has been a major defect of the reform process. I believe it is also a major reason why a "big debate" on the reforms erupted in 2003.

Wu: The need for the provision of basic social security by the government is widely accepted among modern nations. After the onset of the reform and opening, impressive progress was made in terms of economic development, with government revenue registering exponential growth. However, the provision of social security was disappointing. Whereas the former system could no longer satisfy the needs of the people, a new system was not yet in place. This was unsettling to the general public, resulting in both big and small workers' protests since the 1990s. It is also one of the problems that triggered the big debate on the reforms revolving around the question, whither China?

A controversial suggestion arose during the course of the debates: the market-oriented reforms were the main reason for the unsatisfactory provision of social security because the reforms had dismantled the previous system and deprived some people of security for their basic livelihood. Did the previous system really provide a sound social safety net? In order to get a good handle on this problem, we must first examine the pre-reform social-security system.

Ma: After the establishment of the People's Republic, a social-security system was set up following the examples of the USSR and the other Communist countries.

In February 1951, the central government promulgated the Regulations of the People's Republic of China on Labor Insurance. Based on these regulations, work-related insurance for pensions and health and occupational injuries was provided to workers and their families. The system was funded by the state, and the enterprises were the providers. This was considered the beginning of a social-security system. The system was first established in state-owned industrial enterprises and was later extended to state-owned commercial and trade firms.

Wu: Such a system is characterized by a pay-as-you-go (PAYG) scheme for financing. In general, a social-security system is financed either by a PAYG program or a pre-funding scheme. Payments under the former are financed by current government revenue. The early social-security systems in the various Western countries were all funded in this way, as were the systems in the Communist countries.

Under a PAYG scheme, payments are backed by government revenue and are relatively stable, which is an advantage. However, pay as you go necessitates generational transfers of payments, and current workers are paying for the social security of retirees. This usually dampens the enthusiasm of the paying generation to work hard and to make contributions. With an aging population and an increasing number of retirees, social-security systems funded by this kind of scheme will encounter financing problems. The second scheme, a pre-funding system, is financed by contributions from the beneficiaries and from investment returns. The levels of the contributions and the benefits are directly linked, which is conducive to increasing the workers' awareness about the need for self-insurance, thus increasing their enthusiasm to contribute to and to monitor the funds.

A second characteristic of the pre-reform social-security system was its narrow coverage: it only benefited state-sector employees. In the vast rural areas, old-age security was still provided for by the family, as it had been traditionally for generations. After completion of cooperativization in 1956, homes for the elderly and other welfare facilities were set up for widows, widowers, and childless members of the cooperatives. The facilities were usually austere and services were minimal. In addition, under the pre-reform social-security system, there were vast differences between the urban and rural areas. The state allocated most of its monopoly resources for social security to "state units" in the urban areas, including government agencies, SOEs, and collectives run by grassroots urban governments. The system was inequitable because rural and urban residents who did not work in state units were not covered.

A third characteristic was the lack of unified implementation by the state, which set the Chinese system apart from those in the other socialist countries. Social security in China was provided by the "unit," that is, the employer. Because there was no labor mobility, the entire working life of an employee, or even that of her offspring, became an appendage of the unit. Social security was actually "unit" security.

Ma: Since the command economy turned the entire country into one big corporation, it seems illogical that the work units should have provided the social security.

Wu: Yes, this does appear somewhat strange, but it was actually related to the historical conditions.

Initially, enterprises maintained labor insurance funds, which were accounted for as additional wages at a certain percentage of the total wage bill—that is, accounting transfers. But changes occurred with the passage of time. As the workers became older, the number of retirees increased. There were insufficient funds to cover the various social-security expenses. Starting in 1969, the provision of labor insurance funds for accounting purposes ended, and obligations for pensions, medical expenses, and other labor benefits were recorded as "non-operating income and expenses." Social security then became security provided by the enterprises.

This approach had obvious problems.

When social security was provided in kind by the work unit, the benefits for individual workers depended on the unit's capacity to obtain resources, which in turn was determined by the unit's position under the plan. There were huge welfare gaps between the various social groups. Toward the end of the Cultural Revolution, payment arrears began to occur when the SOEs encountered financial difficulties. During the reform and opening era, differences in the performance of the various SOEs began to appear. Although they were all SOE employees, some workers did not receive basic benefits because their enterprises did not receive adequate quotas under the plan, whereas other workers enjoyed a high level of benefits because their employers had access to abundant resources under the plan or held special political positions. This resulted in sharp contrasts in the provision of social security.

In addition, the state sector was oriented toward rankings in the bureaucracy. Social-security benefits differed greatly between Communist Party and government officials and the masses as well as between officials of different ranks. For instance, a large portion of the national health resources was consumed by officials, particularly by senior officials. Even Mao Zedong once called the Ministry of Public Health a ministry that only served its masters in the cities.

Ma: The provision of social security by work units also exacerbated monitoring problems. In this system, funds were managed by the unit and the beneficiaries were not motivated or did not have power to monitor the funds' income and expenditures. Monitoring by higher-level governments was also weak. These problems were fostered by red tape and corruption among the privileged. In this system, the state monopolized all resources for social security. Housing, medical care, children's education and employment, and labor protection were provided to the beneficiaries in kind. Individuals did not have the freedom to select the most satisfactory combination of benefits, nor could they manage their own finances. They had to follow the decisions made by housing management bureaus, public hospitals, or other state units. Citizens became appendages of these agencies.

Wu: Two conclusions can be drawn from this review. First, it is groundless to claim that before the reform and opening China had realized equality through a good social-security system. Second, it is obvious that the former system had to be changed.

After 1978, progress in the reform of the economic system gradually revealed the defects of the previous social-security system.

In many urban areas the social-security system in the SOEs was paralyzed, and employees who were not employed in the SOEs did not have access to any social-security benefits at all. In the vast rural areas, after the people's communes were dismantled, the rudimentary social-security system was gradually transformed into something more suitable to individual farming and a market economy. Under the former system, basic medical services were provided for by "barefoot doctors," who were actually urban youth who had been sent down to the countryside. When these urban youth returned to the cities, private practices by so-called rural doctors started to emerge. The transformation was spontaneous, but it took time to be completed. For a while, more than one hundred million rural households did not have any basic social security at all.

Ma: Faced with these problems, the government began to revise and improve the social-security system. In 1984, Sichuan, Guangdong, Jiangsu, and Liaoning provinces launched pilots on the pooling of funds (called *social pooling*) for pension expenses at lower administrative levels, taking a first step toward a transformation from enterprise-provided pensions to social security. Starting in 1986, new SOE workers were hired under labor contracts and their pensions were funded by this social pooling. Meanwhile, experiments were carried out to reform the healthcare system in some cities, which was called "social fund pooling for major medical treatments." Beginning in 1991, the social pooling of pension funds was extended to the urban areas. However, these reforms were still under a PAYG framework that depended on the employers' income. The reforms could not overcome the defects in the system.

Wu: Major changes took place after 1992.

Given the above reform experience between 1984 and 1991, and based on an analysis of the social-security reform experiences in the early 1990s in Singapore and Chile, a consensus was reached regarding the objective of the reform: the new system would be independent of the enterprise sector to support the development of a market economy; and it would be based on the principle of social equity and would motivate people to work hard and to be willing to save. To be more specific, many people advocated replacing the PAYG system with pre-funded individual accounts, according to international practices. The administration of social security would be separated from the operation of pension funds. Independent institutions entrusted by the beneficiaries would operate the pension funds in order to avoid low efficiency and to prevent corruption caused by the direct involvement of government agencies. Attention would be focused on coordination with the other socioeconomic reforms, in particular those that contributed to the reform of the SOEs and to the formation of a capital market. This consensus was reached at the Third Plenary Session of the Fourteenth Communist Party Central Committee held in November 1993.

Ma: The "Decision on Issues of Building a Socialist Market Economy" adopted at this Central Committee plenary session contains the following basic requirements that you mentioned earlier: (a) universal coverage, consisting of multiple providers; (b) individual accounts for a basic pension system and a basic healthcare system, which are the two most important elements of social security; and (c) the administration of social security separated from the operation of social-security funds.

Wu: These basic principles are in line with the general direction of the social-security systems in the advanced countries. The 1994 World Bank report, *Averting the Old*

Age Crisis: Policies to Protect the Old and Promote Growth, on pension-system reforms proposed that an old-age security system should consist of the following three pillars: a mandatory government-managed PAYG pillar; a market-managed, fully funded pillar financed by mandatory personal savings; and a voluntary savings pillar. Many countries have adopted the World Bank recommendations. The World Bank recommendations were similar to China's 1993 design of a new social-security system. In retrospect, the 1993 reform framework was a good design, albeit the need for minor modifications.

Ma: If the design was good, why was the implementation unsatisfactory?

Wu: In accordance with the government decision, the first step should be the establishment of a pension system that combines social pooling and individual accounts. However, from the very beginning the reform was challenged by financing difficulties, and the individual accounts of older SOE workers were barely funded.

On paper, under the previous PAYG scheme there was no need for SOE employees to own and make contributions to individual accounts in order to realize their legal rights to social-security benefits. In reality, the state withheld the monies for workers' social security by paying them low wages. The withheld funds became state accumulations and were used to finance the SOEs' investments. When employees retired, the government would provide them with pensions financed by tax proceeds and profit handovers from the SOEs. In terms of accounting, this should have been workable.

However, the social-security accumulations were controlled by the government rather than by the beneficiaries. When transforming a PAYG system into a scheme of fully funded individual accounts, these accounts must be financed. In other words, the government should return the accumulations to the older workers and address the contingent liabilities because of its commitment to provide old-age security.

Ma: Did other countries encounter similar problems, and how did they solve such problems?

Wu: All countries that shifted from a PAYG plan to an individual pension account scheme had to address the compensation problems.

A clean and simple solution is to compensate the beneficiaries with government revenue.

Ma: But what if the government is short of funding?

Wu: Chile encountered similar problems in 1981. In 1996, together with Professor Zhang Zhuoyuan, director of the Institute of Finance and Trade Economics of the Chinese Academy of Social Sciences, I took a study tour of Chile to learn about their pension-reform experience. A PAYG scheme had been established in Chile as early as the 1920s. However, after the 1950s the government began to have serious difficulties in terms of financing the scheme, which is said to have been an important reason behind the people's support of the 1973 military coup. A mandatory individual account scheme was established as part of the 1981 pension reform. Deep in debt, the Chilean government resolved the funding problem by issuing government "recognition bonds" to pensioners and soon-to-be-retired employees. The number of bonds a pensioner would receive was based on her tenure of service. Meanwhile, the bonds were indexed to inflation and offered a 4 percent annual coupon rate. When a worker reached retirement age, she could redeem her bonds at the Ministry of Finance. Alternatively, because the recognition bonds were tradable on the secondary market, the beneficiary could also cash out by selling her holdings. Initially, government spending went up due to realization of the contingent liabilities. But by the mid-1990s, the Chilean government was enjoying continuous surpluses and the country was among the few in the world that boasted healthy public finance.

During the 1993–95 discussions among Chinese economists on social-security reform, two approaches were proposed to finance the due compensation. One proposal was similar to the Chilean approach, that is, the Ministry of Finance would issue bonds to pay for the contingent liabilities that the government owed to older workers. Another proposal was to allow a certain portion of existing state assets to finance older workers' individual pension accounts. But neither proposal was accepted owing to opposition from the relevant authorities.

Ma: During the 1995 discussions on implementation of pension reform, the Ministry of Labor proposed a scheme under which the primary funding source would be social pooling and the secondary source would be individual retirement accounts. Workers' mandatory savings would go to the individual retirement accounts to fund their future pensions. To finance the pension obligations to older employees, enterprise contributions would be accounted for under the social pooling funds. Local labor authorities had autonomy to determine the employers' contribution rates based on the need to fund the pensions of older workers. Most of the local governments chose to implement this proposal.

Wu: This program of "primary social pooling and secondary individual accounts" actually applied a PAYG scheme to older workers and a pre-funded scheme to younger workers. The return to a PAYG program had the following adverse effects: (a) The enterprises either did not make the contributions on time or evaded them. Their contribution rates decreased year by year: from 92.4 percent in 1993, 90.5 percent in 1994, 90 percent in 1995, and 87 percent in 1996; (b) The nonstate sector, in particular private businesses and firms with foreign investment, felt it was unfair that they would have to contribute to the compensation for older workers and they were unwilling to participate in the social pooling; (c) Enterprises in old industrial cities carried a heavier burden because of the high proportion of workers eligible for compensation. In these localities, the average contribution rate exceeded 20 percent of total wages. After adding the contributions for other insurance, compensation could be as high as 35 to 45 percent of total wages. In Shanghai, an old industrial base, pension contributions alone accounted for 28.5 percent of total wages (25.5 percent from employers and 3 percent from workers). Meanwhile, some emerging cities benefited from low contribution levels. The scheme created an uneven playing field; and (d) In order to limit the impact on local competitiveness, local governments usually fixed the contribution rates at low levels. When social pooling was insufficient to cover the pension payments to retirees, withdrawals from existing workers' individual accounts were made, leaving these accounts unfunded. In the long run, there was a danger that the entire system would return to a PAYG scheme with defined benefits.

In 1996 the government put forward a plan to overcome the shortcomings of the new pension system. The funding problems were to be addressed through gradual increases in individual contribution rates, adjustments to benefit levels, and improvements in the operation, monitoring, and management of the funds. However, these measures did not solve the problems of pensions for older workers. Beginning in 1998, receipts fell short of current payment obligations in many places. In 1999 twenty-five provinces (including provincial-level municipalities) incurred deficits, and misappropriations of funding under the individual accounts exceeded RMB 100 billion. The central government had to make up for the gaps, and its annual spending on social security reached hundreds of billions of yuan.

Ma: Against this backdrop, different proposals were put forward to further the reform. One proposal advocated replacing the contributions by levying a social-security tax. Although this might have improved the financials of the system in the short run, the approach would have resulted in a return to a PAYG system. Another proposal called for the introduction of Swedish-style individual pension accounts, which is a notional accounts scheme, to alleviate the risks of volatility in the securities market. This proposal was more in line with China's economic situation at the time. But neither proposal was accepted by the authorities.

A prevailing practice with regard to laid-off workers and retirees or employees in the bankrupt SOEs was to have the employers make one-time severance payments based on the workers' years of service and wage grade. But such one-time cash compensations were insufficient to sustain the workers' livelihoods for the rest of their lives, creating serious social problems. Earning gaps occurred because the various enterprises faced different financial situations. Either from a legal perspective or from a rational perspective, it made no sense that rich employers paid a higher amount of compensation, whereas poorer employers paid nothing, since both were SOEs that had contributed to the accumulation of state assets.

Wu: In the early 2000s, a number of mass incidents involving a large number of workers broke out due to their low severance pay. National leaders were awakened to the dangers of SOE restructuring in the absence of a social safety net. They asked economists to make recommendations for a new social-security system. The most noteworthy proposal was by Professor Lawrence J. Lau of Stanford University. Professor Lau proposed the establishment of a two-tiered system: a basic pension, to be financed by general government revenue, and a common reserve fund for individual pension accounts, to be financed by contributions from workers and employers. The common reserve fund was to be managed by a central common reserve agency under a board of trustees. The agency would engage Chinese or foreign fund managers to run the fund. Professor Lau also recommended that SOE retirees and current employees (including laid-off workers) be compensated from existing state assets.

Professor Lau's recommendations were similar to the 1993 proposal for a pension system that combined the social pooling of funding with individual accounts, which had been supported by many economists and government leaders. In August 2000 the Communist Party Central Committee and the State Council decided to establish a national social-security fund, controlled by the central government, to implement a reform based on Professor Lau's proposal. The National Council for Social Security Fund is responsible for the operation of the national fund.

Ma: It was important to address the state's contingent liabilities by compensating the older SOE workers. How did this proceed?

Wu: In 1994–97 various estimates were made of the size of government liabilities owed to older state-sector employees. According to the World Bank, in 1994 contingent liabilities amounted to RMB 1.9 trillion, accounting for 46 to 69 percent of the state's net assets. A research team in the State Council's Office for Economic Restructuring came up with an even higher estimate: RMB 3.6 trillion, accounting for 145 percent of net assets in 1994. After the National Council for Social Security Fund was established in 2000, there was a suggestion to allocate RMB 2 trillion of the commercial assets owned by the state (approximately 25 percent of total net assets) to the fund, with a view to funding the pension accounts of the older workers who had contributed to the formation of these assets. If the state were to compensate them in this way, it could settle the debts owed to their social security. The approach would help reduce the dominance of one shareholder (that is, the state) in many corporations, so as to promote SOE ownership reform. It would also be conducive to the development of fund managers (institutional investors), which was critical for modern corporate governance, and hence it would strengthen the capital market.

However, whenever a new social-security system was proposed in accordance with the decision of the Third Plenary Session of the Fourteenth Communist Party Central Committee, the government agency in charge of social security would oppose carving out a portion of the state assets. In the end, the proposals were shelved and the agency retained power over the collection, maintenance, and distribution of the social-security funds. This was not a pure economic issue but a political economy issue involving powers and interests.

Ma: Therefore, the government did not adopt the proposal to allocate a large portion of state assets to fund older workers' pension accounts.

Wu: That's true. In 2001 the government adopted an approach proposed by the agency in charge—the Ministry of Labor and Social Security—to make social pooling the main funding source by reducing the share of individual accounts. Although the pilot provinces saw improvements in the financial status of their social-security programs, such progress was conditional on an increase in fiscal transfer payments. Even if the government could afford the huge expenses, the system would be mainly a PAYG scheme and it would not be sustainable in the long run.

Ma: The 2001 scheme sidestepped the sustainability problem. Based on international experience, it could not last for long. In addition, under PAYG the administrative agencies were at the same time the fund managers. They were only responsible to the government agencies above them and they were not obligated to report the financial status of the funds to the beneficiaries, nor were they subject to monitoring by the beneficiaries. It was easy for corrupt people to collude with the agencies and to use their powers to advance their own interests. People criticized the embezzlement of monies that they had saved to sustain a basic livelihood in old age, but such graft was commonplace.

From 1986 to 1997 the misuse of social-security funds involved over RMB 10 billion. In 2006 a multidimensional embezzlement case in Shanghai stunned the entire country. The case involved more than RMB 10 billion of social-security funds, and a number of senior officials were implicated.

Wu: With the benefit of hindsight, the way out is to follow the basic principles of the Third Plenary Session of the Fourteenth Communist Party Central Committee. On the surface, the greatest challenge to establishing a new social-security system involves the debts owed to older workers for their old-age security. Until this problem is resolved, the new system will not operate normally. However, the compensation problem is not unresolvable.

According to statistics published by the State-Owned Assets Supervision and Administration Commission in 2010, by the end of 2009 total state-owned assets exceeded RMB 53 trillion. A carveout of the assets would be sufficient to compensate the older workers. But this was not done due to a lack of willingness rather than a lack of capability. If interference and resistance are addressed and the basic principles are followed, it will be highly possible to establish (and improve) a new old-age security system based on international models

Ma: Another main component of a social-security system is healthcare. The histories of the various countries show that it may be even more difficult to develop a healthcare system.

As early as 1993, the government launched a pilot to develop a new employee healthcare scheme in the urban areas. In 1998 the State Council required all urban employers to participate in a basic healthcare scheme managed by local governments. Small expenses incurred from outpatient services were covered by the balance in the individual healthcare accounts, whereas large expenses incurred during hospitalization were paid for from the pooled healthcare funds. However, the reforms did not achieve satisfactory results. On the contrary, in recent years it has become increasingly difficult and expensive to see a doctor, resulting in a source of public resentment.

Wu: The difficulty is due to the generally low level of healthcare services and to a lack of access to treatment in better hospitals. The high costs can be attributed to expensive drugs and high examination fees. Patients have to pay for these expenses out of their individual accounts, which is why individual medical expenses have increased and have become so unbearable for low-income families. These are the two main defects in the current healthcare system.

I have observed that most people agree that the general public is dissatisfied with these problems and they must be resolved by the government. But when it comes to the causes and the solutions, there are numerous divergent opinions and there is no consensus.

Ma: Generally speaking, there are two main views.

Some people believe that the difficulties and the high healthcare costs are caused by the market orientation of the reform because it deprives the masses of medical services. For instance, in May 2005 the Ministry of Public Health sharply criticized healthcare services because their public nature had been weakened and the facilities were inclined to pursue economic interests. A ministry official stated, "The government's dominant role should be upheld and market mechanisms should be introduced. Ownership changes are not the main solution for the reform of the healthcare system. We are absolutely opposed to the proposal to allow the private sector to advance and to let the state retreat." A report on the reform by several researchers at the State Council Development Research Center stated that "the reform by and large has been unsuccessful" and "the difficulties are caused by the increasingly market-oriented and commercialized healthcare services."

According to these analyses, the most important step is to define healthcare as a public good to be provided to all people by government-owned public hospitals.

But there is an opposing view that finds the incomplete reform to be the main cause of the difficulty of accessing medical services and the related high costs. The government retains a monopoly over healthcare resources, tightly controls market entry, and is biased against nonpublic hospitals, thus hindering private-sector investment in healthcare. Furthermore, almost all medical services are provided by state-owned hospitals and medical facilities affiliated with enterprises and government institutions. Although hospitals are positioned to be providers of public goods, they do not receive adequate operational budgets. Instead of being remunerated based on their knowledge, capabilities, and performance, medical professionals are asked to generate income on their own, leading to excessive tests and unnecessary examinations, the selling of expensive drugs to sustain other healthcare services, or the seeking of kickbacks and gift payments known as "red envelopes." But these phenomena do not have a causal relationship with the market-oriented reforms.

Wu: I have read a book entitled *Whom to Consult When Falling Ill*, written by Professor Zhou Qiren of Peking University, which is a comprehensive discussion of his propositions regarding healthcare reform. One chapter, titled "What Sort of Market Orientation Is This?" provides an in-depth analysis. Market orientation refers to the role market pricing plays in directing the flow of resources. Professor Zhou utilizes rich data to show that it is sheer nonsense to contend that China's healthcare system has a completely market orientation.

For me, there are two aspects to safeguarding healthcare. The first aspect is fundraising for basic services; that is, who should be responsible for paying the expenses? The second aspect is who should provide general services?—that is, government-sponsored hospitals free of charge or medical facilities in the market for a fee. These two issues are different and should not be confused.

With regard to the first issue, there are great uncertainties about when a family member might fall ill and what the illness might be, and because most families cannot afford to pay all their medical bills, there is a need for various institutional arrangements for healthcare. In the past, if a family could not pay for medical treatment, other members of the clan would make up for the shortfall. In modern societies, the costs of basic healthcare are usually covered by government healthcare agencies. In most countries, government social-security agencies pay the portion of the medical expenses that are beyond the means of the patients, who pay the remainder. China should adopt a similar scheme.

The previous healthcare system had three problems. First, the coverage of government-provided health security was limited, only benefiting 20 percent of the population. Residents in the vast rural areas and many urban dwellers did not receive government support. Second, government inputs for healthcare were inadequate, passing the burdens on the patients. According to statistics, government expenditures for healthcare declined from 36.2 percent in 1980 to 20.3 percent in 2007, while out-of-pocket payments by patients during the same period increased from 21.1 percent to 45.2 percent. Third, the distribution of healthcare resources is largely biased toward Communist Party and government officials, in particular, senior officials. In 2006, a former vice minister of public health pointed out that 80 percent of government expenditures on healthcare went to healthcare for officials.

Ma: With regard to the provision of general healthcare, the problem was a lack of private hospitals. People had to seek treatment in public hospitals when they were sick.

Wu: The public hospitals underwent a reform to expand their autonomy, partly to address the serious shortfalls in government appropriations. They were required by the government to generate income on their own in order to fill the funding gap, which inevitably led to the phenomena we talked about earlier (for example, the selling of expensive drugs to sustain other healthcare services, etc.). Although healthcare management institutions were established after the reform to be the nominal purchasers of healthcare services, most of the time these institutions do not purchase services on behalf of patients and cannot effectively control the quality and prices of services.

Ma: Based on your analysis, receiving medical treatment inevitably will be difficult as long as government inputs are inadequate and the distribution of healthcare resources is inappropriate. The high costs of medical treatment will be unavoidable as long as there is a limited number of hospitals and public hospitals are engaged in expanding their autonomy.

Wu: How can we reduce the costs? The government should establish a new healthcare system, the key to which is to provide assistance to low-income residents to supplement their basic healthcare costs (the so-called supplement on the demand side).

With regard to the difficulties in receiving healthcare, they should be resolved by increasing the availability of services. Public health services, as a public good, should be provided by the government because they are noncompetitive and non-excludable. General healthcare services beyond the domain of public health do not have the characteristics of public goods. Who should be the providers of these services? Because a government is always less effective than the market in allocating resources for private goods, it is not a good solution to have the government establish and run hospitals (the so-called supplement on the supply side). Other than public health services that are public goods, general healthcare services should be provided by the market. All types of hospitals, be they public, private (including for-profit and nonprofit facilities), or jointly owned, should compete on an equal footing in the healthcare market. The selection of service providers should be left to the service purchasers (the patients or the health insurance companies).

Ma: Can we say that if such a broad framework were to be put in place, everything would be satisfactory when the market is opened?

Wu: It is not as easy as that. There is also a need to appropriately deal with the complex issues related to the financing of the healthcare system and the healthcare market.

With regard to the financing of the system, a tough question is how to define "basic services," the provision of which must be guaranteed. With the development of medical science and the expanded possibility of medical treatment, there will be endless growth in the demand for healthcare. However, the scope and yardstick for basic healthcare can only be set based on the current level of economic development and the government's fiscal capacity.

As for the provision of healthcare, the greatest difficulty is how to address the information asymmetries in the market. As we know, an important prerequisite for an efficient market is information symmetries between the two parties to a transaction. However, there are serious informational asymmetries between patients and medical professionals, between medical professionals and the suppliers of drugs and medical instruments, and between patients and suppliers. When healthcare is provided by the market, the asymmetries must be overcome in order to achieve higher efficiencies. In the past, various countries tried different models to address this problem. For instance, in some countries the government was responsible for providing information and the pricing of medical services and drugs was carried out by the administrative authorities. But the effects of this model fell short of expectations. In 2009 China established a national essential drug system under which more than three hundred drugs are priced by the state, but it is still too soon to evaluate the results. In other countries, health insurance or healthcare security agencies buy medical services from the providers to mitigate the informational asymmetries, which may be an option when healthcare services are provided by the market.

Ma: Another important component of a social-security system is unemployment insurance. What is the situation in this respect?

Wu: In the command-economy era, employment was realized through unified hirings and placements and guaranteed assignments. The authorities did not acknowledge that there was any unemployment, even though it existed implicitly. An obvious example is the case of the sent-down youth. From 1962 to 1978, approximately 18 million young urban people were sent to villages, turning the rural areas into large reservoirs of implicit unemployment. After the end of the Cultural Revolution these people returned to the cities and became "youth waiting for jobs," who were actually jobless youth.

During the reform and opening period the traditional labor system was transformed. In 1988, when SOE jobs were placed under contract systems, the unemployment became explicit. To support the SOE reforms, there were efforts to develop unemployment insurance. The decision of the Third Plenary Session of the Fourteenth Communist Party Central Committee officially stated the need to establish an unemployment insurance system. In 1999 the State Council issued the Regulations on Unemployment Insurance, which require mandatory participation in unemployment insurance by urban employers and their workers. This signaled the formation of an unemployment insurance system in China.

Ma: By the end of 2011, the number of participants in the unemployment insurance system had reached 140 million, with 1.97 million people receiving unemployment insurance payments. The funding sources of this insurance are enterprise contributions, interest income, and government subsidies. In general, the enterprise contributions amount to less than 1 percent of the total wage bill. There is no individual account for this insurance.

Wu: Although the State Council regulations cover all types of urban employers and their workers, the regulations have been implemented primarily in the state and collective sectors. It is difficult for private-sector employees and the self-employed to have access to this insurance. The unemployment insurance system as it is now implemented is no longer suitable to the present economic conditions and should be changed.

DIALOGUE 15

ECONOMIC FLUCTUATIONS AND MACROECONOMIC POLICIES

Ma Guochuan (Ma): During the last thirty years of reform, China has registered an average annual growth rate of 9.8 percent. In 2010 GDP reached RMB 39.8 trillion and China overtook Japan as the world's second-largest economy. However, a more careful review of the period reveals that it has not all been smooth sailing. Until 2008 there were five rounds of economic fluctuations, in 1979–81, 1983–85, 1987–89, 1992–94, and 2003–8. Each time, the macroeconomy suffered from overheating and inflation. This has been a serious problem affecting China's development since the beginning of the reform and opening.

You have been paying attention to and studying China's economic development during the course of all these years. According to your observations, why did this problem repeatedly occur and what macroeconomic policies should be adopted to avoid such large economic fluctuations in the future?

Wu Jinglian (Wu): Yes, economic overheating and inflation have indeed been major challenges to the economy during the reform and opening period. In order to answer your question, we should first look at past experience. Although the specific causes for the overheating and inflation were somewhat different during each round, there was a general pattern.

During the 1980s the economy suffered from three rounds of fluctuations.

The first round occurred from 1978 to 1985, shortly after the end of the Cultural Revolution. It was mainly caused by attempts by the top leaders to recover the time lost during the period of the ultra-leftist policies, but they did not pay attention to the serious distortions in the economic structure. At the time, there was a belief that high-speed growth could be achieved by going full steam ahead in terms of investments, for instance through the massive introduction of foreign technologies. The 1976–85 Ten-Year Plan for National Economic Development, adopted at the First Session of the Fifth National People's Congress in 1978, included 120 new or follow-up large projects, ranging from ten iron and steel production bases and nine nonferrous metal production bases, to eight coal production bases, ten oil and gas fields, and thirty large power-generation plants. The planned total amount of technology that was to be introduced was USD 18 billion (it later was increased to USD 80 billion). Industrial gross output increased by more than 10 percent per annum during the eight years from 1978 to 1985. Since this organized "leap forward" was characterized by a large-scale introduction of advanced foreign technologies, it was called an "outward leap forward." In order to realize the leap forward, which was really beyond the national capacity at the time, many other large projects were implemented simultaneously. However, because the economic institutions were still backward and there were serious distortions in the economic structure, such a leap forward by increasing production and investments caused economic shocks instead of realizing its intended goals.

Ma: Wasn't the reform of state-owned enterprises (SOEs) initiated around the same time that the "outward leap forward" was launched in late 1978?

Wu: As we discussed before, the reform copied USSR and Eastern European practices that had expanded SOE enterprise autonomy. Because these enterprises gained a certain amount of autonomy, they were enthusiastic about increasing production and revenue. However, they were not constrained by market competition, nor were they guided by price signals, which would have reflected resource scarcities. This initiative was not necessarily conducive to the efficient allocation of resources or to efficient factory operations. The SOEs focused mainly on increasing employee incomes and benefits, which quickly led to fiscal deficits, an excess money supply, and economic disorder.

Ma: By 1979, fiscal deficits were spiking and the government was losing control over aggregate demand. In 1978 government finance had enjoyed a surplus of RMB 1.01 billion, but only one year later, in 1979, it suffered a large deficit of RMB 2.06 billion, representing 5.2 percent of GDP at that time. Thereafter, general price levels began to rise. Although most prices still remained under administrative controls, the national retail price index went up by 6 percent in 1980, compared to 0.7 percent in 1978. Since signs of economic overheating were already visible in 1979, why was the decision to readjust the economy not taken until the end of 1980?

Wu: The top leaders could not reach a consensus as to whether there were abnormalities in the economy and whether the economy should be readjusted.

In a letter to central Communist Party leaders as early as April 1978, Xue Muqiao, a senior economist and adviser to the Economic Research Institute of the State Planning Commission (SPC), had warned of the dangers of continuously investing in basic construction projects and the risks of calling for all industrial firms at various administrative levels (the central government, local governments, and the people's communes) to "go all out and faster." Xue predicted the policy would create various contradictions in the economy. By the spring of 1979, Chen Yun, the national leader in charge of economic work, also became aware of this problem: basic construction was too large and the targets were unrealistic. The Communist Party Central Work Conference in April confirmed the "eight Chinese-word policy" proposed by Chen Yun to readjust, reform, consolidate, and improve the economy. However, the shift from the guiding principle of a "leap forward" to readjustment met with strong resistance. For instance, Xue Muqiao, who had stressed the need for readjustment, was singled out by the SPC chairman for being too conservative and for pouring cold water on the people's enthusiasm. Criticism of Xue at the SPC lasted until March 1980, when Yao Yilin became the new SPC chairman.

A true consensus was not reached until the end of 1980. In November 1980, Chen Yun, with the support of Deng Xiaoping, proposed that economic readjustments were necessary. The Communist Party Central Work Conference in December decided that the national economy should be further readjusted; that is, beginning in 1981 there should be withdrawals of investments in basic construction, government finance should be balanced without deficits, and banks should no longer print banknotes.

Ma: The administrative measures adopted after the beginning of 1981 were quite effective in controlling the economic overheating and inflation. However, because the earlier economic growth had entirely relied on expansionary fiscal and monetary policies, once more prudent macroeconomic policies were adopted without corresponding steps to improve economic efficiency, economic growth declined sharply. In 1981 GDP grew 4.5 percent, much less than the 11.7 percent growth rate in 1978.

Wu: You are right. In 1981–82 there was a debate about the reform during the economic readjustment period. There were basically two opposing views. Those economists who advocated the need for readjustment believed that the economic difficulties had been caused by an overemphasis on the roles of the market and money. They called for strengthening management of the plan during the readjustment period, thus highlighting the dominant role of the command economy. The other group of economists believed that the source of the difficulties was that the reform was focused on decentralization and interest-sharing among enterprises. According to the latter economists, the difficulties had nothing to do with the market-oriented reforms and the key to addressing the problems was to improve economic efficiency by implementing reforms, while, at the same time, slowing down growth. Although he strongly supported economic readjustments, Xue Muqiao still vociferously promoted market-oriented reforms. Unfortunately, the former group of economists eventually gained the upper hand.

Ma: Under a command economy, once economic growth slows down, the government usually returns to expansionary fiscal and monetary policies in order to raise the growth rate.

Wu: Exactly. After the first cooling-down period in 1983, the economy started to heat up again, and by the end of 1984, it once again became overheated. Take GDP growth as an example: it shot up from 5.2 percent in 1981 to 15.2 percent in 1984.

Why did the economy overheat again within such a short period of time? There are three reasons. First, after the 1982 Twelfth National Communist Party Congress adopted the strategic goal of doubling industrial and agricultural output by the end of the twentieth century, local governments competed with one another to ratchet up their respective growth targets. They each sought to expand investments so as to double their output. Second, after the October 1984 Third Plenary Session of the Twelfth Communist Party Central Committee set the reform objective of establishing a "socialist planned commodity economy," the country was filled with excitement. People thought they could initiate reforms without any constraints and the economy would take off. However, there was no clear understanding about the reforms. For instance, under the financial-sector reform, it was decided that the plan should no longer control bank credit. Starting in 1984, lending was linked to deposits: more deposits meant more loans. The baseline consisted of the outstanding loans at the end of 1983. The specialized banks rushed to increase their lending targets so as to raise their baselines, thus expanding credit in 1984. Some branches even took the loans to the doorsteps of the borrowers and begged the enterprises to borrow even more. Third, October 1984 marked the thirty-fifth anniversary of the establishment of the People's Republic. At the time, various top Communist Party leaders advocated "earning more and spending more." Some government agencies and enterprises took the opportunity to distribute large bonuses, either in cash or in kind (for example, clothing), which ended up exacerbating the economic overheating.

Ma: According to the *China Statistical Yearbook*, cash (M0) grew by 49.2 percent in 1984. Obviously, there was an oversupply of money. In early 1985, prices began to increase, yet the top leadership could not reach a consensus until the third quarter of the year as to whether it should impose strong control measures. What caused this delay?

Wu: The difficulties in correctly assessing the macroeconomic situation involved the following: inflation (that is, continuous increases in general price levels) was a monetary phenomenon. But there could be a long time lag between money supply and price movements. The oversupply of money had not yet triggered price increases, and neither the political leaders nor the general public realized the dangers of the excess money supply. Intuition is not helpful in making a timely and correct assessment of a macroeconomic situation. In early 1985, there were very different views in academic circles and among decision-makers as to whether the economy was indeed overheating and required a tightening of policies.

People who advocated expansionary policies believed that the economy had an endogenous need for the money supply to exceed economic growth. According to their thinking, a greater money supply, within a certain limit, is an impetus for production. The national economy would always be imbalanced, and aggregate demand would always exceed aggregate supply. If demand were to be artificially suppressed and the money supply restricted by macroeconomic policies, the growth rate would be thwarted and the interests of the various stakeholders would be hurt, thereby weakening support for reform.

In contrast, another group of economists, represented by Xue Muqiao, felt that inflation was not conducive to development, as had been repeatedly demonstrated by the economic-development experiences both in China and abroad. Nor was inflation beneficial to reform. These economists suggested that, in light of the level of endurance in the society, comprehensive economic-system reforms should not be implemented until there was a relative balance between aggregate demand and aggregate supply, there was a favorable economic environment, and there was some surplus in government finance. This would ensure that serious inflation would not occur when major reforms were initiated. They suggested that the government should take decisive actions to suppress demand and to improve supply. It also should quickly initiate a comprehensive set of reforms as soon as the economic environment improved, launching a new economic system to create a virtuous cycle as soon as possible.

In mid-1985 Deng Xiaoping finally set the tone for the direction of the reform. Pointing out that economic overheating was not beneficial to reform and development, he called for firm steps to control the situation. Assessments about the macroeconomic situation among the top leaders gradually converged. The central government dispatched inspection teams to the provinces to investigate the basic construction projects. In addition to tightening the credit quotas, the People's Bank of China raised the deposit and lending rates on two occasions. By the second half of 1985, the money supply began to decline, and by the third quarter investment growth also began to slow down. Thus, by early 1986 a "soft landing" had been achieved.

Ma: The debate apparently revealed the need for scientific decision-making. Did economic leaders learn from this round of economic fluctuations?

Wu: As mentioned in a previous dialogue, in September 1985 when the second round of fluctuations was still unfolding during the above-mentioned debates, the State Commission for Economic Restructuring and the Chinese Academy of Social Sciences, together with the World Bank, sponsored the International Seminar on Macroeconomic Management (the Bashanlun conference). The seminar on the Bashan cruise ship was attended by top-level experts from China and abroad. Although the participating macroeconomists each had had different experiences and did not belong to the same school of economics, they all agreed that China was facing a danger of serious inflation and the only way to deal with the problem was to tighten macroeconomic policies. In particular, Nobel economics laureate James Tobin, who was considered a Keynesian master of monetary policy, pointed out sharply that to avoid a crisis, China would have to tighten its fiscal, monetary, and income policies simultaneously. According to his thinking, the typical policy approach of combining a relaxed fiscal policy and a tight monetary policy, such that was adopted by some Western countries when they faced mild inflation, would not work in China. Tobin's speeches during the Bashanlun conference debunked the widespread claim in China that mainstream Western economists believe that inflation is a positive factor for economic development.

Shortly after the Bashanlun conference, the CCP National Conference, in September 1985, adopted the "Proposal for the Seventh Five-Year Plan," which suggested four basic guiding principles for socioeconomic development during the next five-year plan period (1986–90). Two of the basic guiding principles were directly related to macroeconomic policies. One principle required mutual and complementary reform and construction. The proposal stated that to create a favorable environment for smooth reforms, the economic growth rate must be set at a reasonable level; blind competition and the pursuit of higher increases in production and output should be prevented; and economic overstretching and chaos had to be avoided. Another guiding principle was "to keep a basic general balance between supply and demand so as to maintain an appropriate ratio of accumulation to consumption. The heart of the matter is that while meeting people's daily needs according to the financial capacity of the state, we must also set aside a reasonable amount for investment in fixed assets and try to maintain a balance within state finance, credits, materials, and foreign exchange and a general balance among them."

These two guiding principles were consistent with economic theory and represented a profound reflection on the lessons learned since the beginning of the reform and opening about managing the relationship between reform and growth. Unfortunately, after a short while, the costly lessons seemed to have been forgotten. When inflation was contained in early 1986, GDP suffered a drastic decline. (It grew by only 8.8 percent in 1986, compared to 15.2 percent in 1984.) The government backpedaled on its macroeconomic policies and created an extensive money supply in order to achieve high-speed growth, leading to extremely dire inflation in 1988.

Ma: The 1988 inflation was really serious. The annual retail index went up by 15 percent, triggering widespread panic purchasing. Not only daily necessities but also brand-name cigarettes and liquors were immediately grabbed from store shelves. In Beijing, Shanghai, and Tianjin, cigarettes and liquor were out of stock only a few hours after the shops opened.

Wu: The root cause of the grave inflation was the accelerated money supply after 1986.

Between mid-1987 and mid-1988, there was a debate about inflation among economists. Some young economists advocated expansionary fiscal and monetary policies to promote economic growth because China lacked effective demand. Their views influenced the top decision-makers, resulting in a rapid increase in money supply. In 1987, cash in circulation increased by 19.4 percent and in the following year the rate of increase jumped to 46.7 percent. Retail prices began to climb in the second half of 1987. In the first quarter of 1988, the retail index rose to double digits. Beginning in April 1988, household deposits decreased and there was sporadic panic buying.

Some economists felt that residents were beginning to anticipate another bout of inflation. Given the situation, they recommended that the price reform be delayed until the economic environment had improved. But other economists believed that it was important to promote high-speed growth through an expansionary monetary policy. The case of the Latin American countries was used as an example. The latter economists believed that hyperinflation of several thousand percent had not affected the economic prosperity in some Latin American countries. Influenced by the claim that inflation was harmless, Chinese national leaders continued to believe that they could "storm the barriers to price reform" without altering the expansionary monetary policy. A mid-August 1988 meeting of the Politburo formally decided to "storm the barriers to price and wage reforms." Inflationary expectations soon erupted throughout the country, prices shot up, and panic buying spread. The general public was angered by the serious inflation as well as by the increase in rent-seeking activities, such as the speculative buying and selling of materials under plan allocations and foreign-exchange quotas. The economic problems had become political problems and resulted in dangerous social turbulence.

In order to control the explosive inflation, the government adopted strict administrative measures to send the economy into a "forced landing." These measures quickly cut the rate of inflation, but not without high costs: the market was weak, industries were operating under capacity, employment pressures were increasing, and the fiscal situation was deteriorating. This produced an unprecedented excessive economic cooling down.

Ma: The economy remained in recession following the 1988 economic turbulence and the 1989 political turbulence. To jump-start the national economy, the People's Bank of China allowed extensive lending to SOEs, but most of the SOEs did not take off and in 1990, GDP grew by only 3.8 percent. It was not until 1991 that the economy, driven by growth of the private sector, gradually began to recover. By 1992, the economy was in full swing, but shortly thereafter, it again overheated and inflation reared up once again.

Why did a new round of overheating emerge just as the economy was about to improve? This is really puzzling.

Wu: According to my observations, this round of economic overheating was due to the lack of reforms and a reliance on the former approach of pursuing high GDP growth through large-scale investments.

After Deng Xiaoping took his 1992 "Southern Tour" (to reassert his economic agenda), China embarked on a new wave of reform and development. In particular, local governments and enterprises demonstrated great enthusiasm to take proactive approaches to reform and opening. In contrast, central-government ministries were reluctant to push forward with the reforms. Reforms in key areas, such as public finance, the financial sector, and SOEs, required the initiative of the central government. But instead of taking steps in the direction of these reforms, the authorities adopted expansionary monetary policies to stimulate growth, creating a situation that at the time was described as "those that should heat up remain cool, whereas those that should stay cool become too hot." On the one hand, key reforms did not make substantial progress; on the other hand, both central and regional government leaders focused their attention on establishing basic construction projects to achieve higher growth. The economy once again soon became overheated. Meanwhile, bubbles were forming in terms of fund raising, the opening of development zones, and in real estate, bonds, stocks, and futures transactions. At 14.7 percent, the inflation rate in 1993 was approaching the 1988 high. The general public again began to engage in panic buying. People increasingly started to stock up on US dollars, gold, and consumer durables.

Ma: If the macroeconomic situation was so serious, why didn't the authorities tighten the policies?

Wu: There were widely divergent views, particularly among the top leaders, regarding the macro situation. Basically, there were four different opinions.

The first group felt that the market-oriented reforms were moving forward too quickly and they blamed these reforms for the economic overheating. This produced an undercurrent that sought to slow down the reforms and strengthen control by the plan. The second group admitted that the economy was overheated, but attributed the root causes to delays in the key reforms; thus members of this group advocated taking decisive steps to stabilize the economy and to promote reforms. The third group felt the economy was in good shape, growing at a high speed without the risk of inflation. Members of this group believed that the high growth rate was the result of the implementation of correct policies during the past three years. The fourth opinion advocated further promotion of the reforms, and it took comfort in the economic situation. People holding this view did not believe that the economy was overheating and they feared that inflation control would be used as an excuse to enhance administrative controls.

Ma: It seems to me that each of these various views was based on different theoretical and political circumstances.

Wu: The situation was indeed complicated, and the debates lasted for almost one year. In mid-1993, based on instructions from Deng Xiaoping, the authorities adopted measures that combined both long- and short-term policies to contain inflation and stabilize the economy.

In the short term, a number of administrative steps were taken: loans that violated the relevant regulations were called back with clear deadlines; controls over the lending quotas of the specialized banks were enhanced; and investment projects that were in the pipeline were reopened for review. Meanwhile, economic measures, such as raising the lending and deposit rates—reinstating inflation-indexed deposits and issuing government bonds—were implemented on two occasions to "remove the firewood from under the cauldron" and to halt the price hikes.

The long-term response was the January 1994 launch of reforms in public finance, taxation, the financial sector, the foreign-exchange regime, and enterprises. These reforms created a new system of macroeconomic management that enabled the authorities to use aggregate means, such as fiscal and monetary policies, to regulate the macroeconomy. The bubbles were kept under control and the economy managed to grow at a relatively high speed. The inflation rate (that is, the increase in the consumer price index) dropped from 24.1 percent in 1994 to 8.3 percent in 1996. During the same period, the growth rate declined from 13.1 percent to 10 percent. The Chinese economy had indeed achieved a rare "soft landing."

Ma: Looking at the rounds of economic fluctuations, one cannot help but ask, why did China during its transition period and the Eastern European countries in the 1980s encounter similar problems?

Wu: Economists have studied this question for some time. I think there are four main reasons.

First, the repressed inflation was finally realized. In his masterpiece, *Economics of Shortage*, Hungarian economist János Kornai shows that a planned economy is a shortage economy. In other words, in a planned economy nominal aggregate demand far exceeds nominal aggregate supply. However, because most goods are subject to fixed prices, the excess demand and the weak supply are not reflected in price increases. The imbalance is hidden behind the administrative pricing and is expressed in quotas and additional costs for obtaining goods. The core of market institutions is free pricing. After market-oriented reforms are initiated, sooner or later the prices of goods and factors will have to be liberalized. But when price controls are loosened under conditions of economic shortages, the hidden inflation is realized.

Second, during a transition period government finance is challenged by increased expenditures and reduced revenue. On the one hand, it takes some time for the effects of improved efficiency to become obvious. On the other, in order to strengthen support for reform and to reduce resistance when interest-distribution patterns are undergoing drastic changes, there is a need to increase benefits for those people who had suffered under the former system while, at the same time, trying not to hurt the existing benefits for most people. People who lose some benefits during the reforms also need to be compensated. In order to achieve these goals, the government must increase expenditures, which can be considered to be the costs of the reform. When the two currents converge, they tend to cause fiscal deficits and an oversupply of money during the early phases of the reform, thus increasing inflationary pressures.

Third, during the reforms the shortcomings in macroeconomic management delayed inflation controls. A prerequisite for sound macroeconomic management is a robust institutional infrastructure, such as an independent and efficient central bank, a sound monetary transmission mechanism, and hard budget constraints on enterprises. During a transition period, these preconditions usually do not exist for a long period of time. In addition, the application of fiscal, monetary, and income policies to stabilize the macroeconomy is a very delicate art. Officials in China were accustomed to administrative commands under the command economy. But they were unfamiliar with, or even somewhat averse to, modern economics. There was a deep learning curve, so from the outset it was difficult to achieve satisfactory results.

Under these circumstances, it was imperative to have a good handle on the macroeconomic situation and to make decisions based on a scientific process. The leaders were tempted to favor short-term interests. They often adopted expansionary fiscal and monetary policies. It is possible that before the reforms had achieved their desired results and before economic efficiency had improved, some leaders implemented expansionary policies to accelerate GDP growth in order to showcase their "political achievements." After a period of prosperity, inflation returned in a dramatic fashion, causing serious economic fluctuations. Of course, economists also share some of the blame.

Ma: For more than a decade after the inception of the reforms, the greatest pressures on the economy were an excess of demand and shortages of supply, resulting in frequently inflated investment as well as inflated consumption. By default, the inflated aggregate demand would lead to inflation, creating a cyclical phenomenon. Once a subordinate joked with Chen Jinhua, who was chairman of the State Planning Commission from 1993 to 1998, saying, "You have been in the position [of chairman] for many years and what you have done can be simply summarized by four Chinese characters, that is, containing inflation."

However, after 1998 Zeng Peiyan, Chen's successor, faced a completely different problem. Because of the weak consumption and investment, total investment was growing by only 6 or 7 percent annually, compared to between 10 and 20 percent in the past. There was a lack of demand in the economy. The growth rate began to decline at the beginning of 1998 and the economy entered a two-year period of deflation (a decline in the price index). What caused this situation?

Wu: The deflationary situation from 1998 to 2000 was probably caused by the following four factors. First, the inertia of the tight macroeconomic policies adopted after 1993. There is always a lag between policy adjustments and their effects, which is universal for any tightening or expansionary steps regardless of where they are implemented. The policy tightening began in the summer of 1993, yet the weak demand pressures were not felt until 1996. Second, it was at this time that the only option for the SOEs was to reform and reorganize on a large scale. Excess production capacity had to be eliminated, but this resulted in a huge number of employees losing their jobs. In 1997 the number of laid-off SOE employees reached 12.57 million; by 1998, the number had increased substantially. Although they continued to receive their basic wages, the total income of the laid-off workers declined significantly, causing a drop in demand for consumption. Third, the former system, under which the state had provided housing, healthcare, and pensions, was quickly dismantled, whereas the establishment of a new system inched ahead much more slowly. The people's propensity to save increased because of the anticipated uncertainties, causing current consumption to decline. Fourth, and most importantly, in July 1997 the Asian financial crisis erupted. When China's neighbors devalued their currencies in succession, the Chinese government made a major decision not to devalue the RMB so as to avoid a worsening of the global economy. The competitiveness of Chinese exports was weakened and total exports declined. By the end of 1997 and early 1998, it had become obvious that the market was weak and production capacities were underutilized.

Ma: In early 1998, the government began to implement powerful measures to stimulate the economy from both the demand and the supply sides.

On the demand side, expansionary fiscal and monetary policies were implemented. The authorities adopted a "proactive fiscal stance" to finance investments with government bonds. During the four years between 1998 and 2001, the central government issued long-term construction bonds totaling RMB 510 billion. Co-financing loans provided by the four state-owned commercial banks reached a similar size. The central bank reduced the deposit and lending rates on seven occasions, thereby increasing money supply.

At the opposite end, a series of measures were undertaken to invigorate supply. In particular, a strategic adjustment was made to the state sector, which saw the SOEs advancing in certain areas and retreating in others.[1] About 100,000 state-owned small and medium-sized enterprises were transformed into private-sector firms with clearly defined property rights and operations oriented toward the market. The business environment was thus improved for start-ups and existing firms. Measures were also taken to support the development of small and medium-sized enterprises.

Because the institutional basis was improved and appropriate macroeconomic measures were adopted in a timely fashion, this round of economic recession did not cause major losses, and by 2000 the economy had returned to the growth track.

Wu: The boom from 1994 to 2003 was characterized by a high growth rate and low inflation. The economy grew between 8 and 9 percent annually, while inflation was kept at below 0.8 percent. It can be said that it was the best period for the macroeconomy since the beginning of the reform and opening. However, because some deep-rooted problems related to government functions, the state sector, and in particular the SOEs had not yet been resolved, economic overheating and an oversupply of money again re-emerged. By 2004, they again threatened the stability of the macroeconomy.

There was also a new factor. The export-oriented policy that was successfully implemented for almost ten years had reached a point that required some

1 "Retreat" refers to the withdrawal of the SOEs from general competitive industries/sectors. "Advance" refers to the retention of SOE control over strategic and public goods industries. At the turn of the twenty-first century, the main measure was characterized by retreat.

readjustments. The investment-driven economic development model inevitably led to ever-increasing investments and continuously declining consumption. The export-oriented policy had played a remedial role for a long time. However, a prosperity that relies on export demand cannot last forever. If during the previous twenty years overheating and inflation had mainly been caused by excessive investments, after 2003 delays in readjusting the export-oriented policy represented a new threat to macroeconomic stability.

At the macro level, the direct result of the policy was the increasing dual surpluses (in both the current account and the capital account) in China's balance of payments. Enterprises and residents sold a huge amount of foreign exchange to commercial banks, which in turn sold most of it to the central bank. Foreign-exchange earnings were turned into the state's foreign reserves. In 2001 foreign reserves grew by 28 percent, and in the following years they grew by over 30 percent. In 2004 the annual growth rate of foreign reserves reached a record-breaking 51 percent. The central bank had to buy foreign exchange in large quantities, thus pumping base money into the banking system and leading to an oversupply of money.

Ma: This macroeconomic situation overlapped with the so-called political cycle of scheduled changes of Communist Party and government officials in 2002–3. As a result, many local governments spent extensively on huge "image projects" and "projects to showcase their political achievements." Investments quickly heated up. From 2003 to 2008, the average annual national growth rate for fixed investments was over 25 percent, among which housing investments were growing the most rapidly. Beginning in 2003, the economy was expanding at over 10 percent per annum, and in 2007 it was growing by 13 percent.

Wu: This round of economic overheating can be considered to be a period of prosperity fed by excessive liquidity.

There were differing assessments of the situation among businesspeople, academics, and government officials. As early as early 2003, some academics had pointed to the signs of overheating and called for policy adjustments. However, the mainstream view until early 2008 claimed that this was only a "partial overheating" in some sectors. It was believed that as long as investment was controlled in these sectors, an overall overheating could be avoided.

In light of these different assessments of the macroeconomic trends, controlling the "partial overheating" in the iron and steel, cement, and aluminum industries relied mainly on administrative means, such as investment licenses, market-entry permits, and price ceilings. However, inflation is a macro (aggregate) economic phenomenon. Interventions at the micro levels cannot contain a rise in general price levels, and price increases will gradually accelerate. In July 2007 the consumer price index rose by 5.6 percent, above the benchmark for mild inflation (5 percent). However, the government continued to believe that the economy was growing only somewhat more rapidly than desired and it did not foresee the forthcoming overheating. Between February and April 2008, the consumer price index increased by over 8 percent for three consecutive months.

Ma: In 2008, when the Chinese economy was in a boom phase of the business cycle, the US subprime loan crisis was spreading to become a global financial crisis. The shocks to the Chinese economy came via two channels: (a) The financing chain of the highly leveraged (highly indebted) enterprises was broken, triggering chain reactions in the financial system. Prices in capital markets fell and the bubbles burst; and (b) Because of the economic recession in the West, international demand contracted, the number of orders for Chinese exports declined, and GDP growth started to slow down.

During the first half of 2008, industrial production and GDP continued to grow rapidly, but in the second half of the year the growth rate declined. Industrial value-added grew by only 11.4 percent in September, declined to 8.2 percent in October, and dropped further to 5.4 percent in November. At this point, the government changed its top macroeconomic-control priority from preventing inflation to "expanding domestic demand for growth." The State Council adopted an ambitious investment program involving RMB 4 trillion. In 2009 commercial bank lending increased by almost RMB 10 trillion, a hike of 32.8 percent from the previous year. These measures resulted in a rapid recovery of GDP growth, with the growth rate in 2009 reaching 9.1 percent.

Wu: The growth in 2009 was achieved by massive monetary injections. During the year, broad money (M2) increased by 27.7 percent. In the next year M2 registered an additional increase of 19.5 percent. M2 to GDP reached the exceptionally high level of 180 percent.

However, the negative effects of the highly intensive stimulus program should not be dismissed. The program further depleted resources and the environment. The monetary oversupply and the "re-leveraged" balance sheet exacerbated risks in the financial system and inflationary pressures. A dilemma emerged regarding macro policy options. If the policy tightening was not sufficiently strong, the asset bubbles and the inflation would become worse. Either burst bubbles or worsened inflation would harm economic and social stability. But if the policy were tightened too much, there could be a "hard landing," demonstrated by "half-completed" projects, repayment difficulties for the financing platforms of local governments, and increased nonperforming bank loans.

Ma: Monetary and fiscal policies are short-term instruments. Their use may stimulate short-term growth but they will not completely resolve an economic crisis. If macroeconomic policies are used inappropriately, they may even exacerbate a crisis.

Wu: The last thirty years show that China is not yet able to achieve sustained and steady economic development even though its capacity to deal with economic fluctuations has been strengthened. Economic overheating and inflation are symptoms of a disease of internal and external imbalances.

An internal imbalance exists between investment and consumption. The investment rate has been exceptionally high but the income of workers has increased too slowly. The consumption rate is only one-half that in other countries. If the lack of final demand is not addressed, investment will have to increase and the economy will fall into a vicious cycle of increasingly higher investment rates at the expense of consumption.

An external imbalance refers to large surpluses in trade and the balance of payments as well as large foreign reserves accumulated from the export of low value-added goods. Such an imbalance will result in lower external economic profits, more pressures to appreciate the value of the RMB, and increased trade frictions. It will also lead to a monetary oversupply and higher inflationary pressures.

Ma: These imbalances are beyond the scope of short-term macroeconomic policies. They are related to shortcomings in the economic growth model. Whether a country can achieve sustained and steady growth usually will depend on the model it adopts. We will discuss this later.

DIALOGUE 16

UNFINISHED MARKET-ORIENTED REFORMS

Ma Guochuan (Ma): In the late 1970s China embarked on market-oriented reforms. After more than twenty years of ups and downs, a preliminary market-economy framework was established at the end of the twentieth century. This achievement undoubtedly was an important underpinning for the strong development of the Chinese economy. At present, many people are wondering about the role of the market in facilitating this growth: what path did China pursue and what mechanisms were utilized?

Wu Jinglian (Wu): The most important force has been the space created for entrepreneurship. The creativity that had been suppressed under the former system has now been released. Before the reform and opening, individuals who dared to engage in industrial and commercial activities were ruthlessly suppressed for attempting to "restore capitalism." After the mid-1980s, however, the government gradually relaxed market-entry restrictions for private businesses; in particular, the 1997 Fifteenth National Communist Party Congress recognized nonpublic-sector enterprises as an important part of the socialist market economy, thus providing room for private-sector development. By the end of the 1990s, as the long-suppressed entrepreneurial spirit of the Chinese people finally was flourishing more than 3,000 private businesses emerged. These firms are the fundamental drivers behind China's unexpected developmental achievements.

The second important force has been the more efficient use of previously underutilized human and physical resources. Under the command economy, in which the urban areas were insulated from the rural areas, industrialization was achieved via state mobilization of resources and forced investments, which significantly inhibited the pace of industrialization and urbanization, while also weakening the overall efficiency of the economy. When market institutions were established and private businesses were allowed to thrive, the factors of production began to move from less-efficient to more-efficient industries. Before this, 200 million people were underemployed in the rural areas. But during the reform and opening period, this surplus labor migrated to the cities and found industrial and commercial jobs.

The third force has been the opening, which has provided two powerful catalysts for China's economic development. The increased demand due to the opening supported the high growth rate. One problem of the former growth model was the declining consumption rate, which resulted in a lack of final demand. After China opened its doors, however, net exports increased dramatically. The trade surplus helped to compensate for weak domestic demand. In addition, the opening improved economic efficiency. Although China's capacity for innovation and technological upgrading was weak, the introduction of foreign technologies narrowed China's gap with the advanced countries. Technological progress has been another important factor contributing to the high growth rate.

Ma: Based on your analysis, the high economic growth rate since the reform and opening has been due not only to massive investments but also to improved efficiencies.

Wu: You are right. According to many scholars, since the beginning of the reform and opening economic efficiency, as measured by total factor productivity, has obviously improved. Whereas in the past it was negligible, the current total factor productivity contribution to GDP amounts to about 40 percent. In addition to the improved distribution of factor inputs, such as labor and land, the efficiency improvements can also be attributed to the introduction of advanced foreign technologies through joint ventures, foreign direct investments, and processing trade.

Ma: The economic miracle created by the market is undeniable. However, there are still various criticisms of China's market economy. What is your assessment of the current market economy?

Wu: It is a preliminary and incomplete system that was established at the end of the last century. It is burdened by many of the legacies of the former system. Furthermore, it is still rudimentary and lacks many of the important building blocks needed for a modern market economy. This system is far from a "sound market economy," as was noted by Tsinghua University Professor Qian Yingyi in 2000. Under the current system, the role of the government is still too strong and the market cannot fully play a basic role in the allocation of resources.

These were important motivations behind adoption of the "Decision of the CCP Central Committee on a Number of Issues Concerning the Improvement of the Socialist Market Economy" at the Third Plenary Session of the Sixteenth Communist Party Central Committee, held in October 2003. The decision confirms the establishment of a preliminary socialist market economy. Nevertheless, the decision also admits that "some problems still exist, such as an irrational economic structure, imbalanced distribution relations, sluggish growth of farmers' income, outstanding employment contradictions, intensified pressures on resources and the environment, and generally an uncompetitive economy." According to the decision, the main causes of these problems are that China is still at the primary stage of socialism: its economy still needs to be improved and development of the productive forces still faces many institutional obstacles. To eliminate these obstacles, the decision calls for accelerated reforms and the further liberation and development of the forces of production. The decision announced a series of reforms, focusing on the basic economic system, a modern market economy, administration of macroeconomic management, a legal framework, income distribution, and a social-security system.

Ma: But implementation of the decision has been far from ideal.

Wu: The pace of reform has been slow. In recent years the government's reins over the market have been enhanced, and in some areas there has even been a retreat from reform. Therefore, the current system can only be called a semi-command, semi-market economy.

Ma: Let us examine the main parts of this economic system.

Wu: We can start with the central part of market institutions: a competitive market system. Market exchanges are made by buyers and sellers who have freedom to make their own decisions regarding exchanges. Efficient resource allocations by the market are realized through exchanges at prices that reflect resource scarcities (that is, the equilibrium between supply and demand). Therefore, the degree of the market orientation can be measured by the level of autonomy and freedom for market exchanges. Viewed from this perspective, the basic state of China's market system is the following. In general, the market orientation is greater for goods and less for factors of production. Among goods, the prices of many means of production still remain under administrative controls. For instance, the 2003 power-sector reform program proposed the introduction of price competition for electricity transmission (access to power grids) and the separation of electricity transmission from electricity distribution. This program has not yet been implemented and, to date, the selling price of electricity has not yet been liberalized. The level of the market orientation for factors of production is even lower. Take the land market as an example. The market cannot operate properly because the minimum prerequisite is lacking—that is, clearly defined property rights. With respect to the credit market, basic prices—that is, interest rates—are controlled. The capital market is weak and cannot efficiently allocate capital. It will take a long time for this market to provide innovative products and strengthen the regulatory and supervisory framework.

Although a preliminary market economy has been established, it is still difficult for market mechanisms to play an effective role in resource allocations because of a lack of necessary rules and a lack of impartial enforcement as well as frequent administrative interventions.

Ma: The nature of market exchanges is the passing of property rights from sellers to buyers. Property rights are the foundation of market relationships. Therefore, as called for by the Fifteenth National Communist Party Congress, establishing a sound market system depends on making adjustments and improvements in the ownership structure.

Wu: With respect to the ownership system, land property rights have the most far-reaching influence because these affect most of the population. They are also of greatest concern to farmers. Land reform in the late 1940s and the early 1950s realized the goal of returning "land to the tiller," and hundreds of millions of farmers became masters of their own land. However, in the second half of the 1950s, during the period of cooperativization and the drive to establish people's communes, farmers no longer had direct control over land and privately owned land was turned over to the collectives. Since the late 1970s, household contracting has enabled farmers to establish family farms on contracted fields. However, they only receive land-use rights on contractual terms. Collective ownership of the land continues to exist. In 1993, in order to stabilize the farmers' income expectations from their contracted fields, the Communist Party decided to extend the contract terms to thirty years. Then, in 2008, the Communist Party declared that land contractual rights would remain in place for a long period of time.

Ma: However, extension of the contract terms is not equivalent to returning "land to the tiller." According to current laws, rural land is still collectively owned.

Wu: You are right. Farmers do not have permanent users' rights for the contracted land (what were called *surface rights* before 1949), nor can they pledge, transfer, or lease out these rights. This type of users' rights does not recognize the value created by investments in the land or land improvements because these rights do not appreciate in value. Therefore, farmers are lukewarm about protecting their cultivated land or investing in soil improvements. The relevant laws and regulations clearly state that contracting rights and homestead lots cannot be pledged for the purpose of borrowing, and they cannot be transferred across villages. The ability of farmers to mobilize funding to establish start-ups is restricted because the intangible assets of land-use rights are limited and cannot be converted into liquid capital.

A greater problem is that farmers do not have decision-making powers because of the shortcomings in the current system of village self-governance. In most places, land-use rights are controlled by village officials. When a local government acquires rural land, it is up to the local officials to decide whether or not to sell, what the price will be, and how the income will be distributed. Rural land is frequently confiscated at will or sold in breach of the laws and regulations. Farmers do not receive appropriate compensation from such transactions, thus triggering many "mass incidents."

Ma: Industrialization and urbanization in China have accelerated since the 1990s, and during this period a large amount of rural land has been acquired or expropriated. Much of the farmland has been converted for non-agricultural purposes. By taking advantage of rural officials' control over the land, local governments are able to acquire land at very low prices. The acquired land is then used for the wasteful projects, as noted in the preceding dialogues, or it is leased to industrial and commercial firms or real-estate developers. According to Yu Jianrong, a specialist on rural development, during the thirteen years between 1990 and 2002 non-agricultural projects used 47.36 million *mu* (1 *mu* equals 0.16 acres) of cultivated land, and about 66.3 million rural people lost their land and their means of livelihood. Many of these farmers became vagrants because the amount of compensation they received was insufficient to maintain their basic livelihoods or to start new businesses in the cities. Government income from these land transactions increasingly became the main source of extrabudgetary revenue.

Wu: The situation has become worse since the early 2000s. Take land transactions as an example. In 2005 governments at various levels sold 2.45 million *mu* of land. The total revenue from these transactions amounted to RMB 55 billion, or net income of RMB 21 billion, accounting for 15 percent of the total general revenue of the local governments. In 2010 government revenue from land sales amounted to RMB 2.9 trillion, or net income of RMB 1 trillion, accounting for 25 percent of the total general budget.

The dual-track pricing of land prompted local governments to increase their revenue by seizing and leasing land. Urban boundaries expanded much more rapidly than the growth of the urban population, causing occupancy rates in the cities to decline significantly and land resources to be wasted.

Government reliance on land transactions as a source of financing increased housing prices and widened the gap between the rich and the poor. It generated a trend to construct extravagant and magnificent halls and buildings, including government offices and residential mansions. Projects that were low in efficiency, easily exceeding RMB 100 million in value, were frequently implemented, leading to a huge amount of waste. This also produced an astonishing number of corrupt officials and business tycoons.

Ma: Compared to the rural reform, the process of the state-sector reform has been even more tortuous; there was really no progress at all until the late 1990s. The top economic priority of the 1997 Fifteenth National Communist Party Congress was to adjust and improve the ownership structure. The key was to allow state capital to advance in certain sectors, whereas it would retreat in others; that is, state capital would withdraw from the non-economic lifeline sectors (also called the *competitive sectors*).

Wu: The decision adopted at the 1997 National Communist Party Congress is very important because it clearly states two basic components of the reform of the state economy. The transformation includes not only the reform of the state-owned enterprises but also (and more importantly) the withdrawal of the state from the competitive sectors. Thereafter, some progress was made in the sectoral distribution of the state economy. In particular, by the turn of the century most local small and medium-sized enterprises had changed ownership and were no longer under state control. Nevertheless, the goal of establishing an improved ownership structure, as proposed at the Fifteenth National Communist Party Congress, has not yet been achieved.

According to the 1997 Communist Party decision, the state economy would retain a dominant role only in important industries and in key areas that are relevant to the national economic lifelines. In 1999, the Fourth Plenary Session of the Fifteenth Communist Party Central Committee further specified that the "important industries and key areas" are those sectors that involve state security, hold a natural monopoly, or provide important public goods and services as well as the pillar industries and the backbone enterprises in the high-tech sectors. Implementation of the Fifteenth National Communist Party Congress decision (allowing state capital to retreat from the competitive industries) began at the turn of the century. However, after the state retreated from small and medium-sized enterprises, the pace of the sectoral adjustments in the state economy slowed down, and in some areas the former system staged a comeback.

Ma: After 2004, doubts about the reform and opening began to gain traction and attempts to reverse the state-sector reform surfaced. The sectoral adjustments of the state economy slowed down.

Wu: On December 5, 2006, the General Office of the State Council circulated the Guidelines on State Capital Adjustments and State-Owned Enterprise Reorganizations, which was prepared by the State Assets Supervision and Administration Commission

(SASAC). The guidelines expanded the scope of the "important industries and key areas" as specified by the Fourth Plenary Session of the Fifteenth Communist Party Central Committee and mandated that the relevant ministries "waste no time in determining the specific industries and areas and in compiling the corresponding lists." Thirteen days later, the SASAC announced the lists of industries and sectors subject to control by state enterprises. These included the military industries, power grids and power generation, the oil and petrochemical sectors, telecommunications, the coal industry, civil aviation, and shipping. In these important key sectors, the state would "maintain absolute control." The backbone enterprises in the following sectors would be subject to "relatively strong control by the state": equipment manufacturing, automobile manufacturing, electronics and information technology, construction, iron and steel, ferrous metals, chemical products, survey and design, and science and technology.

The SASAC also announced that by 2010 the state would own a group of backbone enterprises that would be strong leaders in the development of the relevant sectors. Enterprises in the oil and petrochemical industry, telecommunications, the power sector, metallurgy, shipping, and construction were to become world-class companies. Enterprises in the automobile, machinery, and electronics industries were to establish a solid foundation to become world-class companies.

Ma: At the same time, economic resources were continuously injected into the SOEs. In 2009, in particular, in order to comply with the principle of "expanding the demand for growth," most of the resources for the stimulus package, including RMB 4 trillion in central-government appropriations and RMB 10 trillion in bank loans, went to the SOEs, especially those directly owned by the central government. Central-government enterprises gained a powerful monopolistic advantage in the energy, raw materials, transportation, telecommunications, and financial sectors. Benefiting from the possession of public-sector resources and administrative monopolies, the SOEs accumulated huge profits. But the dividends were not distributed to the state, which was the largest shareholder in these SOEs. Since the distribution of the profits remained at the discretion of the enterprises, the resources could not be used to satisfy the urgent need to strengthen public-sector services. According to the Ministry of Finance, in 2010 the SOE sector, including the state holding companies, realized total profits of RMB 1,987 billion, but it only handed over RMB 44 billion to the state, or the equivalent of 5 percent of its profits.

Wu: As the sectoral adjustments of the state economy stalled, the SOE reform was halted. A large number of primary-level companies (enterprise groups and the "remaining enterprises") were not restructured into corporations. As subordinates of "state authorized institutions for investment" (that is, primary-level companies), secondary-level companies (that is, listed companies) could not become truly independent legal entities. The remaining enterprises, which are still operating under the former system, are holding companies for listed firms, thus preventing the latter from becoming truly competitive in the market. In addition, most of the listed companies suffer from a weak corporate-governance structure. There are no checks and balances between owners and managers. In some companies, the governance structure exists in name only, and some have become subject to insider control by management.

Ma: Apparently, the widely existing state-proprietary enterprises and the high proportion of state-holding shares have adversely affected the SOE reform and are one of the reasons for the standstill in the sectoral adjustments of state capital.

Wu: The experience of various countries long ago proved that it is very difficult, if not entirely impossible, to establish an effective corporate-governance structure in enterprises where the state is the controlling shareholder or has absolute control. Therefore, in accordance with the decision of the 1997 Fifteenth National Communist Party Congress, in order to improve SOE corporate governance, great efforts should be made to withdraw state capital from the competitive industries. Based on the "Decision on Several Major Issues Concerning the Reform and Development of State-Owned Enterprises," adopted by the Fourth Plenary Session of the Fifteenth Communist Party Central Committee in 1999, nonstate capital should be introduced into those enterprises in which state capital will remain; thereafter, effective corporate governance can be achieved on the basis of diversified shareholdings.

However, because most of the primary-level companies are proprietarily owned by the state and report directly to the SASAC, some industries are monopolized by a few companies under the same owner. They are said to compete with each other, but there is a revolving door for their senior executives to change jobs.

These abnormalities show that effective corporate governance and rule-based market competition have not yet been established in these industries.

Ma: Because of the incomplete reforms, the operational efficiency of the SOEs has not improved significantly, although the SASAC has tried to enhance its monitoring of the SOEs, even exceeding the power of the owners as stipulated by The Company Law. Serious cases of corruption in these SOEs have frequently shocked the entire country.

Take SINOPEC Group, a "super-company of the central government," as an example. Chen Tonghai, SINOPEC's long-time vice president from 1999 to 2007, squandered a daily average of RMB 40,000 of the company's money. He accepted a confirmed RMB 149.7 million in bribes. He is known to have said, "Compared to the

RMB 200 billion that I pay in taxes every year, these monies are peanuts." To a large extent, the profits of these types of enterprises come from their free use of resources controlled by the state and their monopoly over the market. But Chen asks, "If we, the first-born sons of the People's Republic, do not hold a monopoly, who else should?"

Even more shocking to taxpayers is the case of corruption by Liu Zhijun, former minister of railways, and his cohorts. Shortly after Liu was investigated, seven other senior officials in the ministry were dismissed on charges of corruption involving railway investment projects. Although there are no officially confirmed statistics, it is estimated that Liu and his collaborators collected as much as RMB 1 billion in bribes. The Ministry of Railways is a remaining "fortress" of the command economy that mixes administrative functions with business functions. The ministry has been dragging its feet in terms of reform. Even though it has been the target of popular criticism, it is still horrifying to see the emergence of such a huge case of corruption.

Wu: After 2006, except in a few places, such as Shanghai, that continued to withdraw state capital from some industries, the main objectives of most of the line ministries and localities was to "enhance control by the state economy."

In the aftermath of the 2008 global financial crisis, under the policy aimed at expanding domestic demand to stimulate growth, trillions of RMB in fiscal and bank funding was provided to central-government enterprises and local-government financing platforms. Because the central-government enterprises received more funding, the local governments tried to form alliances with them so as to increase their own political achievements. With their deep pockets, many central-government companies rushed to seize local markets. According to incomplete statistics found on the websites of the SASAC and the National Development and Reform Commission, the total value of investment agreements of central-government companies in various regions jumped forty-two-fold within three years, from RMB 0.26 trillion in 2008 to RMB 11.38 trillion in 2011. These investments covered almost all of the departments in the national economy.

Because the sectoral adjustments of state capital have been halted, or even reversed, it is difficult to realize the objective of establishing a unified, open, and orderly market economy with rule-based competition, as set forth by the Third Plenary Session of the Sixteenth Communist Party Central Committee in 2003.

As early as December 3, 2001, after China became a World Trade Organization (WTO) member and committed to gradually providing national treatment to foreign investments, the General Office of the State Council ordered in an official document that the domestic private sector should be allowed and encouraged to invest in industries that were open to foreign investment. In 2002, the Sixteenth National Communist Party Congress called for "giv[ing] full scope to the important role of the nonpublic sector of self-employed, private, and other forms of ownership of the economy in stimulating economic growth, creating more jobs, and activating the market. We should expand areas for the market access of domestic nongovernmental capital and adopt measures with regard to investment, financing, taxation, land use, [and] foreign trade." The 2003 Third Plenary Session of the Sixteenth Communist Party Central Committee decided to "remove or revise such laws, regulations, and policies that are against developing the nonpublic sectors of the economy and eliminate the institutional obstacles thereto. The areas should be expanded for market access of nonpublic capital, which will be permitted to go to the infrastructures, public undertakings, and other industries and fields where the inflow of such capital is not prohibited by the laws and regulations. Nonpublic enterprises should be treated equally with other enterprises in terms of investment, financing, land use, and foreign trade."

In 2007, the Seventeenth National Communist Party Congress reiterated the need to protect property rights equally so as to have fair competition and mutual promotion among businesses of different ownerships. The State Council also adopted a series of measures to protect citizens' market-entry rights. In 2005 and 2010, respectively, the State Council promulgated two thirty-six-article directives on encouraging, supporting, and guiding the development of the private sector. However, implementation has been a problem. Owing to resistance from the force of habit in the command economy and rent-seeking interests, market-entry restrictions on private businesses still remain in many areas. In more recent years, backpedaling in terms of "further advances by the state and more retreats by the private sector" has occurred in some localities and industries.

Ma: The retreats have taken two main forms. In some industries, private-sector firms are not allowed to continue their operations even though they have received business permits. In addition, some state proprietary companies or enterprises under complete state control have acquired or taken over private-sector firms, further enhancing their monopolies.

Apart from the squeezed space for development, the business environment for the private sector is also unsatisfactory because of a prevalent disregard for credibility, rule-less deals, dishonesty, and fraud. Chambers of commerce should be self-governing organizations, but they have been given industrial administrative responsibilities and thus have been transformed into quasi-government agencies. Their role to protect the interests of businesspeople has been weakened.

Wu: In recent years, the government's access to resources has been increasing rather than decreasing. Administrative powers are not subject to effective monitoring or to checks and balances. Under these circumstances, corruption inevitably has become more widespread. Private businessmen have drifted with the current, and collaboration with those in power has become a rational choice. Instead of working on new ideas and innovations, many entrepreneurs have tried to "make friends" with government officials in exchange for receiving privileged treatment and extra resources. The collusion between government and business is becoming worse.

Ma: Some businessmen have even copied the cunning techniques of the "red-hat merchants" (referring to those businesspeople in the Qing dynasty who had close ties with the imperial government) in an attempt to become rich through exchanges of money for power. Their behavior has seriously undermined market rules, damaged business ethics, and threatened the normal functioning of the market economy. This is the main reason why the plague of crony capitalism has spread.

Wu: Because of interventions by those in power, government-business collusion has weakened the equal protection of owners' rights by market mechanisms, protected the interests of the minority at the expense of the majority, and trampled on the principles of fairness and equality. This phenomenon is rooted in the unrestrained power that exists in many areas. To prevent private businesses from colluding with government officials and engaging in rent seeking, the key is to establish a rule-based market economy. Of course, private businessmen should have a strong sense of social responsibility and should distance themselves from the government and government businesses. However, in the Chinese situation it would be more effective if the government were to take the initiative to clean up its own house and promote further reforms.

In a nutshell, after more than thirty years the market-oriented reforms have registered unprecedented achievements and have established a preliminary institutional basis for the rapid growth of the Chinese economy. However, the reforms have not achieved a final success and many obstacles still remain. Take the preliminary market-economy framework as an example. It is incomplete because it has serious defects. The most prominent problem is the dominant role of the government and the SOEs in terms of resource allocations.

More specifically, these defects include: (a) An incomplete market system due to a lag in the development of the factors markets, obscured property rights for land, and controlled interest rates; (b) Although it does not hold the lion's share of GDP, the state sector controls all the commanding heights of the economy. SOEs monopolize important industries, including oil, telecommunications, railways, and the financial sector; (c) Various government agencies hold great powers over the allocation of land, funds, and other important economic resources; and (d) The rule of law, which is indispensable to a modern market economy, has not been established. Government officials have a huge amount of discretion and frequently interfere in enterprise operations at the microeconomic level through the licensing of investment projects, administrative permits for market entry, and price controls.

Ma: What do you mean by the "commanding heights"?

Wu: The term was first used by Lenin in 1922 to indicate the key sectors that could sway the direction of the national economy. In 1921, in response to the "war communism" difficulties (1918–21), the Communist Party of the Soviet Union (USSR) began to implement the New Economic Policy, which sought to restore a market economy and to move to state capitalism. This was considered to be a retreat from the war communism. At the time, many Communists did not understand the new policy and worried that it would threaten the Communist future of the USSR and the ruling position of the Communist Party. In November 1922, at the Fourth Congress of the Communist International, Lenin addressed these doubts. He explained that the state capitalism being implemented in the USSR was a special type. As the state was in control of all the "commanding heights," that is, land and the most important industrial sectors, it could ensure that economic activities would be undertaken according to the requirements of the state. Furthermore, the state could adjust policy at will. Therefore, this type of state capitalism was not at all dangerous to the Soviet Communist Party. In the Chinese versions of Lenin's works, the term "commanding heights" is translated as "economic lifelines."

Ma: Lenin highlighted the need to control the "commanding heights" because the New Economic Policy represented only a temporary retreat from his state-syndicate model, or the "Party-State, Inc." He also expected that when the time was ripe, the Soviet economy would return to a command economy. If his use of the term is excusable, then it is difficult to understand why the Chinese state, which has engaged in market-oriented reforms since the late 1970s, still needs to occupy the commanding heights.

The Chinese Communist Party's Fourteenth National Communist Party Congress designated the economic reform objective of establishing a socialist market economy. Thereafter, an overall plan to create a socialist market economy and to establish the reform priorities developed gradually. Subsequent reforms should have aimed to move in the direction of this objective. But why did the reforms stop when they were only halfway through?

Wu: This question is worth exploring. To me, the current situation is due to a lack of conceptual or theoretical clarity. In addition, it can be attributed to the rent-seeking privileged interests.

With the benefit of hindsight, it is clear that the consensus on reform that formed in the second half of the 1980s lacked clarity.

During that period, the influence of the Eastern European reform model, which was very popular during the initial phase of China's reforms, began to diminish. Two other models became influential in terms of the final goal of the reforms. The first was the government-led market-economy model (i.e., the East Asian model). The other was the free market-economy model (i.e., the European and US model). The East Asian model was developed after World War II in Japan, South Korea, Singapore, and Taiwan (China). Combining authoritarian government with a market economy, the latter had formed a government-led mercantilist market economy. They implemented an authoritarian development model under the leadership of developmental-oriented governments. In this model, the government used industrial policies and administrative guidance to coordinate, plan, and intervene in the economy. Such a model was very attractive to China. During the initial phase of the reform and opening, many Chinese government officials visited Japan and other areas in East Asia to study the model. Once back home, they introduced these new economic systems, development policies, and government role. This had a huge impact. The European and US model was shared by mature market-economy countries. According to modern economics, the basic role of government in a market economy is to provide public goods rather than to offer private goods in the market. Excessive government interventions will impede the effective functioning of the market and foster corruption. With the increase in the number of people who understand modern economics, this model is becoming more influential. Even in East Asian countries such as Japan, there have been calls for a shift from the authoritarian government-led model to the free market-economy model.

During discussions of the reform objectives in the mid-1980s, most government officials were in favor of the East Asian model. Deng Xiaoping himself was highly appreciative of the Four Little Dragons (Hong Kong, South Korea, Singapore, and Taiwan [China]). In particular, he praised Singapore's model of developing a market economy managed by a powerful government while maintaining strict social order. Academics, especially those trained in modern economics, preferred the European and US model. However, these academics also recognized that when market forces are not yet in place, the government should play a greater coordinating role. Therefore, if there was a consensus regarding the economic reforms in the late 1980s, it supported the establishment of a milestone in terms of the reforms, that is, a government-led market economy similar to the East Asian model.

The official documents of the time were all influenced by the government-led development model. This can be seen in the 1984 decision of the Third Plenary Session of the Twelfth Communist Party Central Committee, which established the "socialist, planned commodity economy" as the objective of the reform. Belief in this model was also behind the adoption by the 1987 Thirteenth National Communist Party Congress of an earlier proposal by some economists in the State Planning Commission, who defined the "operating mechanism" of the socialist planned commodity economy as "letting the state regulate the market and the market provide guidance for the enterprises."

Ma: In a speech at the 2011 World Conference of the International Economic Association, you pointed out that under the Chinese model, government dominance was more extensive than in Japan and elsewhere in East Asia. This point should be highlighted. Under the other East Asian economic development models, such as that in Japan, government interventions were made mainly through the central bank's "window guidance" on bank lending, or by the industrial policy guidance of the Ministry of International Trade and Industry (in Japan). Government in these countries did not directly operate businesses. In China, a somewhat different system evolved from the Leninist state-syndicate model. Under the Chinese system, the huge state apparatus directly managed the national economy and the powerful state sector controlled the economic lifelines. State-sector control over the economy and state-sector interventions were more direct and forceful. This was a semi-command, semi-market system.

Wu: During that period and thereafter, I did not fully recognize the strong influence of the traditional Soviet-type command economy and the role of an omnipotent government. I thought that with the steady development of the market, there could be a smooth transition from a government-led market economy to a mature market economy (what I call a "market economy based on rule of law under political civilization"). As a matter of fact, the basis and the starting point of China's model was the Leninist state syndicate, or the integrated "Party-State, Inc.," as referred to by the Eastern European socialist reformers. Furthermore, the privileged interest groups that were fostered by the dual-track institutions have tried their best to obstruct the transition toward a rule–of–law–based market economy. Huge forces are maintaining and expanding state control. A little slack in the reform efforts will lead to government dominance over the dual existence of a command economy and a market economy.

Ma: As you reiterated several times at the end of the 1990s, once this type of economic system is put in place, it will face two possible futures. Under the first scenario, the government will phase out its interventions in microeconomic activities and strengthen its role when the market fails, such as its role to regulate the market and to provide public goods. The country will thereby gradually become a rule-based modern market economy. The other scenario is to continuously enforce government control and its interventions in the market. A possible future under this scenario will be a continuous entrenchment of state-sector monopolies and state capitalism whereby the government controls socioeconomic development.

Wu: This has been proven by our recent history. At the end of the 1990s, when one million township and village enterprises (owned by county and township governments) were transformed into private businesses, when most of the state-controlled secondary-level enterprises were reorganized into companies held by diversified shareholders and listed on stock markets at home and abroad, and when China gained access to global markets after joining the WTO, the forces of the market were significantly strengthened, industrial and agricultural production and international trade recorded robust growth, and a satisfactory mood prevailed within the society.

However, when the reforms were halted or even reversed and when government control and the dominant role of the state sector were reinforced, the inclination toward state capitalism became ever more obvious.

DIALOGUE 17

WITHOUT POLITICAL REFORM, ECONOMIC REFORM WILL NOT SUCCEED

Ma Guochuan (Ma): Our last dialogue showed that almost all the obstacles to the market-economy reforms have been related to the government and the state sector. If there is no reform of the government, it will be impossible to complete the reform of the economic system. In 1986 Deng Xiaoping said, "If we do not institute a reform of our political structure, it will be difficult to carry out the reform of our economic structure." This comment is indicative of a consensus at that time. However, beginning in the 1990s Deng's comment was just about forgotten, and in more recent years an opposite view has been emerging. Some people began promoting the so-called "China model." According to this model, the Communist Party and the government play a dominant role in society, and the state sector retains a tight grasp over the important and pillar industries, although the private sector is still allowed to engage in economic activities. These are the supposed advantages of the so-called "China model."

It seems to me that from both a theoretical and pragmatic perspective, this issue should be clarified.

Wu Jinglian (Wu): I think Deng Xiaoping's comment makes sense, and I do not agree with those people who promote the so-called "China model."

The following are my main arguments. In any society, politics and economics are inseparable. The two must collaborate closely and be capable of adapting to one another. Under the Soviet-style Communist system, the centrally planned economy coexisted with an omnipotent, highly centralized government. The goal of our economic reforms is to change the economic system, but the political system will need to be changed as well.

Ma: In the previous dialogues we described China's economic system prior to the reforms. Such a system was what Lenin called a "state syndicate," or what the Eastern European economists called the "Party-State, Inc." By default, the political superstructure of the economic system was what Lenin referred to as a *proletarian dictatorship*.

Wu: In his important work "Problems of Leninism," Stalin provided an authoritative explanation of Lenin's proletarian dictatorship.

According to Stalin, this dictatorship would be realized by a tightly organized political system. It was composed of a "directing force" and mechanisms consisting of several "transmission belts" and "levers." The "directing force" referred to the Communist Party, which was said to be "the vanguard of the proletariat." The "transmission belts" and "levers" were the "proletarian organizations of the broadest masses," including: (a) state agencies in the administrative, economic, military, and cultural areas; (b) trade unions; (c) cooperatives of production and consumption; and (d) the Communist Youth League.

The Leninist-Stalinist political system imposed an "iron dictatorship" that was highly centralized.

A distinctive feature of this system was its "direct resort to violence without being constrained by any law." As Lenin stressed between 1918 and 1920, "dictatorship means unlimited power, based on force, and not on law."

The Leninist-Stalinist proletarian dictatorship was also characterized by highly centralized political power. The Communist Party, or the "leading force," was the center of various organizations. As Lenin put it, the Communist Party controls political power and manages the state; in this sense, what we understand as proletarian dictatorship is in essence dictatorship by an organized minority of the proletariat with a level of consciousness. Lenin also believed that to be able to play the leading role, the Communist Party had to be organized in accordance with the principles of strict centralization and subject to personal dictatorship. To quote Lenin: "That in the history of revolutionary movements, the dictatorship of individuals was very often the expression, the vehicle, the channel of the dictatorship of the revolutionary classes has been shown by the irrefutable experience of history"; "There is, therefore, absolutely *no* contradiction in principle between Soviet (that is, socialist) democracy and the exercise of dictatorial powers by individuals; and "Our whole task [is to] lead . . . along the path of coordinating the task of arguing at mass meetings about the conditions of work with the task of unquestioningly obeying the will of the Soviet leader, of the dictator."

Ma: Lenin also remarked, "Everybody knows that the masses are divided by classes; . . . that usually, and in the majority of cases at least in modern civilized countries, classes are led by political parties; that political parties, as a general rule, are directed by more or less stable groups composed of the most authoritative, influential, and experienced members, who are elected to the most responsible positions and are called leaders. All this is elementary."

Wu: It is crystal clear that the political system of proletarian dictatorship and the state-syndicate economic system were linked and mutually reinforcing. The former used compulsory force to establish, organize, and defend the state syndicate and, in turn, the latter provided the economic foundation for the proletarian dictatorship. The Communist Party and its leaders, as the core leading force, relied on a comprehensive system of proletarian dictatorship to maintain absolute control over the state syndicate and the society.

Ma: The Leninist-Stalinist proletarian dictatorship was fundamentally different from the "communities of free men" envisaged by Marx and Engels. Could it be the case that no one in the International Communist Movement opposed this Soviet political model?

Wu: There was some opposition. Karl Kautsky, leader of the Democratic Socialist Party of Germany, was opposed to "one-party dictatorship," but he was criticized for "being revisionist." Rosa Luxemburg, one of the founders of the Comintern (an acronym for the Communist International, the name given to the Third International, founded in Moscow in 1919), also opposed the model. Like Lenin, Luxemburg was in favor of imposing dictatorship over those bourgeoisie who resisted the revolution. At the same time, she pointed out that this dictatorship should not rule out democracy or restrict freedom of speech or freedom of the press. For her, "without unrestricted freedom of press and assembly, without a free struggle of opinion, life dies out in every public institution, becomes a mere semblance of life, in which only the bureaucracy remains as the active element. Public life gradually falls asleep; a few dozen party leaders of inexhaustible energy and boundless experience direct and rule. Among them, in reality only a dozen outstanding heads do the leading and an elite of the working class is invited from time to time to meetings where they are to applaud the speeches of the leaders, and to approve proposed resolutions unanimously—at bottom, then, a clique affair—a dictatorship, to be sure, not the dictatorship of the proletariat but only the dictatorship of a handful of politicians, that is a dictatorship in the bourgeois sense, in the sense of the rule of the Jacobins. . . . Yes, we can go even further: such conditions must inevitably cause a brutalization of public life: attempted assassinations, shooting of hostages, and so forth. . . . That is an overpowering objective law from which no party can be exempt." Unfortunately, Luxemburg's suggestions were rejected by Lenin and other leaders of the Soviet Communist Party.

Ma: How accurate Luxemburg's predictions were! Stalin's Great Purge (1936–38) was a typical case of the brutalization of public life. Leon Trotsky and Nikolai Bukharin, who had been Lenin's comrades-in-arms, met tragic deaths during Stalin's dictatorship. The collapse of the Soviet Union was by no means accidental.

Wu: When the Leninist-Stalinist doctrine of proletarian dictatorship was first introduced to China, several Chinese Communist Party leaders questioned the core doctrine that puts the Communist Party above the state and allows the Communist Party to govern the state.

Ma: These principles were first introduced from the Soviet Union by Dr. Sun Yatsen in the early 1920s. In 1924 Dr. Sun spoke at the First National Congress of the Kuomintang (KMT, i.e., the Chinese Nationalist Party that ruled China from 1928 to 1949). When proposing the establishment of a Nationalist government, Sun pointed out that there was only one example from which to learn. Compared to the political parties in Britain, the United States, and France, the Soviet Party possessed more power. "We must use the party to construct the State. It is fair to say that the success [of the Russian Revolution] is due to the priority given to the party over the State. . . . We must reorganize ourselves and place the party above the State." In 1928, when the Nationalist Party assumed power in China, it copied the Soviet model and established a party-government system.

Wu: After this model was introduced into China, quite a few Chinese Communist Party leaders opposed it. In 1928, shortly after the Jinggangshan revolutionary base area (the birthplace of the main forces of the Chinese Red Army) was established, Mao Zedong pointed out that "the Kuomintang's wrong practice of directly imposing orders on the government must be avoided." In 1929, Zhou Enlai said that " 'let[ting] the Party take charge of everything' is illogical in principle as well as in practice." In 1940, Liu Shaoqi stated that "in opposing the Kuomintang's one-party dictatorship, the Communist Party's intention is not to establish one of its own." In 1941, Deng Xiaoping sharply criticized the Nationalist Party model, stating "The concept of 'ruling the country by the party,' held by some comrades, is a manifestation in our Party of an abominable tradition of the Kuomintang. . . . As a matter of fact, this is the easiest way to paralyze and corrupt the Party and alienate the masses. . . . We oppose the one-party dictatorship of the Kuomintang, which is characterized by one party running the country. We should especially prevent the pernicious influence of the Kuomintang from spreading to our Party."

Things began to change in 1942. On September 1, 1942, the Central Committee of the Chinese Communist Party adopted the "Decision on Centralized Leadership and Adjustment of Relations among the Party Organs in the Anti-Japanese Areas" (the "September 1 decision"). The decision required the establishment of centralized

Communist Party committees to lead everything, including Communist Party organizations, the government, the military, and mass organizations. Based on this decision, a Party-government leadership system was established in the areas governed by the Communist Party. After 1949, this system rapidly spread throughout the entire country.

Ma: At present, a question for the reforms is whether the Leninist-Stalinist political system should be retained even after the economic foundation of Chinese society has been fundamentally altered and there is no choice but to continuously improve the market-economy system.

Wu: The transition from a planned economy to a market economy in China has been achieved through reform rather than revolution. In other words, the transformation has been achieved gradually under the leadership of the Communist Party in power and the government. This approach has avoided large-scale social unrest because the economic reforms have taken place against the backdrop of a stable sociopolitical environment. Nevertheless, changes in the economic system will inevitably bring changes to the social structure, thus requiring political and cultural changes and changes to other aspects of the superstructure. If there is no reform of the superstructure so that it is compatible with the economic base, tensions and conflicts will arise between the two. In such a case, it will not be possible to smoothly accomplish the economic reforms.

Ma: Let's put aside the debate on the merits of the Leninist-Stalinist political system. In China there is a view that one of the advantages of the Chinese reforms is that the basic political system has been maintained. According to this view, the national leaders intentionally sequenced the reforms to first change the economic system and then later to change the political system. What is your opinion about this?

Wu: The history of the reforms shows that this view is inconsistent with the facts. As early as the onset of the reforms of the economic system, the national leaders raised the question of political reforms. Subsequently, efforts were made to initiate a reform of the political system, but on each occasion the flames of political reforms were extinguished. Although the lack of political reforms has indeed slowed the pace of the overall reforms, I do not believe this was a premeditated reform strategy.

Ma: From a historical perspective, your view does make sense. We all know the first official reform step was the circulation by the Communist Party Central Committee, on September 27, 1980, of the "Summary of the First Party Secretaries Conference," which recognized the practice of household contracting for farmers. A bit earlier, at an August 18, 1980 Politburo meeting, Deng Xiaoping delivered a speech entitled "On the Reform of the System of Party and State Leadership." In it, Deng pointed out that for a long time China had been under the influence of a feudal autocracy; during the period of the Communist International, there had been a tradition of a high concentration of power in the hands of individual Communist Party leaders in the various countries; and there had also been a longstanding belief that a socialist society must be managed by a highly centralized system. Deng said that because of these factors, and based on the slogan calling for a strengthening of the leading role of the Communist Party, all powers in China were centralized in Party committees, which, in turn, saw their powers centralized in individual Communist Party secretaries. This system created many problems in the political life of the Communist Party and the state, thereby requiring major reforms. According to Deng, the following major reforms were necessary: (a) The Constitution should be made more complete and precise so as to ensure the people's rights to manage state organs at all levels as well as the various enterprises and organizations; (b) The regular executive bodies of the State Council should become more compact and efficient. A truly effective work system should be set up for the State Council and the various levels of local government. All matters within the capability of the government should be discussed and decided upon, and the relevant documents issued, by the State Council and the local governments concerned. The Central Committee and local committees of the Communist Party should no longer issue directives or make decisions on such matters; (c) Management committees or boards of directors should be introduced in all enterprises and institutions. Under this new system, managers will report to these bodies rather than to the Communist Party committees; and (d) Communist Party committees at all levels should genuinely apply the principle of combining collective leadership. Major issues must be discussed and decided upon by the collective rather than by a Communist Party secretary. This was the main focus of Deng's famous August 18 speech, which can be considered the first official announcement on the reform of the Chinese political system.

Wu: Deng's speech was approved by the Politburo on August 31, 1980. However, in 1981 and 1982, before the reforms were initiated, the traditional ideology staged a comeback, which represented the first of several rounds of such resurgences during the reform era. The 1982 Twelfth National Communist Party Congress upheld the dominant role of the planned economy and assigned a supplementary role to market regulation. Although Deng's call had been approved by the Politburo, reform of the political system was not implemented.

By the mid-1980s, when the economic reforms were intensifying, the lack of reform of the political system increasingly became an obstacle to the continuation of the economic reforms and it created a hotbed of corruption. In summarizing the 1989 political turbulence, Deng Xiaoping said that the increase in corruption was one of the reasons behind the unrest, and because of this, some people among the general public had lost confidence in the Communist Party and the reforms. As a matter of fact, toward the end of the 1980s national leaders had increasingly come to realize that without political reforms, the results of the economic reforms could not be protected or promoted. In 1986 Deng repeatedly called for reforming the political system. He said that "when we first raised the question of reform we had in mind, among other things, reform of the political structure. . . . This question should be put on the agenda"; "the necessity of reforming the political structure, including the need to separate the functions of the Party and the government and to delegate powers to lower levels. . . . The reform of the political structure and the reform of the economic structure are interdependent and should be coordinated. Without political reform, economic reform cannot succeed. . . . So in the final analysis, the success of all our other reforms depends on the success of the political reform." Deng also specifically instructed that "we must set a starting date—one that is not too far off. At the National Communist Party Congress next year, we shall draw up a plan." Deng proposed, "We must separate the functions of the Party from those of the government. . . . [But] we must uphold the leadership of the Party. . . . This is the key and should be given top priority."

Following Deng's instructions, and after almost a year of study and preparations for the Thirteenth National Communist Party Congress in October–November 1987, reform of the political system was put on the agenda for the congress. According to the Thirteenth National Communist Party Congress, the reform would gradually improve socialist democracy and the socialist legal system, overcome bureaucracy and the influence of feudalism, and promote the reform of the economic system and the domestic and external opening.

Guided by Deng Xiaoping's comments, the Thirteenth National Communist Party Congress pointed out that the key to political reform was to first separate the role of the Communist Party from the functions of government, which would be the focal point of the reform. The basic requirements were that after the reform "the Party must conduct its activities within the limits prescribed by the Constitution and those laws"; it "should respect mass organizations, enterprises, and institutions and not monopolize the conduct of their affairs"; and "the principal method by which it exercises political leadership in state affairs is . . . through legal procedures [whereby] what the Party advocates becomes the will of the state, and the people are mobilized by the Party organizations and the good example of Party members." Based on these principles, the following measures were to be taken: Party committees would no longer consist of a secretary or a standing committee member who was given responsibility to provide oversight of the government but did not hold an administrative position in the government; the Party leading groups in the ministries would gradually be removed; the Party organizations in enterprises and in non-enterprise institutions would no longer exert "centralized leadership"; the Party's disciplinary committees would concentrate on managing Party discipline and the working style of the Party, and would not handle judicial cases or those involving government discipline; and those Party organizations that reported directly to the Party organizations of higher-level administrative agencies would gradually be subject to the leadership of the local Party committees. These measures were to be implemented beginning in 1988.

Ma: The goal of the decision of the Thirteenth National Communist Party Congress on the reform of the political system was to seek progress while maintaining stability. But those people entrenched in the former political line were opposed to these changes. Shortly after the reforms were initiated, they were interrupted by the 1989 political turbulence. After the political turbulence was over, doubts were raised about the direction of the reforms that had been implemented since the 1978 Third Plenary Session of the Eleventh Party Central Committee. The political report of the Thirteenth National Communist Party Congress was criticized for its "bourgeois liberalization." Although Deng Xiaoping insisted that the political report had been adopted by the congress and that not a single word in it should be changed, many of the reform measures were halted and the former system remained in place.

Wu: The reform of the political system is both a necessity for the establishment of a market economy and a safeguard for a smooth social transformation in China.

For instance, as early as the end of 1990s when a preliminary framework for a market economy came into being, people felt strongly that this system would not function properly if it were not based on the rule of law.

Modern economics offers an analysis of the dependence of modern market institutions on the rule of law. During the early developmental stage of market-economy institutions, exchanges take place among acquaintances. Bilateral and multilateral concerns with respect to reputations and punishments among acquaintances are effective in ensuring the implementation of contracts. But with the expansion of the market, many transactions become nonpersonal exchanges among strangers. In these circumstances, the previous means of honoring contracts are no longer effective. A legal system that is widely recognized as ethical and a judicial system that is fair and independent become indispensable for the implementation of contracts. Take the services sector as an example. Because of the difficulty of verifying certain features of a service, perfect contracts may be impossible. An effective legal system will obviously be conducive to implementing contracts and to completing transactions in this sector. Similarly, it is only under such a system that enterprises will be forced to make technological improvements in order to remain competitive. Their profit-seeking activities will then be directed toward making innovations that will be expected to create hundreds of thousands of new technologies, both big and small. Without such a legal system, swindlers would dominate and maneuver to corner the market. In seeking profits, enterprises would form alliances with administrative powers and mafia forces, waste their energy and resources, and engage in rent seeking. This would erode the efficiency of the overall economy and weaken its capability to achieve long-term development.

Amid these concerns, after years of silence on the subject, national leaders once again brought up the necessity for political reforms. On October 29, 1997, the Fifteenth National Communist Party Congress adopted the overall objective of the political reforms, which was to expand socialist democracy and establish a socialist rule of law, as well as to govern the country based on law and to develop a socialist political system based on rule of law. In addition to reiterating this objective, the Sixteenth National Communist Party Congress in 2002 also called for developing democracy and enhancing political civilization. The 2003 "Decision of the CCP Central Committee on a Number of Issues Concerning the Improvement of the Socialist Market Economy" noted the need to coordinate reform of the economic system with reform of the political system, and to actively promote political reform in a safe and sound way. However, because there was a lack of concrete measures, progress lagged behind the desires of the general public.

Ma: This recollection of the recent past shows that implementation of political reform in China is still struggling, despite a general consensus among the public and the decisions of the Party in power. One cannot help but ask: Why is it so difficult to abandon the former political system and to replace it with a new system?

Wu: For me, there are two main reasons, which are similar to the reasons for the difficulties in implementing the economic reforms. First, on the ideological front, many people within the Party still believe that the Leninist-Stalinist political system should not be changed and should be upheld unconditionally, as if it were the mandate of heaven. Second, and more importantly, whether this system is maintained is related to the power and interests of certain public officials.

Ma: It appears that in 1942, the wartime environment was the reason the Party-government system under the unified leadership of Party committees was adopted. As a matter of fact, the program for the establishment of New Democracy, which was later proposed by the Party, was somewhat different from this wartime political system. In his 1945 political report to the Seventh National Communist Party Congress, Mao Zedong outlined a program to form a government made up of a democratic coalition and to establish an "independent, free, democratic, unified, and prosperous new China." Later, on October 10, 1947, in the "Declaration by the People's Liberation Army," which had been drafted by Mao, Mao reiterated that after the Chiang Kaishek government was overthrown, the Communist Party would unite with all the oppressed classes of workers, peasants, soldiers, students, and businessmen, all the people's organizations, all the democratic parties, all the ethnic minorities, overseas Chinese, and other patriots to form a democratic coalition government; and Chiang's dictatorship would be replaced by a people's democracy that would safeguard freedom of speech, the press, assembly, and association for the people.

Wu: At the time when the Party introduced the theory of New Democracy, it considered it to be a transitional phase, rather than a stand-alone and stable social state. Although nonsocialist elements would exist during this phase in both the economic and the political spheres, the socialist elements would be decisive. The transition to complete socialism would depend on the objective situation and the will of the socialist elements. In 1953, when criticizing a slogan coined by senior Communist Party leader Liu Shaoqi calling to "consolidate the New Democracy order," Mao said that during a period of transition, changes take place daily and new socialist elements are born every day. Therefore, it would be difficult to "enforce" a New Democracy.

A little more than one month after the "Declaration by the People's Liberation Army" was issued, Mao suggested, in a telegram to Stalin sent on November 30, 1947, that a one-party government be established after the Communist Party assumed power. He wrote that after the victory of the Chinese Revolution, the examples of the Soviet Union and Yugoslavia would be followed: all parties, with the exception of the Communist Party, would exit from the political stage. However, Stalin thought the time was not yet ripe and in his return telegram, he opposed this idea; thus the proposal was temporarily shelved. In the 1949 Common Program of the Chinese People's Political Consultative Conference, which was the de facto interim constitution of the new People's Republic, the transition from New Democracy to socialism was not stated explicitly. The nature of the new government was defined as a people's democratic dictatorship, led by the working class and based on an alliance of workers and peasants and uniting all democratic classes and all nationalities in China.

Ma: After the People's Republic was established, government organizations remained largely in the form of a democratic coalition, consistent with the provisions of the Common Program. Noncommunist Party members held about one-half of the leadership positions in the government. For instance, among the six state vice presidents, three were not Communist Party members, and among the four vice premiers of the State Council, two were not Party members.

Wu: But this situation did not last for long. After completion of land reform and the beginning of negotiations to reach an armistice in the Korean War, Stalin decided that the time was finally ripe for China to move to a one-party government. In October 1952, Stalin asked Liu Shaoqi, who was then visiting the USSR, to pass on to the Chinese Communist Party his recommendation that the Common Program be replaced by a constitution and elections be held in order to shift to a Soviet-style one-party government. The Central Committee of the Chinese Communist Party accepted this recommendation. In 1954, the promulgation of the Constitution of the People's Republic of China and the subsequent reorganization of the government signaled the establishment of a Soviet-style political system. All leading government positions were held by Communist Party members, the Party and government were combined, and the legislative and administrative arms of the government became one body. According to Professor Tsou Tang, a leftist political scientist, this was an omnipotent government that managed everything—from public affairs to enterprise businesses, and even matters concerning individual persons. The political system was conducive to the functioning of the planned economy, which, in turn, formed the economic base for the system. The political and economic systems were thus mutually dependent. Systems based on the Leninist-Stalinist political model existed not only in China but also in the other socialist countries.

After years of repeated "education," the general mindset maintained that a Soviet political model had to be implemented. This mindset continued to be influential in Party and government organizations after the onset of the reform and opening. Take, as an example, the proposal to abandon the practice of state governance by the Party and to initiate a reform to separate the role of the Party from the functions of government. Although Deng Xiaoping clung to his original idea and though his 1941 report was included as the second entry in volume 1 of his three-volume *Selected Works* (which was published in 1989), the forces that regarded the Soviet model as a religious doctrine enjoyed an entrenched position within the Party. Whenever there was a slight change in the wind, the former ideology and system would stage a comeback.

Ma: Another, more important, reason for the lack of political reforms was the obstruction and resistance by the so-called privileged groups. Since the onset of the reform and opening, the economic base had undergone tremendous changes, whereas there had not been fundamental modifications to the political system. Contradictions and conflicts emerged between the two systems. For those people with common sense, the necessity of promoting reform of the political system was obvious. The obstacles to the political reforms were imposed by the existing interest groups—that is, the privileged groups that used their power for rent seeking—rather than based on ideological considerations.

Wu: In his book *The Rise and Decline of Nations*, American economist Mancur Olson offers an in-depth analysis of privileged groups. He claims that privileged groups are essentially parasitical, interest-sharing classes of people who assiduously seek to carve out a portion of personal benefits rather than to compete for them. These groups are not concerned with increasing social productivity; rather, they focus on how to reap the spoils of social productivity. Many people are worried that privileged groups have become too rooted in China today. If this problem is not resolved, the high rate of economic growth will not bring about a widely shared sense of happiness and safety. Instead, there will be frustrations and feelings of deprivation. Unfair growth may even trigger social unrest.

In parallel with the reforms, privileged groups constantly drift apart and undergo regroupings. Thus, new interest groups and classes have emerged in succession. When government officials hold substantial powers to allocate resources, and when these powers are not held in check, some people are able to become rich by colluding with the government. The practice of exchanging "power for money" has become commonplace. It is safe to say that the lag in political reforms has allowed for the emergence of the privileged groups, which, in turn, have become a huge roadblock for future reforms.

Ma: By default, the semi-command, semi-market system that came into being at the end of the 1990s is a transitional economic system. It includes both new market-economy elements and the legacy of the command or controlled economy. It may move forward to become a complete market economy, but it may also return to a controlled economy. Obstacles to the reforms will intensify moves in the direction of state capitalism.

Since the early 2000s, there has been an ongoing trend of escalating interference in economic activities and control over society by the Communist Party and the government. On top of this, as we discussed in the previous dialogue, state capital has become ever stronger. All of these have reinforced control by the state, bringing the semi-command, semi-market system ever closer to state capitalism.

Wu: The so-called state capitalism is a set of political and economic institutions under which state capital, supported by political power, competes with other types of capital to gain control over the market. Given our history, the lack of democracy, and the current weak rule of law, state capitalism is likely to turn into crony capitalism, or in Mao Zedong's words, "bureaucratic capitalism" (that is, "comprador, feudal, state-monopoly capitalism"). If steadfast economic and political reforms are not carried out to implement a market orientation, rule of law, and democracy, the system will be bound to the path of bureaucratic capitalism. As American economist Douglass

North once said, once the path to reform is blocked, it is very difficult to return to it without drastic social unrest.

Ma: In recent years, this economic system that is controlled by a strong government and powerful state capital has been praised as the "Beijing consensus," or the so-called "China model."

Advocates of the so-called "China model" believe that the true reason for China's superior economic performance during the last thirty years has been the development of its own political and economic system. This system is characterized by a strong government and a superpowerful state sector. Because of these advantages, correct state strategies have been formulated and successfully implemented. Owing to the system's capability to concentrate resources on major endeavors, "miracles" were performed, such as the 2008 Beijing Olympic Games and the high-speed railways. Amid the swelling tide of the global financial crisis, China's GDP continued to record an average annual growth rate of more than 9 percent. Considered from this perspective, China is a good example for other countries to follow and the envy of the developed economies.

Wu: For me, this system and its consequences are not at all that wonderful if they are viewed from a longer-term perspective.

First, the corresponding "government-led developmental model," or the "authoritarian economic development model," creates serious socioeconomic contradictions that will overwhelm the government.

Second, government power over resource allocations and its interventions in economic activities have been increasingly strengthened. This has expanded and enhanced the institutional basis for rent seeking, resulting in rampant corruption and an ever-enlarging gulf between the rich and the poor. In a worst-case scenario, social unrest may erupt.

In fact, the newly industrialized East Asian economies that adopted the East Asian model provide both positive and negative lessons. During the initial phase of their economic growth, when the market was at a low developmental level, interventions by the authoritarian governments were a powerful impetus for development. But after the economies of these countries began to take off, suppression of the market and improper interventions by the government often led to poor investment guidance, corruption, and crony capitalism, threatening steady, long-term economic development. This is why, after the market had reached a certain level, these countries all still had to implement political reforms to move from authoritarianism to democracy. South Korea and Taiwan (China) are successful examples of this kind of transformation. Counterexamples can be found in Indonesia and the Philippines. The latter countries did not carry out political reforms and they became bogged down in crony capitalism. For a while, corruption prevailed and the privileged groups could not be contained, social inequalities worsened, and public rights became obscured. These phenomena created what Swedish Nobel economics laureate Gunnar Myrdal called an "Asian Drama"—the collapse of society. The collapse of society will further exacerbate rent seeking and corruption. According Myrdal, as soon as a government faces such a situation, it is on the brink of losing its legitimacy, and even a military government may become a "soft power." Without reforms, it will be difficult for China to avoid the rampant corruption and social collapse as described in Myrdal's Asian Drama.

DIALOGUE 18

DIFFICULTIES IN SHIFTING THE GROWTH MODEL

Ma Guochuan (Ma): The standstill in the market-oriented reforms and the lag in the reform of the political system have presented a dilemma in terms of changing the growth model. Thus far, China's economic growth has relied on investments and exports. There has been a lack of endogenous dynamics for sustained and steady economic development.

In Dialogue 15 on macroeconomic management, we noted that after more than thirty years of high economic growth, one issue has not been adequately resolved—that is, the frequency of short-term economic fluctuations. Such fluctuations still remain a problem today. On several occasions you have pointed out that the short-term economic problems are due to serious shortcomings in the growth model. Would you please provide a succinct explanation of economic growth models? Is this term different from official usage of the term the *mode of economic development* that is employed in government documents?

Wu Jinglian (Wu): In economics, the growth model refers to particular types of driving forces for economic growth during a certain period of time. It is the same as the *mode of economic development* or the *mode of economic growth* (the term that was used in earlier government documents).

Ma: There are also related concepts, such as the "route for industrialization" and the "road to industrialization." For instance, Stalin provided a definition of the "route for socialist industrialization" and Mao Zedong referred to the "Chinese way" to industrialize. I am afraid that these probably all represent attempts to explore the economic growth models.

Wu: In the West, a pioneer study of economic growth models was carried out by Paul Samuelson, who is known for his textbook *Economics*. After years of elaboration and exploration by Simon Kuznets, Robert Solow, and Theodore Schultz, some conclusions have been reached about the evolution of economic growth models.

In the book *Choices for China's Growth Model,* I summarized the propositions of these various economists, as presented in the following table:

Evolution of Economic Growth Models in the West

Time Period	*Stage of Development*	*Main Content*	*Key Determinant*	*Dominant Sector*	*Corresponding Growth Theory*
Prior to 1770	(1) Economic takeoff	Exploitation of natural resources	More inputs of natural resources	Agriculture	Malthusian Trap
1770–1870	(2) Early stage of economic growth	Replacement of manual labor by machinery	Capital accumulation	Heavy and chemical industries	Harrod-Domar Growth Model
1870–1970	(3) Modern economic growth	Efficiency improvements	Technological progress	Manufacturing integrated with the services sector	Solow's Neoclassical Model of Exogenous Growth
After 1970	(4) Information age	Telecommuni-cations and IT driven—transformation of the national economies	Information technology	The tele-communications and IT industries that have penetrated society	Endogenous Growth Theory

This table shows that modernization in the West underwent the following stages: (a) Before the first Industrial Revolution in the eighteenth century, economic growth relied on natural resources, in particular, inputs of land. But because natural resources were limited, the economies grew very slowly. At that time, British economist Robert Malthus and many of his peers believed that once the natural resources could no longer meet the increased demand generated by population growth, mankind would become bogged down in a poverty trap. Thus, at that time economics was referred to as a "dismal science"; (b) The Industrial Revolution negated Malthus's predictions. Under the Western early growth model, economic growth was mainly generated by machine processing that replaced manual labor. There was a need for massive investments in capital-intensive heavy industries that produced machinery, machine tools, coal, and basic materials. By default, this kind of industrialization relied on capital accumulation. But the problem with this growth model was that it required an ever-growing investment rate (investments as a share of GDP). In parallel with the continuous increase in investments and the corresponding decline in consumption there was sluggish improvement in the workers' living standards and a lack of end demand; and (c) After the second industrialization wave that began in the late 1890s, scientific knowledge and modern technology were widely disseminated. The West entered a stage of modern economic growth whereby technological progress and efficiency improvements were the main drivers of economic growth. At that time, the definition of "industrialization" also underwent a change. The term became much broader, referring to comprehensive economic development that would be achieved through the integration of services, agriculture, and manufacturing, and efficiency improvements in all sectors. The fourth stage is an extension of the third stage.

Ma: In the late 1800s and the early 1900s, China followed the early growth model. After the Beiyang Fleet (the North Seas Fleet) was destroyed during the 1895 First Sino-Japanese War, reformers believed that industrial development was the basis for a prosperous country and a powerful military force. For instance, leading reformer Liang Qichao wrote in 1896 that China's prosperity was dependent on the growth of industry. Another leading reformer, Kang Youwei, wrote to the Guangxu Emperor in 1898 and called for the establishment of large factories to develop industry, suggesting that the goal of Chinese development should be industrialization.

Wu: This is not surprising. At that time, the emergence of the Western industrial powers was accompanied by a shift from agricultural to industrial resources. The Qing dynasty reformers realized that the share of industry in the Western countries was continuing to rise and that industry was replacing agriculture as the main economic sector. However, at that time the more developed Western powers were no longer at a stage of early economic growth, and they were about to enter a new stage of modern economic growth in which technological progress and efficiency improvements were the main determinants of economic development.

Ma: In other words, the Chinese view of industrialization at the time was understandable because a modern economic growth model had not yet been achieved. But why did China still set narrow industrialization as its goal after the establishment of the People's Republic?

Wu: This had something to do with misleading guidance from the Soviet Union. As a matter of fact, Marx had much earlier provided detailed analyses on the socioeconomic problems in the West caused by the early economic growth model. Based on these analyses, he concluded that capitalism would be replaced by socialism. Unfortunately, during the debates on industrialization in the Soviet Union in the 1920s, in order to gain the upper hand in a controversy with Bukharin, his rival in the Communist

Party, Stalin took the position that the Western early economic growth model was the route to socialist industrialization, as opposed to the route to capitalist industrialization. Priority in the Soviet Union was thus placed on the development of heavy industry, and the proposition that capital accumulation (investment) was the only way to expand reproduction (growth) became a fundamental principle in Marx's theory of reproduction. The other socialist countries, including China, treated these propositions as a proven model, and they all sought to achieve economic growth based on an investment-driven, extensive-growth model.

Ma: At the 1945 Seventh Congress of the Chinese Communist Party, Mao Zedong proposed that after the establishment of New Democracy, China would gradually develop light and heavy industries, so as to make the transition from an agricultural to an industrial country. The goal of development in the Common Program of the Chinese People Political Consultative Conference (1949) and the 1954 Constitution was such a transformation to an industrial country.

Wu: In 1953, with the beginning of the First Five-Year Plan (1953–57), China adopted a Soviet-style socialist industrialization policy, placing priority on the development of heavy industry. This became the guiding principle for economic construction. The programmatic document, "Outline for Study and Promotion of the General Line for the Transition Period," which was drafted with personal input from Mao, stated that in order to realize socialist industrialization, the key is to develop heavy industry, which is the foundation for industrialization and the linchpin for the modernization of national defense. Stalin had stated that "not any development of industry can be called industrialization. The core of industrialization, its very basis, consists of the development of heavy industry (fuel, metal, etc.) and of the expansion, as a last resort, of the output of the means of production of our own engineering." The outline also stated that because of the implementation of socialist industrialization, the Soviet Union had achieved industrialization in a little more than ten years (between 1921 and the completion of the First Five-Year Plan in 1932). China should thus learn from the history of the Soviet Union.

Just as China was embarking on an ambitious plan to industrialize based on a model similar to the Western early growth model, the Western countries entered a new historical stage of post-industrialization growth. During this stage, growth was driven by widespread adoption of information technology and a lowering of transaction costs. However, China still followed the Soviet Union and followed the extensive growth model, which had been utilized in the West during the stage of early growth.

Ma: During China's First Five-Year Plan period, human, material, and financial resources were concentrated on 156 priority projects, with assistance from the Soviet

Union. Most of these projects focused on the development of heavy industry, and over the course of the next five years, investment in these industries reached 85 percent of total industrial investment. Based on Stalin's 1933 summary on implementation of the USSR's First-Five Year Plan, commerce and other services were not considered production. It was believed that as long as the value of gross industrial output was more than 70 percent of the total output value of agriculture and industry, and the output of heavy industry accounted for more than 60 percent of the value of gross output of industry, industrialization would be achieved in China. It was estimated that the goal of the socialist transformation of agriculture, handicrafts, and commerce would be completed after three five-year plan periods, and by that time China would be a "great socialist country."

Wu: However, the early results of the First Five-Year Plan were unsatisfactory. Although the industrial sector, in particular heavy industry, grew rapidly, the national economy was unstable because of the lopsided development of heavy industry and the increasing structural imbalances. The economic imbalances became worse after the political campaign to criticize "rightist conservative tendencies" and the launch of the "socialist upsurge in the countryside" in 1955. In his 1956 "On the Ten Major Relationships," Mao suggested that the over-development of heavy industry had had a negative effect on agriculture and light industry and that it was necessary to strike a balance among these three sectors. However, beginning in the fall of 1957 Mao initiated criticism of a slogan coined by senior Communist Party leaders Zhou Enlai and Chen Yun that called for "preventing both conservatism and rash advance." In 1958 Mao launched the Great Leap Forward and all human, material, and financial resources were used to develop the heavy-industry sector, led by the iron and steel mills. Mao believed that as long as steel led the way full steam ahead, industrialization would be accelerated.

The Great Leap Forward pushed the lopsided economic structure to an extreme. From 1958 to 1960, the ratio between average investments and average consumption in China was 39.1:60.9, compared to the 20:80 ratio in low-income countries in the 1950s and 1960s.

Ma: The massive investments during the Great Leap Forward that attempted to spur rapid economic growth resulted not only in an enormous waste of wealth and the loss of tens of millions of lives but also a worsening of China's economic situation.

Wu: Even with a disaster of this magnitude, the traditional political line of "socialist industrialization" was not corrected. Economic growth mainly relied on investments in the heavy and chemical industries. This was the basic characteristic of China's economic development during the first thirty years of the People's Republic—from the time of the First Five-Year Plan to the initiation of the reform and opening.

Ma: However, after almost thirty years of national industrialization that was characterized by isolation of the urban areas from the rural areas and forced state investments, China remained an agricultural country. In 1977 the agricultural population accounted for 82.5 percent of the total population. Additionally, China also remained a low-income country. The distance between China and the Four Little Dragons had expanded significantly, even though their starting points had been similar. Why did China, which was growing at a rapid speed, become mired in a situation of "growth without development"?

Wu: GDP figures alone do not adequately explain the quality of economic growth. The traditional path of industrialization resulted in a lopsided economic structure and low economic efficiency.

First, with regard to the industrial structure, China followed the doctrines of the Soviet Union that regarded only the production of materials as economic activities. Commerce and other services were considered "nonproductive." The basic yardstick for industrialization was the dominance of industrial output in total agricultural and industrial output and the dominance of heavy industry in total industrial output. Heavy industry became a sector serving itself, with products circulating among themselves at the expense of agriculture and light industry. The services sector seriously lagged behind.

Second, economic growth was mainly driven by investments. The imbalance between capital and labor led to an imbalance between returns on capital and labor income. The shares of government and state-owned enterprises continued to rise, whereas workers' incomes suffered relative declines. With regard to the distribution of national income, the state was becoming richer, but the people were becoming poorer. Improvements in living standards rose slowly and the general public could not share in the fruits of the high growth.

Hence, during the twenty years from 1957 to 1977, the livelihood of the Chinese people did not improve and both rural and urban residents suffered from inadequate food and clothing.

Ma: According to your studies, the phrase "transformation of the economic growth mode" is derived from the Soviet Union in the 1960s. At that time, after studying why the Soviet Union was at a disadvantage in terms of competition with the developed market-economy countries, some Soviet economists concluded that the reason was the difference in their respective main sources of economic growth: the Soviet Union mainly relied on increases in investment, whereas the West benefited from efficiency improvements. Based on volume 2 of *Das Kapital*, these economists called growth driven by resource inputs *extensive growth* and they called growth driven by efficiency improvements *intensive growth*. They believed that the only solution for the Soviet Union was to change the "growth mode" from an extensive model to an intensive model.

Wu: You are right. In China, reflections on these lessons began much later. After the Cultural Revolution, the most urgent problem for the government was how to deal with the negative effects of the extensive growth model, such as the decline in agriculture, the paralysis in rural life, the high unemployment rate among urban youth, the weak light industries, and the backward services sector. This is why in 1979 the government decided to reduce the size of industrial investments, enhance agricultural production, and raise the shares of light industry and commerce in the economy as part of its three-year economic adjustment plan. At the end of 1980, the government once again called for "further readjustments to the national economy."

After these adjustments and readjustments, the economic structure was improved to a certain extent. Agricultural production recovered, serious shortages of agricultural products were alleviated, and the incidence of absolute poverty was reduced. Furthermore, there was a turn for the better in terms of the supply of consumer goods, and commerce and other services began to grow.

Ma: Although the economic structure improved, the adjustments did not touch upon the root causes of the problems because they only focused on the adverse effects of the traditional growth model. Shortly after the end of the readjustments, the structural problems reappeared. Learning from this lesson, the Government Work Report approved by the National People's Congress at the end of 1981 stated that the future guiding principle for economic growth would be adoption of a new program to attain realistic speed, better economic effects, and more benefits for the general public.

However, initiating a correct principle did not necessarily mean things changed for the better on the ground. At that time, there was no systematic streamlining of the concept of traditional industrialization and the related institutional arrangements. During the following years, the main driver of the high GDP growth continued to be large-scale investments. In particular, a "heavier economic structure" appeared in many localities and the extensive growth model was intensified.

Wu: In 1996, given the fact that the negative results of this growth model had increased rather than decreased, a fundamental task of the Ninth Five-Year Plan (1996–2000), adopted by the Eighth National People's Congress, was to implement a transformation to an intensive growth model. In 2001 the Tenth Five-Year Plan focused on economic structural adjustments and upgrading as the main tasks of economic development during the 2001–5 Five-Year Plan period. The 2002 Sixteenth National Communist Party Congress further stated that the country should pursue a new industrialization path, with a higher level of science and technology, better economic effects, lower consumption of resources, and less environmental pollution. The new path was projected to bring into full play the advantages of China's human resources. The following two five-year plans, the Eleventh Five-Year Plan (2006–10) and the Twelfth Five-Year Plan (2011–15), both emphasized making a change in the economic development model as the backbone for all economic work. Although the objective was clear, the results were not noteworthy because policies and incentives continued to promote high levels of investment.

GDP growth that is dependent on high levels of investment has produced a number of problems, as highlighted by the following weaknesses in the allocation of resources. The principle of "playing to one's strengths" has not been followed. Priorities are placed on industries that consume more resource inputs, generate high environmental losses, create fewer jobs, and have low value-added. Although individual enterprises, sectors, and localities have benefited from certain rates of growth and profitability, overall economic efficiency has decreased. The extensive growth has also overstretched scarce resources, for instance, land, freshwater, coal, oil, electricity, and transport capacity. The worsening of the ecological environment is accelerating and development of the services sector is being suppressed. It has also become more difficult to deal with the challenges of unemployment. Excessive investments have led to increased nonperforming loans in banks and an accumulation of systemic risks in the financial sector.

The continuation of the extensive growth model has also resulted in a higher investment rate. Meanwhile, the consumption rate has been declining, accompanied by a relatively lower share of labor in total income, slower improvements in living standards, inadequate demand for consumption, and an expanding gap between the rich and the poor.

Ma: Socioeconomic development in Western Europe during the nineteenth century revealed that if a country adopts an investment-driven early growth model, imbalances between investments and consumption are inevitable, leading to overcapacity and economic crises. It is quite puzzling that China's growth rate has not declined, despite the lack of demand and the declining share of consumption caused by the ever-rising investment rate and the continuously expanding production capacity. How has China been able to maintain such a high rate of economic growth over the course of several decades?

Wu: In Dialogue 8 we mentioned that an important reason for the continuous high rate of economic growth in China was the adoption, at the end of the 1970s, of an export-oriented strategy, similar to that in Japan and the other East Asian countries. Demand for exports compensated for the lack of domestic demand and added steam to the engine of reform.

Like the reforms in other sectors, the shift from import substitution to an export orientation was gradual. Market elements, such as foreign-exchange rates formed on swap markets, were introduced cautiously under a dual-track system. A fundamental change took place in 1994 when the foreign-exchange regime was reformed.

Ma: On January 1, 1994, the government abolished the official foreign-exchange fixed-rate regime and adopted a single managed floating system. Enterprises and individuals were allowed to buy from and sell to banks their foreign-exchange holdings in accordance with the relevant regulations. Banks were authorized to trade on the interbank foreign-exchange markets, which gave rise to a market-determined exchange rate. The central bank set the range for exchange-rate fluctuations and maintained a stable RMB exchange rate by buying and selling foreign exchange on the market. On December 31, 1993, the fixed official exchange rate stood at RMB 5.76 to USD 1.00, and the rate on the foreign-exchange swap market stood at RMB 8.6 to USD 1.0. After the reform, the exchange rates were unified to RMB 8.7 to USD 1.0. This exchange rate was not only significantly lower than the previous fixed official rate, but it was also lower than the swap market rate.

Wu: The dramatic depreciation of the RMB in 1994 represented a milestone in the comprehensive implementation of an export-oriented strategy.

The reform led to rapid growth in China's international trade, in particular, growth of exports. The trade surplus rose sharply. There had been trade deficits during ten of the fifteen years between 1979 and 1993. During the remainder of this period, the surpluses were not from strong exports; rather, they were mainly the result of a weak economy and contracted demand for imports. After the reform of the foreign-exchange regime in 1994, there was a constant rise in the trade surplus. International trade registered a surplus of USD 5.39 billion in 1994, compared to a deficit of USD 12.22 billion in 1993. Beginning in the twenty-first century, China's trade surplus grew exponentially, from USD 31.98 billion in 2004 to USD 298.13 billion in 2008. Demand for net exports was an important part of aggregate demand in the economy.

Ma: Comprehensive implementation of an export-oriented strategy has been highly positive for China's economic development since the 1990s. Because of the expansion of exports, the advantages of low-cost but good-quality labor and the large work force have come into full play. The surplus rural labor has been absorbed by non-agricultural sectors in the urban areas. People's livelihoods have improved and overall national economic prosperity has been achieved.

But can we maintain long-term prosperity based on this strategy?

Wu: There is no policy that will be effective forever, even if at one time it may play a positive role. The most noteworthy stories of trade-driven successes can be found in the other East Asian countries. After World War II, Japan, South Korea, and Taiwan (China) took advantage of the huge savings deficits in the developed countries, especially in the United States, to adopt export-oriented strategies, and they achieved high-speed growth for ten to twenty years. This became known as the "East Asian miracle" of the 1980s. If the export orientation was the engine of this miracle, the savings deficits and the demand for imports in the developed countries can be considered to be the high-octane fuel. At the time, the Japanese economy was regarded as the rising sun. In 1979, Harvard Professor Ezra Vogel published *Japan as Number One: Lessons for America*, a popular book throughout the world at the time.

However, by the 1990s these economies began to suffer from serious crises. It was difficult for them to get back on track without major reforms and policy adjustments.

Ma: Changes should be made as conditions change. A policy can be all positive or produce more benefits than harm only under certain conditions. But when conditions change, the same policy can be more harmful than beneficial, or it may even be completely negative.

Wu: This is also true in China. With the passage of time, the adverse effects of the policy-supported export expansion have gradually increased. Negative results have occurred in succession.

The first negative result has been the specialization of some enterprises in low-tech manufacturing industries. Because of the long period of explicit or implicit subsidies, such as the low exchange rates and the export tax rebates, these enterprises do not have any motivation, nor do they face any pressures, to upgrade their technologies, improve management, or lower costs. As economist Joseph Stiglitz has pointed out, although the export-oriented growth strategies allow demand to be free from the limitations of domestic revenue, they can also lead to "specialization" in labor-intensive manufacturing, thus weakening the long-term growth potential. According to Stiglitz, under these circumstances, the non-exporting sectors will remain at a low level of development for a long period of time. China is now in just such a situation. By implementing an export-oriented strategy, processing trade has become the main form of China's international trade. Typically, export producers rely on imported equipment and low-cost local labor to assemble intermediate inputs imported from Japan, South Korea, and Taiwan (China). The final products are then exported to the developed countries. By engaging in this type of trade, China has become deeply involved in the global division of labor and is engaged in low value-added processing and manufacturing for global value chains.

Since the 1980s, the growth rate of processing trade has been surpassing that of other types of trade, and the annual surpluses of processing trade have been consistently higher than those of total trade. If viewed by its volume of exports, the dominance of processing trade over a long period has enabled China to become a global factory. But most of its exports are at the lower end of the global value chains. China engages in assembly but it lacks innovation and patented technologies, resulting in "Made in China" rather than "Made by China." Quite often, Chinese original equipment manufacturers receive processing fees as low as 1 to 5 percent of the final selling price of an exported product.

Ma: Given the low value-added and the low profitability of exports, many enterprises have relied on increased volumes. This strategy has inevitably led to trade frictions and to an escalation in the number of anti-dumping cases. According to statistics from the Ministry of Commerce, in 2010 most of the international anti-dumping investigations were against China.

Wu: China has consumed a large number of nonrenewable resources, polluted its environment, and has a poor reputation with respect to dumping, yet it does not receive the main share of the profits from its exports. When there were large quantities of rural surplus labor and when the resource bottlenecks were not as tight as they are now, the development of labor-intensive processing industries introduced more advantages than disadvantages. However, after 2005 when conditions changed, when the so-called Lewis turning point was reached or was about to be reached, and when the domestic capacity of technologies had matured, many economists, including myself, strongly called for a shift in strategy.

Other negative results of the export-oriented strategy are an excess money supply and liquidity flooding caused by the huge increases in the balance-of-payments surpluses. China's foreign-exchange reserves only totaled USD 157 million at the end of 1950, and they did not reach USD 1 billion until the end of 1981. Throughout the 1980s, China's foreign reserves were only several billion USD. At that time, the government could barely make ends meet, and it had great difficulties in making payments. After 1994, foreign reserves began to rise sharply, surpassing USD 100 billion in 1996 and exceeding USD 1,000 billion by the end of 2006. At the end of 2011, reserves had reached USD 3,180 billion.

Ma: China has bid farewell to its former foreign-reserve shortages, which are a major challenge for most developing countries. Huge reserves imply a strong capability to make international payments, which is a good buffer to external shocks. Isn't this good news?

Wu: A small size of foreign reserves is problematic, but this does not mean that more reserves are necessarily better. Because of the high volume of foreign-exchange reserves, some of the country's resources have been converted into low-yield financial credits abroad at the expense of goods and labor imports, increases in production resources, or overseas investments. In addition, increases in foreign reserves have to be sterilized by increases in money supply. Excessive reserves will force the central bank to supply excess money.

There are two possible options for addressing this problem. The first is to let the market decide the exchange rates (that is, liberalization) in order to alleviate the sterilization pressures and to achieve a monetary balance. The other option is for the central bank to continually purchase foreign currencies, relying on strong interventions to maintain stability in the exchange rates of the local currency. The first option will usually meet with a lot of resistance because an appreciation in the local currency will exacerbate export difficulties. But the second option will narrow the space for central bank policy operations. An excess money supply will lead to a bubble economy and intensify inflationary pressures.

Japan, South Korea, and the other East Asian countries adopted the latter option, resulting in rocketing real-estate and stock prices and creating huge asset bubbles. When the bubbles burst in the 1990s, Japan entered a period of recession that lasted for more than a decade. The golden era of high growth also came to an end in Taiwan (China) for the same reason. During the following two decades, similar events were played out in the other East Asian countries as well.

Ma: In the fall of 2003, there was an extensive debate in China regarding reform of the foreign-exchange regime and appreciation of the RMB. At the time, both you and economist Yu Yongding pointed out that the long period of a fixed exchange-rate regime and the rapid growth of foreign reserves would lead to economic bubbles and inflation. You called for a resumption of a floating-rate regime and stated that there was nothing to fear from an appreciation of the RMB.

Wu: Unfortunately, and similar to what occurred in the East Asian economies, China delayed the adoption of a floating-rate regime because of its concerns about exports and the consequent impact on economic growth. In March 2005, as pressures to appreciate the value of the RMB were constantly increasing, the government announced a program to reform the exchange-rate regime. On July 21 of the same year, the exchange-rate formation mechanism was changed and the RMB–USD exchange rate slowly began to increase. The slow pace of the appreciation may have helped to avoid big shocks to the economy, especially for export producers. However, it also resulted in big inflows of "hot money." People placed their bets on a RMB appreciation, further increasing appreciation pressures. In order to suppress the pace of appreciation, the central bank frequently intervened in the market and accelerated the purchase of foreign currency (for example, US dollar–denominated assets).

By February 2006, China's foreign-exchange reserves had reached USD 875 billion, surpassing Japan to become the world's largest holder of foreign reserves, and by 2011, the size of China's foreign reserves had reached an astronomical USD 3,000 billion. The enormous reserves were the result of the issuance by the central bank of high-powered money totaling several trillion RMB. After the money went through the commercial banking system, it multiplied into a current purchasing power measured in millions of billions of RMB.

Simply put, because of the continuation of an export-oriented strategy that is underpinned by low valuations of the exchange rate, the internal imbalances in the Chinese economy have worsened. An excess money supply has resulted in asset bubbles, persistently high real-estate prices, and increased inflationary pressures. The only way out is to adjust the strategy. The objective of international trade should no longer be to "earn foreign exchange through exports." Rather, international trade should seek to improve quality and to increase the value-added and profitability of exports.

It should be noted that such an adjustment does not imply a change in the opening policy or a cut in the scale of international trade. The goal is to transform the function of international trade; in other words, it is to make best use of the advantages of imports and exports and to avoid the disadvantages in order to improve the structure of resources.

Ma: The current model allows investments and exports to drive economic growth. The problems created by this model have been escalating. The Communist Party and government have repeatedly called for an acceleration in the transformation of this growth model. Economists, including yourself, have analyzed why such a transformation is needed. Despite all these efforts, however, the trend toward a heavier economic structure has intensified. What is behind this phenomenon?

Wu: I think there are probably two main reasons.

The first is related to our understanding of the evolution of industrialization, that is, of the growth model. For years, Soviet theories of industrialization dominated Communist Party and government documents and they are still influential today. These theories have misled people to believe that countries must all follow a development path that begins with agriculture, then moves from light industry to heavy industry, and then to high-tech industry before finally reaching services. According to this belief, if China can grasp the opportunities to develop the heavy and chemical industries, it will be able to maintain a high growth rate for the next twenty years. Development of human capital, that is, knowledge and capabilities, has been ignored; instead, attention has been focused on investments in the capital-intensive heavy and chemical industries.

The second reason is the institutional obstacles, which consist of the following four main problems: (a) The Communist Party and the government, instead of market mechanisms, continue to play a basic role in resource allocations. In particular, since the early 2000s when urbanization began to accelerate, governments at various administrative levels have amassed more power to deploy land resources by buying land from rural collectives at low prices; (b) The growth rate of GDP remains the most important objective of the state and is the main criterion used to evaluate the political achievements of Communist Party officials and government leaders. Such an institutional arrangement has prompted the government to invest heavily in land to achieve high GDP growth or to finance growth through bank loans; (c) Under the current fiscal and tax systems, government revenue is linked to output in the production sector. Meanwhile, responsibilities for expenditures on important public goods have been excessively decentralized and are now mainly shouldered by governments at the county or lower administrative levels. The lower-level governments thus need to achieve high output growth; and (d) Most of the production factors are still subject to administrative pricing, with prices set at low levels. The seriously distorted price signals have encouraged rather than restricted the production of products that consume more energy, produce greater pollution, and are highly capital-intensive.

To summarize, the key to a transformation of the growth model is to eliminate the just-mentioned conceptual and institutional obstacles in order to establish a system that is conducive to innovation and entrepreneurship.

Ma: Some people believe that because of its weak capacity for technology and innovation, China does not have an advantage in terms of increasing the value-added of its products. It is therefore unrealistic to attempt to change the economic growth model.

Wu: In the past, I also had a similar impression that China's innovation capacity was not strong. But in recent years, after many study trips, my views have changed.

First, since the onset of the reform and opening, a relatively complete industrial system has been established, consisting of a powerful manufacturing sector equipped with a basic technological capacity, even though the overall technological level is still not very high and the share of scientists and engineers in the total population is still quite low. But because of its huge population base and the development of education, China has already surpassed the United States and become number one in the world in terms of the absolute number of scientific and technological workers with high educational backgrounds. In 2007 budget allocations for research and development ranked number two in the world, even exceeding those in Japan. The innovation capacity of Chinese scientists and engineers has improved significantly. There have been numerous innovations, some of which are at the international frontiers of technology.

The current problem is the unfriendly environment for business start-ups. Management of scientific and technological education by the government is also problematic. If enabling systems and policies encouraging innovation and entrepreneurship are adopted, the technological level of Chinese industries will be capable of recording obvious improvements within a short period of time. At present, many global industries are facing a myriad of breakthroughs in technology. If China can seize these opportunities and take advantage of its strengths, it is entirely possible that it will develop some unbeatable internationally competitive industries.

Second, a transformation of the growth model and industrial upgrading are not at all unrealistic. These are not calls for the development and application of cutting-edge technologies in every industry. As a matter of fact, because of China's huge processing capacity, if only a portion of Chinese manufacturing enterprises can make progress in the direction of more advanced technologies and higher value-added (or extensions at both ends of Stan Shih's "smiling curve"), its total increase in value-added will be astonishing. Of course, this will require hard work and on-the-ground efforts. Only hard work and perseverance will equip the hundreds of millions of low-skilled workers with adequate levels of knowledge and skills. But this is by no means impossible.

Ma: A conclusion can be drawn from our discussion in this dialogue: the key to transformation of the economic growth model is adoption of good institutional arrangements. To realize a shift in the growth model and to achieve industrial revitalization, China should seek to promote reforms, transform its former systems, complete the establishment of a market economy, and improve its relevant policies.

DIALOGUE 19

WHY DID CHINA BECOME A RENT-SEEKING SOCIETY?

Ma Guochuan (Ma): In the last dialogue we discussed a popular question that has attracted a lot of attention: Why has it been so difficult to change the growth model? In this dialogue, I would like to discuss with you another question that attracts even more attention: What are the reasons for the worsening of corruption and how might we be able to contain it?

Wu Jinglian (Wu): This is a critical topic, but it is one that we must confront.

As early as when the reform and opening was first initiated, some people took advantage of the dual existence of a command economy and a market economy to engage in rent seeking. In the late 1980s, as we discussed in Dialogue 9, some people with government backgrounds had access to huge rent-seeking opportunities. Within a short time, these "profiteering officials" became very wealthy by buying and selling plan quotas for resource allocations. This type of corruption was hated as much as rats running across the street, with everyone yelling: Kill them! Kill them! It was also an important cause of the subsequent political disturbance in 1989.

At that time, some senior Communist Party and government officials realized the dangers: if they did not effectively fight corruption, there was a possibility that the Communist Party–controlled state would be overthrown. After recognizing this, the Communist Party and the government imposed severe punishments on all those who engaged in corruption and they also launched education campaigns to fight corruption and to promote cleaner government. Unfortunately, instead of being contained, over the years the corruption has become even more widespread.

Ma: This shows corruption cannot be contained merely by education campaigns and strict punishments. Despite repeated efforts to eliminate it, corruption has become all the more rampant. There must be some deeper causes for this phenomenon.

Wu: For me, the root cause of rampant corruption in any country is unrestrained powers that create an environment for rent seeking. In order to eradicate corruption, an economy should become market-oriented to the extent that those powers cannot be used to intervene at will in resource allocations. Meanwhile, whenever there is a need for administrative permits or interventions by the state, the powers must be restrained by strengthened oversight.

In Dialogue 9 we talked about China's experience in this respect in the 1980s and the 1990s.

Ma: Corruption is a social evil that is generally abhorred by the public. It has also captured the attention of many academics. I remember that in 1988 you organized a discussion on profiteering officials and rent seeking. The proceedings of the discussions were published in the book *Corruption: The Exchange of Power and Money*, which has since been reprinted several times and has generated a strong reaction in the society.

Wu: Since publication of this book, "rent seeking" has become a well-known term, and it has become increasingly detested. However, instead of being eliminated, corruption has been penetrating ever deeper into the social structure. In the third edition of that book, published in 1999, the title was changed to *Finding the Root Causes of Corruption: Will China Become a Rent-Seeking Society?* In a way, the change in the book's title reflects the fact that the spread of corruption had become a serious issue affecting China's future. In the preface to the third edition, I write, "Since publication of the second edition, five years have passed. The corruption issue has become ever more acute. On the one hand, the general public is increasingly resentful of corruption, and works by economists and other writers have clearly conveyed such social reactions. On the other hand, corrupt officials continue to arrogantly hurt the public interest. The existence of many rent-seeking opportunities in the current system allows these officials to engage in corrupt practices without any oversight. Sometimes they even establish new rents using the excuse that they are strengthening so-called comprehensive macroeconomic management."

Ma: We should discuss this in more detail, and especially the ups and downs in the anti-corruption efforts.

Wu: Deng Xiaoping took his well-known trip to Southern China in 1992 in the aftermath of the 1988 economic turbulence and the 1989 political turbulence. At about that time, the prices of most goods were quietly determined by the market because of a loosening of the strict macroeconomic policies and relaxed price controls. Once the goods market was liberalized and the system for the allocation of materials was abandoned, the dual tracks for pricing converged. Profiteers could no longer reap fortunes by buying and selling plan-allocated materials. In the early 1990s, we all observed the disappearance of the previously rampant rent seeking in the goods sector.

Ma: It is difficult to understand why corruption was not contained after the disappearance of rent seeking in the goods sector. In fact, after a short while corruption became even worse in other sectors. Many people have asked, How could such a situation have occurred?

Wu: It is not very difficult to understand the causes. As long as fertile ground exists for rent seeking, these activities will continue. The price liberalization in the goods sector in the early 1990s eliminated only a small portion of this fertile ground. The institutional arrangement whereby power could still interfere with and control transactions remained intact. Because the prices of production factors were not determined by the market and because foreign-exchange rates were not formed through the market, power continued to dominate the allocation of these resources. Rent-seeking activities shifted from the goods sector in the 1980s to the factors sectors in the 1990s. The new ground for rent seeking became lending and land transactions.

During the period of the command economy, in order to "promote investments and accumulation" the government adopted a policy that, in the literature on financial development, is called *financial repression*. Lending rates were kept at very low levels. This policy continued into the new era. In the first half of the 1990s, after inflation began to soar, the real lending rates of state-owned banks became negative. Borrowers at these banks were therefore receiving implicit subsidies. For instance, in 1994 the annual inflation rate was 24 percent, but the banks' lending rate was only 11 percent per annum, resulting in a real lending rate of negative 13 percent. If someone took out a one-year loan of RMB 10,000, the principal would amount to RMB 12,400 in real terms because of the inflation and currency depreciation. However, the borrower would only have to repay the RMB 10,000 loan, plus a total interest payment of RMB 1,100. This means that in real terms, the borrower would earn an economic return of RMB 1,300, instead of paying interest on the loan. At the time, the total lending of state-owned banks amounted to RMB 4 trillion, generating a huge economic spread (rent) totaling hundreds of billions of RMB.

Ma: At the time, I heard that enterprises with good connections received loans from state-owned banks at low interest rates, and then they on-lended the loans at higher rates to those who could not borrow directly from the banks. The interest differential was pocketed by the enterprises or shared with the bank employees. During the past two years, the inflation rate has once again exceeded the banks' lending rates (a reappearance of negative lending rates in real terms). I assume there must be many enterprises with access to bank loans at low rates that are busy making money by on-lending to those suffering from funding shortages (mostly small and medium-sized enterprises in the private sector).

Wu: Another target of rent seeking is land. According to current Chinese law, rural land belongs to farmers' collectives, whereas urban land is owned by the state. During the period of the command economy, land owned by the state was provided to state-owned enterprises free of charge. At the beginning of the reform era, the state began to lease land to users, mainly utilizing two methods: selling leases in auctions or offering leases at negotiated prices. When urbanization was accelerated in the early 1990s, the state began to acquire rural land on a large scale at low prices. Land acquired in this way was leased to urban users. Most localities used the negotiation method to lease the land. Some places replaced the existing auctions by negotiating the lease prices. Government officials usually had the final say about whether to lease, how much land would be leased, and what the final price would be. Well-connected people could lease good-quality land at a low price and then sell the lease at a very high price. Even the second, third, or fourth buyer could reap windfall profits by re-selling the lease. If the buyer had received a loan from a state-owned bank at a negative real rate, he/she was able to develop a profitable business without providing any original capital out of his own pocket. There are stories about people becoming billionaires in only a few months through bribery. Several prefectural-level cities became famous for attracting large amounts of funding from all over the country by leasing land and supporting speculation in the local real-estate market. Once such a "drum-flower" drinking game[1] was over, the play would come to an end and the bubble would burst. The losses were shouldered by the state-owned banks and the governments in other localities that had hoped to reap windfall profits. In other words, the taxpayers eventually had to cover the losses. Enormous amounts of wealth were thus lost.

Ma: I heard that in the second half of the 1990s Premier Zhu Rongji used an iron fist to try to clean up the financial sector and the corruption in land-leasing deals. Many Communist Party and government officials in some mid-level cities and land-administration departments who had become famous through land-leasing deals were found guilty of corruption. It was expected that after the harsh punishments, the situation would change.

[1] In this Chinese game, one participant is responsible for beating a drum as a spray of blossoms is passed among the other participants in time with the beat of the drum. Once the beating stops, whoever is left holding the blossoms will have to give a performance (and/or drink a cup of wine).

Wu: Many people believed that the high incidence of corruption in the land-administration agencies was due to lax oversight. If further anti-corruption education were provided and serious disciplinary actions taken, then the trend could be reversed. But it was not quite so simple. As we mentioned earlier, the root cause of corruption is unrestrained power. As long as power can control the land markets and the environment is conducive to rent seeking, corruption will prevail. This is an inevitable truth. As a matter of fact, over the years the government has adopted tough laws and regulations to fight corruption in the agencies that are in charge of land administration and utilization. Many officials have been severely punished, but successive officials have continued to engage in corruption. This phenomenon clearly shows that the prevalence of corruption can only be explained by the existence of rent-seeking opportunities under the current institutional arrangements.

Ma: At the turn of the century, there was an upsurge in urbanization in China. Rural land was turned into urban land owned by the state. This was not only an important source of local-government revenue but also a main channel through which corrupt officials could amass huge amounts of wealth from the general public. Between the end of 2002 and the beginning of 2003, new executives who had replaced the previous Communist Party and government leaders in many localities promoted large-scale and wasteful projects, thus creating an unprecedented wave of investments. These projects were a profiteering bonanza for the red-hat merchants, that is, those businessmen who enjoyed close connections to power. Serious cases of corruption involving land deals emerged in rapid succession. In recent years, land-related corruption has been the main cause of the so-called mass incidents in which government officials are confronted by angry residents who are resisting the forced appropriation of their land.

Wu: Because of the persistent rent-seeking activities, people began to better understand the mechanisms that were conducive to the spread of corruption. Those in power began to pay more attention to removing the institutional basis for rent seeking.

During an April 2000 inspection tour of Guangdong province, Wei Jianxing, Communist Party secretary of the Central Discipline Inspection Commission (CDIC), pointed out that government power, when it is used inappropriately, is actually the source of the corruption. He commented that over the years, many senior officials had abused their administrative-licensing powers. They had leased land, approved loans, or cleared construction projects in breach of the laws and regulations in return for huge bribes. Secretary Wei concluded that reform of the administrative-licensing system would play an important role in preventing a recurrence of corruption.

In November 2000, the Fifth Plenary Session of the Fifteenth CDIC adopted a decision to further intensify the fight to eradicate corruption at its roots. The top priority was to reform the administrative-licensing system by streamlining its procedures. The CDIC called for abolishing the redundant prior-review requirements and for allowing matters that should be handled by the market to be handled by market mechanisms. With respect to the prior-review requirements that were to be retained, the CDIC proposed a sound oversight mechanism. Review procedures were to be streamlined to cut the multiple bureaucratic layers. The procedures and review results were to be publicized to allow for monitoring by the general public.

The CDIC decision affected the origins of the corruption and won public support. In 2001 the State Council established an office to be in charge of the reform of the administrative-licensing system. It has been reported that during the following three years 1,795 administrative-licensing requirements were abolished or consolidated, accounting for 48.9 percent of the total requirements. However, people who had benefited from rent seeking under the administrative-licensing system made great efforts to resist the reform. As Montesquieu, the French philosopher during the European Age of Enlightenment, once put it, "Constant experience shows us that every man invested with power is apt to abuse it." In early 2004 there was an announcement that "important results" had been achieved in the administrative-licensing reform. But when the tide in the fight against corruption at its origins receded, many direct or disguised administrative-licensing requirements re-emerged with a vengeance.

Ma: Another main step to reduce administrative interventions and rent seeking was promulgation and implementation of the Administrative Licensing Law of the People's Republic of China in 2003.

Wu: Prohibitions against arbitrary requirements for administrative licenses are critical to protect citizens' basic rights and to ensure correct government behavior. It is the natural right of citizens to freely engage in activities that are not prohibited by law. Modern nations have adopted a basic principle for citizen behavior; that is, if it is not prohibited, then it is allowed. In other words, if the law does not explicitly prohibit an activity, a citizen can engage in it as he or she wants. However, during the Soviet-style state syndicate, citizens belonged to the state and the applicable principle was that they were required to receive prior administrative licenses for their activities. China, in following this tradition, required numerous administrative licenses in various sectors.

According to official statistics, in 2002 sixty-five agencies under the State Council reported 4,159 administrative-licensing requirements, indicating an overwhelming inundation of administrative licenses. What is even more absurd is that township and county governments also required administrative licenses. For example, in order to set up a stall to sell goods, a prospective vendor had to pay repeated visits to various government agencies so as to obtain some one dozen official stamps (that is, permissions). This clumsy system of multiple administrative licenses was a hotbed of exchanging money for power.

Ma: In August 2003 the Standing Committee of the National People's Congress adopted the Administrative Licensing Law (it entered into effect one year later) to prohibit arbitrary administrative licenses, probably with a view to preventing abuses of administrative powers.

This law stipulates the principles for requiring administrative licensing: any problem that can be addressed by market mechanisms should be left to those mechanisms; if a problem cannot be resolved by market mechanisms but can be dealt with by nongovernmental intermediaries, it should be left to such self-disciplined organizations; and if a problem must be handled by the government, then the government should focus on ex-post supervision. In other words, the former sequence of addressing problems—"first by the government, second by the self-disciplined organizations, and lastly by the market"—should be reversed.

Wu: For me, the most significant provision of this legislation is that only the National People's Congress, the State Council, and the provincial and municipal people's congresses with legislative powers have authority to require administrative licensing. All administrative licenses required by other agencies were declared invalid. Because of this provision, the law is important in setting norms for and restraining administrative behavior. It is also essential for protecting the legal interests of citizens, legal persons, and other organizations.

If this legislation were to be properly implemented, administrative licensing would be contained within a strictly defined scope and the number of matters subject to administrative licenses would be significantly reduced. This would lead to a large downsizing in the number of government agencies and their staff, and it would be a powerful impetus for reforming the administrative system. Before the legislation entered into effect, the State Council confirmed the validity of several hundred licenses and indicated that the remainder of the licenses would be declared invalid. But in reality, the legislation has not been truly implemented. Because power to approve investment projects has been retained, the principle "it is permitted if it is not prohibited" is merely empty rhetoric.

Ma: In China there is an erroneous belief about the relationship between administrative licensing and corruption. People think that prior administrative reviews are an effective instrument for containing corruption. There is a traditional blind faith in administrative powers. Whenever socioeconomic contradictions occur, people first seek to enhance intervention and control by the government.

Wu: According to the theory of rent seeking, in fact the exact opposite is the case. When a new layer of administrative licenses is added, another rent-seeking opportunity is created. Take the stock exchanges as an example. There have been attempts to contain fraud in IPO (initial public offering) practices by tightening the licensing requirements. Before a company can go public, it must be recommended by the provincial Communist Party and government agencies and go through several layers of review by the regulatory authorities. Because of such complexities and multiple layers, the IPO process has in fact become an arena for rent seeking. Companies seeking to go public must pay huge amounts. For instance, there used to be a quite abnormal phenomenon: the company name of a listed shell company that was in default (a so-called empty shell company) could sell for several dozen million RMB. This indicates that the opportunity costs to go through the mandatory review procedures—that is, payments to the various parties—were equal to several dozen million RMB.

Ma: What the general public has observed is totally consistent with the above analysis. In recent years, the enlarged administrative powers have resulted in a worsening of corruption, which has eroded deep into the body of the Communist Party and government. The buying and selling of government positions has become ever-more fashionable.

Wu: Another undercurrent beneath this grave situation is the distorted macroeconomic measures that have created opportunities for privileged groups to establish rents.

In the fourth quarter of 2003, the Chinese economy began to overheat. In order to maintain steady growth, the government adopted macroeconomic measures to cool down the economy. However, the macroeconomic situation was erroneously seen as only "partially overheating," or only occurring in certain industries. Based on this judgment, the government did not use the indirect instruments of a market economy, that is, fiscal and monetary macroeconomic management policies. Instead, it relied on administrative means, such as ministry directives and prior reviews, to directly control investments and production in the overheated industries, for instance, the iron and steel, and aluminum industries. Since then, using administrative means for macroeconomic management has become an official guiding principle. Governments at various levels have enhanced their interference and control in the microeconomy in the name of macroeconomic management. As administrative powers for allocating resources have been increased, the basic role of the market has been weakened.

Since 2004, the most prominent examples of this have been the microeconomic interventions and the price controls by ministries and local governments.

Enhanced administrative interventions have expanded the institutional basis for rent seeking. A phenomenon of the command economy has again become popular as people are rushing in and out of the ministries to obtain funding.

To summarize, when the market-oriented reforms had not yet been completed, administrative allocations of resources became mixed with market allocations of resources. Under this system, corruption spread and more rent-seeking opportunities were created. In other words, the number of matters subject to administrative licensing increased and administrative interventions in economic activities were enhanced, thus exacerbating the corruption.

Ma: There is another important reason for the prevalence of corruption in recent years. Some people holding power have become billionaires overnight by stripping public assets during the ownership restructuring in the period of transition.

This was a period with major changes in ownership structures and relative interests. Before the transition, there had been no clear definition of property rights over public assets. During the transition, the clarification of property rights was led by the government and oversight of administrative powers was ineffective. Some government officials took advantage of this opportunity (that is, the adjustment of property relations) to encroach upon or devour public assets.

Wu: A property regime is a basic social system. Under the command economy, all property belongs to the state. In these circumstances, there is no need, and it is indeed impossible, to define property ownership. After the inception of the reforms, the blurred property rights became problematic. Market relations are exchanges of property rights between different entities. To establish a market economy, the previous blurred property relations had to be changed into clearly defined rights. More often than not, the adjustments to the property rights were controlled by government officials. When power was not subject to tight monitoring and strict restrictions, some officials used their unrestrained power to seize public property.

For instance, during the reforms of state-owned enterprises, the real "bosses" (the whole people) did not assume responsibility. Rather, they let the enterprise managers handle the ownership changes. In management studies, this is called *self-dealing*. Although they were authorized to be the agents of the owners, the enterprise managers gave themselves more powers and more benefits. It was easy for selfish agents to protect their own interests at the expense of the interests of the owners.

A common practice was to maintain "little coffers" at the enterprise level, depriving the state coffers of their due revenue. Some large SOEs, in particular, foreign trade companies trading in international futures markets, could generate high returns but they also faced high risks. Their losses would be assumed by the government, but the earnings would go into the "little coffers" at the enterprise level, or even into their personal pockets. Another practice was for enterprises to set up subsidiary companies to rob the public. A ministerial-level enterprise could have more than one thousand legal entities, going down to the fourth or fifth subsidiary level. These were all scattered, both domestically and abroad. The head of the big family might never know exactly how many subsidiaries he had. Under these circumstances, the transfer of interests was easy. When the administrative-control arrangements were changed, the involved parties were often unaware of the existence of these entities. For instance, when foreign trade companies were moved from the Ministry of Foreign Trade and Economic Cooperation to the State Economic and Trade Commission, or when agricultural SOEs were handed over to the Communist Party enterprise working committees, or when defense enterprises were divested from the military and placed under an office in charge of the divestment of these enterprises, their subordinate firms at the fourth or fifth levels "automatically" dropped out of the organizations. In addition, when an enterprise went public, the tradable shares were priced at a high premium to seize more funding from the investors, whereas the nontradable "original" shares were distributed internally or were sold at low prices. This was another popular method to strip public property. These kinds of dealings in company shares resulted in the dismissal of two ministers. And this story is just the tip of the iceberg.

Ma: As you mentioned in Dialogue 5, there were many loopholes in the SOE reform that focused on decentralization and benefit sharing. During that reform, the main approaches were "enterprise contracting," "delegation of operational authority," and "delegation of authority to invest." Because of these practices, the agents (contractors) became the real masters of the property. They could use their powers to strip enterprise assets. The delegation of operational authority gave factory directors power to decide on the possession, operation, and disposal of enterprise assets. This practice provided some legal basis for managers to seize assets at will.

Wu: During the transformation of the SOE sector, the state did not assume the owner's responsibility to effectively supervise those whom it had entrusted with the exercise power. This failure created much space for corruption, resulting in tremendous losses of public property.

In general, the transformation took the form of corporatization, with the owners of the state shares and the shares of state-owned legal entities clearly defined. On the surface, property rights appeared to have been clarified. The authorized investment agencies, that is, the previous SOEs (alternatively called *holding companies, enterprise groups,* or *asset management companies*) exercised their rights to the state shares as the controlling shareholders. However, because these agencies were enterprises whose managers were the authorized representatives of the owner, the owner was not involved, and it was impossible to establish checks and balances between the owner and the managers. It can be said that the "insider control" was thus maintained. When an authorized investment agency was both the authorized representative of the owner and an insider hired by the owner, the executives could use their power to seek personal benefits or benefits for their cliques. A common practice was to let a parent company (the authorized investment agency) delay the repayment of loans taken from a listed subsidiary.

When the owner was not involved, internal financial control inevitably became lax. Insider trading tended to appear in some state-owned securities firms or futures trading companies, whereby the staff would pocket the returns and shift the losses to their employers. By the turn of the century, a total of RMB 1.4 trillion of nonperforming loans was taken out of the state-owned banks. By 2002, when these banks were to be listed on the stock markets, their nonperforming loans had reached RMB 1.8 trillion, entirely wiping out their equity. A significant factor behind these enormous losses was the corruption in the state sector.

Ma: Because of the existence of an enabling institutional basis, corruption has run rampant. According to some economists, the incomes of corrupt officials and "red-hat" businessmen have reached astronomical levels.

Wu: Since corruption usually takes place behind closed doors, it is difficult to precisely calculate the amount of income from corruption. However, because the amount of bribes (that is, the costs of rent seeking) must be higher than zero but lower than the rent to be received, there is a positive correlation between the amount of income from corruption and the scale of rent-seeking activities. This is why economists use the size of the economic rent to assess the level of corruption in a country. As mentioned in Dialogue 9, in 1974 American economist Anne Krueger conducted pioneering analysis in this regard. Since 1988, many Chinese economists have used Krueger's methodology to estimate the size of the rent in contemporary China. The findings are shocking, but they are consistent with the intuitive feelings of the general public about corruption.

Ma: In 1989 economist Hu Heli found that total economic rent in 1988 was RMB 456.9 billion, accounting for 30 percent of GDP. In 1995 economist Wan Anpei estimated that in 1992 total rent accounted for 32.3 percent of GDP. These were shocking figures when compared to what Krueger had found in India and Turkey. In her 1994 article "The Political Economy of the Rent-Seeking Society," Krueger estimates that economic rent accounted for 7 percent of GDP in India and 15 percent in Turkey, and these two countries were widely considered to be corrupt.

Wu: After the onset of the global financial crisis in 2008, the Chinese government adopted an economic stimulus program to "expand demand and maintain growth." Under this program, local governments obtained more resources and their administrative powers were enlarged significantly. Their role in economic activities became increasingly important. The space for rent seeking thus expanded enormously. It is no exaggeration to say that corruption and monopolies have become the two biggest economic problems facing China.

Corruption in the economic arena has led to corruption in the political arena. Since unrestrained administrative powers have a high "value," people are willing to pay high prices for them. In the mid-1990s, the practice of buying and selling official positions began to spread in Communist Party and government agencies. After the turn of the century, the phenomenon became even worse. In 2005 a case was disclosed in which more than nine hundred people had obtained various government positions through buying and selling. The case involved a vice Communist Party secretary of Heilongjiang province, the Communist Party secretary of Suihua municipality, several provincial-level government officials, and more than one hundred prefectural-level officials. It was the largest case of buying and selling of official positions since the establishment of the People's Republic. In addition, according to mass media reports, between 2008 and 2010 the total number of official appointments made in violation of the laws and regulations reached 10,716. This political corruption is extremely dangerous. It not only has an effect similar to "bad money driving out the good," but also it alienates the public nature of government. All possible internal controls are eliminated and government organizations become downright cliques of corruption.

Ma: Another serious adverse effect of the rampant corruption is the exacerbated social polarization of the rich and the poor. Corrupt officials with power over the use of resources and people who have the connections for rent seeking are in a minority, but they can quickly become rich by using the powers in their possession. Ordinary workers, including SOE employees and especially ordinary farmers, have not benefited much from the reforms. Some cannot even maintain their basic livelihoods because of the lack of social-security guarantees.

During the reforms, the earnings of laid-off SOE workers and of farmers without any non-agricultural source of income increased negligibly, or even decreased.

According to official statistics, between 1998 and 2003 a total of 28.18 million SOE workers were laid off. In the absence of a new social-safety net, the living standards of most of these workers declined. Although farmers' incomes had increased significantly during the early phase of the reform and opening, after 1985 the gap between the urban and rural areas began to expand. By 1993, the difference in consumption between farmers and non-agricultural residents exceeded that during the pre-reform era. Thereafter, the gap continued to widen because of the slow pace in the shift of surplus labor from the rural areas to the urban non-agricultural sectors. According to the National Bureau of Statistics, in 2011 the ratio of per capita disposable income of urban residents to the net income of rural residents was 3.13:1, whereas in most countries this ratio is below 1.6:1.

Wu: Beginning in the second half of the 1980s, the gap between the rich and the poor increased dramatically. According to the National Bureau of Statistics, the Gini coefficient was 0.30 in the early 1980s. By 2003, it had climbed 0.479 and by 2008, it reached 0.491. Although it declined somewhat after 2008, in 2012 it still stood at 0.474. In terms of deciles, official statistics reveal that in 2011 the income of households in the top decile was 23.6 times that of the income of households in the lowest decile, exceeding the readings in the developed countries and in most of the developing countries as well. The National Economic Research Institute under the China Reform Foundation reported a ratio of 67:1 in 2011. Furthermore, during the last decade the gap in household wealth has been expanding much faster than the increase in household income. According to the findings of the China Family Panel Studies conducted by the Institute of Social Science Survey at Peking University, in 1995 the Gini coefficient of net wealth was 0.45; by 2002, it had climbed to 0.55; and by 2012, it had reached 0.73. The top 1 percent of households possessed 34.6 percent of the national wealth, as compared to the bottom 25 percent of households that held only 1.2 percent of the national wealth. The continuous widening of the rich-poor divide will inevitably cause serious social conflicts and pose a threat to social stability.

Ma: As the polarization of the rich and the poor has become a major social problem, different understandings of its causes have emerged. One representative view claims that the society had been equal before the reform and opening and that the current problems are caused by the market-oriented reforms. According to this view, the reforms gave priority to efficiency with due consideration to fairness, but too much emphasis was placed on efficiency at the expense of equality. If there had not been any market-oriented reforms, the shocking gulf between the rich and the poor would not have occurred. This is an important argument for enhancing government intervention and increasing the share of the state sector in the national economy, which runs counter to the market-oriented reforms.

Wu: There are two questions to be asked about a view that holds the market economy is responsible for the worsening of the divide between the rich and the poor. The first question is, Was Chinese society really equal before the reform and opening? The second question is, Are the market-oriented reforms really the culprit?

Historian Yang Kuisong has conducted in-depth studies on the first question. According to his research, in August 1955 the central government led by the Chinese Communist Party abolished an income distribution arrangement whereby free daily necessities were provided to certain government employees. Instead, a graded salary system was put in place. There were thirty grades, with the highest paying a monthly salary of RMB 560 and the lowest paying RMB 18 per month. The difference between the highest and lowest grades was more than 30.11 times. In 1956 the State Council issued a set of new salary criteria, leading to a difference of 36.4 times between the highest and lowest grades. At that time, the average difference between the highest and lowest salaries of civil servants (including chief officials) in the UK, France, and Germany was about eight to ten times. Although the gap in the United States and Japan was larger, it was only about twenty times. Even worse than the graded salary system was the preferential treatment of those in the administrative hierarchy in terms of housing, medical care, domestic workers, security guards, personal secretaries, and automobiles. There were huge differences in the treatment of officials at different administrative levels. If the costs of the various privileges are included, the income gap between the top and bottom groups would be simply astonishing.

These statistics show that China was not an equal society before the reform and opening. Because of the large differences in incomes and treatments based on the grading system, the bureaucratic system was strengthened, resulting in social inequalities.

Did the market-oriented reforms that "gave priority to efficiency and due consideration to fairness in income distribution"[2] cause the divide between the rich and the poor? The distributional principle behind the dominant egalitarianism of the 1980s was based on the theory that there is a negative correlation between equality and efficiency. Even at the time that this principle was adopted, its theoretical framework was being questioned.

Equality can be viewed in terms of opportunities and results. According to American economist Arthur Okun, there are "substitution effects" (a negative correlation) between efficiency and equality. Okun's proposition refers to the negative correlation between efficiency and equality in terms of results. By and large, efficiency and opportunity equality are complementary. There is a positive correlation between them. In other words, both are achievable.

In fact, the current polarization of wealth is mainly due to the inequality of opportunity, and a main cause of this inequality is corruption. Social inequality and the

[2] "Giving priority to efficiency with due consideration to fairness" is the guiding principle for income distribution, as adopted at the 1993 Third Plenary Session of the Fourteenth National Communist Party Congress. It remained in effect until 2005.

consequent rich-poor divide can only be resolved by furthering the market-oriented reforms and realizing equality of opportunity.

Inequality of opportunity also occurs in a market economy. For instance, in a knowledge economy, people who have received a higher education will have more job opportunities and higher incomes. Those without a higher education or those who are not equipped with the requisite skills will face unprecedented employment pressures and their incomes will be relatively low. This is the so-called digital divide. Elimination of this inequality is a responsibility of the public sector and it should be dealt with through a compulsory education program supported by the government. In addition, in a market economy there will also be inequality of results due to capability differences. This problem should be addressed by certain social policies, such as the establishment of a social-security system, support for the development of social-welfare charities, and collection of an inheritance tax and a capital gains tax.

Ma: There are no theories or empirical findings that support the claim that strengthened government intervention and a higher share of the state sector will help contain corruption and achieve relative fairness. Because enhancement of state power will expand the institutional basis for rent seeking, adoption of this claim as a guiding principle will create a vicious cycle: expansion of state power will lead to entrenchment of the institutional basis for rent seeking, which will then result in a further expansion of state power and a further entrenchment of the institutional basis for rent seeking.

Wu: Although both social-science analyses and actual practice in China suggest that it is the enhancement of the state sector that has contributed to the worsening corruption and the increased inequality, there are still people who advocate that the state sector should be strengthened. These people have resorted to populism to direct the general public's dissatisfaction about corruption and inequality in terms of income distribution against the market-oriented reforms.

Ma: There have been two ideological trends. One supports the dominant role of the state and the state economy and advocates government control over the market and over society. This trend is opposed to the reform and opening. Another trend backs the development of a prosperous, civilized, and democratic China. These two trends have risen and subsided in turn. In the early 2000s, when the reform was halted and corruption was spreading, the former trend gradually gained an upper hand. Some people even dug out Mao's slogan of "continuous revolution under proletarian dictatorship" in an attempt to return to the "comprehensive dictatorship over the capitalists" that had been implemented during the Cultural Revolution. In May 2004, American writer Joshua Ramo published a paper entitled "The Beijing Consensus," in which he suggests that China's economic growth model should replace the Washington Consensus, which advocates privatization, liberalization, and transparency in economic development and that the developing countries should adopt the so-called "China model."

Wu: If Ramo's "Beijing's consensus" is generic, then the later proposition of a so-called "China model" provides details and explains its advantages.

Supporters of this model believe the greatest advantage, and the main characteristic, of the model is that China has a powerful government. Because the Chinese government has the "most powerful administrative capacity in the world today," it can "concentrate efforts and resources on important matters" in pursuit of the "great national objective." These supporters regard the so-called "China model" as not only the foundation for China's rise but also an unparalleled miracle.

However, the Great Leap Forward and the Cultural Revolution, which were launched by the powerful government and were guided by the slogan that it was establishing "a Communist paradise on earth," brought about grave disasters that, despite some people's attempts to cover them up, cannot be erased from history. Furthermore, such touted "miracles" have revealed that the serious negative effects were concealed by the short-term political achievements. Such revelations have led many people to realize that the so-called miracles did not produce a bright path to build a prosperous modern China.

Ma: Corruption has jeopardized China's economic development and social stability. The public has strongly appealed for actions against corruption, and senior national leaders have repeatedly pointed out that corruption is a life-and-death matter affecting the future of the Communist Party. Despite these appeals and statements, corruption is becoming ever-more rampant because government officials have gained too much power and too much control over too many resources. An effective system, by which to supervise government officials and to restrain government power, is lacking. Whether corruption can be contained remains a question of whether there is a political will and whether there is a capacity to carry out reforms that are oriented toward a market economy, rule of law, and democracy.

DIALOGUE 20

RESTARTING THE REFORM AGENDA

Ma Guochuan (Ma): In Dialogue 19 we further reviewed both the bright and dark developments in China over the last thirty years.

These developments highlight the best and the worst of China's economic system. Based on these circumstances, several different views on the question, whither China? surfaced at the beginning of this century.

Wu Jinglian (Wu): I have reiterated many times that with its system of a semi-command, semi-market economy, Chinese society faces the question, whither China? It is a grim question that can have two possible answers: the first is a reform path, that is, improving the market-economy system, restraining administrative powers, and achieving rule of law. The other answer is the path of state capitalism, that is, intensifying the role of the state in the direction of crony capitalism. China's economic development can be viewed as a race between these two trends. The results will depend on which trend runs faster.

Against this backdrop, at the beginning of this century two main socioeconomic views were formulated.

The first view advocates upholding the reforms to create a market-oriented economy, the rule of law, and democracy. The reforms will gradually replace the legacies of the former system with rule-based market institutions, which can also be called a *market economy based on rule of law*.

The objective of the second view is to achieve a semi-command, semi-market system. The claims of the so-called "China model," which have been hotly debated since 2008, are typical of this view. It is argued that China's outstanding economic performance during the last twenty to thirty years can be primarily attributed to the existence of a powerful government that has strong control over the economy. These institutional arrangements can ensure the successful formulation and implementation of the national strategy. Not only should China uphold this model, but other countries should learn from it as well. In addition, some representatives of privileged groups are actively promoting the current system. They are trying to further strengthen the unrestrained powers of the government in order to expand the institutional basis for rent seeking.

The debates between these two views unfolded at a time when the impact of crony capitalism on social life was becoming increasingly noticeable. In these circumstances, a third view appeared that called for a return to the former political line and the Maoist system. Advocates of this view claimed that the market-oriented reforms are the cause of all the problems in today's China—from the rampant corruption and inequality in income distribution to the difficulties of receiving adequate healthcare and education and even the losses of state assets and the frequent mining disasters. Their solution was to expand the power of the government, enhance administrative interventions in the economy, re-nationalize industry and commerce so that the state sector will advance and the private sector will retreat, and "consolidate the dispersed land" in order to re-collectivize agriculture. These people even advocated a return to the Great Proletarian Cultural Revolution, relying on the political slogans of that time, such as "continuous revolution under the dictatorship of the proletariat" and "all-round dictatorship over the bourgeoisie."

As we mentioned in the previous dialogues, the appalling social phenomena today are due to the incomplete economic reforms and the lagging political reforms, and they have also been caused by the further intensification and interference of administrative powers to suppress legitimate economic activities. They are the results of widespread rent-seeking practices. Resentment of these phenomena among the general public is justified, and this resentment should be an important impetus for further reforms to remove the institutional traps and to eradicate the corruption. However, when ideological guidance deviated from the correct direction and when dispassionate reasoning was suppressed, defenders of the former political line and the former system took advantage of the public resentment about the spread of corruption and the increasingly felt disadvantages among the vulnerable social groups. They tried to divert the public's attention and turn the target from crony capitalism to the market-oriented reforms.

Ma: Since the various phenomena of crony capitalism are caused by unrestrained power that interferes in economic activities and dominates economic resources, it would be counterproductive to enhance the government's "dictatorship-like" powers and the state-sector monopoly in order to contain the corruption and reduce the rich-poor divide.

Although supporters of the former system joined the general public in condemning the corruption, their prescription for curing the disease was based on a mistaken diagnosis of its origins. Nevertheless, their view was influential because it aroused populism and nationalism.

Wu: People should be aware of the rise of populism and nationalism. If left unchecked, these tendencies will result in extreme social chaos and will block the country's modernization process. Various pioneers spent close to one hundred years trying to transform Chinese society during the twentieth century. As my sage Gu Zhun once said, this experience shows that despite the most sincere and best of intentions, the path represented by the French Revolution (1789), the Paris Commune (1871), and the Russian October Revolution (1917) did not lead mankind to a promised earthly paradise; instead the path resulted in huge disasters and a further backpedaling of history. This situation is similar to that of Nora in Henrik Ibsen's *A Doll's House*, who left her husband and children but, in the end, ends up back with her children (in the Norwegian writer's alternative ending of the play).

Chinese history over the course of the last several thousand years has been characterized by a vicious cycle of uprisings leading to a new dynasty, the new dynasty leading to new tyranny, and coming full circle back to more uprisings. In modern times, "the salvoes of the October Revolution" brought Leninism to China, or, to be more accurate, as Gu Zhun put it, it brought us along the path from 1789 to 1871 to 1917. When the People's Republic was established in 1949, many of us thought that the vicious cycle of history had finally been broken and that it would never again be repeated. But contrary to expectations, seventeen years after the victory of the revolution, China became engulfed in the disaster of the Great Proletarian Cultural Revolution. In Gu Zhun's words, "Under the guise of honoring the revolutionary martyrs, the revolutionary idealism turned into a backward-looking reactionary despotism." Why did the radical revolutionary path fail to improve the people's welfare and achieve social progress? Why did it instead lead to Jacobin or Stalinist despotism? Gu Zhun's answer was that the goal of the leaders was to establish a paradise on earth and they believed that they embodied the will of the people. Based on this belief, it was completely legal for them to engage in totalitarianism, terror, and slaughter in order to achieve their final goal.

The history of the world demonstrates that both the ultra-leftist and the ultra-rightist paths will result in social havoc. Although the reforms have yielded amazing results, China still has a long way to go to become prosperous, democratic, and modernized. In particular, social contradictions have been exacerbated in recent years because of the delay of important reforms in various economic and political arenas. Because of differences in their social backgrounds and in their personal values, people also differ in terms of their ideas about the origins of these contradictions and the possible solutions. At a time when the contradictions are attracting more attention and debates about them are intensifying, a major task related to the destiny of our nation is to prevent the extreme ideological trends from tearing up the society and placing the various social groups in sharp opposition. It is critical that we not go down this ruinous one-way street again.

Ma: Some people believe it is China's fate to alternate between tyranny and mob rule and between order and chaos. They regard this as our unavoidable destiny. Because of the delays in the reforms, this pessimistic view is currently quite popular.

Wu: However, I do not believe this is a valid conclusion. The samsāra of history was a product of the traditional social structure. In modern times, because of the changes in the socioeconomic structure, it is possible that the middle forces will dominate the trend of social development and that a new middle class will become a nucleus for the pursuit of freedom, equality, and social harmony. At present, the rapidly growing middle class in China is primarily composed of white-collar workers. In due course, as this class matures, it is entirely possible that China will break the historical cycles and proceed on a march toward becoming a modern nation.

Ma: When different views confront each other, debates should be dominated by reason, solid justifications, and the provision of evidence. It is worrisome to see calm discussions become swamped in slander and rumor. When verbal violence is employed to win a debate, it is a sign that various political propositions may turn extreme.

Wu: As Polish economist Włozimierz Brus once said, a prerequisite for successful reform is free and rational discussion. If the current debates over the various ideological views can be carried out reasonably, there may be a smooth social transformation in China. However, why has there been a trend in the direction of extremism? In essence, this has been due to an accumulation of many social contradictions over the years. During the last thirty years the entrepreneurial spirit of the people released by the new market-economy institutions created China's economic miracle. Unfortunately, in recent years the role of the government has been expanded and control by state-owned enterprises has been strengthened. This has brought the various socioeconomic contradictions almost to a breaking point. If the root causes of these contradictions are not eliminated by steady and orderly reforms, extreme solutions will win more support.

The correct path to overcoming the social maladies and avoiding a historical tragedy is to establish a full-fledged market economy. In other words, in order to eradicate the roots of crony capitalism efforts should be made to resist the interference by privileged groups, promote further market-oriented economic reforms, and support political reforms toward the rule of law and democracy. The deployment of public powers should be restrained by the Constitution and should be subject to public monitoring. There is no other path. Because the reforms have been halted in recent years, it has now become all the more urgent that they be reinstated on the government's agenda and be earnestly implemented.

Ma: It is only after a reform agenda for a market economy, the rule of law, and democracy is re-launched and overall reform objectives are formulated (that is, a top-down reform design) will it be necessary to discuss the details.

Wu: With regard to reform of the economic system, the central issue remains the development of a fully competitive system whereby the market plays a basic role in resource allocations.

The existing problems reveal that the threats to fair market competition come from two directions: the state-sector monopoly over important industries and the excessive government interference in the market.

Ma: The state-sector monopoly exists in two forms. Under the economic monopoly, the state-owned enterprises (SOEs) deploy their huge economic strength acquired from government support to stifle their rivals. Under the administrative monopoly, the administrative powers protect the SOEs (and some nonstate-owned local companies in which the government holds stakes), keep their rivals out of the market, and restrict competition.

Wu: To uproot the first type of monopoly, the economic-ownership structure should be readjusted to allow the state to retreat from certain sectors while advancing in others. At present, SOEs and governments at various administrative levels control too many economic resources, especially land and capital. They have invested most of these resources in profit-making enterprises that compete with the private sector. This is abnormal for a market economy. The decision of the 1997 Fifteenth National Communist Party Congress should be upheld to allow the state sector to gradually exit from the competitive sectors.

The basic function of a government is to provide public goods, but many public goods are currently in short supply in China. For instance, the coverage of social-security funds and the provision of public housing, which should be financed by state capital owned by the so-called whole people, cannot meet demand. Years ago, there was a proposal to allow the National Council for Social Security Fund to hold about RMB 1 trillion of equity in various state-owned companies in order to repay the social-security debts that the state owed to older workers and to fully fund their individual accounts.

In more recent years, various economists have put forward good proposals that should be carefully studied as candidates for adoption. Professor Chen Qingtai has recommended that state assets be turned into state capital and that 30 to 50 percent of state capital in the competitive sectors be transferred to social-security funds and public-welfare funds so that the state assets will be truly owned by the whole people and the benefits will be shared by all citizens. I support Professor Chen's proposal. To implement this proposal, a special agency should be established to deploy and manage the state capital. Such an agency should be responsible for formulating rules to manage the investment of the funds and to supervise their operations.

Ma: Given the experiences in Russia and other transition economies, as well as in some localities in China, people are concerned that wide-ranging transformation of the SOEs may lead to large-scale losses of state assets.

Wu: Such concerns are justified. However, just as "all crows are black" is a false claim, it is also not true that the past experience of SOE transformation was all negative. In some countries (and also in some localities in China), where the legal framework was sound and the monitoring of the reforms was effective, or where more appropriate approaches had been adopted, the SOE reforms achieved better results. Avoiding the reforms will not eliminate the dangers of asset stripping. Those in power or connected with power may use other means to erode or devour public wealth. The government should assume its responsibility to use all necessary instruments to prevent abuses of power in the state-sector reforms in order to avoid polarization in the possession of the original property.

Ma: Since the state economy is huge in size, a significant part of state capital may have to be retained in the profit-making sectors for a long time.

Wu: With the exception of a few SOEs as special legal entities in some particular industries that will continue to be solely operated by the state, most SOEs in the profit-making sectors should be transformed into companies with diversified ownerships. As enterprises, these SOEs should do their best to become both stronger and bigger. However, they should also compete with other economic ownerships on an equal footing and should not be given any special powers or preferential treatments. Because shared development among different economic ownerships is a reliable basis for the party in power, the Communist Party should not treat entities with different ownerships as if they are different castes. All economic entities should be treated equally.

Ma: You have touched upon an important question: How can we implement the calls by the Seventeenth National Communist Party Congress to provide equal protection of property rights and to create a new environment for fair competition and mutual promotion among economic entities with different ownerships?

Wu: On the one hand, the monopolistic privileges of the SOEs and some nonstate-owned enterprises that are favored by the government should be removed. On the other, the discriminatory provisions against the private sector should be cancelled; this should be based on the principle that "you can do anything as long as it is not prohibited." In addition, private businessmen should be trained and provided with support so as to refrain from engaging in unethical conduct, such as consorting with government officials, willingly depending on the government, and associating with SOEs to engage in rent seeking.

Ma: Another important issue that you have raised is the need to eliminate the administrative monopolies. Unlike the developed market economies, the current system in China evolved from a command economy operating with many legacies of the Leninist state-syndicate model. The government grants monopolistic powers to some SOEs and to some private-sector enterprises. These firms exclude or restrict competition in violation of market rules. Some scholars have called the administrative monopolies "a big economic nuisance." Legal theorists and economists, based on their in-depth studies on the relevant phenomena and the currently impotent Anti-Monopoly Law, have put forth recommendations to curb these types of monopolies. However, their proposals have not yet attracted the attention of the authorities.

Wu: Administrative monopolies have indeed hindered the development of an environment for fair competition. This presents a serious economic challenge. The problem has become even worse because of ineffective anti-monopoly enforcement and major shortcomings in the current system. The 2007 Anti-Monopoly Law of the People's Republic of China contains a chapter on administrative monopolies (chapter 5, on the abuse of administrative powers to exclude or restrict competition). However, the law narrowly defines this type of monopoly as "abuses of administrative powers." Furthermore, the law narrowly defines "abuse" as an action that creates an obstacle to the free exchange of goods between localities. This means that, with the exception of local protectionism, other administrative monopolistic behavior is legal. Based on this law, administrative monopolies by economic entities are to be handled by the national-level anti-monopoly authorities, such as the Ministry of Commerce, the State Administration for Industry and Commerce, and the National Development and Reform Commission. When government agencies or organizations entrusted with public administrative functions are in breach of the law, it is up to their superiors to issue corrective instructions.

It is well known that administrative monopolies are generally formed by the instructions or regulations of the authorities. Asking these authorities to instruct their enterprises to amend the relevant regulations is like asking a tiger to give up its prized pelt. Under these circumstances, it is not at all surprising that the administrative monopolies have become rampant.

Ma: Many scholars believe that a main component of the Anti-Monopoly Law should be to provide for the monitoring of government behavior and for the prevention of abuses of administrative powers that restrict or undermine market competition. In order to improve China's market institutions, the anti-monopoly legislation must be modified and legal enforcement must be strengthened.

Wu: In addition to steadfast readjustments in the sectoral distribution of state capital and continuous SOE reforms, the judicial system must also be reformed to prevent the monopolies from blocking the proper functioning of the socialist market economy. First, judicial reform should either amend the current Anti-Monopoly Law or should adopt a separate anti-administrative-monopoly law that targets Communist Party and government agencies. Second, there should be an authority above the Communist Party and government agencies that is responsible for handling both economic- and administrative-monopoly cases. Third, because administrative monopolies are often linked to improper behavior by government agencies, the Administrative Law should also be revised to authorize the courts to monitor the government and to correct any inappropriate behavior.

All in all, China should establish inclusive economic institutions. In their new book *Why Nations Fail*, American scholars Daron Acemoglu and James Robinson point out that the secret of successful and prosperous nations is "inclusive institutions." According to these scholars, inclusive institutions allow and encourage the general public to participate in economic activities and to give full play to their ingenuity and expertise. Inclusive institutions are part of a system that enables individuals to make their own choices. The main characteristics of inclusive institutions are protection of private-property rights (private ownership), creation of an environment for fair competition (guarantees for individual entrepreneurship and the rule of law), and encouragement of investments and technological innovations. All failed nations share the same characteristic—bad extractive institutions. "Extractive institutions" serve a tiny minority at the expense of the majority and suppress the people's creativity and initiative. Although an extractive system may sometimes achieve economic growth, it is based on existing technologies; therefore, it cannot be sustained over the long term and thus may be vulnerable to collapse.

Economic institutions and political institutions are mutually complementary. If there are only inclusive economic institutions but no inclusive political institutions, economic development will not be sustainable and eventually will either stagnate or even fail. As the authors of *Why Nations Fail* point out, "While economic institutions are critical for determining whether a country is poor or prosperous, it is politics and political institutions that determine what economic institutions a country has."

Ma: These problems, whether they are economic monopolies or administrative monopolies, are all related to excessive government interventions in the market. Our discussions have demonstrated that economic and political reforms are closely linked. Compared to the reforms of the economic system, the reforms of the political system have not yet met expectations. This lack of progress has attracted attention throughout the country. More and more people have come to realize that without reforming the political system, it will be difficult to carry out further economic reforms or to resolve the various social problems.

What should China do to reform the political system?

Wu: First, the objectives of the political reforms should be clarified. What type of political system should be established in China? This touches upon issues related to the rule of law, democracy, and constitutionalism.

Rule of law as a concept of governance and an institutional arrangement originated in the ancient past, but it has gradually been improved in recent times. The concept has three main dimensions: (a) the law is the only basis for determining punishment; (b) no one is superior to the law; and (c) court decisions are the final defense for individual rights. This notion is fundamentally different from the term *rule by law* that is frequently used these days. It is also not the same as "rule by law" that was practiced by the legalists in ancient China.[1] China's traditional rulers treated law as a tool to enforce their will and to rule their subjects. Modern rule of law is based on laws embodying widely accepted principles of fairness. Everyone is equal before the law.

Historically, development of the rule of law and of democracy did not take place at the same time. Take England as an example. The Magna Carta of 1216 triggered the development of rule of law, but the establishment of democratic institutions did not begin until the 1688 Glorious Revolution. Nevertheless, the two processes were interdependent. Only democracy can guarantee rule of law.

Ma: In China, although no one openly denies democracy as an institution, some people, in particular some government officials, believe that given its current stage of development, China should follow the East Asian authoritarian developmentalism

[1] Translators' note: The legalists, active in ancient China (475–221 BC), were proponents of a school of thought that advocated governance by rigid laws to increase the power of the state.

of the 1960s and 1970s. Under that model, the governments of Singapore, South Korea, and elsewhere in East Asia concentrated significant powers to quickly mobilize resources on a large scale, thus enabling them to achieve their extraordinary economic growth and to produce the "East Asian miracle."

Wu: *Authoritarian developmentalism* is a tool for rapid growth used by a particular country at a particular moment in history; therefore, it should not be the final objective of development. The validity of this model may at best last only for several decades when the developing countries are endeavoring to catch up with the developed world. When a spacecraft reaches a certain altitude, the booster rocket is discarded. Once an economic takeoff is completed, the development model should be transformed from authoritarian developmentalism to democratic developmentalism. This is because the legality of authoritarian developmentalism is derived from the sustained economic growth. However, when economic development reaches a certain stage, the growth rate will inevitably slow down and social problems, such as inequality and corruption, will intensify. It is at that time that a democratic system should be established to establish the legality of the government.

In fact, authoritarian developmentalism has an inherent transformative mechanism: when an economy develops, social values begin to diversify and the newly emerging middle class will demand more democratic rights. As the Japanese economist Toshio Watanabe has said, the economic-development success of an authoritarian system is the seed for the self-destruction of this system. This is why South Korea, Malaysia, Indonesia, and Taiwan (China) all turned to democracy, although some achieved this goal peacefully and others underwent a violent process.

Ma: There are two basic types of democracy: radical *people's democracy*, as under the Jacobin dictatorship after the 1789 French Revolution, and *constitutional democracy*, as after the 1688 Glorious Revolution in England. China's Cultural Revolution is an example of Jacobin democracy.

Wu: A democratic system in China can only be a constitutional democracy. As we know, the constitution is the basic charter for quantifying state powers. The essence of constitutionalism is to place restraints on those entities that are given powers. There should be no supreme and unrestrained power. Radical people's democracy was a model of popular sovereignty in name only. It was actually governance by several charismatic leaders. Constitutional democracy is different. This model, seeking a balance of power, will prevent a few individuals from seizing public power and thus it will better ensure the realization of popular sovereignty.

Ma: You have mentioned that rule of law, democracy, and constitutionalism are closely linked, or even mutually related. But they cannot be established and improved all at once. Given the Chinese realities, what is a feasible way to begin the reforms of the political system?

Wu: Considering international experiences and the realities China faces in establishing constitutional democracy, I think adoption of the rule of law may represent a quick win. Furthermore, people are already calling for the rule of law, as it is a prerequisite for the effective functioning of a modern market economy.

As stated in a previous dialogue, the Chinese market has evolved from a market of personalized exchanges into a market of impersonal exchanges, that is, from transactions between acquaintances to transactions between strangers. Bilateral and multilateral concerns about reputations and penalties are no longer effective. There is a need for a third party (mainly the court system) to ensure the enforcement of contracts. Because of the significant weaknesses in China's court system, local capture of the judiciary has become a serious problem in terms of enforcing contracts. In the past, China was rated low on the World Bank's Worldwide Governance Indicators, and its ranking even declined from 45.2 in 2008 to 38.9 in 2012 (the highest score is 100). Under these circumstances, it is difficult for businesspeople to protect their interests in normal ways. As a result, some of them employ inappropriate means, such as collusion with government officials, to obtain protection or to gain a competitive edge.

Ma: These practices have distorted the market economy and have adversely affected China's socioeconomic development: entrepreneurs are less motivated to make innovations; the potential for sustained economic development has been weakened; administrative corruption is worsening; and the income gaps between different social strata have become wider. Calls for the establishment of the rule of law are becoming increasingly vocal because the rule of law is the foundation for a modern market economy.

Wu: In order to establish rule of law, the following three areas must be strengthened.

First, all citizens, in particular government officials at all levels, should embrace the rule-of-law concept. Rule of law is an important component of the core values of modern societies. The concept is the opposite of the traditional autocratic imperial ideology that claimed that "the sovereign is above all" or "all land under heaven belongs to the king." Rule of law is also fundamentally different from the self-proclaimed "revolutionary" concepts that advocated that "a dictatorship is power elevated above all law." Under rule of law, laws are superior to everything. Organizations and individuals, including the political party in power and its leadership, should only act within their legally defined scope: they are not above the law. It is absolutely necessary that a thorough "enlightenment movement" replace the traditional ideological constraints with a set of core modern values.

Second, a legal system that conforms to widely accepted principles of basic justice should be established. Above all, laws and administrative directives should comply with the constitution. The main content and role of a constitution is to distribute power. A constitution should establish the citizens' basic rights and guarantee the inviolability of these rights. It should also define the limits of government power to prevent government from violating the rights of citizens. Under the rule of law, laws must be transparent and they must meet the following basic requirements: broad participation of the general public in the legislative processes and wide dissemination of the laws. According to the modern concept of the rule of law, laws that are unknown to the general public are ineffective. Nowadays, some government officials, disregarding the people's right to know, treat laws and regulations that are related to the people's interests or that reflect the handling of public affairs as confidential internal documents. Public affairs are sometimes dealt with within the government without notifying the general public. Transparency also means that laws must apply to all actors in the society, be secure, and not be retroactively effective, in order to allow citizens to have steady expectations about the legal consequences of their actions and to give them the peace of mind needed to develop their own businesses or careers. If members of a society cannot be the masters of their own fates, they will turn to the abuse of personal connections and bribery to obtain privileged treatment from officials who have significant discretionary powers.

Third, there should be judicial independence and equitable enforcement of the laws. These are basic prerequisites for the rule of law. Corruption by judicial officials and administrative interventions are the main obstacles to meeting these conditions. Improvements in the judicial system will contribute to the removal of these obstacles, but the main means are to improve the quality of the judges and to strengthen the public's monitoring of the judicial processes. As the party in power, the Chinese Communist Party should monitor and guarantee that its members strictly abide by Communist Party discipline and do not violate the laws, and that the judicial agencies comply with the constitution and the laws and regulations. However, the role of the Communist Party should be restricted to ensure the fairness of personnel appointments and judicial procedures. The Communist Party should not make direct personal appointments or intervene in judgments or decisions on specific cases.

Among these three tasks, the legislative improvements have made the most progress. More problems have been encountered with respect to the second task. As several recent serious cases have revealed, the judiciary lacks independence and the laws are not yet superior to all else. Thus, some judicial agencies and personnel have served as tools enabling government officials to engage in corruption. These problems require sincere judicial reforms. Because of China's long history of despotism and ideological indoctrination, as evidenced by the claim that "proletarian dictatorship is not subject to any legal restraints," there are still great hurdles to surmount before the rule of law can be embraced by all citizens.

Ma: In reforming the political system, if adopting the rule of law is the beginning, then reforming the government is the key. At present, China's government is still omnipotent. Despite slogans such as "serve the people" and "be public servants for the people," some officials consider themselves to be the "masters of the society" or the "leaders of the masses." Under the pretext of national goals or the public interest, these officials impose their own will on society and make decisions in the name of the general public, even when the decisions are really related to their own self-interest. This upside-down relationship between the government and the people is accepted by the general public. It is commonplace for local government officials to be called *fu-mu guan* (parent-like officials). Honest officials are often called the "parents of the people." Because of these outmoded habits and customs that conflict with modern political civilizations, some officials have adopted irresponsible attitudes on major issues affecting the people's interests. Instead of serving their constituencies and the taxpayers, some unscrupulous officials use their powers to infringe on the people's interests. Forced demolitions of houses and involuntary resettlements are examples.

Wu: In their summary of the lessons of the Paris Commune 130 years ago, Marx and Engels repeatedly pointed out that it was important to prevent the state and the state organs from evolving from servants of the society into masters of the society. The most serious problem of an "omnipotent government," a notion that originated from Lenin's state syndicate, is the reversal in the master-servant relationship between the people and the government.

Reform of the government involves reversing this inverted relationship so that the government will comply with the requirements of a modern political civilization. In 1980, based on the lessons learned after the Chinese Communist Party came to power, Deng Xiaoping concluded, "It is true that the errors we made in the past were partly attributable to the way of thinking and style of work of some leaders. But they were even more attributable to the problems in our organizational and working systems. If these systems are sound, they can place restraints on the actions of bad people; if they are unsound, they may hamper the efforts of good people or, indeed, in certain cases, may push them in the wrong direction." Deng also said that "Stalin gravely damaged socialist legality, doing things which Comrade Mao Zedong once said would have been impossible in Western countries like Britain, France and the United States.

Yet although Comrade Mao was aware of this, he did not in practice solve the problems in our system of leadership. Together with other factors, this led to the decade of catastrophe known as the 'Cultural Revolution.'"

Since the government is both the target of and the main driving force behind the political reforms, government transformation is the key to the success of these reforms.

Ma: Although many people have realized the need to reform the government, there are different views about the objectives of the reform. Some people are in favor of enhanced government control, whereas others maintain that "smaller is better."

Wu: I think both views are biased. For me, the objective should be to establish a limited and effective government. A limited government is the opposite of the omnipotent (unlimited) government of the command economy. From an economic perspective, the role of the government is limited in a market economy. The government should only possess resources for the provision of public goods, and it should not expand at will. The market should play a basic role in the allocation of scarce resources. An effective government should also be able to provide services to the general public with high efficiency and low costs. It should be subject to public monitoring and should improve its management to prevent corruption and waste.

Ma: Can we say that the goal of a limited government is to restrain the power of government, and the goal of an effective government is to improve government efficiency in terms of serving the public?

Wu: Yes, you are right. A good government is one that performs its duties while providing quality services to the public. Obviously, it will take hard work to achieve this objective. At present, reform of the government must address the following issues.

First, it must ensure that the fundamental rights of citizens are not violated. Both the Constitution of the People's Republic of China and the United Nations Universal Declaration of Human Rights (to which the Chinese government is a signatory) provide for the basic rights of man. They include freedom of speech, press, assembly, association, protest, and religion, as well as personal rights and rights to elect and to be elected. These basic rights of the people must be effectively protected.

Another right is the right to know about the government's official activities. Modern governments all have legislation requiring information disclosures and sunshine laws. Except for national security information that is exempt from publication, all other information should be shared with the general public. Only when information is transparent can citizens exercise their rights as the masters of the country to monitor the government and its officials. In this age of well-developed mass media, such as newspapers and magazines, radio and TV broadcasting, and the Internet, the government should support rather than restrict the exercise of the citizens' constitutional rights to know and to monitor. This should be a basic duty of the government.

Second, the government should strictly comply with the constitution and engage in its businesses based on the law. At present, the government holds too much power over the allocation of land and funds. The boundaries of government activities are not clearly defined, and government officials have excessive discretion and rent-seeking opportunities. Given these problems, effective measures are needed to ensure that all government officials observe the law and discipline so as to prevent them from violating the citizens' basic rights in the name of state interests. Furthermore, the government's power over the allocation of economic resources should be reduced. In recent years, the National People's Congress and the State Council have issued a series of laws and regulations that restrict the government's administrative powers. Currently, the challenge is to ensure that these laws and regulations are implemented.

The Communist Party as the party in power has an important role to play in law-based administration. The Charter of the Chinese Communist Party states that "the Party must conduct its activities within the framework of the Constitution and laws of the country" and that Communist Party members must "abide by the laws and regulations of the state in an exemplary way."

Based on several decades of personal experience as national leader, Deng Xiaoping repeatedly called for addressing the leftist legacies, separating the functions of the Communist Party from those of the government, and preventing the Communist Party from performing the function of the government. Deng also proposed a number of specific measures. Some of these measures were implemented for a while after the 1987 Thirteenth National Communist Party Congress. Lessons from this period should be summarized and the good ones should be promoted.

Third, the electoral system of grassroots-level governments to gradually extend democracy should be improved. The development of political democracy in China began with the election of these lower-level governments. The Third Plenary Session of the Eleventh Communist Party Central Committee called for the gradual realization of direct democracy by the people at these administrative levels and in grassroots social activities. In the early 1980s, villagers' self-governing committees were established after the rural areas adopted household contracting for agricultural production. The 1982 Constitution clearly confirmed this grassroots system of self-governance. The 1987 Organic Law of Village Committees (trial version) stipulated that the directors, deputy directors, and members of the village committees should be directly elected by the villagers. The law, fully adopted in 1998, improved the procedures for direct elections. By 2010, there had been six rounds of elections of village committees throughout the country and several million village officials had been elected rather than appointed.

Some localities also conducted pilots for the direct election of township governments. However, there is still a need to foster an electoral culture. There have been cases of manipulation, bribery, and fraud in these elections. The problems related to governance by village self-governing bodies need to be addressed. There is still a lot to be done to improve government elections at the grassroots level.

Fourth, a civil society must be cultivated, and the self-organizing capabilities of the society must be developed. Diversified interests, with different varieties of social activities, exist in modern society. Public affairs cannot be dealt with only by Communist Party and government agencies. Civic organizations must also be developed to improve self-governance. An important characteristic of the traditional "big government and small society" is full expansion of government powers and maximum contraction of space for civil society. After the end of the Three Great Socialist Transformations in 1956 and, in particular, after the establishment of the people's communes in 1958, social and civic organizations disappeared. The only exception was the family as the basic unit of society, but its independence was at risk as well. All trades were consolidated into a hierarchical, mono-administrative system. It was a system of "fibrotic induration" that lacked vigor and vitality. It can be called "a state without a society." When government leaders made decisions or issued marching orders, the system could use state authority to mobilize as many resources as necessary to achieve state objectives. However, the system had a fatal weakness: social groups lacked a self-organizing capability and therefore they relied on government instructions. Projects without state approval and activities without government permission had to be halted or they would encounter great difficulties. In a country in which the people are supposed to be the masters, the self-organizing capabilities of the civil society must be improved. Civic groups should be allowed to handle various public affairs on their own. Only with these changes will a vigorous social life and a lively political situation emerge, leading to economic, political, and cultural prosperity.

Ma: Further reforms of the political system require that governments at various administrative levels revolutionize themselves. In other words, governments need to forgo certain powers and adopt new social-service functions. Since it is quite difficult to cede power and revolutionize oneself, some government officials have become obstacles to the reforms. They either obstruct implementation of the market-based reforms in an attempt to retain the existing space for rent seeking or they distort the reforms in order to create new rent-seeking opportunities.

Wu: Indeed. China is burdened with a tradition of despotism and lacks experience in democracy and rule of law. It is an important but extremely difficult task to establish a market economy based on constitutionalism, democracy, and rule of law. For more than one hundred years, several generations of Chinese pioneers have strived to modernize the country, but they have invariably suffered frequent setbacks. Over the last thirty years, historic progress has been made in the right direction, but the reforms have not yet passed the critical point and the road ahead remains difficult. Political reforms should be actively but cautiously implemented, while the establishment of a market economy should continue. This is not only the main task for future reforms in China but it also is related to the rise or fall of the Chinese nation and the fundamental interests of all Chinese citizens. On an issue of such great significance, there should be no tolerance for even the slightest hesitation. Only by removing the obstacles and breaking through the barricades can the dream of generations of Chinese people be realized and can China develop into a prosperous, democratic, and civilized modern country.

FURTHER READING

Acemoglu, Daron, and James Robinson. *Why Nations Fail: The Origins of Power, Prosperity and Poverty*. New York: Crown Publishers, 2012.

Bernstein, Eduard. *Selected Writings of Eduard Bernstein, 1900–1921*. Atlantic Highlands, NJ: Humanities Press, 1996.

Brus, Włodzimierz. *The Market in a Socialist Economy*. Translated by Angus Walker. London: Routledge and K. Paul, 1972.

Brus, Włozimierz, and Kazimierz Laski. *From Marx to the Market: Socialism in Search of an Economic System*. New York: Oxford University Press, 1989.

Bukharin, Nicolai, and Evgenii Preobrazhensky. *The ABC of Communism*. 1922. London: Penguin Books, 1969.

Cai Fang, ed. *Transforming the Chinese Economy*. Leiden: Brill, 2010.

Chen Qingtai. "SOE Reform Again in the Spotlight." 2012. *Caijing*, May 22, 2015. http://english.caijing.com.cn/2012-05-22/111855690.html. Accessed September 21, 2015.

Chen Yun. "Problems Arising Following Socialist Transformation." September 1956. In *Selected Works of Chen Yun, Vol. 3 (1956–1994)*. Beijing: Foreign Languages Press, 1999.

Chen Yun. "Problems Concerning Planning and the Market." March 1979. In *Selected Works of Chen Yun, Vol. 3 (1956–1994)*. Beijing: Foreign Languages Press, 1999.

Chen Yun. "Upholding the Principle of Proportional Development in Adjusting the National Economy." March 1979. In *Selected Works of Chen Yun, Vol. 3 (1956–1994)*. Beijing: Foreign Languages Press, 1999.

Coase, Ronald H. "The Problem of Social Cost." *Journal of Law and Economics* 3 (October 1960): 1-44.

Coase, Ronald H., and Ning Wang. *How China Became Capitalist*. New York: Palgrave Macmillan, 2012.

Commentator. "Why Must We Unremittingly Oppose Bourgeois Liberalization." *Contemporary Trends* (April 1991), excerpted in *Renmin ribao* [People's daily]. Translated in Foreign Broadcast Information Service, FBIS-CHI, April 26, 1991.

Dangdai Zhongguo congshu bianjibu. *Dangdai Zhongguo de jingji tizhi gaige* [Contemporary China's economic system reform]. Beijing: Zhongguo shehui kexue chubanshe, 1984.

Deng Xiaoping. "Building Socialism with a Specifically Chinese Character." June 1984. In *Selected Works of Deng Xiaoping, Vol. 3 (1982–1992)*. Beijing: Foreign Languages Press, 1994.

Deng Xiaoping. "Excerpts from Talks Given in Wuchang, Shenzhen, Zhuhai and Shanghai." January–February 1992. In *Selected Works of Deng Xiaoping, Vol. 3 (1982–1992)*. Beijing: Foreign Languages Press, 1994.

Deng Xiaoping. "The Party and the Anti-Japanese Government." April 1941. In *Selected Works of Deng Xiaoping, Vol. 1 (1938–1965)*. Beijing: Foriegn Languages Press, 1992.

Deng Xiaoping. "On Reform of the Political Structure." September–November 1986. In *Selected Works of Deng Xiaoping, Vol. 3 (1982–1992)*. Beijing: Foreign Languages Press, 1994.

Deng Xiaoping. "On the Reform of the System of Party and State Leadership." August 1980. In *Selected Works of Deng Xiaoping (1975–1982)*. Beijing: Foreign Languages Press, 1984.

Deng Xiaoping. "We Must Rationalize Prices and Accelerate Reform." May 1988. *Selected Works of Deng Xiaoping, Vol. 3 (1982–1992)*. Beijing: Foreign Languages Press, 1994.

Dong Fureng. "Guanyu woguo shehuizhuyi suoyouzhi xingshi wenti." 1979. *Jingji yanjiu* [Economic research], no. 1. Translated as "On the Question of the Forms of Socialist Ownership in China," in *Chinese Economic Studies* 23, no. 1 (Fall 1989): 8–23.

Du Runsheng. "On a Responsibility System for Agricultural Production." September 1980. In *Chinese Economists on Economic Reform: Collected Works of Du Runsheng*, edited by China Development Research Foundation. London: Routledge, 2014.

Economics Institute, Academy of Sciences of the USSR. *Textbook on Political Economy*. 1954. London: Lawrence & Wishart, 1957.

Engels, Frederich. "Historical Materialism." 1878. In *Socialism: Utopian and Scientific*. Translated by Edward Aveling. New York: International Publishers, 1935.

Engels, Frederich. "Introduction: On the Twentieth Anniversary of the Paris Commune." 1891. In *The Civil War in France: The Paris Commune*, by Karl Marx and V. I. Lenin. New York: International Publishers, 1968.

Engels, Frederich. "Part 3: Socialism." 1877. In *Anti-Dühring: Herr Eugen Dühring's Revolution in Science*. Peking: Foreign Languages Press, 1976.

Friedman, Milton. "Memorandum from Milton Friedman to Zhao Ziyang." 1988. In *Two Lucky People*, by Milton Friedman and Rose D. Friedman. Chicago: University of Chicago Press, 1998.

Friedman, Milton. "A Monetary and Fiscal Framework for Economic Stability." *American Economic Review* 38, no. 3 (June 1948): 245–264.

Gao Xiqing. "Developments in Securities and Investment Law in China." *Australian Journal of Corporate Law* 6, no. 2 (July 1996): 228–247.

Gu Mu. *Gu Mu huiyilu* [Memoirs of Gu Mu]. Beijing: Zhongyang wenxian chubanshe, 2009.

Guo Shuqing. "Comprehensive Reform Is in Urgent Need of Planning." With Liu Jirui and Qiufang. April 1985. In *Chinese Economists on Economic Reform: Collected Works of Guo Shuqing*, edited by China Development Research Foundation. London: Routledge, 2012.

Hu Heli. "1988 nian woguo zujin jiazhi de gusuan" [Estimated value of rents in 1988]. *Jingji shehui tizhi bijiao* [Comparative economic and social systems], no. 5 (1989): 10–15.

Huangfu Ping. "On Being 'The Sheep That Leads the Flock' during Reform and Opening Up." *Jiefang ribao* [Liberation daily]. February 1991. Translated in Joint Publication Research Service, JPRS-CAR-91-031, May 31, 1991.

Huangfu Ping. "The Consciousness of Expanding Opening Needs to Be Strengthened." *Jiefang ribao* [Liberation daily]. March 1991. Translated in Foreign Broadcast Information Service, FBIS-CHI, April 1, 1991.

Huangfu Ping. "Reform and Opening Require a Large Number of Cadres with Both Morals and Talents." *Jiefang ribao* [Liberation daily]. April 1991. Translated in Foreign Broadcast Information Service, FBIS-CHI, April 17, 1991.

Huerta de Soto, Jesus. "Oskar Lange and the Competitive Solution." In *Socialism, Economic Calculation and Entrepreneurship*. Northampton, MA: Edward Elgar, 2010.

Jiang Yiwei. "The Theory of an Enterprise-Based Economy." *Social Sciences in China* 1, no. 1 (1980): 48–71.

Jiang Zemin. "Concerning China's Establishment of a Socialist Market Economy." 1992. In *Selected Works of Jiang Zemin, Vol. 1*. Beijing: Foreign Languages Press, 2010.

Jingji shehui tizhi bijiao, ed. *Fubai: Huobi yu quanli de jiaohuan* [Corruption: The exchange of power and money]. Beijing: Zhongguo zhanwang chubanshe, 1989.

Jingji shehui tizhi bijiao, ed. *Fubai xun gen: Zhongguo hui cheng wei xunzu shehui ma?* [Finding the root causes of corruption: Will China become a rent-seeking society?]. Beijing: Jingji chubanshe, 1999.

Kornai, János. *Economics of Shortage*. New York: Elsevier North-Holland, 1980.

Kornai, János. *The Socialist System: The Political Economy of Communism*. Princeton, NJ: Princeton University Press, 1992.

Krueger, Anne O. "The Political Economy of the Rent-Seeking Society." *American Economic Review* 64, no. 3 (June 1974): 291–303.

Lardy, Nicholas R. *China's Unfinished Economic Revolution*. Washington, DC: Brookings Institution, 1998.

Lenin, V. I. "A Contribution to the History of Dictatorship: A Note." 1920. In *Collected Works*. Vol. 31. 4th ed. Moscow: Progress Publishers, 1965.

Lenin, V. I. "Speech to the Fourth Congress of the Communist International." 1922. In *Collected Works*. Vol. 33. 2nd ed. Moscow: Progress Publishers, 1965.

Lenin, V. I. *The State and Revolution*. 1917. New York: International Publishers, 1943.

Lenin, V. I. "Two Tactics of Social-Democracy in the Democratic Revolution." 1905. In *Collected Works*. Vol. 9. Moscow: Progress Publishers, 1972.

Lim, Edwin, Ian Porter, Paul Romer, and Michael Spence. *Medium and Long-Term Development and Transformation of the Chinese Economy: An International Perspective*. Beijing: Beijing Cairncross Economic Research Foundation, 2011.

Lim, Edwin, Adrian Wood, Ian Porter, William Byrd, Timothy King, Gerhard Pohl, Robert P. Taylor, Gene Tidrick, and Wouter Tim. *China: Long-Term Development Issues and Options: The Report of a Mission Sent to China by the World Bank*. Baltimore: Johns Hopkins University Press, 1985.

Lin Zili. *Shehuizhuyi jingji lun: Lun Zhongguo jingji gaige*. Beijing: Jingji kexue chubanshe, 1985–86. Excerpts translated as "China: Going Toward the Market," in *Chinese Economic Studies* 27, nos. 1–2 (January–February, March–April 1994): 9–208.

Liu He. "Liangci quanqiu da weijide bijiao yanjiu" [Comparative study on the two global crises]. In *Liangci quanqiu de weijide bijiao yanjiu*, edited by the Office of the Central Leading Group for Financial and Economic Affairs. Beijing: Zhongguo jingji chubanshe, 2013.

Liu Shaoqi. "On Anti-Japanese Democratic Political Power." December 1940. In *Selected Works of Liu Shaoqi*. Vol. 1. Beijing: Foreign Languages Press, 1984.

Liu Zunyi [Lawrence Lau]. "Guanyu Zhongguo shehui yanglao baozhang tixi de jiben gouxiang" [On a basic framework for the Chinese social pension and security system]. *Bijiao* [Comparative studies], no. 6 (2003): 3–28.

Lou Jiwei. *Chinese Economists on Economic Reform: Collected Works of Lou Jiwei*, edited by China Development Research Foundation. London: Routledge, 2013.

Luxemburg, Rosa. *The Russian Revolution*. 1922. New York: Workers' Age Publishers, 1940.

Ma Hong. "Towards a Rational System of Economic Management." In *New Strategy for China's Economy*. Beijing: New World Press, 1983.

Mao Zedong. "The Debate on the Cooperative Transformation of Agriculture and the Current Class Struggle." October 1955. In *Selected Works of Mao Tsetung*. Vol. 5. Peking: Foreign Languages Press, 1977.

Mao Zedong. "On Coalition Government." April 1945. In *Selected Works of Mao Tsetung*. Vol. 3. Peking: Foreign Languages Press, 1965.
Mao Zedong. "On New Democracy." January 1940. In *Selected Works of Mao Tsetung*. Vol. 2. Peking: Foreign Languages Press, 1965.
Mao Zedong. "On the Ten Major Relationships." April 1956. In *Selected Works of Mao Tsetung*. Vol. 5. Peking: Foreign Languages Press, 1977.
Mao Zedong."The Party's General Line for the Transition Period." August 1953. In *Selected Works of Mao Tsetung*. Vol. 5. Peking: Foreign Languages Press, 1977.
Mao Zedong. "Refute Right Deviationist Views That Depart from the General Line." June 1953. In *Selected Works of Mao Tsetung*. Vol. 5. Peking: Foreign Languages Press, 1977.
Marx, Karl. *Capital*. Vol. 1: *A Critique of Political Economy*. 1867. Moscow: Progress Publishers, 1887.
Marx, Karl. *Capital*. Vol. 2: *A Critique of Political Economy: The Process of Circulation of Capital*. 1863–1878. Rev. 2nd ed. Moscow: Progress Publishers, 1956.
Marx, Karl. *The Eighteenth Brumaire of Louis Bonaparte*. 1852. Peking: Foreign Languages Press, 1978.
Marx, Karl, and Friederich Engels. *The Communist Manifesto*. 1848. Edited by Frederic L. Bender. New York: W. W. Norton, 2013.
More, Thomas. *Utopia*. 1516. Edited by Dominic Baker-Smith. London: Penguin Books, 2012.
Naughton, Barry. *The Chinese Economy: Transitions and Growth*. Cambridge, MA: MIT Press, 2007.
Naughton, Barry. *Growing Out of the Plan: Chinese Economic Reform, 1978–1993*. New York: Cambridge University Press, 1995.
Naughton, Barry, ed. *Wu Jinglian: Voice of Reform in China*. Cambridge, MA: MIT Press, 2013.
North, Douglass C., John Joseph Wallis, and Barry R. Weingast. *Violence and Social Orders: A Conceptual Framework for Interpreting Recorded Human History*. New York: Cambridge University Press, 2009.
Okun, Arthur. *Equality and Efficiency: The Big Tradeoff*. Washington, DC: The Brookings Institution, 1975.
Olson, Mancur. *The Rise and Decline of Nations: Economic Growth, Stagflation, and Social Rigidities*. New Haven, CT: Yale University Press, 1982.
Peng Dehuai. "Comrade Peng Dehuai's Letter to Chairman Mao." July 1959. In *Memoirs of a Chinese Marshal: The Autobiographical Notes of Peng Dehuai (1898–1974)*. Beijing: Foreign Languages Press, 1984.
Qian Jiaju. "Tan wujia jiaoyu he shehui fenqi" [Qian Jiaju talks about prices, education, and the public ethic]. April 1988. *Wenhuibao* [Hong Kong]. Translated in Foreign Broadcast Information Service, FBIS-CHI-88-068, April 4, 1988.
Qian Yingyi, and Jinglian Wu. "China's Transition to a Market Economy: How Far Across the River?" In *How Far Across the River? Chinese Policy Reform at the Millennium*, ed. Nicholas C. Hope, Dennis Tao Yang, and Mu Yang Li. Stanford, CA: Stanford University Press, 2003.
Resolution on CPC History (1949–1981). Beijing: Foreign Languages Press, 1981.
Schultz, Theodore. *Transforming Traditional Agriculture*. New Haven, CT: Yale University Press, 1964.
Sen, Amartya. *Development as Freedom*. New York: Knopf, 1999.
Sen, Amartya. *Poverty and Famines: An Essay on Entitlement and Deprivation*. New York: Oxford University Press, 1982.

Stalin, Joseph. *Economic Problems of Socialism in the U.S.S.R.* 1951. Moscow: Foreign Languages Publishing House, 1952.

Stalin, Joseph. "The Economic Situation of the Soviet Union and the Policy of the Party." April 1926. In *Works*. Moscow: Foreign Languages Publishing House, 1954.

Stalin, Joseph. *Problems of Leninism*. 1926. Peking: Foreign Languages Press, 1976.

"Ten-Thousand-Chinese-Word Manifestos" (1995–1997):

1. "A Preliminary Investigation of the Internal and External Conditions of the Major Potential Threats to Our National Security in the Next Ten to Twenty Years." Fall 1995. Translated in *Chinese Economy* 32, no. 2 (1999): 5–21.
2. "Several Factors Affecting China's State Security." Spring 1995. Translated in BBC, Summary of World Broadcasts, September 16, 1996, FE/2718, S1/1–9.
3. "Several Theoretical and Policy Issues for Upholding the Dominant Role of Public Ownership." *Dangdai sichao* [Contemporary trends], no. 4 (1996). Translated in Foreign Broadcast Information Service, FBIS-CHI-97-096, May 1997.

Tsou, Tang. *The Cultural Revolution and Post-Mao Reforms: A Historical Perspective*. Chicago: University of Chicago Press, 1986.

Vogel, Ezra F. *Deng Xiaoping and the Transformation of China*. Cambridge, MA: Belknap Press of Harvard University Press, 2011.

Wan Anpei. "Zujin guimo de dongtai kaocha" [A study on value changes of rents]. *Jingji yanjiu* [Economic research], no. 2 (1995): 75–80.

Wang Xiaolu. "Woguo de huise shouru yu jumin shouru chaju" [Gray income and income inequality in China]. *Bijiao* [Comparative studies], no. 31 (2007): 33–70.

World Bank. *Averting the Old Age Crisis: Policies to Protect the Old and Promote Growth*. New York: Oxford University Press, 1994.

Wu Jinglian. *China's Long March toward a Market Economy*. San Francisco: Long River Press, 2005.

Wu Jinglian. "Does China Need to Change Its Industrialization Path?" 2006. In *East Asian Visions: Perspectives on Economic Development*, edited by Indermit Gill, Yukon Huang, and Homi Kharas. Washington, DC and Singapore: World Bank and Institute of Policy Studies, 2007.

Wu Jinglian. "Economics and China's Economic Rise." 2011. In *Chinese Economy: A New Transition*, edited by Masahiko Aoki and Jinglian Wu. New York: Palgrave Macmillan, 2012.

Wu Jinglian. "Jingji gaige chu zhan jieduande fazhan fangzhen he hongguan kongzhi wenti." *Renmin ribao* [People's daily]. February 11, 1985. Translated as "Developmental Guidelines in the Early Stages of the Battle for Economic Reform and Some Questions of Macroscopic Control," in *Chinese Economic Studies* 19, no. 1 (Fall 1985): 40–52.

Wu Jinglian. *Understanding and Interpreting Chinese Economic Reform*. 2nd ed. Singapore: Gale Asia, 2015.

Wu Jinglian. *Zhongguo zengchang moshi juece* [The choices for China's growth model]. 4th ed. Shanghai: Yuandong chubanshe, 2013.

Wu Jinglian et al. *Da zhong xing qiye gaige: Jianli xiandai qiye zhidu*. Tianjin: Tianjin renmin chubanshe, 1993. Excerpts translated in *Chinese Economy* 30, no. 1 (January–February 1996): 8–121.

Xu Chenggang. "Institutional Foundations of Structural Problems." In *Chinese Economy: A New Transition*, edited by Masahiko Aoki and Jinglian Wu. New York: Palgrave Macmillan, 2012.

Xue Muqiao. "Comments on Employment in Cities in Towns." July 1979. *Beijing ribao* [Beijing daily]. Translated in *Current Economic Problems in China*, by Xue Muqiao, edited by K. K. Fung. Boulder, CO: Westview, 1982.

Xue Muqiao. "Explanatory Notes to the Preliminary Opinions on Economy Restructuring." September 1980. In *Chinese Economists on Economic Reform: Collected Works of Xue Muqiao*, edited by China Development Research Foundation. London: Routledge, 2011.

Xue Muqiao. "Overcome Difficulties through Deepened Reform: A Letter to the Standing Committee of the Communist Party of China." September 1990. In *Chinese Economists on Economic Reform: Collected Works of Xue Muqiao*, edited by China Development Research Foundation. London: Routledge, 2011.

Yang Jisheng. *Tombstone: The Great Chinese Famine, 1958–1962*. Translated by Stacy Mosher and Guo Jian. New York: Farrar, Straus and Giroux, 2012.

Yang Xiaokai. "Bainian Zhongguo jingjishi biji" [Notes on the one-hundred-year history of the Chinese economy]. 2001. http://jpkc.gduf.edu.cn/xfjjx/downloads/kuozhan/k001.pdf. Accessed September 16, 2015.

Zhang Wei-wei. *The China Wave: Rise of a Civilizational State*. Hackensack, NJ: Century World Publishing, 2012.

Zhang Weiying. *The Logic of the Market: An Insider's View of Chinese Economic Reform*. Washington, DC: Cato Institute, 2015.

Zhao Ziyang. "Advance Along the Road of Socialism with Chinese Characteristics." In *Documents of the Thirteenth National Congress of the Communist Party of China*. Beijing: Foreign Languages Press, 1987.

Zhou Qiren. "Resource Shortages the Key." *Beijing Review* 50, no. 34 (August 23, 2007): 19.

Zhou Xiaochuan. *Guoji jinrong weiji: Guancha, fenxi yu yingdui* [The global financial crisis: Observations, analysis, and countermeasures]. Beijing: Zhongguo jinrong chubanshe, 2012.

Zhu Rongji. "Meeting the Press as the New Premier." March 1998. In *Zhu Rongji Meets the Press*. New York: Oxford University Press, 2011.

Zhu Rongji. "'Three Ground Rules' for Financial Work." July 1993. In *Zhu Rongji on the Record: The Road to Reform, 1991–1997*. Translated by June Y. Mei. Washington, DC: Brookings Institution Press, 2013.

INDEX

www.ingramcontent.com/pod-product-compliance
Ingram Content Group UK Ltd.
Pitfield, Milton Keynes, MK11 3LW, UK
UKHW020849150926
475595UK00003B/91